ALSO BY KEVIN FEDARKO

The Emerald Mile

A WALK IN THE PARK

THE TRUE STORY OF A SPECTACULAR MISADVENTURE IN THE GRAND CANYON

KEVIN FEDARKO

SCRIBNER

New York London Toronto Sydney New Delhi

Scribner
An Imprint of Simon & Schuster, LLC
1230 Avenue of the Americas
New York, NY 10020

Copyright © 2024 by Kevin Fedarko

First Scribner hardcover edition May 2024

SCRIBNER and design are trademarks of Simon & Schuster, LLC.

Simon & Schuster: Celebrating 100 Years of Publishing in 2024

For information about special discounts for bulk purchases, please contact Simon & Schuster Special Sales at 1-866-506-1949 or business@simonandschuster.com.

Interior design by Kyle Kabel

Manufactured in the United States of America

10   9   8   7   6   5

Library of Congress Cataloging-in-Publication Data has been applied for.

ISBN 978-1-5011-8305-8
ISBN 978-1-5011-8307-2 (ebook)

For my wife and children

ANNETTE,
CORA, THAD, AND MADDOX

Contents

CONTENTS   xi

And the end of all our exploring

Will be to arrive where we started

And know the place for the first time.

—T. S. Eliot

The Grand Canyon

"In the Grand Canyon, Arizona has a natural wonder which is in kind absolutely unparalleled throughout the rest of the world. I want to ask you to keep this great wonder of nature as it now is. I hope you will not have a building of any kind, not a summer cottage, a hotel or anything else, to mar the wonderful grandeur, the sublimity, the great loneliness and beauty of the canyon. Leave it as it is. You cannot improve on it. The ages have been at work on it, and man can only mar it." — Theodore Roosevelt

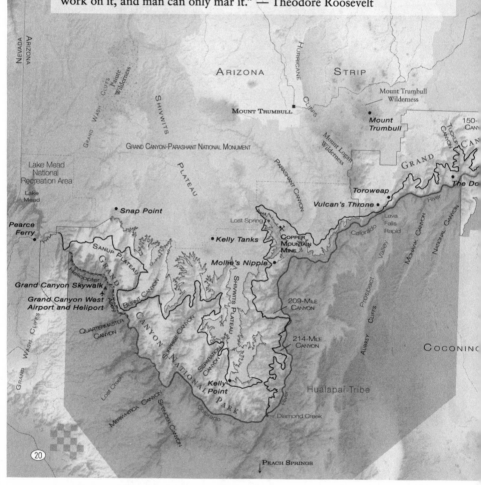

NEVADA
ARIZONA

ARIZONA   STRIP

HURRICANE CLIFFS

Paiute Wilderness
GRAND WASH CLIFFS

SHIVWITS

Mount Trumbull Wilderness

MOUNT TRUMBULL

Mount Logan Wilderness

PARASHANT CANYON

Mount Trumbull

150-
CAN

GRAND CANYON-PARASHANT NATIONAL MONUMENT

PLATEAU

GRAN

CAN

Lake Mead National Recreation Area

Lake Mead

Snap Point

Lost Spring

Toroweap

Vulcan's Throne

The Do

River

Pearce Ferry

Kelly Tanks

COPPER MOUNTAIN MINE

Lava Falls Rapid

Colorado

SANUP PLATEAU

Mollie's Nipple

SHIVWITS PLATEAU

Prospect Valley

MOHAWK CANYON

NATIONAL CANYON

Helicopter
GRAND

Grand Canyon Skywalk

Grand Canyon West Airport and Heliport

BURNT CANYON

209-MILE CANYON

AUBREY CLIFFS

COCONINC

QUARTERMASTER CANYON

CANYON

SURPRISE CANYON

SEPARATION CANYON

214-MILE CANYON

GRAND WASH CLIFFS

NATIONAL

Kelly Point

PARK

Hualapai Tribe

Lost Creek

MERIWHITICA CANYON

SPENCER CANYON

Colorado

Diamond Creek

(20)

PEACH SPRINGS

- ∿ Fedarko/McBride Traverse
- ☐ Grand Canyon National Park
- ▨ Tribal Lands
- ▨ National Monuments
- ☐ National Forest
- ∷ Wilderness Areas
- ⠿ National Recreation Areas
- — State Boundary
- — Highways and Roads
- ∿ River, Stream, or Wash
- ∿ River Rapids

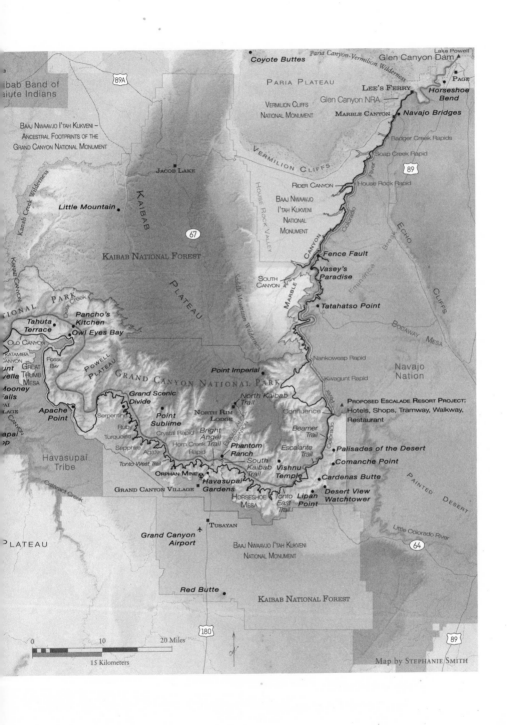

Map by STEPHANIE SMITH

Prologue

There are some good things to be said about walking.

Not many, but some.

—Edward Abbey

Every now and then, I find myself confronted by someone who wants to know about the very worst moment that Pete McBride and I endured during the year we spent together inside the Grand Canyon, and I'm forced to explain that addressing this query properly is no simple matter. So many horrible things happened to us down there, I point out, that it's almost impossible to single out just one because, really, any of them could have qualified as the most wretched and intolerable of all.

There was, for example, the afternoon I tripped and fell into a cactus, and the night that I unwittingly unfurled my sleeping bag atop an anthill—which happened to be the very same evening that Pete and I toppled into the Colorado River with our backpacks. Or the morning after the snowstorm when I was trying to thaw out my frozen shoes with our camp stove, and accidentally set them on fire.

And there was also the time the canyon got so bad that we quit and went home, resolving never, ever to come back.

But then, I admit, having given the matter due consideration, Pete and I now agree (and perhaps you will, too) that the moment the wheels completely fell off the bus was probably when the rat burrowed under Pete's skin and started snacking on his intestines.

This happened at a place called Rider Canyon, one of hundreds of minor tributaries that branch off of the main canyon, and it unfolded during a time of day that I had come to despise more than any other, which was the hottest part of the afternoon when the fleeting freshness of early morning was nothing but a distant memory, and evening's reprieve lay too far off in the future to even start dreaming about. A period of such incandescent misery that it felt as if a cackling, fork-tailed demon had flung open the door to the furnace of hell itself.

The sun stood squarely overhead, straddling the canyon's rims, pouring a column of fire directly into the abyss and driving the shadows into the deepest recesses of the rock while causing the cushion of air that hovered just above the surface of the stone to tremble, as if the ground itself were gasping for breath. But the most striking element of all, the detail that could burn a hole in the center of your consciousness, was neither the brilliance nor the ferocity of that heat, but its heft: its thickness and weight as it draped itself over the top of your head and across the blades of your shoulders, as if it were a blanket braided from material that was already in flames when delivered into the hands of its weaver.

It was the kind of heat that would slap you dead if you lingered in its glare for too long, which was why Pete and I were so keen to lower ourselves off the exposed ledge we'd been stumbling across for the past hour and drop into the bottom of Rider to seek some shade. Getting there involved about sixty feet of down-climbing through a steep notch with an overhang, and the first move required Pete to place his palms on the edge of the ledge—ignoring that the surface of the rock was almost too hot to touch—then jackknife his body into the notch while scrabbling blindly for a foothold with his toes.

I was kneeling beside him, peering over the lip to see if I could pick out a place for him to jam one of his feet into, when something on his backpack drew my eye. It was a miniature thermometer clipped to one of the shoulder straps, and as he shifted his body, the device caught the light and twinkled, as if it were saying:

Hey, check me out.

The column read 112°F.

That was somewhat shocking—it was nearly October and the forecast had called for a temperature of only 105°F. But it sort of made sense, too.

Rider's steeply angled walls, which comprise five separate layers of stone spanning a color palette that runs from caramelized honey and braised butterscotch to unfiltered bourbon, are aligned on a direct east-west axis. This meant that Rider's interior had been hammered directly by the sun since the break of dawn, seven hours earlier, long enough to turn the space between those walls into a kind of convection oven.

The narrow patio at the bottom, however, was bathed in shadows and even featured a few small pools of water, each linked to the next by a thin stream penciling between them. The scene looked deliciously cool and inviting, and Pete's progress toward it seemed to be unfolding smoothly—until, without warning, he grunted softly and froze.

We were now at eye level with each other, which meant that I could read the expression on his face: a hazy suspension of shock, bewilderment, and pain. A quivering dollop of sweat the size of a pinto bean glided down the center of his forehead, skidded off the bridge of his nose, and fell onto the front of his shirt, already soaked with perspiration and encrusted in rings of salt, with an audible *plop*.

He held himself in place for a moment before muttering something inaudible, then carefully hitching his body back up onto the ledge, where he leaned on his elbow and stared at me vacantly.

"What's going on?" I asked, confused.

He swallowed hard and tried to speak, but was unable to push the words past his lips. So instead, he lifted the front of his shirt, exposing his belly and chest. Protruding from the skin directly above the rib cage was a distended lump, and as I watched in horror, the lump began to move.

It wriggled to the opposite side of his chest, then slowly descended toward his abdomen. Then it wormed across his belly before turning again and squirming back up the side of his torso toward his shoulders.

The lump was about the size of a Bushy-Tailed Woodrat, a mammal renowned for its foul temper and a fondness for lining its nest with cactus spines, and it probably stands as a testament to just how poorly

I was dealing with the whole situation that for several long seconds I found myself wondering exactly how an actual rat—a *live rodent*—had managed to tunnel his way beneath Pete's skin.

This was like nothing I'd ever seen before, a spectacle whose freakishness was intensified by its mystery, and the only thing surpassing my bafflement was an ardent sense of relief that whatever kind of rabidly deranged parasite this might be, it had seen fit to drill its way into Pete instead of me.

Relief, I hasten to add, that was swiftly expunged by a surging backwash of panic laced with deep concern for a person who, yes and true, was often profoundly annoying as well as a titanic pain in the ass—but who also happened to be my closest friend in the entire world.

"What the hell is wrong with you?" I screeched.

*   *   *

As it turned out, there was more than one answer to that question.

Technically, Pete was suffering from a heat-related imbalance of sodium in his bloodstream that is one of the leading triggers for rescue and hospitalization among hikers in the canyon. What appeared to be a rat scurrying beneath his skin was a rolling series of intense muscle cramps. Soon those spasms would subside as tight knots formed in the major muscles along his arms and legs. If these were left unchecked, he would undergo severe cognitive impairment as the tissues in his brain began to swell, inducing a drunken-like stupor. Then sometime in the next twenty-four to forty-eight hours, he would succumb to violent convulsions and lapse into a coma from which there would be no recovery.

He clearly needed help. But I was in no position to offer assistance because I was saddled with my own problems, which had started a few days earlier, when I'd noticed several tender areas on my feet where the skin looked like uncooked bacon. Instead of fishing out some moleskin from our med kit, which I was too exhausted to extract from the bottom of my pack, I decided that if I ignored the problem, it would either get better or go away.

By the following morning, the hot spots had turned white and were filling with fluid. Soon blisters were everywhere—along the bottoms of my feet, around the balls of my ankles and the Achilles tendons, plus all ten toes. By the end of that afternoon, the blisters had burst and it looked as if I'd been given a pedicure with a belt sander. At this point, acting on Pete's advice, I elected once again to bypass the med kit and go straight for the duct tape, which, for reasons that now seemed mystifying, I had applied somewhat overzealously, encasing each foot inside a plastic perma-sock whose sticky side, having bonded directly to the open blisters, was impossible to remove.

All the following day, my airtight duct-tape galoshes provided a moist, nurturing habitat for a colony of bacteria to steep in the brine of sweat, dirt, and foot funk. Within hours, both feet were infected and rotting. Now every stride I took felt as if I were stepping into a bucket of broken glass. Before long, I wouldn't be able to walk at all.

Needless to say, we were in far over our heads, a condition stemming not only from our specific medical problems, but also from a deeper and more debilitating disorder. An affliction that could be addressed neither with antibiotics nor bed rest because it was not a physical ailment so much as an impairment of character—an infirmity rooted in the complexion of our personalities as well as the delusions we harbored regarding our competency and prowess in the outdoors.

Ours was a conflation of willful ignorance, shoddy discipline, and outrageous hubris: an array of flaws that we had been denying (perhaps, like the sores on my feet, in the hope that it would simply improve or disappear) ever since the moment Pete had gotten the two of us into this mess by pressing me to join him for what he'd billed, quite literally, as "a walk in the park."

A misguided odyssey through the heart of perhaps the harshest and least forgiving, but also the most breathtakingly gorgeous, landscape feature on earth. A place filled with so much wonder, replete with so many layers of complexity, that there is nothing else like it, anywhere.

PART I

Wild Country

*What a world of grandeur
is spread before us!*

—John Wesley Powell

CHAPTER 1

Into the Abyss

A nugget of conventional wisdom peddled by the boatmen of the Colorado River suggests that if it were somehow possible to take every inch of the terrain wedged between the walls of the Grand Canyon, including the faces of all the cliffs, and pull everything out flat, you'd wind up with a chunk of real estate bigger than Texas. That's a bold claim—and for anyone familiar with the average river guide's fondness for doctoring up facts for the sake of entertainment, it should come as little surprise to learn that it's a load of nonsense.

Strictly speaking, the topography of the canyon—which can perhaps best be imagined as a range of mountains roughly the length of the Pyrenees flipped upside down and countersunk below the horizon—has a total surface area no bigger than that of Delaware. But even so, those whitewater guides deserve some credit for putting their fingers on an important truth, because few things come closer to capturing the canyon's stupefying depth and labyrinthine complexity than the possibility that it might somehow be capable of swallowing up the entirety of the Lone Star State.

If there's a key to framing the scale and vastness of that abyss, it lies within the tiered walls that descend from the canyon's rims—one set running along the north side, the other along the south—whose longest drop exceeds six thousand vertical feet: tall enough that if five Empire State Buildings were stacked one on top of another, they would barely reach the highest point on the North Rim. In fact, the total loss of elevation from rim to river is so great that the climate actually shifts, becoming significantly hotter as one descends. With every thousand feet of drop, the temperature increases by roughly 5°F, giving rise to a ladder of meteorological zones and niches so discrete that the flora and fauna at the top bear little if any relation to the forms of life on the bottom.

The North Rim, the loftiest section of the park, is a world unto itself, stocked with its own special repository of plants and animals, where the fir and spruce trees can be buried in twelve feet of snow during the winter, and the only road in is closed from November to May. The timber up there shelters grouse and wild turkeys as well as Mountain Bluebirds and a multitude of Mule Deer, and the forests are interspersed with open meadows that are spangled with wildflowers in the summer. In the fall, the leaves on the aspens drop to the ground like gold coins, and at night, the woods resound with the hooting of Great Horned Owls.

Inside the canyon below, life-forms from three of North America's four deserts—the Great Basin, the Sonoran, and the Mojave—all collide and commingle. Here the air temperature during the summer will push beyond 120°F, while the surface temperature of the stone can easily claw its way up to 170°F—hot enough to kill a snake caught in the open within a few minutes, or cook a Giant Hairy Scorpion in just less than an hour.

Under these conditions, only the hardiest things can persevere: tiny tree frogs that bide their time in rocky crevices for months on end; spiders capable of waiting two hundred days in a burrow without a drop of water; seeds with the patience to remain dormant for an entire century until, under just the right circumstances, they give themselves permission to sprout. There are species of cactus whose limbs retreat into the ground, and in some areas even the streams are rendered so tenuous by the heat that their waters recede into the stone by day and emerge only by night, trickling timorously beneath the bleached gaze of the moon and the stars.

* * *

All across the cliffs and terraces between the rims and the river, a range of distinctive habitats have woven themselves along various elevations. Nestled just below the stands of fir and spruce are parklike groves of Ponderosa Pine that can live for five hundred years.* The trunks of those trees are furrowed with an orange-and-black bark so tough that it can withstand wildfire, so sweet it smells faintly of vanilla or butterscotch, so nutritious it can be pounded into a flour and used to bake bread.

On the slopes and benches beneath the Ponderosa belt lie swales of sagebrush and bonsai-like shrubs called blackbrush, each spaced as if they'd been set down by a Japanese gardener. Together, they create a loose tapestry of cover for Black-Tailed Jackrabbits, Side-Blotched Lizards, and the Black-Throated Sparrow—perhaps the quintessential desert bird because it metabolizes moisture from seeds and insects, and thus never needs a drink of water.

Together, these strata of vegetation enable the canyon to function as a nexus in which some seventy-five ecological communities are spread across four distinct biomes and two geological provinces. The mosaic is so rich and varied that a hiker who descends from the highest point on the North Rim to the lowest point inside the canyon will pass through a spectrum of life equivalent to moving from the cool boreal forests of subarctic Canada to the sunstruck deserts of Mexico that lie just above the Tropic of Cancer—thereby compressing a distribution of plants and animals that typically stretch over more than two thousand horizontal miles into a single vertical mile.

* This may sound ancient, but the Ponderosa is decisively eclipsed by the life span of the creosote bush and the Kaibab Plateau Century Plant, desert flora whose individual members propagate by seed as well as cloning, enabling them to live for more than a millennium.

Thanks to its extremes of heat and aridity, the canyon cannot come close to nurturing the plenitude of animals and plants that flourish in national parks such as the Great Smokies and the Everglades, which support either a larger biomass or a greater number of individual species. But what sets the chasm apart is the breadth and range of its biota. There are, for example, 167 types of fungus, 64 species of moss, and 195 varieties of lichen—all arrayed in specific elevation zones and thriving tenaciously among the vegetation one might more reasonably expect to find in the desert: saltbush and brittlebush, greasebush and rabbitbrush, plus nine different types of sagebrush and more than a dozen cacti, including the Prickly Pear, the Teddy Bear, and the Hedgehog.

As for animals, the canyon and its adjoining rims host more than ninety species of mammal ranging from Mountain Lions and Desert Bighorn Sheep to a carnivorous mouse that specializes in consuming scorpions and howls at the moon. There are thirty-eight types of reptile, twenty-two varieties of bat, and eight different amphibians, including a toad that eats bees. Plus, there are a ton of birds: 373 species and counting, fully one-third of the entire spectrum of winged fauna in the continental United States. Over the years, researchers have cataloged Snow Geese, Sandhill Cranes, and Trumpeter Swans, along with Bald Eagles, Belted Kingfishers, and Brown-Headed Cowbirds. During the winter months, avian concentrations along some sections of the river can exceed a thousand birds per square kilometer every hour. In summer, they run the gamut from Peregrine Falcons, which can dive at speeds of 235 miles an hour (the fastest organisms on earth), and California Condors (the largest of all North American vultures with a ten-foot wingspan), to the tiniest bird on the continent, the Calliope Hummingbird, which is about the same size as that bee-eating toad but weighs only one-tenth of an ounce, lighter than the page displaying the words you're reading right now.

And let's not forget the insects and other invertebrates. The canyon hosts 60 different species of terrestrial snails and slugs, 116 variants of stink beetle, 89 dragonflies and damselflies, and 140 different types of butterfly, 5 of which are unique to the canyon, including Nabokov's Wood Nymph, which was discovered on the Bright Angel Trail by the author of *Lolita* in the summer of 1941. There's also a tarantula endemic to the canyon floor that is hunted by a three-inch-long wasp capable of delivering a sting so painful it has been likened to dropping a hair dryer into the tub while one is taking a bath.

In no other national park can you find a broader span of geographic and climatic conditions supporting such a varied spectrum of life wedged inside such a tightly compressed space. Yet as remarkable as all of this may seem, what lies beneath that tapestry of life is perhaps even more astonishing.

*   *   *

Although the Colorado River spent roughly 6 million years carving out the canyon itself, the rock into which the river has cut is far older. The mile-deep walls on both sides of the gorge reveal no fewer than twenty-seven formations whose lineages straddle eight geological periods, during which nearly 40 percent of the planet's chronology was etched directly into the stone. By some measures, those walls showcase perhaps the finest cross-section of terrestrial time visible anywhere on the globe, a vertical concatenation of history stacked in horizontal strata, much like the pages of an immense book—the most venerable manuscript of its kind.

The very first page of that monograph, known as the Kaibab Limestone, which forms the canyon's caprock—the youngest and freshest folio of them all—was written approximately 270 million years ago, a point anchored so far back in the past that many dramatic events in the annals of our world still had not taken place. The first birds had yet to take wing, the first flowers had yet to bloom, and the massive asteroid that was destined to create the firestorm that would wipe out the dinosaurs would not slam into what is now the Yucatán Peninsula for another 205 million years.

Thousands of feet beneath the Kaibab, encased in the ledges and terraces, embossed on the faces of the cliffs, are strange and wonderful fossils: the wings of dragonflies, the stems of sea lilies, the teeth of sharks that swam through vanished oceans between the shores of continents that no longer exist. Each layer is older than the one above it until finally, all the way at the bottom, you arrive at rock whose bloodlines extend further back in time than the human mind can even imagine: almost a full 2 billion years, a third of the age of the planet, and roughly one-seventh the life span of the universe itself.

For thousands of years, human beings have occupied this space in successive waves of migration that are every bit as rich and varied as the layers of geology and ecology. Yet there are still a number of spots where neither ancient nor modern people have ever set foot, and other places sheltering creatures that the outside world is only just beginning to bump up against. Less than a decade ago, a group of researchers selected an uncharted cavern on the canyon's North Rim to test thermal remote-sensing imagery that NASA one day hopes to use for cave exploration on Mars. During their work, they stumbled across four species—a cave cricket, a bark louse, and a pair of eyeless albino millipedes—that were completely unknown to science.

Nowhere else is the ground so broken and the past so exposed. Nowhere else can a person move simultaneously along so many different dimensions: forward in space, backward in time, and across the face of an entire hemisphere of life zones, ecosystems, and biological communities. Nowhere else is the simple act of putting one foot in front of the other so provocative, so destabilizing, so densely freighted with rich and interlocking layers of meaning.

And perhaps most extraordinary of all, the contours of no other landscape are so broadly recognized by so many even as its essence remains known—truly known—to so few, because glimpsing its deepest secrets and ferreting out its hidden treasures requires something that only a small number of us are willing to embrace. An undertaking that extends well beyond what Theodore Roosevelt called for when he referred to the canyon, in a speech he delivered on the South Rim in the spring of 1903, as "one of the great sights which every American, if he can travel at all, should see."

Aside from simply looking at it, you must lace up your boots and actually step inside the place.

*   *   *

When Pete first approached me with his proposal for a walk in the park, I didn't need much of an introduction. For most of my life I had been obsessed with the canyon and had even spent a number of summers living and working on the Colorado as an apprentice whitewater guide, a story we'll get to in good time. This may not have qualified me as an expert. But I viewed myself as someone with enough knowledge and experience to feel that he knew what he was getting into by agreeing to tackle the place the hard way: moving through it on foot.

Alas, although I didn't know it at the time, I didn't have the faintest clue how truly *unfit* Pete and I both were, in every possible way, for a journey that would pull us into parts of the canyon where, for good reasons, few travelers have ever been. A journey that was supposed to last no more than a couple of months, but would ultimately turn into the longest, most arduous ordeal that either of us had ever endured while forcing us to confront at multiple points along its arc the question of why we had bothered to start, and whether it was worth the trouble of finishing. But it was also a journey in which the canyon would show us things we had never dreamed of.

At the start of this quest, I had no way of imagining that long after it was over I would still be struggling to formulate a coherent response to the miseries the canyon inflicted on us, the satisfactions that would later overtake the memories of that misery, or the yearning and splendor that transcended them all. I had no way to fathom the force with which the canyon's austerity, its grandeur, and its radiance—traits that stand implacably aloof to human hopes and ambitions—can impart a perspective that will enable you to see yourself as nothing more, and nothing less, than a grain of sand amid the immensity of rock and time and the stars at night.

All I knew was that the place was calling out to me—and that when the canyon calls, its voice is as impossible to ignore now as it was back in the summer of 1962, when a man from Wales with bright blue eyes and a bushy beard who would eventually be known as "the father of wilderness backpacking" stepped to the edge of the rim for the very first time, and found himself gazing into the abyss.

CHAPTER 2

The Man Who
Walked Through Time

B y the time that Colin Fletcher arrived at the Grand Canyon, he was already forty years old and had courted more adventure and risk than most people touch in their entire lives. After joining Britain's Royal Marines and participating in the 1944 D-Day invasion of Normandy, he'd worked as a farmer in Kenya, a road surveyor in Rhodesia, and a prospector in Canada—all without ever truly settling down. In 1958, having drifted to San Francisco and taken a job as a janitor, he decided it would be a good idea to hike the length of California—all the way from Mexico to Oregon along the spine of the Sierra Nevada—to figure out whether he should propose to his girlfriend.

The journey took six months, yet the marriage that was consummated upon his return lasted only a few weeks. But the book that Fletcher wrote about the hike itself, *The Thousand-Mile Summer*, firmly established him as a "compulsive walker," as well as a pioneer in the art of solo backcountry travel.

In the decades to come, Fletcher's reputation as a world-class wanderer would be burnished by another half dozen books chronicling equally impressive pilgrimages—a year among the animals of Africa's Serengeti Plain and the Great Rift Valley; another six months on a seventeen-hundred-mile paddle down the length of the Colorado River from the Rockies to the Sea of Cortez. But in the early 1960s, the fullness of Fletcher's fame was still awaiting him when he veered off Route 66 in the midst of a road trip from New York City to the West Coast and took an eighty-mile detour to the edge of one of the great wonders of the world.

It was midmorning when he parked his car, and as he strolled toward the rim, Fletcher, who had already seen plenty of postcards and magazines with images of the canyon, thought he knew what awaited him. But none of that even came close to preparing him for what it actually felt like to step to the brink of the chasm and peer inside.

The photos had faithfully reproduced the basic lineaments of the vision laid before him: the immense benches and cliffs descending like a crudely hewn staircase toward the bottom far below, and the matching set of cliffs and ledges clawing their way out of the depths on the opposite side. But nothing had conveyed the clarity and crispness of the canyon's light, or how piercingly all of that rock—rock that had been carved by water and abraded by the wind and polished by the passage of time—glimmered in the pale, clean countenance of day, absent any filter but the crystalline air of the high desert.

It felt like stooping to peer through the eyepiece of a telescope trained on the gray-white craters of the moon, with features so sharp and granular that they appeared impossibly distant, yet somehow close enough to reach out and brush with the tips of one's fingers. Unlike the moon, however, the canyon was neither cold nor sterile. Light seemed to be pouring upward from its depths, and color was everywhere. Each square inch of stone was saturated in the lustrous tones—almond and rose, chestnut and salmon, chocolate and peach, coffee and eggplant and plum—of rock that had been left to marinate and mellow in the urn of time.

There were shadows, too: a limitless array, each extending at precisely the same distance in proportion to the height of its source, each pointing in exactly the same direction, suffusing the core of the chasm with texture and reach and dimensionality.

The sheer force of the canyon's magnificence—the dignity of its bearing, the sternness of its architecture—all of that left the restless Welshman wide-eyed and spellbound. But what truly clobbered him was the stillness and tranquility of the stone, an absolute dearth of sound or movement.

The quiescence was heavy, mysterious, distinctly unnerving—yet strangely beckoning, too. "A silence so profound," he would later write, "that the whole colossal chaos of rock and space and color seemed to have sunk beneath it."

In those initial moments of shock, as he took in the unruffled solemnity of this monumental crevice, he felt a shift take place inside him as both his perception and his equilibrium were nudged into a new alignment.

"I knew that something had happened," he said, "to the way I looked at things."

*   *   *

Fletcher's response, it should be noted, was in no way odd or unusual, either then or now. Each summer, thousands of tourists who flock to the main overlooks along the South Rim experience a destabilizing adjustment upon gazing into the canyon for the first time. The impact of the landscape's immensity, combined with the absence of any references— roads or buildings or people—that might convey perspective and scale can be so disorienting that some visitors feel as if they're on the verge of fainting. Over the years, a small number have even become so dizzy that they have lost their footing and toppled over the edge.

Perhaps the most horrific of these incidents unfolded in the spring of 1989, more than a quarter century after Fletcher's first trip, when a young woman from Japan named Yuri Nagata was admonished that three days earlier a woman from Germany had lost her balance while watching the sunset and plunged four hundred feet to her death. Just after this warning, Nagata herself became wobbly and tumbled over the lip. She landed on a steep slope and rolled for several yards before skidding over a 360-foot cliff. Those on the rim could hear her screams as she fell.

As for Fletcher, he was in no danger of falling to his death back in the summer of 1962, but he found himself pulled into the canyon in a different way.

He spent hours sitting on the edge, staring out at the striated cliffs, studying the angles and orientations of the ledges, peering east and west as far as his eyes would carry him until late in the afternoon, when an idea finally presented itself—a resolution whose simplicity seemed to cut like an arrow across the twisted topography at his feet.

If there was a path or a route through that marvelous wasteland of rock, he resolved—right there on the spot—he was going to follow it, and traverse the entire length of the canyon on foot.

*   *   *

It may be worth taking a moment here to acknowledge what a unique and unlikely paradox the canyon represents in the context of America's most stupendous landscapes. Back in October of 1540 when a small party of Spanish conquistadores approached the South Rim and became the first outsiders ever to gaze into the abyss, the rest of what would eventually become the United States was all but untouched by Europeans, who would not reach the shores of Cape Cod for sixty-seven years. It would be almost three centuries before they crossed the Continental Divide in Montana's Bitterroot Mountains, and the better part of another half century would pass before they glimpsed the pewter-colored precipices of the Sierra Nevada.

Thus of all the great natural wonders in America—the graceful sandstone arches of Utah, the towering trees of Northern California, the snow-draped steeples of Wyoming's Tetons—the Grand Canyon was the very first to be spotted by Europeans. Yet after pausing just long enough to dispatch a trio of soldiers over the rim with orders to inspect the river at the bottom (and making it less than a third of the way there), the Spaniards departed, convinced that the great gorge held nothing of material value—a judgment echoed by the handful of whites who would arrive in sporadic bursts during the next 329 years to look the place over and leave again.

All of which meant that when a one-armed veteran of the Civil War named John Wesley Powell finally led a survey party of nine men in four wooden boats down the Colorado River in the summer of 1869, the canyon would win the additional distinction of being the very *last* of the country's major landscape features to be officially explored— although the tantalizing possibility that other voyagers may well have preceded Powell is suggested by the legend of Tiyo, a Hopi boy who is said to have floated through the canyon in a hollow log, riding the river all the way to the Sea of Cortez before returning to his people.*

Upon emerging from that ordeal and a follow-up expedition two years later, Powell pronounced himself stunned by the hostility the canyon exhibited to anyone with the temerity to take its measure. "It can be seen only in parts from hour to hour and from day to day and from week to week and from month to month," he later reported, adding that the terrain was "more difficult to traverse than the Alps or the Himalayas."

When Colin Fletcher finally showed up at the South Rim, almost an entire century had passed since Powell's pioneering voyages, and during the intervening years the canyon had been swarmed by prospectors, dam builders, and even a gang of surveyors intent on constructing a railway along the bottom so that freight trains could haul coal from the mines of Colorado to the factories of San Diego. In addition, as early as the 1930s, the chasm had also become a magnet for adventure seekers. Every summer, hundreds of river runners were boating downstream in a recreational redux of Powell's trip, while others were hiking or riding mules along a handful of trails down to the bottom, where they stayed in rustic cabins at a secluded tourist lodge called Phantom Ranch.

---

* The story of Tiyo, which is recounted in slightly different form among the Navajo, belongs to a larger repertoire of tribal stories whose antiquity and splendor attests to a human history in the canyon that radically predates the arrival of whites, who saw themselves as "discovering" the land for the first time.

During this era, the canyon's legal status was progressively elevated, first from a federal forest reserve to a game preserve, then a national monument, and from there to one of the country's flagship national parks. By the end of World War II, this was perhaps the most recognized landscape feature in the entire country—rivaled only by the cataracts of Niagara and the geysers of Yellowstone—and the South Rim itself had become a mandatory vacation stop for millions of tourists, who harbored no doubts, after taking in its vision, that this was truly a crown jewel of America's public lands, the standard against which all the rest were appraised.

Yet as Fletcher was about to discover, despite all this acclaim and activity, there wasn't a single trail that would get a person from one end of the canyon to the other on foot. In all the time that had passed since the place was discovered by white explorers, nobody had figured out how to walk through the damn thing from one end to the other, because the canyon simply isn't built to accommodate that.

*   *   *

To be sure, human beings can move from the rims down to the river and back by dozens of routes, most of which were originally established by the Ancestral Puebloans, who occupied this space long before the arrival of whites. But while the terrain grudgingly permits passage up and down, the general layout of the interior prohibits extended travel on a lateral axis.

Much of the ground next to the Colorado is too convoluted to allow for efficient trekking, and significant reaches have no shoreline at all because the cliffs drop directly into the river. Anyone hoping to forge a path along those stretches confronts a topographic puzzle that requires repeatedly ascending and descending through many different layers of rock. The hardest and most resistant of those strata—the limestones, sandstones, and schists—tend to form impassable vertical faces, so it is necessary to link together a chain of ledges, many of which are warped or broken by geological fractures and faults.

In addition, every half mile or so, the canyon's main corridor is met by a smaller canyon forking in from one side or the other. Some of these offshoots have been excavated by a handful of permanent or seasonal creeks, but most are the work of horrifically violent flash floods or debris flows triggered by rainstorms. These branches come in all shapes and sizes—a number of them extend back for ten or even fifteen miles, and the largest constitute entire canyon systems unto themselves, replete with their own networks of tributaries. Subworlds so immense and convoluted that fully exploring any of them can justify a separate expedition.

In essence, the canyon is far more than just one giant cleft, as its name seems to imply. Instead, it is a fiendishly elaborate maze in which so many tributaries fork off the main-stem gorge—some 740 of them, by one count—that for anyone attempting a traverse on foot, every mile of lateral progress along the main-stem canyon has to be paid for with an additional two and a half miles of detouring. In getting from one end of the canyon to the other, a hiker will almost triple the 277-mile distance covered by the river.

Wild country. Wild enough to convince almost anybody who ventures into the place that moving overland for long distances by foot or on horseback is a fool's errand, and that the only sane approach to extended travel inside this labyrinth is by riding the river in boats, as Powell had done.

For all these reasons, when Fletcher conceived the idea for his walk, vast stretches of the canyon's backcountry were rarely trodden, and a number of features probably hadn't been seen or touched in centuries, if ever. He had, in effect, stumbled across a code that had yet to be cracked by anyone in the modern era—perhaps the grandest riddle in all of long-distance hiking.

*   *   *

From the moment Fletcher began researching his project, it was clear that the goal he'd set suffered from too much ambition and not nearly enough pragmatism. After making inquiries about the basic topography and badgering park officials on the feasibility of feeling one's way along the cliffs and ledges, he wasn't sure he even understood where such a route might start, or how it should finish. "No two people," he later grumbled, "seemed able to agree about where the canyon began and ended."*

Accordingly, he dialed back the plan. Instead of tackling the entire length of the abyss, he would set his sights on a thru-hike of Grand Canyon National Park, whose borders then embraced only the central portion of the chasm—albeit, in Fletcher's view, its "major and most magnificent part." This offered two advantages: in addition to shortening the total distance, a chunk of the more modest transect was traversed by one of the park's few footpaths, an east-to-west artery known as the Tonto Trail on the canyon's south side, significantly reducing the untracked ground he would have to navigate. But even with these modifications, Fletcher would face some daunting challenges within those parts of the park that lacked any well-defined hiking routes.

It's difficult to overstate how taxing and unpleasant movement inside the canyon becomes from the moment one steps off a trail. Forcing a passage where none has been laid out requires picking across shattered terraces or weaving along precarious slopes strewn with rocky debris known as scree or talus and, whenever progress is impeded by a cliff or precipice, laboriously struggling up or down to find a new way forward. Under these conditions, every step becomes a struggle; forward progress is achieved in increments, and often through a series of mad scrambles that involve grueling detours in every direction except the one you hope to go.

Hours, sometimes entire days, are spent thrashing through thickets of brush, fields of cactus, or acres of thorn trees. And when hikers find themselves shunted into the network of cliffs and ledges thousands of feet above the river, the search for water becomes an existential

---

* This claim is a bit odd. A cursory glance at any decent map would have confirmed for Fletcher that the canyon starts at Lee's Ferry, a break in the cliffs along the shoreline of the Colorado River less than ten miles south of Arizona's border with Utah, and concludes just short of the Nevada border at a set of saw-toothed escarpments known as the Grand Wash Cliffs.

challenge. Up there, springs are either scarce or nonexistent, and survival can hinge entirely on potholes, cup-shaped indentations in the
rock that collect thin pools of snowmelt or rainwater, many of which
evaporate within a day or two after the last storm. Along those high
escarpments, you hopscotch from one puddle to the next while knowing
that if you venture too far from the last without finding another, you
will be cut off, unable to retreat or advance—and that within hours,
you'll be dead.

With these challenges in mind, Fletcher spent the better part of the
next year consulting the finest topographic maps he could find, compil-
ing weather data, and pulling up old exploration reports. He reached
out to park rangers, geologists, river runners, archaeologists, wildlife
biologists—anyone who might have information to share about the
problems he would confront.

In the end, he found only one truly qualified expert, whom we will
meet in due course—a professor at a college in Flagstaff who specialized
in Euclidean numbers theory, and who liked to hike the canyon during
his free time. With the mathematician's help, the ambitious Welshman
was able to chart a course and identify sources of water that would
enable him to work his way through the remote sectors of the park.

Next Fletcher turned to the question of supplies and logistics. To
survive, he had to put together eight weeks of dehydrated-food rations,
together with a long list of gear, clothing, and sundry items on which
his survival or comfort would depend: matches and flashlight batteries,
toilet paper and soap, foot powder and water-purification tablets, wax
for his boots and white gas for his camp stove. When everything was
assembled, he then had to divide it up and build his resupply caches.

Because one day's allotment of dehydrated food typically weighs
about twenty-four ounces, it's possible for most people to carry only
about eight days' worth of meals at a time, so long-distance hikers
tend to divide their rations into separate stashes and deposit them at
designated locations with roughly a week of walking between them.
Fletcher's project required seven separate caches, two of which were
air-dropped using a small plane, a practice that would not be allowed

today. Each was placed in a five-gallon metal can and stuffed with additional goodies, including clean socks, extra notepaper, plus a few treats such as smoked oysters or canned frog's legs, and a small bottle of claret, his favorite wine, to help keep his spirits up.

Then almost before he quite realized it, spring arrived, and it was time to go.

*   *   *

He descended into the canyon on April 17, 1963, and over the next two months he covered almost 250 miles, which equated with roughly one hundred river miles in the central portion of the canyon. Along the way, he met with a marvelous series of adventures, mishaps, and revelations. He was almost swept away by the Colorado while ferrying himself and his backpack across an eddy on his air mattress. He crossed paths with Bighorn Sheep, several rattlesnakes, and a beaver. He took long breaks, often pausing for days to meditate and write, and he saw so few people that he spent weeks at a time walking naked except for his hat, socks, and boots.

He emerged in the middle of June, almost exactly a year after he'd first peered into the canyon, with many pages of notes and a slew of photographs, and immediately headed home to California to start writing. The book took almost four years to complete, but when he was through, he'd composed a tale of beauty and substance, a story worthy of the place that had inspired him.

Instead of grandstanding as a trailblazer, as other authors in the outdoor-adventure genre tended to, he kept the spotlight squarely on the landscape: its vastness, its intricacy, and, perhaps the most intriguing of all its paradoxes, its capacity to alter the sensibilities of those who fell under its spell by making them feel not only profoundly diminished, but also radically expanded, often in the same breath.

"I saw that by going down into that huge fissure in the face of the earth, deep into the space and the silence and the solitude, I might come as close as we can at present to moving back and down through the smooth and apparently impenetrable face of time," he wrote in one passage that evoked the title he had chosen for his manuscript, *The Man Who Walked Through Time*. "I was hopelessly insignificant and helpless, a mere insect."

When the book was published in the winter of 1968, the story spoke to such a large number of people that it became a runaway bestseller. Like another work along similar themes that came out the same year—Edward Abbey's *Desert Solitaire*—Fletcher's book built an audience of readers who would elevate it to a classic in the canon of American wilderness literature.

In the years to come, more than four hundred thousand copies would be printed and sold—including a dog-eared paperback that was purchased for ten cents at a used-book sale by my father, who then placed it in my hands without knowing that by doing so he would change the shape and course of my life as profoundly as an irrigation channel alters the course of a stream in the desert.

CHAPTER 3

Hell with the Lid Off

I was eleven years old when my dad handed me Fletcher's book, so what initially captured my imagination had little to do with the writing, and everything to do with the image on the cover. It was a photo Fletcher had taken of himself, clad in a burly-looking pair of hiking boots as he stood at the edge of a cliff with a massive backpack strapped to his shoulders. His fists were wrapped around a stout walking stick, and he was staring resolutely into a landscape unlike anything I had ever seen or imagined.

Far beneath his feet stretched a river whose contours were dwarfed by a sweep of bare rock and shimmering blue air that, like the sea itself, appeared to go on forever. It was fiercely beautiful and starkly rugged, and it stood in radiant contrast to the place I belonged, which was a part of the country where nature had been ravaged so thoroughly and for so long that until quite recently, it had been regarded, literally, as a kind of hellscape.

Between the turn of the twentieth century and the end of World War II, the mines and mills of Pittsburgh, Pennsylvania, produced roughly half the steel in the United States, turning out the thermite-welded rail lines that knit the country together, as well as the beams and girders that provided the skeletal core for America's bridges, ships, and skyscrapers. All of that industry and growth, however, had come at a price.

The air was so polluted with residue from burning coal that the center of the city was coated in soot. Businessmen changed their shirt collars twice a day because they turned black by lunchtime, housewives washed their living room curtains once a week, and streetlights were forced to remain on during the daytime so that drivers could see where they were going. In the winter, not even the snow was white.

This was the world that Mike Fedarko, my grandfather, was born into, and it marked him indelibly. He grew up in what was known as a coal patch, a cluster of company-owned houses and a company-run store, directly adjacent to a mine and often named after the nearest headframe or winding tower—in this case Tower Hill Number Two. He left school in the sixth grade and by the age of fourteen was spending his days far underground in one of the many mines run by the Jones brothers, steel-industry barons who were consolidating control of the coal in the Monongahela Valley.

He would spend the next fifty years in those shafts, laboring alongside a squad of his male siblings and cousins that included his brother Mac, who always made sure to take his cake out of his lunch bucket and gobble it down first, so that if the tunnel collapsed before they finished eating, at least he wouldn't have died without his dessert.

Some sections of the mines worked by Uncle Mac and my grandfather, whom we called Pap, were enormous, with cavernous vaults extending three or four stories underground. But many of the tunnels were extremely narrow, and they were often forced to work on their knees, or while lying on their sides. Either way, the coal they dug helped to stoke the roaring industrial forge that Pittsburgh had become, while simultaneously completing the city's transition into an American version of a Dickensian nightmare.

This was a place in which the connective tissue that binds people to the land had been severed, and nothing illustrated that sundering more graphically than the disaster that was about to unfold less than five miles from where my grandparents lived.

*   *   *

The little mill town of Donora sits on a horseshoe bend along the Monongahela River about twenty miles south of Pittsburgh, with steep hills at its back and even steeper ones along the far shore. The town grew together with the city, and by 1945 it housed thirteen thousand residents, plus an American Steel and Wire plant, where most of the workforce was employed. Owned by U.S. Steel, the complex was the largest of its kind in the world, and on any given day it pumped enough fluoride and chloride gases through its smokestacks to kill all the emerging vegetation within a two-mile radius. Residents claimed they could tell which sector of the mill was firing from the color of the air: reddish brown from the open hearth, black from the blast furnace, and, thanks to the sulfur dioxide it contained, a sickly shade of yellow from the zinc smelter.

None of that deterred my grandparents from paying periodic visits to Donora. Although Pap refused to go to restaurants or the movies (both of which he considered a waste of money), the town was a magnet for my grandmother, whom we called Nanny, because it boasted a Dan's Dollar Store as well as a JCPenney, where she purchased clothing on layaway. Donora might have been dirty, but it was also prosperous, and for many years people in the area considered that to be a fair trade-off. Pollution was a nuisance, something you lived with to have jobs and income. But in the autumn of 1948, that view was permanently recast.

On the morning of Tuesday, October 26, an unusual temperature inversion trapped a dense layer of air laden with toxic chemicals directly over the town, preventing the noxious mixture from dissipating as it normally did. No warning was given as the cloud thickened over the next several days into a stagnant yellowish haze, so the Halloween parade featuring children in costumes, as well as the high school football game, both went ahead as planned, even though bystanders could see little more than shadows moving through the gloom. On the sidewalks of Main Street, pedestrians had trouble finding the curb.

The first death occurred on Friday, from acute fluoride poisoning and asphyxiation. By Saturday, the town's eight physicians were rushing

from case to case, able to spend only a few minutes at each bedside. By
Monday, half the population was sickened with vomiting, headaches,
stomach pains, or respiratory distress, and a temporary morgue had
been set up in the basement of the main hotel because all three funeral
homes were full. Through it all, the zinc works and the steel mill stayed
open and continued pumping fumes into the air.

By the time the rain finally arrived on the following Sunday, lifting
the longest temperature inversion observed anywhere in America during
the twentieth century, another nineteen people had died, although the
exact number is still in dispute. For weeks after the event, the "Donora
Death Fog" made headlines across the United States as one of the worst
environmental disasters in the history of the country. Hundreds of the
survivors would live out the remainder of their lives with permanently
damaged lungs and hearts.

Although my grandparents' home was only a ten-minute drive away,
neither they nor my father and his two sisters were directly affected by
the tragedy. Nevertheless, it was a landmark event in their world and
took its place in our family lore.*

As for Pittsburgh, it didn't even begin to get a handle on its pollution
problems until well into the 1950s. Even by the early 1960s, when my
mom and dad met and opened a small hairdressing salon in a community
on the eastern side of the city, heavy smog was still recorded in the area
between 250 and 275 days a year. One of the more potent memories
from my childhood was how tightly my brother, Aaron, and I would
squeeze our noses and hold our breath as we sat in the back seat of
the family station wagon whenever our parents drove past Jones and
Laughlin's blast furnaces along the Monongahela River.

Even with the car windows rolled up, the sulfurous air reeked of
rotten eggs. If we were driving at night, the sky and the water glowed

* Donora later became a national "scientific test tube" for the study of air pollution, which
eventually led to the nation's first clean air legislation. The tragedy also inspired one of my
cousins, Brian Charlton, to become the archivist and curator of the Donora Smog Museum,
which today memorializes the role that the town played in helping to shape the environmental
movement that was to follow.

orange from the flames, evoking Pittsburgh's most notorious epithet, Hell with the Lid Off.

*   *   *

As a boy, I was only dimly aware of the history behind all of this. Despite the region's problems, parts of southwestern Pennsylvania were still beautiful—and remain so to this day. But the effects of Pittsburgh's industrial legacy were visible everywhere, and I could never quite shake the feeling that in my home state something had gone terribly awry in the way that nature was treated, even by members of my own family.

Among my grandfather's most cherished pastimes, there was nothing he enjoyed more than driving up the road along the Youghiogheny River on a Sunday afternoon, dumping all the tin cans and glass bottles that my grandmother had saved up that week into the current, then jumping back in his car and racing downstream, where he would stand with his rifle and use the litter for target practice as it floated past. But perhaps the most telling sign of our relationship with the natural world was how my father introduced my brother and me to the form of outdoor recreation that he most enjoyed.

Whenever we visited my mother's parents, who lived in a rural area north of the city, my dad would tell Aaron and me that it was time to go on a hike, and the three of us would traipse off through the grove of pine trees directly behind the house, climb a low hill, and head into the "spilly piles," where local strip-mining operators had scraped off the topsoil and dug out the beds of coal, leaving behind rolling hillocks made of oily black slag and crushed gray shale.

In those years, almost nothing green would take root on the surfaces of those waste mounds, and the water that ponded in the sockets and craters turned a bright, poisonous shade of orange. In a reflection of how worthless and ignored the land had become, the slopes were littered with abandoned cars, rusted washing machines, and berms of garbage. Yet we spent our afternoons traversing the ridges and summits of those tailing fields. They were our mountains.

Judging by the manner in which the water and the land had been treated, it seemed to me that the place where I was born had been knocked off-center in a way that prevented us from treating it with respect, or even from recognizing how badly we had abused it. Which may, in turn, help to explain how radical it was for my father to hand me that copy of Colin Fletcher's book—and also why the image on its cover took such a firm hold of me, refusing to let go.

*   *   *

If my father's placing that book in my hands was an act of generosity and kindness, it was also a bit of a departure from the code by which he lived and navigated his life. Although my dad perceived the world through eyes that marveled at its vastness and wonder, he had little interest in moving beyond where he came from, taking comfort in the firmness of his resolve to remain close to home, and true to who he was. For me, however, that photograph seemed to offer concrete proof that there were places out there that hadn't yet been marred by smokestacks or foundries or heaps of slag. Places where you could strap on a pack, tie up your boots, and follow your gaze out to the horizons and beyond.

And the image held forth something else, too, which was the possibility that any who were willing to follow that restless Welshman into the abyss might find themselves forever changed—expanded, deepened, maybe even made whole. Because whatever had passed between Fletcher and the Grand Canyon, there was enough of it to fill up the pages behind that photograph with an entire book's worth of words.

In more ways than I could comprehend at the time, that image didn't simply open a window to another world; it also confirmed a hunch I had that the road from a place like Pittsburgh to a place like the Grand Canyon was neither direct nor short, and that if I wanted to traverse it, I would have to be prepared to travel a very long way.

Over the next couple of decades, that's exactly what I did. First to New York City and then England for college and grad school, followed by a job with a newsmagazine that covered events all over the globe, and finally to New Mexico for a stint with another magazine—in this case, one that published stories about adventure and the natural world.

All told, a quarter of a century would pass before I got my first glimpse of the canyon, and the sequence of events that delivered me to it kicked off with a white-knuckle drive over the Continental Divide in the winter of 2003.

PART II

The Witchery of Whitewater

He sat on the bank, while the river still chattered on to him,

a babbling procession of the best stories in the world,

sent from the heart of the earth.

—Kenneth Grahame, *The Wind in the Willows*

CHAPTER 4

The *Jackass* Chronicles

I t was early March, and a blizzard had engulfed much of the highway between Santa Fe and Flagstaff, where I was scheduled to visit the offices of an outfitter that ran guided whitewater expeditions on the Colorado to research a magazine story on river trips. At the time, I knew nothing about whitewater, so I had no idea what to expect when, after driving all night, I kicked the snow off my boots and stepped through the door of the boathouse into one of those moments you later identify as pivotal—a juncture where your life takes an abrupt turn, and you know that nothing after will ever be the same.

Inside, I found myself staring at a fleet of rowboats, each about seventeen feet long. They had been painted in an array of bright colors, and the sterns of several were decorated with hand-drawn images of plants and animals from the desert rivers of the Southwest: a Swallowtail Butterfly, a Bighorn Sheep, a cluster of Verbena blossoms. What struck me most forcefully about the boats, however, was that they boasted some of the loveliest lines I had ever seen in a watercraft. The camber of their gunwales—the rails running along the upper edges of the hull—mirrored the swelling flare of their hulls, and all of those curves came together at their stems to form a point as bold and fair as the tip of an Ottoman scimitar.

Five boats took up most of the cement floor, parked so closely together that their oarlocks almost touched. The rest were stacked in racks against the far wall, each nesting into its neighbors like the shells of Easter eggs. It took a moment for my gaze to be pulled up to the ceiling, where a set of steel trusses cradled half a dozen jagged shards of wood painted in the same bright colors, and after a moment or two, I shuddered with the realization that those pieces—bow posts, transoms, hatch lids—were all that remained of several vessels that had been demolished by the rapids in the canyon.

Then off in the far corner, I spotted something else: a boat all by itself, suspended from the ceiling on several loops of frayed nylon webbing. She had a beryl-green hull and bright red gunwales. Her decks were covered in dust, and she was tilted at an angle that exposed her decking, which made it possible to see that just above her right oarlock, someone had taped a piece of cardboard inscribed with a hand-drawn cluster of three-leafed clovers, and an epigraph that read FASTEST LUCKIE THROUGH THE GRAND CANYON.

The words were as much a mystery to me as everything else. I had no idea that those diminutive craft were legends on the Colorado, renowned not only for their elegance and dexterity, but also for the demands they made on anyone hoping to row them through the river's explosive hydraulics. I had no inkling that the men and women who had honed the skills required to pilot those boats, which were known as whitewater dories, belonged to one of the most rarefied confederacies in all of the outdoors: a company of tanned swashbucklers who were paid to spend their summers living and working in the heart of America's most famous national park.

Perhaps the only thing I did know that morning was that I was entranced. So I decided—right there—that although I was thirty-eight years old and had no business walking away from a steady income, I was going to have to find some way to sign on as an unpaid apprentice and follow those dories into the water-ravished world at the bottom of the grandest canyon on earth.

It's not unusual for men on the threshold of middle age to find themselves flirting with fantasies of turning the road map of their lives upside down. But most men are smart enough to abandon those visions after giving the matter some thought. Aside from my not having a family of my own who might have pulled me back to reality, I'm not confident that I can offer a satisfying explanation for failing to walk away from my own delusions, except to acknowledge a truth that anyone who has ever succumbed to the witchery of wooden boats finds impossible to deny—which is that dories are drop-dead gorgeous, and that a man who falls under the spell of that much beauty is apt to fling prudence and sanity straight out the window.

And if I'm being honest, something else was probably at work, too. Ever since I could remember, I had been seeking a place whose depths and distances extended beyond the furthest borders of my imagination. Consciously or not, some part of me understood that the prospect of stepping into a hidden kingdom of whitewater spoke to a longing that had taken root during my boyhood and had never relinquished its grip: the dream of leaving behind the world of my father and grandfather by immersing myself in the kind of wildness and grandeur that southwestern Pennsylvania had lost a long time ago.

*   *   *

When I say I wanted to "follow" those boats into the canyon, that's not completely accurate. What I really had in mind was sitting at the helm of a dory, oars in hand, and rowing it down the river myself—a conceit that underscores the magnitude of my naiveté and cluelessness when, for reasons that baffle me to this day, the operations manager at the company that owned the boathouse agreed to take me on.

"We'll put you on one of the early trips in April," he said. "All you need to bring with you is your toothbrush and a pair of shorts—the rest will get sorted out on the river."

In those years, a commercial dory trip through the canyon typically consisted of sixteen clients distributed across four dories, each captained by a guide who would fall in line behind the head guide, or trip leader—generally known as the TL—as the expedition made its way downstream. The boats covered roughly twenty miles a day, and it usually took just over two weeks to get all the way from Lee's Ferry to the Grand Wash Cliffs.

A hallmark of the company that took me on was that each dory was named after a natural wonder that had been irreparably harmed by humans. Among these were the *Hetch Hetchy* (Yosemite's sister valley, which was drowned by a dam in 1923), the *Diablo Canyon* (a pristine stretch of the California coastline where conservationists lost a bitter battle to block the construction of a nuclear power plant atop an earthquake fault in 1968), plus the *Hidden Passage*, the *Tapestry Wall*, and the *Ticaboo*—once-lovely features along the Colorado River now submerged beneath the waters of Lake Powell, the massive reservoir behind the Glen Canyon Dam, which sits a short distance above the entrance to the Grand Canyon.

The dories were also supported by a pod of two or sometimes three rubber rafts that were responsible for hauling most of the gear and supplies, along with the watertight bags containing the clients' clothing and tents. In the eyes of some, those rafts were bulbous and ungainly, basically a set of giant inner tubes, and although they had the advantage of not smashing to pieces when they were accidentally driven into a rock—which is why they were assigned to the novice rowers—the rafts boasted none of the dories' sleekness or finesse.

In keeping with the status of the trainees who piloted them, the baggage boats were named after things considerably less lyrical than vanished ecological treasures. Specifically, barnyard animals. There was the *Mule*, the *Ox*, the *Clydesdale*, and the boat I was posted to—which, fittingly, was called the *Jackass*.

It's shocking to look back now and acknowledge the depth of my own ignorance during that first river season. Among novice boatmen mistakes are inevitable as they struggle to unlock the 160-odd rapids studded along the canyon, the most vicious of which will flip a raft upside down and tear it to pieces like a pack of hyenas devouring a wildebeest. But by the summer, the consensus was that I seemed intent on setting some kind of new record for the most unpardonable screwups of any rookie in the canyon.

On one especially awful trip in July, shortly after breaking one of my oars in House Rock, the first truly serious rapid, I partially melted the plastic floor of the *Jackass* with a bucket of hot coals from the previous night's campfire. Then I slammed her into a granite wall just downstream from the Slate Creek Eddy, which runs next to one of the wickedest stretches of whitewater in the entire canyon, obliterating a second oar, plus one of my spares—they actually *exploded* from the force of the collision, something I hadn't thought possible. (One of the other baggage boatmen had to lend me an extra oar so that I could keep going.)

A few days later, I arrowed straight into a beach where we were planning to camp without bothering to slow down, smashing up against a pair of dories. That evening when the trip leader summoned me aboard his boat for an unscheduled performance review, I was told that if I didn't straighten up immediately, this would be my last trip.

You might think a warning like that would have been enough for me to get my act together. But on the very next trip, at a rapid known as Horn Creek, I rammed the stern of the *Jackass* into one of two large and highly visible midstream rocks that mark the entrance to the rapid like a set of goalposts, ricocheting the raft directly into a boat-eating hole deep and powerful enough to keep you submerged until you drown. When the compression wave at the front of that hole—aptly known as the Green Guillotine—surged over the bow, it hit me so hard that it slapped the wind from my lungs and the lenses from my sunglasses while catapulting me over the side of the boat.

Finding oneself tossed into the center of a major rapid is referred to as getting "Maytagged," and in this case the wash cycle started with a nasty crack to the side of my head—the blade of my right oar—as the current sucked me toward the bottom. As best I could determine, I was down for the better part of a minute, surrounded by darkness, struggling to move my arms, and almost out of air, when the hydraulics let go and spat me to the surface. There, I seized the gunwale of the nearest dory and was dragged through the tail waves like a sodden cat, gasping for breath while scanning the shoreline through my empty sunglass frames for bits and pieces of my poor raft, which I assumed had been demolished as thoroughly as the three oars from the previous trip.

"Relax, Kevin—everything's okay," said Billie Ray Prosser, the skipper of the dory to which I was clinging, whose astonishment at my stupidity was surpassed only by her kindness and decency. "The *Jackass* had a much better run than you did."

Sure enough, there she was: tucked neatly into an eddy on the far side of the river, having skated through the maelstrom on nothing more than the beneficence of the river and the shining force field of her own righteousness—an aspect of her character evidently called forth by my no longer being in the boat.

*   *   *

As late summer approached, it was becoming obvious to everyone that when it came to reading and rowing whitewater, I was a total washout. Sadly, I was even worse at my duties onshore, especially those that involved cooking. I oversalted the tuna salad at lunch, I undercooked the pasta for dinner, and in a ham-fisted effort to make up for those errors, while fixing breakfast I burned the bacon to a crisp and turned the pancakes into hockey pucks—twice. But the truly unforgivable blunder took place one night when I was asked to carry a tray loaded with two dozen pork tenderloin medallions that had been marinating in a honey-garlic sauce over to the grill, tripped on a rock, and dumped everyone's favorite meal in the sand.

"You might want to find a place to sleep away from camp tonight," the TL suggested. "Everybody's pretty upset with you right now, including me."

Somehow, the *Jackass* and I made it to the end of that season intact. The fact that I wasn't sent packing stands as a testament to both the power of free labor and the forbearance of the guides who were forced to work with me. But another factor was at work, too—an epiphany that came to me after observing how the crew handled the least appealing aspect of a river expedition.

Because most of Grand Canyon National Park is managed as a wilderness zone in which infrastructure and services are kept to an absolute minimum, none of the shoreline camps along the bottom of the canyon has toilets or outhouses. Instead, every whitewater expedition is compelled to store, transport, and properly dispose of its solid human waste.* To comply with this rule, one of the baggage rafts carries a specially designed latrine system, which in those years featured a set of rectangular metal army surplus canisters that were originally designed to store antitank grenade rockets for the U.S. military's M1A1 bazooka.

Each "rocket box" could handle approximately fifty deposits of human waste, and when full would tip the scales at about forty-five pounds. Its key feature was a hinged lid with a latch that created a watertight seal to prevent spillage while locking in the odors (mostly). Every evening after one of the canisters was set behind a screen of bushes at the edge of camp and the lid was pried up, a toilet seat was slapped on top, and the outhouse was open for business.

During an early river trip back in the 1970s, shortly after this system was invented, a toilet seat was accidentally left behind, and the sharp metal rims of the rocket box left telltale indentations on everyone's bum, earning a permanent nickname for the box: the *groover*. A large expedition that spent two and a half weeks on the river could easily fill nine or ten groovers, several of which were lashed on either side of the rowing cockpit in the toilet boat, while the rest were stowed in a hatch on the rear deck. If you were in charge of that raft, you would therefore find yourself surrounded by two sets of groovers as you rowed during the day, and then sleeping atop the rest of them at night.

Responsibility for the poop boat typically rotated among the baggage boatmen, all of whom cheerfully accepted it as part of the job. But the insight I gleaned a few weeks into that first summer was that because transporting excrement through the world's most sublime

---

* Because the average person tends to produce about a pound of poop each and every day, conditions would become exceedingly unpleasant if waste management weren't handled with exceptional care inside a narrow canyon that receives less than seven inches of annual rainfall, and where daytime temperatures in the summer can exceed 120°F.

natural wonder ranked close to last on most people's list of dreams and priorities, nobody was dumb enough to volunteer for this assignment on *every single trip*.

I also realized that although my skills were woefully deficient in every other aspect of river guiding, this was something I could handle. So the *Jackass* became the designated toilet boat, and I became known as the guy who would not only manage all the raw sewage, but would carry the rest of the trash, too.

By the end of the summer, I had a nickname of my own—Groover Boy—which would stay with me for the rest of my time on the river and beyond. I also had a tight system for rigging the rocket boxes, the toilet seat, and the garbage bags, plus the expedition's entire supply of liquid bleach, Clorox crystals, hand soap, scented air freshener (both jasmine and evergreen)—and most critical of all, our entire stash of toilet paper. One roll per person for every five days, a total of at least seventy rolls, none of which could get a drop of water on them.

Lashing all this down properly took thirty separate cam straps, including double backups to ensure that nothing would be lost if the boat was flipped upside down. This meant that each morning when I untied my lines and cast off, I was piloting a dung barge roughly the size of a one-ton pickup truck surrounded by a pile of trash, toilet products, and other people's poop—all of which would have to be steered through some of the biggest whitewater in the West.

Although the job placed me at the very lowest rung of the river ladder, captaining the *Jackass* yielded some useful dividends. In addition to conferring a measure of the dignity and pride that arise from the simple act of performing one's duties faithfully and well, my self-appointed gig enabled me to contribute something of value to the rest of the crew. That was enough to prevent me from getting sacked, and it allowed me to do what I wanted most, which was to keep returning to the canyon in the hopes of one day rowing a dory.

CHAPTER 5

The Emerald Cannonball

B ack then, it could take at least two or three years for a promising
beginner to be promoted out of the baggage pool into the driver's
seat of a dory, and far longer for anybody who struggled. But in
view of my inept oarsmanship, my bosses determined that I could be
entrusted only with cargo, never the lives of others, and I was permanently relegated to schlepping sewage and rubbish on the *Jackass*.

This, it must be confessed, was something of a setback—or, to put it
in terms that reflected my true feelings about the matter, transcenden-
tally soul crushing. But as time passed, frustration and despondency
were assuaged by the growing awareness that I was being introduced
to a mode of travel very different from Colin Fletcher's—and that for
the most part, it was actually pretty great.

Moving through the canyon in a boat had little in common with
lugging all of your gear and food on your back as you stumbled along
crumbling ledges from one stagnant pothole to the next. The river permitted us to carry anything we needed, and a lot more that we didn't,
and although storage space on the dories was extremely limited, each
baggage raft could haul a full ton, so we didn't hold back.

We brought thirty-seven-pound propane tanks, aluminum serving
tables, and eight-burner stoves for cooking; guitars and banjos for
entertainment; giant beach umbrellas for shade; and a seven-pound

collapsible camp chair for the comfort of each client and crew member—plus dinnerware. We carried high-tech rotomolded coolers with
three inches of insulation to keep our eggs cool, our lettuce crisp, and
our gin and tonics refreshed with ice. We even brought a rocket box
labeled THE LIBRARY, which was packed with about forty-five pounds
of books, including a comprehensive set of guides to the canyon's
mammals, birds, plants, fish, insects, reptiles, amphibians, and rocks.

These amenities afforded a level of comfort that long-distance trek-
kers such as Fletcher could only have dreamed about—but that was
just the start of the difference between boating and backpacking. The
corridor through which the river flowed was sumptuous and green, suffused with a lushness that made it feel like a watery domain unto itself,
a realm set entirely apart from the arid catwalks looming high above.

In the mornings, the air along the river was alive with pink-and-green
dragonflies that would perch on the shafts of your oars, quivering their
wings as you rowed, while the trill of the canyon wrens, the sweetest
birdsong on the river, dribbled down the walls. Along certain stretches,
every mile or two seemed to yield yet another bubbling spring where
a lacy umbrella of mosses and Maidenhair Fern jutted from the walls,
and as you skimmed beneath them in the afternoon heat, you would
be sprinkled with droplets of emerald-colored water. If the trip leader
decided to pull over next to a grotto or stream for lunch, you could steal
away for a catnap amid a bed of Golden Columbines, Scarlet Monkey
Flowers, and watercress the color of chartreuse. Then late in the day
you might find yourself drifting past clean, unmarked beaches in quiet,
nameless coves, marveling at the ripples on the sand, the texture of
the rock, and the softening tapestry of the light as evening drew near.

"Today was one of those days when I can't believe we actually get
paid to do this," one of the guides would exclaim as we pulled into
that night's camp.

"Livin' the dream," the rest of the crew would reply in unison.
"Livin' the dream!"

*   *   *

Through my position at the tail end of our flotilla (given my inability to properly gauge the currents, the *Jackass* was invariably the last boat in our running order), I witnessed things that left me dumbfounded. I watched as summer rainstorms triggered hundreds of waterfalls at the same time, each of them stained red or orange with dirt, pulsing with truckloads of gravel as they thundered en masse from the tops of the cliffs into the river. I floated beneath Bighorn Rams battling on the terraces above, the clonking of their horns echoing off the stone. Once, I even rowed up on a mother bobcat with her three kittens crouching next to the water less than twenty feet from my boat. I was so enraptured by the sight of their tiny pink tongues lapping in unison at the olive-colored current that I froze in midstroke, neither breathing nor moving the blades of my oars, as the river silently ferried me past them, then drew me around a bend.

Early one morning, at a smooth, horn-shaped beach called Stone Creek, which abuts the end of a long rapid known as Dubendorff, a flock of a dozen waterbirds arrived just after breakfast. They were pelicans, a remarkable enough sighting on its own, given that we were several hundred miles from the inland lake where they breed. But what happened next surprised us even more.

They flew in a miniature echelon, cutting low through the angled light, and touching down in the smooth water at the very top of Dubendorff—where they tucked their wings to their sides and piloted themselves straight into the middle of the rapid, maintaining the same formation they'd held in the air as they slid pertly down the glassy tongue of entry water called the V-slick, bobbed through the tumbling helix of whitewater, and permitted the tail waves at the bottom to nudge them into an eddy along the far shore, directly opposite from where we stood. Then they circled up, took to the air, flew straight back upstream to the head of the rapid—and dropped in to do the whole thing all over again.

When we realized that their first run wasn't just a one-off, we settled in to watch the show, which lasted for the rest of the morning as the pelicans ran the rapid again and again and again. As we admired their technique and studied the lines of current that they selected (which were quite elegant), we tried to guess what forces might be driving those birds. Were they lost and trying to recalibrate their bearings prior to flying out of the canyon? Were they hunting for fish in the eddies? Were they tormented by insects and using the turbulence to clean their feathers?

In the end, we were forced to concede that only one explanation made sense. The pelicans were simply besotted with whitewater—drawn to its beauty, captivated by its thrills, unable to break free of its joyous pull. Like us, they just couldn't get enough of it. And like me, they apparently had no desire to fly back to wherever they had come from.

                    *   *   *

Witnessing these and many other splendors, I came to love not only the Colorado but also its guides, a community of misfits, outcasts, and dreamers who were bound together by their addiction to its beauty. Glimpsing the world of the river through their eyes helped me understand the impulses and aspirations that induce everyone who falls prey to the canyon's seductions to hand over perhaps the finest parts of themselves to this landscape.

Like many close-knit communities, those guides could be reserved and haughty. They also sensed what I was slowly coming to recognize, which was that I would never truly be one of them. Yet they accepted my presence, overlooked my shortcomings, and even took me under their wing—in part because I was living and laboring in their midst (and hauling their sewage); but mainly, I think, because they were kind and openhearted people, and because they could see that I, like them, had been smitten by the river.

They never let me touch their oars or permitted me to pilot one of their boats—sensing, rightly, that the trick to mastering the dories was well beyond my grasp. But they did take the trouble to teach me how to read water and, eventually, to row a raft well enough to avoid making an ass of myself. Even more important, they permitted me to sit in on a ritual that unfolded around the same time each day: the moment when the sun slipped beyond the rimrock, gilding the tops of the canyon's walls while lavender traces of twilight suffused its bottom. At this hour, with the passengers padding off to their tents, and the first of the planets and stars winking in the darkening sky, the guides gathered around the campfire or on the decks of one of their boats to do what they did even better than tackling whitewater, which was to entertain themselves by telling river stories.

Some of those tales were precise and accurate, while others amounted to nothing more than shameless fabrication, and together they ran the spectrum from the high-minded to the heroically vulgar. But they were all entertaining, and the more nights I spent beneath the stars listening to those tales unspool, the clearer it became to me that so many of them were revolving and cohering, like the constellations in the Milky Way above, around something larger than themselves. A set of narratives that had unfolded during one magnificent river season more than twenty years earlier, involving a man whose influence on me, at least when it came to the canyon, would far exceed that of Colin Fletcher.

*   *   *

Kenton Grua was raised, for the most part, in a small rural town in the northeastern corner of Utah, a place where there were few opportunities to see the outside world. But from the moment he got his first glimpse of the canyon on a river trip as a teenager in the summer of 1962, he knew he had no need to travel farther, because he was hooked. A few years later, he dropped out of college and returned for a series of gigs that eventually led him to the only outfitter that was committed to running the river exclusively in dories.

His friends observed, correctly, that he was built like a wolverine—short and wiry, ferociously strong, with a thick coat of hair covering his arms, legs, and back—and they were equally accurate when they admitted that it would be something of an understatement to say that he was obsessed with every aspect of the dories. In his hands, the boats responded like floating mandolins, vibrating in tune with the harmonics of the river. But the folks who knew him best also understood that this fixation was a proxy for an even deeper fascination with the canyon, which he could never seem to get enough of.

"It just seems like it's going to go on forever, and then—*boom*—it's over," he would exclaim at the end of his trips. "I want to do this again!"

One manifestation of that obsession was his conviction that when you were in the canyon, there was an absolutely right way and an absolutely wrong way to do absolutely everything, regardless of whether it was gathering sticks for a campfire, boiling water for coffee in the morning, or rigging a temporary patch for a hole in the side of a boat that had been driven into a rock. He also developed a fondness for measuring himself against the landscape.

Once, for no justification other than that it seemed like an elegant thing to do, he tried to row an entire river trip without ever taking his oar blades out of the water; another time, for similar reasons, he decided it would be fun to see if he could ascend and descend a series of rock ledges along a chain of waterfalls without using his hands. His most celebrated test was at Deer Creek, a place of special significance for members of the Paiute tribe that features a gap between two towering walls of sandstone. Although the space appeared to be too wide for a person to jump across, a set of prehistoric handprints affixed to the stone suggested that the fissure may once have served as a prehistoric initiation site.

Finally one summer after screwing up his courage and making the leap, Grua discovered that he enjoyed the thrill so much that he kept repeating the jump for the rest of the season until the approach of autumn, when he launched himself into the air—only to realize halfway across that something was off. He barely cleared the gap, landing so awkwardly that he was on the verge of toppling into the crevice and plummeting to his death when, mysteriously, he felt a pair of invisible hands take hold of his body and pull him back until his balance was restored.

Prior to this, Grua hadn't devoted a great deal of thought to spirituality or the afterlife. But from that moment forward, he was convinced that the ancient peoples of the canyon maintained a physical presence on the landscape, a force as tangible and real as the rock itself.

To outsiders, stunts such as the leap at Deer Creek—which he never tried again following his near miss—may have appeared pointless and contrived. But to Grua, they were simply an expression of his desire to know the landscape in its entirety and to touch its essence as directly as possible: with the tips of his fingers and the soles of his feet. In time, he would come to consider the canyon to be as essential to his vitality as the air he breathed—and perhaps the tensile nature of that bond accounted for his response in the summer of 1983, more than a decade into his career, when the Colorado's runoff reached a level of savagery that hadn't been witnessed in a full generation.[*]

*   *   *

The crisis was set in motion earlier that winter when a series of El Niño–driven "superstorms" collided against the Central Rockies, blanketing the headwaters of the Colorado with a snowpack that continued building throughout the spring. Then in late May, the temperatures shot up without warning, sending a rush of meltwater cascading down the west side of the Continental Divide toward Lake Powell and the Glen Canyon Dam.

When federal officials realized that water was pouring into the reservoir faster than it could be released through the dam's power plant, raising the possibility that the dam might be overtopped, they began dumping as much water as possible downstream by opening Glen's enormous spillway tunnels—which, despite their size, weren't designed to handle an overflow of that magnitude. The force of the water inflicted catastrophic damage to the spillways, while simultaneously transforming the bottom of the canyon into a torrent studded with boat-sucking whirlpools and immense standing waves.

---

[*] For more background on why the runoff of that year was unique, please turn to the notes for chapter 5 at the end of this book.

In that moment, with engineers scrambling to save one of the largest gravity-arch dams in the United States, Grua spotted an opportunity to test his limits once again while deepening his connection with the canyon even further. He proposed to two of his fellow river guides, Rudi Petschek and Steve Reynolds, that they use the flood as a hydraulic catapult to propel them through the canyon fast enough to break the speed record from Lee's Ferry to the Grand Wash Cliffs, which at the time was just under forty-eight hours.

The key to pulling this off was Grua's dory, which boasted self-bailing footwells and a double set of oarlocks. She was named the *Emerald Mile* after a towering stand of California redwoods that had been slated for clear-cutting by a lumber company intent on disqualifying the grove from inclusion in a national park. She was also the very same boat—the one with the beryl-green hull and the bright red gunwales hanging from the corner of the boathouse—that would catch my eye twenty years later, on my first morning in Flagstaff.

When Grua and his crew shoved her into the Colorado at 11:00 on the night of June 25, they did so in defiance of the park's superintendent, who had shut down all river traffic to enable his rangers to concentrate on rescuing a number of boating expeditions that were already trapped inside the canyon. Grua's plan was for each man to take turns hauling on the oars as hard as he could in twenty-minute bursts. They would row day and night without pause, while calling on all their skills and stamina to keep the dory upright and in one piece until they punched through the Grand Wash Cliffs.

It was reckless, misguided, illegal—and utterly glorious: a once-in-a-lifetime chance to cannonball through the Colorado's deepest and most magnificent canyon under some of the most treacherous conditions imaginable, while coming face-to-face with the ancestral fury of a river that, before it had been shackled by a phalanx of twentieth-century dams and irrigation canals running from its headwaters to its delta, was once the wildest and freest waterway in the West.

To the astonishment of everyone, including themselves, they not only broke the record, but smashed it to pieces, besting the previous time by more than ten hours. It was the kind of feat that could have turned Grua into a minor celebrity, inscribing his name in the annals of the canyon, had he made the slightest effort to trumpet what they'd pulled off. But in the years to come he resisted any temptation to promote himself, opting instead to devote his energies to what he loved more than anything else, which was rowing dories.

As a result, the legend of the speed run was confined mostly to the world beneath the rims, an anecdote trotted out around the campfire by guides who had known and worked with Grua, and whose deepest feelings about the Colorado were neatly encapsulated by the events surrounding the runoff of 1983.

All of which gave me something to ponder each night when the storytelling was over, and everyone headed off to sleep.

*   *   *

Listening to those yarns may not have been especially helpful to my career, at least not right away. Given my less than stellar boatmanship, the smartest move would have been for me to abandon the canyon and head off to find a half-decent desk job before my dory-addled delusions drifted even further onto the rocks. But the more I listened, the more my fascination deepened. Not just with the trio of deranged boatmen who were hell-bent on riding the crest of a giant flood through a place that most people strive to linger in rather than race through, but with all the other drama that had unfolded during that magnificent and terrifying deluge, including a second race to save a colossal, state-of-the-art dam that was supposed to have rendered such flooding a thing of the past.

It was one of the few stories that could, in my view, rival the greatest river legend of them all, which was John Wesley Powell's seminal odyssey in the summer of 1869. And in addition to being an exciting, turbocharged adventure, Grua's speed run also seemed to embrace a set of larger themes tied to the complexities and contradictions of the canyon: its beauty, its brutality, and the power it can wield over those who love it most deeply.

So, for better or worse, by the end of that first season I had decided that I was never going back to work in an office. Instead, I would somehow find a way to keep myself afloat during the winter by stringing together freelance magazine assignments, hopefully earning enough so that I could keep returning to the river and working next to the dory guides, until I'd gathered the material for a book.

A book that would lay out the history of the canyon and recount the story of the speed run in a straightforward manner, while simultaneously addressing something more mysterious and emotionally fraught, which was the impulse to compose a kind of extended note of appreciation—a love letter, really—from me to the world of wooden boats and whitewater at the bottom of the canyon.

Kenton Grua in his dory

CHAPTER 6

"Kind of a Crazy Idea"

All told, I would spend the better part of six seasons chasing dories and the story of the *Emerald Mile*. Each spring as the snowpack in the high country began to melt and the runoff started racing from the mountains to the canyon country, I would finish up my last magazine piece, clamber into my truck, and once again head west over the Divide to be back in Flagstaff for the first trips of the year. I would then spend a chunk of the next five months rowing and living on the *Jackass*, until autumn arrived and the aspen leaves on the North Rim turned gold, when it was time to return to Santa Fe.

During the river season, the smoke from our campfires worked so deeply into the fabric of my clothing that the aroma never faded. In that way, the canyon was always with me, no matter how far afield my assignments might lead.* Those were some of the finest summers of my life, filled with adventure and beauty in the company of friends who were convinced that we were in the best of all possible places working the best of all possible jobs (although, admittedly, in my case the job didn't actually result in my getting paid). And it was in those years that I came to learn—truly learn—about the world along the bottom of the chasm.

---

* And it's with me still, even today: almost a quarter century later, a faint whiff of juniper smoke is enough to deliver me back to my days and nights on the Colorado.

As with my understanding of rowing whitewater, much of the knowledge I acquired about the canyon came directly from the river guides, whose expertise included more than the handling of rowboats. Some were scientists with advanced degrees in geology or botany or entomology; others were artists who painted, sculpted, or blew glass, and there was even a smattering of musicians and dancers and poets. They were people who responded deeply to their surroundings and paid keen attention to the landscape. They were also generous with sharing, and between them and the library—from which I read voraciously at night—I slowly acquainted myself with the detailed workings of the river.

Much of this new information was rather technical. It wasn't unusual (indeed, it became something of a joke) for a guide to get up at midnight to check the mooring lines and spot the captain of the *Jackass*, headlamp on and pen in hand, perched atop his poop boxes poring over a color-coded bathymetric riverbed survey that someone had handed him earlier that afternoon, or earnestly underlining a monograph on the chemical profile of groundwater discharges along the South Rim. I read about everything I could get my hands on: the distribution of riparian insect hatchings, the patterns of river-sediment migration, the mating protocols of Spotted Sandpipers and Harlequin Ducks.

But alongside this torrent of hard data, all of which added depth and nuance to my understanding of the river's scientific profile, I was also lapping—like that family of bobcats—at the edge of another stream. A cascade of softer impressions that had less to do with natural history and more to do with the moods and cadences of the river as it pushed through the canyon. The silky, sensuous feel of the weather-polished granites and limestones along the shore, or the feathery hiss made by grains of sand suspended in the water column as they swept against the bottom of the boats. How the wind could come tearing up the canyon at more than fifty miles an hour, ripping off the tops of each ripple, flinging sheets of spray straight in your face in a way that was wild and fierce and deeply thrilling. Or how, sometimes when the river narrowed, the hull of your boat would ride the downstream current while the blade on each of your oars plied an eddy in which the water was running upstream, so that the river was literally pulling you in two directions at once, as if it couldn't decide between sending you on to whatever it wanted to show you next, or pulling you back for a second look at something it thought you'd missed.

Clearly, my impression of this place was being filtered through the prism of water, which meant that I was also taking in a conceit shared by everyone around me: the belief that the Colorado was the truest and deepest essence of the canyon. And how could it be otherwise? The river, after all, was the instrument that had carved the abyss and sculpted its walls, as well as the elixir that quickened and sustained the ribbon of life along the base of what otherwise appeared, from the river's vantage, to be a soaring matrix of mostly lifeless precipices: a stonescape of stark ruination, haunted by far too little water and far too much of God's indifference to ever make it anything but hostile and terrifying.

As far as we boatmen were concerned, the Colorado was the canyon's centerpiece and highlight, the wellspring of its vitality and grandeur. Everything else—the cliffs and terraces, the wind and sky, the starlight and the moonbeams—all those elements merely served as backdrop and supporting ensemble for the one defining feature that mattered most. And clearly, no one had embraced the idea of the river's primacy more wholeheartedly than Kenton Grua himself.

Or so it seemed—until I started to realize that things weren't quite that simple. Not by a long shot. Which brings me to a very different kind of tale about Grua that I eventually started hearing around the campfire.

It was a story that took place long before the runoff of 1983, and the events were no less daring or dramatic than the speed run. But this story was somewhat unsettling, because if you listened to it carefully and thought about it hard enough, it could completely upend how you saw not only Grua himself, but the entire canyon.

*   *   *

To understand how that works, it's necessary to return to Colin Fletcher and recall the decision that he made when he was first planning his thru-hike, to abandon his initial vision of traversing the entire length of the canyon, and instead to focus on a shorter crossing of Grand Canyon National Park.

When *The Man Who Walked Through Time* was published in 1968, a year before Grua's first season as a river guide, it was saddled with a contradiction. In the text, Fletcher was admirably forthright in explaining exactly what he had done and not done—although he'd also claimed, nonsensically, that he was forced to dial back his original goal because the natural borders of the canyon were so "fuzzy" that no two people could agree on where it began and ended. The stickier problem was with the book's jacket, which was emblazoned with the statement that the author was "the first man ever to have walked through the entire length of the Grand Canyon."

Although that was patently false, most readers couldn't have cared less about the difference between the canyon and the park. In the minds of these people, the distinction sounded not only irrelevant and trivial, but downright hairsplitting. Surely the two must be one and the same; and even if they weren't, well—honestly, was there anybody out there fussy and pedantic enough to raise an objection?

Indeed, there was.

Even before he'd finished the book, Grua was incredulous. He was well aware that the canyon's geographic boundaries were clearly marked on any decent map, and that at the time of Fletcher's hike, the size and scope of the canyon far exceeded that of the park. (When Fletcher had set out, the park's eastern boundary was 53 miles downstream from Lee's Ferry, and its western border was almost 120 miles from the Grand Wash Cliffs.)

Grua also knew that although Fletcher's 250-mile odyssey may have sounded impressive, if the Welshman had traversed the full length of the canyon, he would have needed to walk somewhere between 600 and 700 miles, depending on which route he took. And finally, Grua knew that almost every square inch of the parts that Fletcher had skipped were devoid of even the barest hint of a trail, which meant that the lion's share of the hardest and most remote sectors, as well as the hottest and driest, still hadn't been traversed by anybody during the modern era.

In Grua's mind, this was more than a minor discrepancy. By confining himself to the park, the "man who walked through time" had omitted almost *two-thirds* of the canyon.

"Somebody else needs to do it," Grua grumbled to a friend, "and do it right."

Before long Grua figured out who that person should be, and in the autumn of 1973, he decided to tackle the job himself.

*   *   *

By this point, he had studied the route and the terrain far more meticulously than Fletcher had, mostly by scoping out long sections from his boat and taking careful notes during his river trips. He had also had time to think about the style in which he wanted to conduct the journey, an approach that differed from Fletcher's in a number of important ways, starting with footwear.

Among his many strong opinions, Grua was convinced that if the original inhabitants of the canyon had moved through the landscape without heavy hiking boots, he should do the same. So when he launched his walk on the final day of September, he was clad in a pair of Native American–style moccasins, which he pronounced "the next best thing to going barefoot."

Thanks to the route he'd selected, his small North Face rucksack was astonishingly light compared with the cargo that Fletcher had hauled. By sticking as close as possible to the river and steering clear of the high terraces frequented by Fletcher, where the walking was easier but springs were extremely scarce, Grua was betting that he would never have to haul more than a single gallon of water, which weighs roughly eight pounds. He also cut weight by abstaining from the kind of fancy treats that Fletcher loved, which meant no smoked-oyster hors d'oeuvres in the evening before dinner, nor any claret with which to wash them down. (While Fletcher's "skin-out load"—the total weight of everything he carried, including food, water, and the clothing he wore—tipped the scales at sixty pounds, the contents of Grua's pack never exceeded thirty.)

At first, things went better than expected as Grua skipped down-canyon with his ultralight dunnage. "My body is holding up well," he noted in the pages of his journal that first evening, "and my head is soaring like a raven on the wind." By the end of the following day, he was moving so fast that he reached that night's objective with three hours of daylight to spare.

"If things continue to go this well," he observed self-assuredly, "perhaps I will finish in less than two months"—the time it had taken Fletcher to get through just the park. Only later would Grua recognize that this moment of brash optimism marked the high point of his venture, and from that moment forward, things would rapidly start to unravel.

The heat didn't make things easy—it was 98°F in the shade. But the bigger problem was the moccasins, which were already exhibiting serious signs of wear.

To preserve the leather he tried walking barefoot, but found this impossible the moment he hit a razor-sharp layer of limestone. Soon, he was toying with the idea of using the nuts and seeds in his food bag to concoct some sort of glue to patch his fraying footwear.

"I guess I would have to say that doing this with moccasins was kind of a crazy idea," he confided to his journal that night. "But then, doing it at all was kind of a crazy idea too!"

The following morning, he reached a set of cliffs that cut him off from the river for an interminable stretch, forcing him to spend hours picking across fields of loose boulders amid the scorching heat. By the time he found a route back to the river, the moccasins were falling to pieces and his water was gone.

"A pretty close call," he admitted after flinging himself into the river. "In many ways, I am damn lucky to be alive."

Just before reaching camp that evening, he was debating whether to hike out and purchase a pair of boots when he accidentally stepped on a dead cactus, driving several spines through a hole in his right moccasin, straight into the ball of the foot.

He spent the next day limping in pain while holding out hope that things might get better. By that night, his right foot was swollen with an infection that would need at least a week to heal, while his left foot was tender and badly bruised.

The following morning, he conceded that his hike was over and prepared to hitch a ride downstream with a party of river runners.

"I am beaten—I was beaten before I began," he remarked in disgust, noting that he'd barely lasted a week, and drew a conclusion that had the ring of finality:

"I've decided against trying it again."

So much for lowering the boom on Colin Fletcher.

*   *   *

After returning home, Grua's resolve against making a second attempt only grew stronger. The more he thought about it, the more convinced he became that his impulse to one-up Fletcher was petty and conceited, unworthy of the majesty of the land.

"I can see little point in continuing further for the purpose of becoming the first person to walk through the canyon," he declared. "Perhaps this is a lesson in life for me."

Accordingly, he scrapped the project and devoted the next couple of river seasons to honing his whitewater skills. But as time passed, his thoughts began returning to the deceptive claim on the cover of Fletcher's book—especially after the winter of 1975, when Congress, responding to years of pressure from conservationists, finally agreed to dramatically expand the park by pushing its borders all the way to Lee's Ferry and the Grand Wash Cliffs (a story that we'll return to in more detail later).

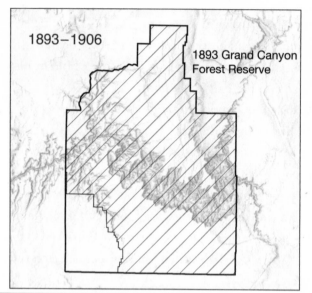

1893–1906

1893 Grand Canyon
Forest Reserve

1906–1908

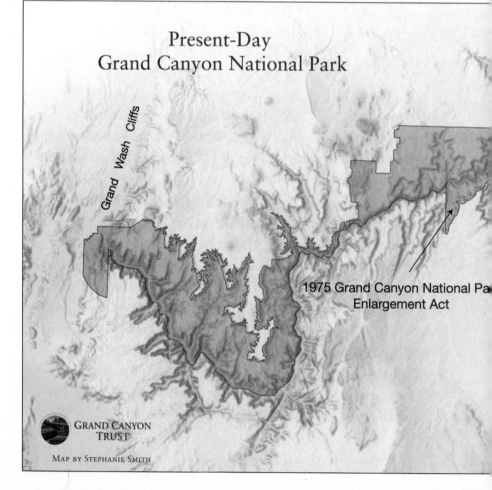

Present-Day
Grand Canyon National Park

Grand Wash Cliffs

1975 Grand Canyon National Pa
Enlargement Act

GRAND CANYON
TRUST

MAP BY STEPHANIE SMITH

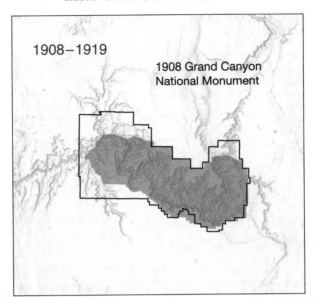

1906 Grand Canyon Game Preserve

1908–1919

1908 Grand Canyon National Monument

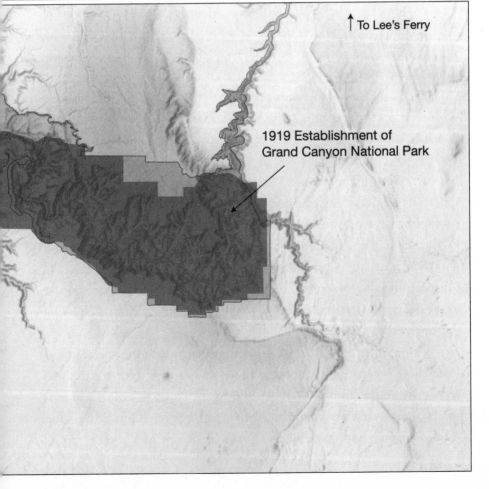

↑ To Lee's Ferry

1919 Establishment of Grand Canyon National Park

This meant that not only were canyon and park now congruent, but that neither had been traversed on foot by anyone in the modern era—a reminder of the unfinished business awaiting Grua's attention in the world beneath the rims.

"The idea won't leave me alone," he noted in his journal. "I'm very seriously, at times, considering trying it again."

Eventually, the pull was too strong to resist. But this time, he resolved, things would be different. So in the midst of gathering his gear, finalizing his maps, and prepping his food caches in the winter of 1977, he went to JCPenney and bought himself a pair of high-topped leather boots with thick Vibram soles.

He departed from Lee's Ferry on February 28 with the aim of traveling solo except for two relatively short stretches, in which he would be accompanied either by his girlfriend, Ellen Tibbets, or a friend from Alaska. But regardless of whether he was in their company or by himself, he advanced with incredible speed, as if he were a pebble being hurled from a slingshot.

He was underway every morning by six and would hike all day without stopping, pushing forward until darkness overtook him. The routine remained largely unchanged, except that as March arrived and the days got longer, he was able to spend more hours on the move between sunrise and sunset. He covered between fifteen and twenty miles a day, a punishing pace to sustain even on a trail, and on a number of days he covered closer to twenty-five or even thirty miles.

On the day after St. Patrick's, he shot past the halfway mark, and shortly after that found himself in the most daunting section of the journey, which lay along the limestone cliffs beyond the western border of the old park. There he found a passage through the cliffs by following the tracks of Bighorn Sheep.

All along the route, he saw plenty of evidence that the ancients had been there before him. Although there was no sign of a continuous trail, it was clear from the artifacts they'd left behind—colorful sherds of clay pottery, neatly knapped arrowheads, the remnants of roasting pits—that they had connected with the landscape at a level he could only imagine, and he was awed by the knowledge that he was moving in their footsteps.

By April Fools' Day, he was in the home stretch, and less than a week later—just thirty-seven days after he had started—he reached the end of the canyon and popped through the Grand Wash Cliffs. By his best reckoning, he had hiked just over six hundred miles, covering more than twice the distance Fletcher had traversed in almost half the time—a feat that had less to do with superior discipline or drive (Fletcher had plenty of both) and a great deal more to do with Grua's being a decade younger than Fletcher while carrying less than half of his pack weight.

In addition to being the first person in the recorded history of the modern era to walk through the entire canyon, Grua had inadvertently set a speed record that wouldn't be broken for thirty-five years.

* * *

Perhaps it's no surprise that the story of these two men is sometimes framed as a rivalry between implacable adversaries. From this perspective, Grua's trek is presented as a well-deserved rebuke to Fletcher's fraudulence. For a number of reasons, however, that's neither accurate nor fair. Better, perhaps, to see them less as bitter antagonists and more as unwitting collaborators in a joint effort to explore and celebrate the hidden folds of a monumental landscape—an unintended partnership whose twin legacies are as disparate as their personalities, yet equally inspiring to those who love wilderness.

Shortly after the publication of *The Man Who Walked Through Time*, Fletcher came out with an encyclopedic primer on the techniques and tools of backcountry trekking called *The Complete Walker*, which was embraced as a kind of bible for long-distance hikers. Over the next twenty years, the two books would sell more than a million copies, inspiring wilderness devotees of all stripes to explore marathon routes such as the Pacific Crest Trail (2,650 miles), the Continental Divide Trail (3,100 miles), and the most famous of them all, the Appalachian Trail—the classic 2,192-mile thoroughfare extending from Georgia to

Maine. "He was to backpacking what Walter Cronkite was to reporting or what Leonard Bernstein was to music," wrote his biographer, Robert Wehrman. "When Colin Fletcher had something to say, people listened."

All of which contrasted starkly with Grua, who treated his own thru-hike with the same reticence that he would later display toward his speed run in the *Emerald Mile*. He gave no interviews, called no press conferences, delivered no lectures, published no articles or books, and never shared a word with anyone, including his wife, from the 285-page journal he kept during his hike.

Despite his discretion, however, word of Grua's exploits slowly percolated among friends and acquaintances, and like groundwater that has filtered through porous rock, the trickle of details that emerged was pure and exhilarating. He may not have inspired a generation of outdoor enthusiasts on the level that Fletcher had. But when Grua passed away in the late summer of 2002, he was considered a legend among a community of canyon fanatics who were (and remain to this day) as awed by his disinterest in fame or profit as they were by the astonishing feats he had pulled off in the world beneath the rims.*

The record he set in the *Emerald Mile*—thirty-six hours, thirty-eight minutes, and twenty-nine seconds—would stand for more than thirty years before it was finally topped, twice in the same week, during the winter of 2016, by two separate parties of kayakers. Remarkably, this means that the speed record for an oar boat has yet to be broken—a benchmark that may stand indefinitely as the Colorado's flows continue to drop amid an era of accelerating climate change, and floods such as the one that powered the runoff of 1983 become a distant memory. But even if Grua's speed record holds forever, it is his achievements on foot that will probably be remembered as the greater of the two triumphs.

Meanwhile, thanks to Grua's epic walk, a new challenge opened up for a coterie of extreme backpackers who had the skills and the

---

* His death was caused by an aortic dissection, a spontaneous tear in the large blood vessel branching off his heart, which occurred during a mountain-bike ride near his home in Flagstaff. He was fifty-two years old.

determination to forge their own thru-hikes. All of them understood that traversing the canyon on foot was fundamentally different from any other long-distance trek anywhere: a category unto itself, without analog or antecedent, whose uniqueness was underscored by just how few people, in the coming years, would dare to attempt what Grua had done.

Among the few who tried to pull it off, most were responding not only to the summons of the adventure, but to something that spoke to them on a deeper and more instinctive level. It was a facet of Grua's character, as radical then as it is now, that may have achieved its keenest articulation in the moment when he decided, all those years ago, to make that leap across the precipice marked by the ancient set of handprints affixed to the wall at Deer Creek.

For anyone attempting to follow in Grua's footsteps, perhaps the most provocative and inspiring aspect of his legacy was the sincerity of his efforts to acknowledge the presence of the ancient people of the canyon by reaching across the gap between our world and theirs. And he bridged another kind of divide, too—because his thru-hike affirmed the presence of a largely hidden and still-unknown realm suspended between the bottom of the canyon and its rims: the kingdom of pure rock that most river guides and boatmen had little interest in learning about or exploring.

For a number of years, that group also included me—until one summer, when the domain into which Grua had ventured began calling out in a manner that was too insistent and too compelling to ignore.

CHAPTER 7

The Real Deal

On most of our river expeditions, we did our best to encourage the passengers to explore parts of the canyon on foot by offering up a series of hikes. Every second or third day, the trip leader would announce that a guided excursion was on the menu and usher everybody up a side canyon to show them something of interest, often a waterfall or a set of prehistoric relics.

Partly because many of our clients were older or had little experience moving over uneven terrain (and partly because we boatmen, for the most part, weren't exactly CrossFit endurance athletes ourselves), these sojourns were usually brief, never more than a few hours ambling in shorts and sandals, with each person clutching a sandwich and a single bottle of water. Although some of those hikes could *feel* ambitious and rugged, especially during the heat of midsummer, I had no sense of just how limited they were: how little we had seen, and how negligibly we had penetrated into the rock, when the guide who was leading the hike stopped—often at a ledge or slope that would require some hard scrambling to surmount—and announced that it was time to turn around and return to the boats.

Virtually everything beyond those turnaround points was terra incognita in the minds of the crew. Few of them seemed to know much about Colin Fletcher, and when they referred to Grua, it was almost always in connection with his exploits on the river. Sometimes, it seemed as if the soaring matrix of rock on either side of the Colorado didn't truly exist, at least not as a place that anyone would consider going. And for the most part, our passengers were happy to adopt this same mindset—although every now and then, one of them would pause at the turnaround point, overcome by curiosity.

"So, what's up there?" the passenger would ask, peering up at the sun-blasted rock and the impassable cliffs.

"Dunno—nobody's ever been past this point," the guide would say, shrugging. "People just don't *go* there."

Judging by the evidence at hand, this appeared to be entirely accurate. In those days, aside from day hikers on the main trails leading down to the river and the backpackers who camped at Phantom Ranch, we never saw much evidence that anyone went anywhere on foot in the deep backcountry. Until one evening in the summer of 2006, when something unusual took place.

*   *   *

It happened at Pancho's Kitchen, a sand beach in the central part of the canyon that was one of our favorite spots to camp because it featured a massive overhang that offered ample shade in the summer, and solid protection from wind and rain during a storm. It was late May, with temperatures that had pushed into the upper nineties that afternoon, and I was in the kitchen beneath the overhang chopping vegetables for dinner when I caught sight of the TL, who went by the nickname Bronco, standing at the water's edge staring at something directly across the river.

When I followed his gaze, I spotted four men with backpacks, picking their way along the shore in single file through a set of boulders. They were dressed like bedouins in loose-fitting pants, baggy long-sleeved shirts, and hoods to protect their skin from the sun. Clearly, from the grimaces on their faces and the way their legs were quivering, each step demanded intense focus and every move hurt. To my eye they appeared absolutely exhausted—a conclusion Bronco had evidently drawn, too, because he was already untying his dory and shoving her off the sand into the water.

The men were so fixated on where to put their feet that they didn't even look up as he rowed out of the eddy next to our camp and knifed his boat into the main current at an angle that shot him neatly into the eddy next to the hikers. After listening to him for a moment, they took off their packs, clambered into his boat, and sat quietly as he performed the same crosscurrent trick in reverse.

"Let's get some more food going," he said to me after he'd delivered them to our camp. "These guys are having dinner and spending the night with us."

I was too busy cooking and washing dishes that evening to chat with the backpackers during dinner, and by the time I was ready to sit down, they had already devoured several plates of food and retreated to their sleeping bags. But I did get a good look at them—their torn and ragged clothing, their chapped and split lips, and the coating of sweat-caked grime on their bodies that they were too exhausted to wash off in the river.

I never forgot the look in their eyes. It was like nothing I'd ever seen in the faces of the boatmen I worked with, even on our toughest days: a mixture of misery, fatigue, and defeat—plus something that looked strangely like euphoria. I had no idea what to make of that look, but it suggested to me that the world of cliffs and ledges was considerably less pleasant, far more confounding, and perhaps every bit as magnificent as anything on the river.

The following morning, we fed the backpackers a huge breakfast, then Bronco ferried them back across the river, delivering them to the exact spot where he'd picked them up. They all shook hands with him, then shouldered their packs and resumed toiling through the boulders.

After Bronco returned to camp, he raised his hand in a two-fingered salute, a gesture he normally reserved for a boatman who had threaded through an especially nasty piece of whitewater.

"Look at 'em go," he murmured. "Those guys are the real deal."

*   *   *

Our encounter with those hikers stayed with me. Sometimes the memory of the battered look of euphoria they bore in their eyes would return to me late at night when I had put aside my reading and was gazing out at the river from the deck of the *Jackass*, watching the current rippling in the starlight beneath the darkened cliffs. Their faces had made it clear that they were haunted by something they had seen up there.

In those moments, just before drifting off to sleep, I would find myself thinking about the hundreds of thousands of acres of rock looming in the darkness above the water, and I would remind myself that as exhilarating and seductive as the river was, its footprint amounted to less than 1 percent of the surface area of the rest of the canyon, the bulk of which couldn't even be seen from the river.

How much did you truly know about the canyon if all you knew was the river? I wondered. What about the rest of this place—the other 99 percent?

In those moments, too, my thoughts would turn to Grua and his long walk.

Where had he gone, and what had he seen? What might it be like to follow him up into that labyrinth and roam the ramparts as he had done—to inhale its fragrances, to feel its heat, to meet its citizens, plant and animal alike? And did he carry the same haunted look as the backpackers at Pancho's?

Plus, there was another question—a query provoked by all the reading I was doing that was so subversive I never dared to share it with any other boatman or guide, because it amounted to a form of river heresy.

The longer I spent at the bottom of the canyon, the more it seemed to me that the Colorado embodied a curious contradiction: the conundrum of a river that felt wild and free, especially at the top of rapids such as Horn Creek or Dubendorff, but that also served as a thoroughfare for travelers equipped with many of the comforts you'd find in a high-end motor home, including lawn chairs, kitchen tables, and iceboxes.

What's more, thanks to the giant dam anchored at the head of the canyon, plus eighteen other dams up and down the rest of the river, every cubic foot of the Colorado's flow was metered and rationed by a vast network of infrastructure for water storage, hydropower, and flood control upon which the entire Southwest depended. No other river in America was more rigorously controlled or more stringently regulated—and none had been exploited so ruthlessly that, according to one set of calculations, every drop of its water was used and reused up to seventeen times before the Colorado dried up and died in the Sonoran Desert south of the border.

In effect, the river that had carved the Grand Canyon was no longer nature as much as plumbing—a system so efficient that even in the wettest years, not so much as a teaspoon of its waters was permitted to reach the sea.

How wild was *that*?

And was it possible, perhaps, that the purest, truest wilderness in the canyon might no longer reside along the Colorado, but instead be found amid the austere and all but untrammeled world of cliffs and ledges above?

*   *   *

Evidently, these questions could be answered only by leaving the river behind and venturing into the deepest recesses of the canyon's backcountry. But if the notion of attempting to follow Grua's lead had ever occurred to me during that summer, I would have dismissed it out of hand—and for good reason.

In addition to lacking the expertise required for a thru-hike of my own, I wouldn't have known whom to turn to for advice or where to begin. And if all of that weren't enough of a deterrent, I was confronting a set of far more pressing challenges.

As the summer came to an end, I found myself in a position nobody would envy. Thanks to my obsession with the canyon, at the age of forty-one I had no wife, no children, and almost no money in my bank account. According to a survey of incomes across the United States in a magazine article handed to me by another boatman, I had apparently made less money the previous year than a part-time doughnut fryer in Baltimore, a pet psychologist in Albuquerque, and a hospital clown in New York City.

I had a feeling that the wife, the kids, or even a dog probably weren't going to happen, at least not anytime soon, and I was more or less okay with that. But if I was to have a prayer of finishing the research for the book I wanted to write, I was going to have to find a better way to make some money.

And that, for better or worse (maybe both), is where Pete McBride comes into this story.

PART III

You Can't Fix Stupid

Pete McBride on the back of a yak, Everest Base Camp

We've been friends for so long,

I can't remember which one of us is the bad influence.

—T-shirt, gift shop, South Rim of the canyon

CHAPTER 8

Fricking *Grand*

The story of how little Pete and I have in common—and thus how ill-suited we are to work together, much less be friends—begins with his being raised in a part of the American West that represents the antithesis of Pittsburgh. A place that comes as close to paradise as one could possibly imagine.

The McBride family ranch, which included two hundred acres of lush, green meadows bordered by dense stands of aspen, was nestled at the base of Colorado's Elk Mountains and framed by a wall of twelve-thousand-foot peaks whose summits gleamed with snow, even in July. Its fields were irrigated from the headwaters of Capitol Creek, and any water that wasn't taken up by the timothy and the clover used to feed the cattle made its way toward the Roaring Fork River, and from there into the Colorado for a five-hundred-mile journey down the western slope, through the badlands of southeastern Utah, and directly into the Grand Canyon.

Back in the late seventies, when Pete was a boy, the property was so far from the nearest town—the still-emerging skiers' paradise of Aspen—that it was known as the Lost Marbles Ranch, a name that captured exactly how Pete's parents assessed his state of mind in the summer of 1997 when he informed them that, after attending an expensive Ivy League college without having bothered to take a single course in photojournalism, he intended to become a photographer in the world of outdoor adventure.

Over the next several years, he barnstormed from one continent to the next on a series of assignments for magazines such as *National Geographic*, trekking from the mountains of Bhutan to the high deserts of the Andes, kayaking along the west side of the Antarctic Peninsula, and walking the rainforests of the Amazon, where an eight-foot-long electric eel once shimmied between his legs. He visited more than seventy-five countries, and the images he shot in those faraway places were a testament not only to his skills with a camera, but his tenacity: a stubborn and sometimes perverse refusal to give up on whatever he'd started, no matter how difficult things might get.

In part, this pigheadedness was a product of the years he'd spent playing hockey and ski racing, sports that had honed his strength and fitness to a keen edge. Without much effort, he could spend days breaking trail through waist-deep snow—as he did in the Indian Himalayas while tracing the length of the Ganges River—or a week slogging through water up to his chest in Gabon. But the primary reason Pete neither broke nor wavered during those and many other expeditions was linked to his older brother Johno, who coached for both the U.S. and the Canadian men's Olympic ski teams, specializing in the downhill, the most dangerous of all the World Cup and Olympic events, in which racers often exceed ninety miles an hour.

During the years that Johno spent working with elite athletes, he became convinced that the limits of both performance and endurance were defined not by physiology, but the mind, and although this wasn't exactly a revolutionary idea, the training methods he developed from this insight were, to say the least, unusual. The men who made the cut for his teams found themselves heading to California to attend a training camp run by former Navy SEALs, sprinting up sand dunes, racing wheelbarrows loaded with rocks or sand, and spending hours immersed in frigid surf. Because Johno accompanied them every step of the way, his racers were subjected to the added torture of having to listen to him continually hammer home the central tenet of his philosophy:

"When you know there's a good chance you're going into the red room, you have to reach down and find a different place mentally," he'd tell his squad.* "The thing that distinguishes successful athletes from everybody else is a realization that your limits are not necessarily where you think they are—and that your body is capable of doing more, often far more, than you expect it can."

Although Pete never really tried to make the downhill team, he absorbed many of these ideas, in particular the conviction that any challenge could successfully be met with the right combination of drive, grit, and sunny optimism—and if this proved insufficient, well, it was okay to just wing it.

That more or less summed up the essence of who Pete was when our paths first crossed as freelancers back in the early 2000s, and he proposed we start working together as a two-man writer-photographer team. From the get-go, I realized that his approach to journalism— which seemed to be based on a habit of getting in far over his head, combined with a disinclination to pay close attention to important details—in many ways mirrored how I had been handling the *Jackass*, with similar results.

*   *   *

Our first trip was to the Canadian Arctic, where we were supposed to witness the migration of the Porcupine caribou herd, the largest and most magnificent movement of mammals in North America, and document their crossing of a remote river called the Firth, which Pete assured our editors at *National Geographic Adventure* "shouldn't be too big of a deal," given the size of the herd (roughly 123,000 animals, flanked by wolves, grizzly bears, and other predators). Unfortunately, we planned so poorly that we failed to locate a single caribou, returning home with little to show, aside from a lone photo capturing a set of antlers lying

---

* When a skier loses control and veers into the crash fences on either side of the racecourse, it's known as "going into the red room."

forlornly on the tundra—which, one of the magazine's fact-checkers indignantly informed me, had actually belonged to a moose.

Six months later, we found ourselves in the Republic of Georgia hoping to explore the untapped backcountry ski-mountaineering opportunities in the Caucasus Mountains along the border with Chechnya, where the Russian army had been battling Islamic rebels. (Pete had pitched the story as a cutting-edge venture into a kind of skiers' DMZ where adventure overlapped with, or was at least enlivened by, the specter of guerrilla warfare—an idea whose ludicrousness was surpassed only by our astonishment when we learned that it had been green-lighted by an editor at *Skiing* magazine.)

Unfortunately, the road to the Chechen border was blocked by a series of avalanches triggered by a huge storm system over the Black Sea, which a cursory peek at the weather report would have warned us about, had we bothered to check. Trapped in a village next to the Terek River, we took refuge inside a bank that had gone out of business several months earlier, where we spent the better part of a week cooling our heels, until we caught word that a group of Azerbaijani farmers with a stranded truck containing several tons of fresh parsley had hired a helicopter to rescue their consignment, enabling us to hitch a ride out. The closest we ever got to the mountains we were supposed to have skied was gazing down at them through the open door of the rescue chopper.

Once again, our editors were less than impressed. But through a trick of timing that is no longer possible thanks to social media, we secured a job with *Men's Journal* before the skiing fiasco leaked out. For this project we traveled to the base of Mount Everest to profile a four-man team of Nepali Sherpa known as the Ice Doctors, who enabled mountaineers to have a shot at reaching the summit by building a route through a frozen minefield known as the Khumbu Icefall, which sits directly above Base Camp and is the single deadliest feature on the entire mountain.

The only way to document the Ice Doctors' handiwork was to follow them into the icefall. Less than ninety minutes after we'd started climbing through the maze, I heard a sharp explosion above us that sounded like something being shot out of a cannon, and looked up to see that a cornice attached like a shelf to Everest's West Shoulder had broken off the side of the mountain. It appeared to be about the size of an aircraft carrier, and the entire mass remained mostly intact as it fell more than a thousand feet before plunging into the top of the icefall and detonating.

The concussion, which was unspeakably violent, generated an unearthly ripping sound, as if a section of the sky had been peeled back like a layer of sheet metal. The impact blew chunks of ice the size of delivery trucks into the air while creating a cloud of pulverized ice and snow, all of which coalesced into an avalanche that swiftly enveloped the upper portion of the icefall.

I had just finished tiptoeing over an aluminum ladder spanning a deep crevasse, and Pete was still stranded in the middle of the ladder, balanced on his crampons, while clinging to a climbing rope. Staring directly into the advancing maelstrom, we could see the shock wave, an undulating pulse that was causing the air, along with the ice crystals suspended in it, to shimmer with an energy that was menacing and weirdly beautiful. With nowhere to run or hide, all we could do was watch, stupefied, while the monster sledgehammered toward us. In that moment I would later recall thinking, in an oddly detached way—

Okay . . . so this is what it's gonna feel like to die on Everest.

Unbeknownst to us, however, the Ice Doctors had purposely strung their route directly below a line of deep crevasses running perpendicular to the path of the avalanche. A few hundred yards downslope from the top of the icefall, the vortex hit the first buffer crevasse, then the second, followed by the third and fourth:

Whump . . .

Whump . . .

Whump . . .

Whump!

By the time it reached the final crevasse, the heaviest debris inside the cloud had disappeared, robbing the avalanche of much of its punch. But even so, a vast, white cloud was still bearing down on us. Just before it arrived, we turned our backs and covered our faces with our gloves—and a second or two later we were slapped by a powerful gust of wind, followed by a storm of tiny ice crystals that stung like bits of thrown gravel.

It took a full minute for the air to clear, and when it did, we looked up—Pete on the ladder, me at the lip of the crevasse—and each found himself staring into the face of a man he'd never met, yet who looked oddly familiar.

Every inch of exposed skin on our faces, as well as our eyebrows, eyelashes, and the unshaven hair on our cheeks, was silvered in hoarfrost. It was as if the avalanche had somehow hurled us forty years into the future and flash frozen us into a pair of little old men.

* * *

And so it went, one screwup following another as we assembled a string of failures, like a tawdry necklace of fake pearls. Each botched assignment afforded yet another opportunity to test the validity of Pete's conviction that regardless of how much trouble we might bumble into thanks to poor preparation, sketchy research, and generalized negligence, if we simply refused to give up, one way or another things would work out just fine.

Much to my surprise, this theory more or less held up.

What's more, in extricating ourselves from these self-generated predicaments, I learned a few things. I was forced to admit that thanks to my own shortcomings in the same areas that Pete found challenging, I often bore just as much blame as he did when the train came off the rails. I also recognized that he was far better than me when it came to not only getting us out of trouble, but also how to *look* at trouble in the first place. Even when nothing seemed to be going our way, he held fast to the belief that something absolutely marvelous lay hidden within the folds of each disaster, and that if we kept our wits and maintained our senses of humor, we would sooner or later be permitted to partake in the magic.

Although Pete never framed it in precisely this manner, his attitude reminded me of something I had already been taught during the writing of *The Emerald Mile*, the book on Kenton Grua's speed run, which was finally published in the spring of 2013: the insight that making one's living in magnificent and beautiful landscapes wasn't a job, but a privilege in the best sense of the word. The things Pete and I saw, the places we went, and the people we met—regardless of whether we were staring at the northern lights, walking through the Blue Mosque in Istanbul, or watching the moon rise over the Himalayas—offered up a series of bright reminders that despite its many absurdities and cruelties, the world sometimes vibrates with a harrowing richness and wonder, and that each of those encounters represented a bestowal of grace that we were obliged to acknowledge by weaving our images and words into stories.

Finally, somewhere amid those misadventures, I learned that Pete and I were more than just colleagues. Although each of us often found the other to be madly annoying, amid our mutual irritation we somehow became the very best of friends. By the time we had been afforded a glimpse of ourselves as timeworn codgers on the side of Everest, the trust we bestowed upon each other was absolute.

*   *   *

By then, a kind of ritual had taken shape. At the conclusion of each project, Pete would permit some time to pass, then circle back to me with another idea that sounded wildly stupid, but also wickedly compelling. After hearing him out, I would tell him he'd lost his marbles, inducing him to unleash a flurry of expostulation and hand-waving until, against my better judgment, I found myself careening along the tracks on another runaway assignment, clinging to the rail of the caboose while Pete rode the locomotive and blew the steam whistle.

Which is where things stood early in 2015, when he showed up at the door to my home in Flagstaff and announced that *National Geographic* was willing to sponsor him on a sectional traverse of the canyon if I agreed to come along and write the article that would accompany the photos he took. The story, he explained, would be timed to coincide with the hundredth anniversary of the founding of the National Park Service, scheduled to take place the following summer.

He had piqued the interest of the magazine's editors by pointing out that the centennial offered a reason to spotlight America's flagship park by conducting an inventory, on foot, of its hidden gems and secret splendors, a number of which were threatened by some disturbing development projects that deserved scrutiny. He also suggested that this would be a fitting moment to touch base with several Native American tribes whose members view the canyon as part of their homes, and whose stories had received far too little attention in the past. But what sealed the deal, in the eyes of the editors, was when he let them know how few people had walked the entire canyon in the thirty-eight years since Grua had completed the original transect.

Among the 5 million visitors who convene along the South Rim each year, Pete pointed out, fewer than 10 percent hike down one of three main trails, each of which features rest stops and other amenities. A far smaller fraction of those tourists—roughly 3 percent—actually move into the surrounding cliffs, ledges, and side canyons on a back-packing trip that entails camping for more than a single night, while a tiny sliver of that group—an average of about thirty-five people a month—penetrate the deep backcountry, where the terrain is steep, rugged, and for the most part devoid of water.

As for those willing to consider a "thru-hike," when Pete pitched his idea, only ten people had followed Grua's lead by traversing the canyon in a single, unbroken push, fewer than the number of astro-nauts who had stood on the surface of the moon. In addition, another dozen or so had successfully tackled the less rigorous but more lengthy and time-consuming challenge of dividing a continuous transect into pieces—taking breaks between individual sections while tying the head of each new segment into the tail of the last, which was what Pete was suggesting for our venture.*

In completing their various projects, those hikers had also discovered that little had changed since Grua first passed through. As before, there

---

* Repeatedly hiking into and back out of the canyon on a sectional traverse can easily add another hundred miles to this option, bringing the total distance closer to eight hundred miles.

was still no trail for more than 95 percent of the distance along the north side of the river, and 80 percent of the south side. Beyond the margins of those footpaths lay a three-dimensional labyrinth devoid of mile markers, signposts, or designated campsites, with no access to emergency caches of food or water, no places to seek medical attention, no regularly scheduled ranger patrols, and not a single designated shelter or lean-to in which to take refuge from the elements. Thanks to the fragility of the desert and the ever-present danger of wildfires, several of which sweep along the rims each year, campfires were now forbidden—even during winter. Plus, there was no guidebook.

The bulk of the canyon's interior, the vast and mostly untrammeled zone between the river and the rims, was exactly as it had been forty years earlier: remote, isolated, visited by almost no one. Rangers who had previously been posted to distant outposts in the National Park System such as Gates of the Arctic or Denali before arriving in the Southwest would claim that when they were on patrol in the canyon, they often felt more cut off than they did in Alaska. Out there on the stone terraces, deep in the center of the maze, you could spend entire weeks without encountering another human being. As in the days of John Wesley Powell, it was still wild country.

And perilous, too—although Pete conspicuously avoided mentioning this to anyone, including me.

*   *   *

During the previous century and a half, more than eight hundred people have perished inside the canyon, making it one of the deadliest national parks in the country. With so many fatalities, an entire book has been devoted to the subject. Entitled *Over the Edge: Death in Grand Canyon*, it is packed with gruesome details about not only the 43 boaters who drowned in the river, the 88 victims of suicide, and the 138 pilots and passengers killed in air-tour accidents involving helicopters or fixed-wing aircraft, but also the 202 visitors who have met their deaths on foot while hiking—often in exceptionally unpleasant ways.

While several of those hikers were swept away by flash floods or snatched up in debris flows, others were crushed by falling rocks, bitten by venomous snakes, or felled by dehydration and heatstroke. Two were struck by lightning, and a third plummeted to his death after a cactus, around which he'd wrapped his arms in a bid to arrest his fall, abruptly tore loose. At least one drowned while attempting to cross the river on an air mattress with his backpack; another was headbutted off the edge of a precipice by an irate Bighorn Sheep; a few others perished after committing heartbreakingly simple mistakes, such as stepping off the edge of a cliff after getting up to pee at night. And these were the *normal* hikers, folks who were sticking primarily to the heavily trafficked, assiduously maintained, and regularly patrolled trails. Among the eighteen people who had embarked on a full traverse up to that point, one-sixth had suffered terrible fates.

Thirty years after becoming the first person to complete a continuous thru-hike on the north side, a former river guide named Bill Ott disappeared in a remote section of western Grand Canyon. Despite a massive search-and-rescue effort, his body remains missing to this day. The same year that Ott vanished, a twenty-four-year-old woman from Phoenix, who was only a few miles short of completing the next-to-last leg of her sectional transect, slipped on a slab of rock and was catapulted over the edge of a four-hundred-foot cliff to her death. And a third hiker, a young man from Albuquerque who was in the midst of a continuous double-traverse in opposite directions, was lowering himself from a narrow ledge when both his handholds broke off, sending him backward over a thirty-foot cliff. Although the fall fractured his pelvis and broke a chip off one of his vertebrae, he refused to give up and spent the next week crawling in so much pain that he was forced to beg for aspirin from passing river runners. Months later, he completed his goal (a feat that has never been repeated) and returned home to Albuquerque, where he succumbed to a bout of severe depression—brought on, in part, because he found it impossible to cope with being away from the canyon—and tragically took his own life.

As those examples illustrate, the canyon's backcountry is a place where, even for veterans, a single misplaced step or poor decision, or a moment's loss of focus, can be fatal. Moving safely through this landscape demands meticulous research, thorough preparation, and total commitment, plus a set of specialized skills that don't always go together. In addition to being adept at rock climbing, rappelling, and long-distance desert backpacking, canyon thru-hikers need to feel comfortable moving along the edges of massive cliffs and drop-offs, be proficient at land navigation and route finding, be skilled at piloting a pack raft, and be fluent in reading geological as well as topographic maps.

In short, this is no place for amateurs, which is why the Park Service has gone out of its way to discourage people who haven't bothered doing their homework from even *thinking* about attempting a traverse. "The terrain encountered is some of the most difficult on the planet," warned Elyssa Shalla, a ranger who was preparing to complete a continuous thru-hike with her husband, Matt Jenkins, one of the park's elite backcountry rangers, when Pete was pitching his idea to *National Geographic*. "Off-trail hiking is unique to the Grand Canyon, and it requires a honed set of skills," Shalla declared. "It is not possible to hike the length of the canyon 'off the couch.'"

In light of all this, it would seem obvious that no one in their right mind simply shows up at the South Rim and waltzes off into the abyss with the aim of cutting a cross-canyon transect by the seat of their pants. Yet, that's a fairly accurate summary of exactly what Pete was proposing that he and I do.

*   *   *

In keeping with every other proposition that he'd dangled in front of me, he made it sound as if nothing could possibly go wrong. He made no mention of the complete absence of guidebooks to a backcountry transit; skipped over the Park Service's dire warnings about preparation and fitness; and refrained from commenting on the many ways one could die—all while sidestepping mention of the minuscule number of people who had somehow surmounted those challenges to pull it off. Instead, he presented the journey from its most glittering angle: a quest to find a line through the heart of the country's most recognized, least understood national park, as well as one of its most beloved touchstones, America's open-air cathedral in the desert. A place, he knew, that I was obsessed with.

He also suggested, in not so many words, that the goals of some adventures involve far more than simply traversing the physical distance between the beginning and the end, and this was one of those, because it would embrace elements that ran deeper than distance and ambition—rock, sky, bone, and time—and you don't polish off an odyssey like that without some sort of transformation.

Journeys such as this aren't things that you complete, he told me. Instead, it's the journey that completes *you*—which meant that if we did this thing together, if we walked the length of the Grand Canyon, a thing that fewer than two dozen people had ever done, by starting at Lee's Ferry and not quitting until we reached the Grand Wash Cliffs, I might return not only with a cleaner understanding of a landscape that had been a fixation since my boyhood, but with a better grasp of who I was, and perhaps a renewed sense of whom I might yet become, before it was too late to grow and change.

In truth, Pete didn't need to say anything to convince me, because I had unfinished business in the canyon. For me, taking a walk in the park wasn't just a good idea. It was fricking *grand*.

"Okay—I'm in," I said. "But I've got questions."

I wanted to know when we would leave and how long it would take. I wanted to know about the gear we'd have to bring, the food we'd be eating, and details about clothing. I wanted to know how we would avoid adding our names to the long list of the canyon's fatalities. Most pressing of all, I wanted to know one thing:

"How the hell do you imagine us actually pulling this off?"

As with everything else, Pete was ready with an answer.

"Oh, no worries," he replied airily. "I've got a guy who's totally gonna help us figure all this out."

CHAPTER 9

A Shortcut

B ack in the spring of 2012, Pete was attending a film festival in Telluride when a friend announced that he wanted to introduce him to a "major player" in the world of extreme desert exploration—a man who had probably spent more days and nights below the rim of the Grand Canyon with a backpack than anyone else during the modern era. Based on that description, Pete was expecting to meet a twenty-first-century cross between Colin Fletcher and John Wesley Powell. Instead, he found himself shaking hands with a stocky, mild-mannered, scrupulously polite man who appeared to be about fifty years old, was mostly bald, and in Pete's estimation looked less like a canyon rat than a Silicon Valley tech bro.

In some ways, that impression wasn't too far off the mark. Rich Rudow had spent the better part of the past two decades running a company in Phoenix that specialized in satellite-navigation technology, a role that demanded a fairly high level of business acumen. Nothing about his appearance indicated that during that same period he had spent the bulk of his free time penetrating some of the harshest and most isolated reaches of the canyon, places that few people had ever been to or even imagined. Nor was there any sign that he was capable of hauling enormous loads across shockingly difficult terrain at a pace that regularly left people half his age demoralized and driven into the dirt—or that his mastery of the full kit of canyoneering skills was matched by fewer than a dozen hikers and surpassed by nobody.

Standing in line outside a movie theater with a latte in his hand, Rich may not have looked the part, but he was the real deal. Like many genuinely talented people, however, he wasn't much of a salesman in touting his achievements, which is probably why Pete failed to grasp that he was standing next to a living legend who was in the midst of putting together a journey whose vision was so innovative and daring that nothing like it had ever been conceived.

*   *   *

Up to this point, many of the early thru-hikers had adhered to a baseline principle originally established by Grua when he had found himself cut off from the Colorado during his first attempt and nearly perished after running out of water. The lesson Grua learned from that ordeal was simple and draconian: the river is your lifeline, so stick as close as possible to the bottom of the canyon and, at all costs, avoid the rocky terraces thousands of feet above—because even though the terrain up there may look appealing, it can easily kill you.

This makes a lot of sense. Being near the river ensures access to water while guaranteeing that if anything goes wrong, sooner or later a pod of boaters will show up and bail you out. But this approach has problems, too, many of them linked to the belt of dense vegetation known as the riparian zone. Long stretches of the corridor on both banks of the Colorado are absolutely choked with the kind of foliage that makes walking exceptionally difficult and slow: dense thickets of shrubs and bushes, plus mesquite and acacia trees covered in thorns the size of three-penny roofing nails. In many places, it can feel like thrashing through an endless briar patch, making the river line a double-edged compromise: safe—but messy, arduous, and miserable.

Rich, however, had something different in mind: a route whose appeal resided in its audacity and elegance. His vision was to ascend into the world of pure stone and tease out a route along the loftiest cliffs and ledges that would enable him to shift into overdrive by gliding across the bare slickrock for weeks at a stretch, suspended in the bright between: thousands of feet off the river, thousands of feet below the rim, cutting through country with neither boatmen, rangers, or any other people—only light and rock, and the desert creatures who dwelled in that rarefied realm.

A route like that had been tried by a number of others, but never in such a deliberately sustained manner, among other reasons because it was so phenomenally dangerous, especially out on the arid expanses of the canyon's western end. If you failed to find water, if you got sick or injured, if a hundred other things went wrong, you'd be cut off— unable to retreat to the river or climb to the rims—and you would die up there, helpless and alone. But those risks carried rewards, too.

In addition to its novelty and flair, Rich's line would take him through each of the canyon's intricately layered ecosystems, rock strata, and life zones. Along the way, he would tick off a punch list of things he'd dreamed of doing for more than a decade: meandering across isolated mesas and buttes; ascending the summits of obscure towers and pinnacles; poking into all the little places he'd been curious about for years or that simply looked intriguing on the map. In his eyes, the journey would not only be a feat of stamina and boldness, but also a thing of beauty.

*   *   *

Over several years, he'd applied himself to translating that vision into a plan by poring over maps and pulling down hundreds of satellite images from Google Earth. Slowly he added in new layers of detail—noting terrain features, measuring distances, estimating travel times—until the plan came to fruition in the form of a seven-hundred-mile course that was overlaid against a fifty-seven-day itinerary. He knew the escarpments and hollows where he would camp, the ledges that would enable him to make forward progress, and the geological breaks that would permit him to shift from one layer of rock to the next when those ledges disappeared—and above all, he knew the locations and waypoints of the hidden niches in the rock where he could reliably find water.

He also enlisted a pair of desert rats to join him. Dave Nally, forty-nine, was from southern Utah and had spent years exploring the rugged backcountry around Zion National Park, which he knew well enough to have written a comprehensive history of all the rescues and fatalities that had taken place there. Chris Atwood, thirty, possessed equally deep knowledge of the Painted Desert just north of his home in Winslow, Arizona. Both men had completed many difficult journeys through the desert on foot, experiences that enabled them to sit down with Rich and sketch out a set of alternative routes and bailout options that they would follow when events they could not yet foresee—the storms and the rockfalls, the debris flows and the wildfires—made it impossible to stick to the original route.

Around this time, Mike St. Pierre, another long-distance hiker with a great deal of experience, albeit not so much in the desert, reached out to ask if he could join. Mike's company, Hyperlite Mountain Gear, had already committed to sponsoring the project by providing exceptionally tough, ultralight backpacks, plus a tent and other items. Now he indicated that he was keen to knock out the first two hundred miles of the canyon with Rich's team, and perhaps return to finish the rest of the route later.

When everyone agreed that St. Pierre would make a solid addition to the group, the four of them turned to arranging their caches, filling more than forty plastic buckets with supplies and carrying them in from the rim, then organizing their packs. Thanks to their meticulousness, nothing was rushed, and by the middle of that summer, the pieces were all sliding neatly into place as they looked toward the launch date on which they had all agreed: Friday, September 25, 2015.

Meanwhile, things were looking wildly different over in the Fedarko/McBride camp.

* * *

As usual, Pete was in charge of logistics, and from the get-go, he found that once again he had gotten us in way over our heads. At every turn, he was smacked by another reminder that a responsible traverse can only be built upon a foundation of what we most lacked—experience.

The logical response—the *smart* response—would have been for us to take a step back and embark, patiently and methodically, on a series of smaller expeditions in which we refined our skills and learned the lessons that would enable us to survive. The problem, however, was that all of that would be terribly tedious and time-consuming. The whole process could take *years*.

What we needed, Pete finally decided, was a shortcut—which is when he remembered his encounter in Telluride with the nerdy-looking expert on canyon exploration.

Maybe it was time to dig up the guy's number and reach out for some advice.

When Pete got Rich on the phone, it swiftly became clear that the two projects were radically different. Rich's strategy, which demanded tremendous speed with no stopping, amounted to an all-out blitzkrieg. If everything went as planned, he and his team would enter the canyon two days after the autumn equinox and be out just before Thanksgiving. This also meant that they would have almost no time to record or reflect upon their journey while it was unfolding.

Our vision was the direct opposite of that approach. By walking the canyon in five or six sections, each covering roughly one hundred miles, and pausing for breaks between each segment, in some cases for several weeks, we would have plenty of time to document our progress and catalog our impressions. If Rich and his team cast themselves as hares, then we wanted to be the tortoises; and if our journey unfolded far more slowly than theirs, it would nevertheless generate thousands of photographs, many hours of film, and a set of notebooks filled with ideas and observations, in keeping with our job as storytellers.

Instead of concluding that the two approaches were totally incompatible, however, Pete latched on to another idea altogether:

Apparently, there *was* a shortcut!

If Rich could somehow be talked into allowing us to accompany him and his team on the first part of their trip, it would both cushion and accelerate our own acclimation to the canyon.

Wasting no time, Pete emailed Rich the very next day and announced that we wanted to tag along.

*   *   *

As I later learned, Rich wasn't quite sure how to respond.

In addition to harboring his own questions about our lack of preparation and competency, he suspected that neither Dave, Chris, nor Mike would appreciate a couple of amateurs being tossed into the salad at the last minute. So for guidance, he turned to someone whose counsel he valued.

Glenn Rink was a desert botanist based in Flagstaff who had spent forty-five years hiking, climbing, and boating in the canyon. Only a handful of people had knowledge that could match Rich's, but Rink was definitely one of them.

"So what do you think?" Rich asked after phoning Rink and laying out what was going on.

Rink didn't hesitate. "You're being stupid," he growled, incredulous that Rich was even considering the idea. "Do *not* bring those two idiots with you."

"Why not?"

"Because they will fuck up your entire trip."

*   *   *

To this day, I don't know exactly what Pete said to Rich to countermand Rink's counsel. But based on what happened next, I'm forced to assume that Pete served up his trademark cocktail of hoodwinkery and bamboozlement.

A few days later, Pete phoned me to deliver the news. Despite having been advised by one of the canyon's most respected elder statesmen to drop us like a hot rock, Rich had abandoned his judgment, along with any shred of common sense, and given us permission to join his team for the first phase of their trip.

The plan, Pete explained, was that he and I would hook up with Rich's team for the first twelve days of their hike, then we'd climb out of the canyon at a prearranged location and catch a ride back to Flagstaff, where we could start planning the rest of our adventure.

That initial segment would serve as a "shakedown" phase in which we took the canyon for a gentle test-drive to set us up for the tougher sections to follow, all while moving under the supervision of more experienced hikers. As for what happened after that—how we would design, map out, and provision the rest of our route—Pete was breezy and vague. He was also eager to lay out what excited him most about the way things were unfolding.

"Believe it or not," he exclaimed, "you and I don't even have to worry about being in shape."

That sounded odd. How could we pull off an expedition such as this without being in top physical condition?

"Because," Pete said, sensing my skepticism while warming to his revelation, "the hike *itself* is the thing that's gonna get us in shape *for the hike*."

"Really?" I mumbled, struggling to wrap my head around the logic.

"You bet. In fact, that's the coolest part of the entire plan."

By now, I'd placed him on speaker so that I could set the phone on my desk and rummage my fingers through my hair while staring bleakly at the wall.

"Look," he continued, "this warm-up cruise with Rich and his guys, it means that the whole time we're down there, the canyon is gonna be polishing us off like little gemstones, and by the end of that first phase, guess what?"

I could not imagine.

"You and me will turn into a pair of hard-core hiking buffs—and all we have to do for that to happen is *show up*."

As I placed my head in my hands, his final words wafted up hollowly from the speaker, as if emerging from the bottom of a wishing well filled with moist, green horseshit.

"Dude—we can do this thing *off the couch*."*

---

* In the interest of accuracy, balance, and maintaining my friendship with Pete, I'm compelled to disclose that he takes exception to the manner in which we have been depicted up to now.

He points out that during the months and weeks prior to the start of our hike, we went to great lengths to plan for this project, efforts that included researching our route, courting sponsors, purchasing gear, planning menus, packing food caches, and arranging for our permits with the National Park Service, pouring in so much energy and care that it is unfair to suggest, as I do in these pages, that we were behaving frivolously and irresponsibly, because it will invite readers to mistakenly conclude that we were a pair of incompetent ding-dongs who deserved to be treated like piñatas.

Some of this may be true.

My own view, however, is that despite these measures, he and I were unforgivably derelict in the area that mattered most, which was our duty to cultivate the experience and judgment that are prerequisites for responsibly traversing the length of the canyon.

Those fundamentals can only be acquired slowly and patiently over a period not of weeks or months, but years—and by investing the resource we were least willing to expend, which was our time.

Because of that, we were guilty of both hubris and negligence, and thus deserve—at least at this stage of our journey—a certain amount of mockery and disdain. Especially me.

And in addition to all of that, I just like the story better when it's told this way.

CHAPTER 10

Who *Are* These Clowns?

One afternoon toward the end of July, I heard a knock at my front door and opened it to discover that half a dozen large cardboard boxes had been dumped on my porch. The labels indicated that shipments of gear were being sent to me from every point of the compass. Boots from Scarpa in Italy. Headlamps and trekking poles from Black Diamond in Salt Lake City. Sleeping bags from Feathered Friends in Seattle. Backpacks and a tent from Mike St. Pierre's company in Maine.

"There's a lot more coming," Pete warned when he called me that night to explain that my house would serve as the staging area for all of the equipment, clothing, and food that he was ordering. "Your job is to wrangle everything together and get it squared away. Can you handle that?"

"Absolutely. Consider it done."

Given how many packages were still on the way, I decided it was best to wait for everything to arrive before getting to work. After all the boxes had been delivered, I'd unpack them and start testing important items such as the camp stove, the tent, and the DeLorme inReach, a handheld communicator that enabled two-way text messaging via satellite, but could also be paired with topographic maps on a cell phone—and would, if necessary, transmit an emergency SOS. But for the moment, I simply plucked each new package off the porch, carried it down the driveway, and tossed it into the garage.

I knew that the organizing-and-testing business was important, and I had every aim of flinging myself into the mission, when the moment was right. But, alas, a hundred other urgent and pressing tasks intervened—laundry, napping, mowing the lawn—and despite my best intentions, the pile inside the garage continued to grow. Then, almost without warning it seemed, September 24 arrived, and it was time to leave for the canyon.

Around 5:30 p.m., Pete and I clambered into a friend's truck and headed north on Highway 89, driving for more than a hundred miles along the edge of the Painted Desert, a stretch of colorful badlands on the western end of the Navajo Nation. The sun had set long before we crossed a two-lane bridge over the Colorado River, and twilight was already fading when we arrived at a spot on the road marked by a steel gate clasped to a fence post with a rusting piece of chain.

We pulled off the pavement and followed a set of tire tracks leading through clumps of saltbush and rabbitbrush interspersed with the occasional yucca. It was pitch-dark when we finally reached the end of the road, killed the headlights, and gasped in awe as we stepped from the truck. The Milky Way shimmered across the heavens from one horizon to the other, and the rest of the sky was speckled with so many constellations that I felt dizzy and was forced to look away—which is when my eye caught the flicker of a small campfire, about twenty yards in front of us. Amid the orange glow, I could see the silhouettes of Rich and his crew, set against the star-dappled immensity of the night.

The scene looked inviting, but we had work to do before joining them. So we shuffled around to the rear of the truck, flung open the tailgate—and jumped back as a small avalanche of boxes tumbled into the dirt around our feet.

After several minutes of fumbling around blindly, we located the batteries for our brand-new headlamps, then took even longer to figure out how to turn them on. When we finally had some light, Pete removed the camp stove from its container and, after hastily scanning the directions, attempted to screw on each of our brand-new gas canisters to confirm that everything worked. Meanwhile, I was busy opening a carton of Patagonia underwear, made from a high-tech fabric that, according to the tags, was "odor-free."

Within minutes, the ground was littered with torn cardboard, pieces of plastic wrapping, and sundry articles of clothing with their price tags still attached. As we were wondering where to start, we caught the sound of footsteps.

* * *

"Hey, guys, how's it going over here?" Rich called out cheerfully. "Need any help?"

"Nope," we replied in unison. "Everything's under control!"

By now the others were approaching, and when everyone turned on his headlamp at the same time, the area around the tailgate was lit up like a crime scene, affording us our first glimpse of the team.

Chris Atwood was tall and lanky with a bushy blond beard. Mike was short and wiry with black hair, and Dave Nally had blue eyes and a salt-and-pepper goatee. All three looked supremely fit, and like Rich they were clad in the unofficial uniform of high-desert walkers: lightweight pants and loose-fitting shirts with long sleeves and hoods to protect them from the sun, and tattered baseball caps whose edges were stained white from the salt of their sweat. Although most of their clothing came from the same high-end brands that Pete and I had purchased, almost every item had tears or holes, a number of which were patched with duct tape.

The glare of the headlamps also enabled them to get a good look at us, and what grabbed their attention immediately was Pete's photography equipment, which was mixed up with everything else. He was militant about carrying a backup for every piece of gear he used, so he had brought double the amount he needed: two high-tech digital cameras capable of shooting video as well as still shots, each worth $8,000; eight battery packs to run the cameras, plus four sets of solar panels to charge the batteries, four lenses, a pair of tripods, and an assortment of cables and tools. The entire kit weighed at least twenty-eight pounds, and by long-standing agreement, we would pretend that we were splitting it evenly between the two of us, but with Pete carrying almost all the heavy stuff.

"Ridiculous," Mike muttered to himself, "but maybe this is how these guys like to roll."

Rich, Chris, and Dave were so stunned by what they were witnessing that they decided it was best to return to the fire and leave us be. Mike was no less shocked, but held back to see if he could help.

"Hey, did you guys bring the Footprints?" he asked, referring to a compact groundsheet made by Hyperlite that weighed 3.77 ounces, lighter than a handful of paper clips, and retailed for $175 apiece. Everybody in Rich's group was carrying one.

"Nope," said Pete. "But Kev found something that'll work for both of us."

This was true. Two days earlier, I'd dashed over to Home Depot and purchased a tarp in the lawn-and-garden section whose label indicated that it was large enough to protect an RV or a medium-sized boat. It was acid blue, the color of Windex, and I was rather proud of the thing. Coated with heavy-duty polyethylene, it cost $14 and weighed approximately five pounds, thanks to the round metal grommets embedded in the fabric every foot or so as anchor points in case we were struck by a weather event such as, say, an F5 tornado.

When I unfolded the tarp for Mike to admire, he assumed I was joking. "Yeah, right—so where's your *actual* ground cloth?"

"No, really," I replied, sounding wounded, "this is it."

For Mike, the notion that someone might intentionally drag a monstrosity such as this into the backcountry was too much to process. Incredulous, he turned his attention to something else. "Okay, do you guys really need this?" He held up a gallon-size Ziploc filled with what appeared to be cocaine.

"Oh, definitely," declared Pete, not realizing that he had brought enough powdered Gatorade to supply fifteen people for an entire week.

"If you say so, but . . . what the *hell*?!"

Mike was pointing to my toilet kit—two king-size tubes of tooth-paste, a thirty-two-ounce bottle of Dr. Bronner's peppermint-scented shampoo, and a box of Pampers hypoallergenic baby wipes. Total weight: three and a half pounds.

Mike now stopped with the questions and started seizing anything he found offensive—a glass jar of instant coffee; a foldable camp chair; a plastic shovel that one of us had brought along, for God knows what reason—and tossing it onto a rapidly growing reject pile. This must have felt like progress, until he realized that Pete and I were surrep-titiously snatching back items that we couldn't bear to part with, so Mike simply began hurling things off into the night.

First to go was the Gatorade, which he flung into the brush by the side of the truck without realizing that we'd parked next to a study plot designed to protect a patch of highly endangered Brady's Pincushion cactus, a succulent with a pale-yellow flower whose only remaining habitat is a twenty-seven-square-mile area along the eastern end of the canyon. Leaving the cactus frosted with powdered drink mix, Mike yanked out his knife and went after the tarp, slashing it in half, then slicing off the grommets one by one, eliminating more than four pounds while leaving us with a pair of narrow ground cloths that looked as if they'd been run through a wood chipper.

On it went—taking away this, putting back that, tossing something else into the bushes—until Mike finally glanced at his watch, saw that it was past 9:00 p.m., and gave up.

"Who the fuck *are* these clowns," he wondered as he stalked back toward the campfire, "and how the hell did they talk their way onto this trip?"

*   *   *

Mike arrived at the fire to find each of his companions sitting cross-legged on a gossamer strip of ground cloth—the aforementioned Foot-print, which wasn't much longer or wider than a sleeping bag. The corners of everyone's cloth were neatly anchored with small pebbles, and on its surface, the things that each man intended to take with him had been laid out like the components of a clock.

Some of those items, such as a hyperefficient propane stove that could bring a half liter of water to a boil in 120 seconds, were rather high-tech and quite expensive. But many items in their kits, such as the plastic cups duct-taped with insulating foam that would serve as their dinnerware, were homemade and cost next to nothing. Several pieces of gear were intended to fulfill more than one purpose, such as the trekking poles that would double as support rods for their ultra-minimalist emergency shelter, a pyramid-shaped piece of fabric called a mid, whose walls didn't even come all the way to the ground.

During the final week leading up to this night, each of these items had survived an intense and finicky process of elimination as the team had sifted and sorted and pondered before grudgingly retaining only those items they couldn't do without. Thanks to that vetting, the aim of which was to maximize the amount of food and water each man could carry on any given day, the things that had failed to survive the culling—the things they would *not* be carrying with them—now told a story about how disciplined they were, and what it might be like to travel in their company.

None of them, for example, had a magazine or book, and all three would have scoffed at bringing a razor, an extra pair of sunglasses, or a stick of deodorant. Nobody was carrying a single bar of soap or a stitch of spare clothing, which meant that they would forgo bathing and would walk a week or more in the same pair of underwear. At least one of them wasn't even bringing toilet paper, for which he would substitute smooth pebbles or soft leaves.[*]

It wasn't that they didn't covet those things. But just as Kenton Grua had pared the load of his pack to less than thirty pounds, they had cast

---

[*] The only concession to luxury was that each of them brought an ultralight air mattress to ensure that he didn't have to sleep directly on thorns or shards of rock. It weighed less than a box of Kleenex tissues and took up half the space.

away everything except what mattered for their survival, attesting to how well they understood the difference between what they merely wanted, and what they'd actually need—a distinction whose drawing demanded a measure of ruthlessness. And those choices said something about the canyon, too: how, in forcing you to pare down your dunnage, this landscape would pare you down, too, peeling away the layers until it had stripped you into something that, not unlike the land itself, lay very close to the bone.

The extent of that remaking now made itself evident through a ritual that Mike joined as he took a seat by the fire, spread out his things, and conducted a final inventory in the hope that perhaps he might find some tiny article—the plastic cap of a toothbrush, an extra set of tweezers, the label on a tea bag—that he could discard, thereby shaving off another nanogram or two of unneeded weight.

When they had finished sorting, each man began placing his items into a white ultralight backpack, carefully stacking everything according to the order in which it would be needed the following day so they could avoid dumping out their entire packs each time they had to retrieve a water bottle or a pair of sunglasses. This was more than just a system for keeping things organized; it was a mental exercise in knowing precisely where everything was at all times, and it was important enough that it actually had a name: *pack discipline.*

An outsider might well dismiss these rituals as obsessive and silly. But anyone familiar with extreme desert hiking would recognize these rites as a vital part of the liturgy of departure—a praxis whose purpose had less to do with saving weight or mapping out one's gear, and more to do with quickening each man's acknowledgment of the seriousness of what they were about to attempt, and the trials they would endure in the days and weeks to come if they were to have any hope of reaching their goal.

*   *   *

Meanwhile, back at the rear of the truck, now that Pete and I had finally finished unwrapping and sorting our gear, it dawned on us that we somehow had to stuff all of this junk into our packs. We spent the next forty-five minutes haphazardly cramming things into every last available pocket, then lashing whatever didn't fit to the outsides.

The work was sweaty and frantic, but when it was done, Pete reached into the front of the truck and pulled out a small digital scale. The moment of truth had arrived.

My pack tipped the scale at just over fifty-three pounds. His was fifty-five.

When we shouldered the loads and stood up, which wasn't easy, mine felt as if it were loaded with pig iron.

"Not as bad as I thought," grunted Pete as he staggered to his feet. "How about you?"

"I'm think I'm okay," I lied, ignoring that my hands and elbows were already turning numb. "How much heavier are these packs than what those other guys are carrying?"

"I think I heard Mike say they're each at around thirty-three pounds."

"Okay, so we're carrying—what, like forty percent more than they are?"

"We're only about twenty pounds heavier, so relax. It's not that big of a deal."

Only later would it dawn on me that two middle-aged men were about to head out with as much weight as my dad had carried as a nineteen-year-old marine in full combat gear during boot camp. Or, putting it in terms that I could actually imagine, each of us would be schlepping all of the weight that our companions had on their backs, plus two cast-iron skillets and a Dutch oven.

By now the moon had come up, casting a milky-white glow that revealed a number of loose items still scattered on the ground around the truck. As Pete and I paced the area trying to account for everything, Rich and his crew sat glumly around their campfire, watching the beams of our headlamps slash jaggedly through the darkness, and listening as we continued to bicker, unaware that everything we said carried directly to their ears.

"Hey, I don't think we unwrapped the gaiters yet."

(This was a reference to cloth sleeves that are worn around the tops of one's footwear to keep out sand and dirt, critical for preventing blisters, and something that no long-distance desert backpacker would be dumb enough to leave behind.)

"Yo—do you know where the gaiters are?"

"Dude, chill, gaiters make you look stupid. Forget about them."

"But they were on the list. Did you not bother to read the *list*?"

"I can't believe I'm getting lectured about reading by some guy who couldn't be bothered to open his fricking mail!"

Good lord, we haven't even started and these nitwits are already squabbling, thought Rich, while trying to gauge the mood of his team.

For Mike, the incompetency he'd witnessed defied belief—never before had he encountered such cluelessness on the threshold of a major expedition. But for Chris and Dave, a more complicated response was unfolding as they both realized that Rich may not have been entirely honest with them about how inexperienced Pete and I were—and that perhaps Rich had purposely withheld this information until it was too late to do anything about it.

The canyon was no place to bring a pair of greenhorns, a move that neither of them would have agreed to had Rich bothered to consult them. How could he justify doing such a thing?

Chris was too diplomatic to say anything at first. But Dave wasn't about to sit in silence.

"Rich?" he protested in a hushed voice. "This is not gonna go well."

"He's right," added Chris, looking out to where Pete and I were still messing with our packs and arguing. "This is pretty bad."

Rich took a deep breath before responding. Thanks to Pete's flair for fast talk, Rich himself hadn't fully understood how ignorant we were, until just now.

"Look, guys, I apologize," he finally told them. "I am really, *really* sorry about this."

Chris, Dave, and Mike stared glumly into the dying embers of the fire.

"We may have some rough moments with these guys over the next few days, but we'll get them sorted out," Rich assured them. "So trust me—it'll be okay, and everything will work out just fine."

Many months later, Dave would find himself unable to recall exactly what he'd said next. But he knew, emphatically, what he *wished* he'd said:

"No, Rich, it isn't gonna work out fine, because nothing about this is okay."

Instead, Dave nodded politely, shuffled over to his bag, and tucked himself in, hoping that things might look better in the morning.

CHAPTER 11

Happy Trails

R ich's plan called for everyone to rise promptly at 6:00 a.m., hop in their vehicles, and drive nine miles down the highway to Lee's Ferry, a stretch of bottomland where the Colorado briefly emerges from a sinuous sandstone chasm known as Glen Canyon, just before it plunges into the far-deeper corridor of the Grand Canyon. For many years, "the Ferry," as it is known, has been the point of departure for every Grand Canyon river expedition—and for people foolish enough to make their way through the chasm without the use of a boat, this was also the spot to start walking.

Unfortunately, Pete and I were so disorganized that we were forced to dump our belongings on the ground and reorganize everything several times before we were ready to get going. As a result, our group didn't arrive at the Ferry until just before 9:00 a.m., having frittered away the coolest part of the morning, the best time for hiking.

The delay was especially distressing for Dave, who was emerging as the most conscientious member of the group, and who could see that the math wasn't looking good for the distance we needed to cover that day. But despite his concerns, the rest of us were upbeat when we finally arrived.

The only thing moving amid the stillness was the river itself, which was lively and bright as it slid along the shore, burnished by the amber light of late September. The banks were lush and green with willow and cottonwoods, whose foliage concealed the warblers and finches that drench the air in birdsong at dawn and dusk, and in every direction, we could see the features that would soon come to dominate and define our days, which were the walls of rock.

Just upstream, where the Colorado was exiting from the last segment of Glen Canyon, the shoreline was buttressed by orange cliffs soaring almost three thousand feet into the air whose layers were seeded with the fossils of dinosaur trackways, turtles, and some of the planet's earliest mammals. Around the open terrain at the Ferry itself—which is little more than a gently sloping parking lot where boating parties can load their equipment and supplies—the ramparts stood back at a discreet distance, as if giving the river a moment to catch its breath, before funneling through the portal of its biggest and most magnificent canyon. But everywhere else, the walls climbed straight-sided and steep, as if beckoned from deep within the earth by the sky, which was beguilingly blue and shorn clean of even a single cloud.

Beneath all this drama, another spectacle was unfolding as a crowd of well-wishers waited to greet us. In addition to Dave's and Chris's girlfriends, some two dozen long-distance canyon hikers had gathered to see us off. A number had driven all the way from Phoenix, and almost all of them were presentably dressed in clean khaki shorts, collared shirts, and snazzy fleece vests.

The only exception was a rumpled-looking character whose shambolic disarray suggested that he may have been vacationing in the nearby bushes. His face bristled with several days' worth of stubble. His hair jutted up daringly toward all four points of the compass, and his eyes bore a look of bleary insouciance that may have had something to do with the can of Budweiser clutched in his fist. But the most notable thing about him was that in addition to a torn T-shirt and a loose-fitting pair of Chaco sandals, he was sporting a pair of brown short pants that featured a conspicuously broken zipper in the crotch.

It seemed clear that he should be given a wide berth. Until, that is, Rich mentioned his name, and I realized that this was someone I'd been hoping to meet.

Andrew Holycross was a professor of zoology affiliated with Arizona State University who was widely regarded as one of the most respected herpetologists in the Southwest. An authority on all manner of desert reptiles and amphibians, he had a particular fondness for snakes, especially rattlers: Ridge-Nosed, Speckled, Banded-Rock, Western, and Great Basin, as well as the Mojave "Green," the Arizona Black, and, of course, the Grand Canyon Pink, which is found nowhere else except where we were about to go.

For the better part of the past two decades, Holycross had been exploring every aspect of rattlesnake behavior and biology, ranging from their diet and reproductive habits to their parasites, predation strategies, and neonatal aggregations—all of which was being meticulously compiled into the pages of a book that, when it was finally published, would stand as the definitive scoop on each and every limbless vertebrate between the North Rim of the Grand Canyon and the Mexican border.

As impressive as all this was, Holycross had somehow found the time in the midst of that work to hike the length of the entire canyon— not once, but twice. His first effort, a sectional transect on the south side of the Colorado in 2012, had been followed by a nonstop push along the north side in 2013. That back-to-back triumph, which had been pulled off by only two others, gave Holycross a better understanding than most people of the challenge on which Rich, a close friend, was now about to embark.

"This isn't gonna be anything like the Appalachian Trail," Rich announced as they stood beside the water, gazing downstream.

"No comparison," affirmed Holycross. "It's pretty much the toughest hike in America."

"The terrain's so much more difficult than anywhere else, and then there's the heat. This place will fricking kill you."

"That's the dark side, for sure. Definitely not something you'd wanna try to go and do off the couch."

*   *   *

Listening to this exchange, I couldn't help but wonder if a message was being transmitted—and if so, how Pete and I should react (although one fitting response, certainly, would have been for us to depart immediately for the Appalachian Trail). Perhaps we might have considered that had Holycross not decided, for no discernible reason, to abruptly change his tune.

"But you know what else?" he exclaimed. "This is also an amazing thing to do, because if you've never done it before, a whole new world's gonna open up to you."

Momentarily thrown off-balance by this wildly inappropriate display of good cheer, Rich examined his shoes and stabbed his trekking pole into the dirt a time or two.

"And besides," Holycross added, "I really *like* being down here."

While we awaited elaboration, he paused and sent a fat stream of tobacco juice squirting from between his teeth, as if to emphasize the importance of what was coming next.

"When I'm in this place," he declared, his voice quavering with stridency, "nobody's *judging* me."

Evidently, the canyon had a lot to offer a man with an open zipper drinking a can of Budweiser at 9:30 a.m.—a fact whose solemnity and righteousness Holycross consecrated by taking an extended pull from the beer in his hand, swallowing hard, and emitting a robust belch.

Meanwhile, Pete, who also had a taste for snuff, gazed longingly at the gooey brown dollop of spit that was glinting on the ground.

"You know, I could really use some of that before we leave," he finally remarked. "Mind if I take a pinch?"

"Go for it," replied Holycross, forking over the can.

Pete helped himself to a wad the size of a lug nut, rammed it behind his upper lip, then handed the can back.

Holycross waved it off. "Keep it," he said generously. "You guys are about to learn the difference between what you *want* and what you *need*. And where the two of you are going? You're definitely gonna need that."

*   *   *

By now, poor Dave could restrain his anxiety no longer. The temperature had broken into the nineties, ten degrees above normal for this time of year. To stay on schedule, we would have to cover nine river miles in the eight hours of daylight that remained before the sun went down. The fact that everyone was still standing around the boat ramp jabbering away and posing for photographs was absurd.

As Dave motioned for Rich to quit wasting time and get a move on, Pete and I took one last round of selfies. Then we shouldered our packs, gathered up our trekking poles, and started walking.

The first mile or so of shoreline leading downstream from Lee's Ferry features a stretch of smooth, fine-grained sand that would do credit to any oceanfront resort in the Caribbean. As an added bonus, for a short distance this promenade runs parallel to an excellent road. So despite its fearsome reputation, the opening twenty minutes of the toughest hike in America presents a choice between two agreeable options: a cakewalk along a level section of blacktop or a stroll down the beach next to a cool green river.

Pete and I opted to stay on the road for as long as possible, in the hope that it would ease us into a rhythm and a pace that felt right. As we shuffled down the asphalt, the well-wishers stayed with us to extend their goodbyes. Among them I spotted Holycross—moving several yards in front of us, beer in hand, sandals smacking hollowly on the pavement—and was reminded that I had an important question to run past him.

The manuscript of his book was now rumored to be approaching biblical proportions, stoking a brushfire of anticipation among the nerdiest sector of the desert-hiking community, whose members were poised to greet the arrival of this landmark treatise with the sort of excitement normally reserved for, say, the discovery of a new microspecies of Sonoran songbird. In short, everybody, including me, wanted to know when the hell they would be able to get their hands on the thing.

"Hey," I exclaimed brightly, waddling to his side, "I hear you've been working on a book!"

"Yup."

We marched for a minute or two to a symphony of ill-tempered squeaking and creaking from my overloaded pack, which apparently was even less happy than me about how much weight it contained.

"When do you think it'll be finished?"

"Dunno."

More plodding. More squeaking.

"What's it about?"

"The snakes of Arizona."

Feeling rebuffed but still curious, I tried to compose a probing question that might coax him out of his sullenness like, well, a snake from its hole.

"So whatcha gonna call it?"

"*Snakes of Arizona.*"

Clearly, this was going nowhere.

"Solid title," I muttered, taking the hint and dropping back to let him walk in peace. "When you finish, maybe I'll be able to figure out what kind of snake I almost stepped on last spring."

Abruptly, Holycross stopped and wheeled to face me.

"Where and when did you see the snake?" His eyes bulged. "And what—*exactly*—did it look like?"

Taken aback by the ferocity of his interest, I cast my mind to what had happened several months earlier.

*   *   *

Not long after Pete had assured me that the hike itself was the thing that would get us in shape for the hike, I'd begun to suspect that this might be total nonsense and launched a last-minute fitness program,

setting my sights on a volcanic peak called Mount Elden, just grazing
Flagstaff's city limits, which features a steep trail that climbs twenty-
four hundred vertical feet to the summit in less than three miles.
Starting in late July, I fell into a routine. Four or five times a week,
I'd drive to the trailhead straight after work, ascend at sunset, and
descend at twilight, returning to the parking lot just after it got dark.
(This wasn't even remotely close to the kind of fitness regimen that
would have truly prepared me for the canyon, but it was better than
nothing.)

Because I was moving up and down Elden during the times of the
day when the animals and the birds are especially active, I spotted
more than my fair share of wildlife. The ground abounded with rabbits, while the air was alive with hawks and ravens. Once or twice I
even caught sight of a coyote ghosting between the juniper trees. But
the most surprising encounter took place one evening at dusk when,
without warning, a snake materialized on the trail, no more than six
inches from my right foot.

Our meeting was brief—within a heartbeat or two, the creature
slid to the side of the trail with an oiled grace and disappeared into a
thicket of scrub oak, leaving me to wonder what genus it belonged to
and whether it was venomous. I had seen that it was brightly colored,
with some stripes on its back, and I made a mental note to do some
research in the hopes of identifying it. But by the time I returned home,
I'd decided that the snake didn't matter all that much and allowed the
matter to drop.

Right now, though, the snake apparently *did* matter, because here
at the front doorstep of the Grand Canyon one of the premier herpetologists in the Southwest was demanding details.

"Describe it," Holycross barked.

"Well . . ." I paused and scratched my head.

Ten minutes earlier, I could easily have called to mind the snake's
salient features—its size, its colors, the shape of its head and body. But
now the creature's likeness seemed to have slithered off and vanished
into the underbrush of my own bewilderment.

"It was mostly red," I stammered. "But also mostly white."

He looked at me blankly.

"And there may have been a brown stripe running down its back—or wait, was it black?"

It felt as if I were mostly talking to myself.

"The stripe, if it was there, was definitely either black or brown, but probably not both."

Holycross blinked once, leveling me with a glare that must have been reserved for his least promising students—and it was in that moment, confounded by the shallowness of my own observancy, that I saw the professor in an entirely new way.

The torn shorts and the broken zipper? The goofy sandals and the beer can? Suddenly, those things didn't seem quite so funny or foolish anymore, while Holycross himself no longer came across as a joke.

Snakes were serious business. If you ran across one in the desert, you paid attention, taking the trouble to study the snake with closeness and care to enable you to commit its features to memory, so that if called upon to describe it by somebody who knew more than you, you'd be prepared to relay some basic facts about its looks and behavior. What's more, you did this not simply because snakes were important in and of themselves, but because the attention that you paid a snake—your willingness to examine and study the thing until you were able to truly *see* it—was tied directly to your ability to observe and understand the place to which the snake belonged.

In other words, how you looked at a snake said a lot about how you were moving across the land: your alertness, your concentration, the vigilance and the care that you brought to the task of being present and attentive to everything that surrounded you. And by the same token, while the details you could later recall might well convey something important about the snake, they revealed far more about *you*.

I'd done a lousy job taking stock of that snake back on Mount Elden. But standing there on the road beside the river, I had no trouble making out the current of thoughts coursing through Holycross's mind, a stream as chilly and cutting as the Colorado in runoff season:

Anybody who cannot attend to a snake isn't paying heed to a thousand other things, and a person like that has no business bumbling through the canyon on foot.

As if to confirm my suspicions, Holycross now conducted a brief, two-sentence conversation with himself.

"You know what?" he mused, staring off into the distance with a look of contemplative revulsion. "That is the single worst description of a snake I've ever heard in my entire life."

Shaking his head in disgust, he headed off down the road at a rapid clip, leaving me to walk in the company of my own thoughts.

*   *   *

Holycross might well have had something to teach me right then. But instead of attending to the lesson, I chose to write him off as a brooding, tight-lipped sourpuss.

"Who cares about a stupid snake?" I mumbled, while noting with satisfaction how glaringly his crabbiness clashed with the buoyant spirits not only of our hiking companions and well-wishers, but even the folks driving past us on the road, many of whom were merrily tooting their horns and shouting words of encouragement.

"Woo-hoo!" yelled a man at the wheel of a passenger van, who waved his arm while giving us the thumbs-up.

"Happy trails!" cried a woman from inside an SUV (clearly having no idea that where we were heading had none).

The enthusiasm was contagious. As I clomped along the smooth, flat, debris-free surface of the road in my brand-new Scarpa Zodiac GTX boots, my feet felt solid, my legs didn't seem to be shaking too much, and things seemed more or less okay.

This doesn't actually feel that bad, I remarked to myself. *Maybe we're not in as much trouble as everybody seems to think we are.*

With that, my thoughts turned snidely toward our companions:

Rich and his pals, they seem like they're pretty tough. But maybe hiking through the canyon isn't really that big of a deal after all.

As I was making a mental note to set some time aside in camp later that evening to get a few of these ideas down on paper, my thoughts were interrupted by the sound of a vehicle slowing to a stop behind me.

A massive rig truck that had just dropped a group of river guides at the Ferry was now on its way back to Flagstaff. As the window lowered, a voice called out from inside the cab.

"Hey, Groover Boy, jump in—this is your last chance to skip all this madness before it's too late!"

I couldn't see who had recognized me from my days on the river, but it didn't matter.

"No way," I called back smugly. "We've got this hike in the bag."

"Well, alrighty then . . ." came the reply as the driver of the truck shifted gears and sped off. "It's your funeral."

This, I would later come to recognize, marked the exact moment when our journey truly began.

PART IV

The Shakedown

This shouldn't be so bad, I told myself.

But secretly, I knew that I was quite wrong.

—Bill Bryson

EASTERN GRAND CANYON

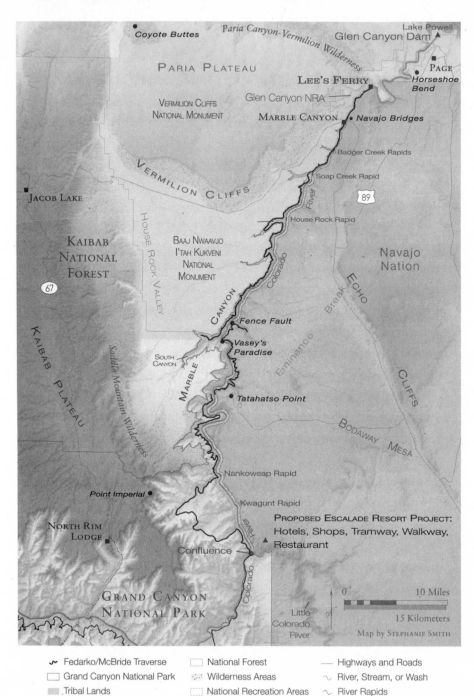

Coyote Buttes

Paria Canyon-Vermilion Wilderness

Glen Canyon Dam

Lake Powell

PARIA PLATEAU

PAGE

LEE'S FERRY

Horseshoe Bend

VERMILION CLIFFS NATIONAL MONUMENT

Glen Canyon NRA

MARBLE CANYON

Navajo Bridges

Badger Creek Rapids

Soap Creek Rapid

89

JACOB LAKE

VERMILION CLIFFS

HOUSE ROCK VALLEY

House Rock Rapid

KAIBAB NATIONAL FOREST

BAAJ NWAAVJO I'TAH KUKVENI NATIONAL MONUMENT

Colorado River

Navajo Nation

67

ECHO

MARBLE CANYON

Fence Fault

Eminence Break

Saddle Mountain Wilderness

SOUTH CANYON

Vasey's Paradise

KAIBAB PLATEAU

CLIFFS

Tatahatso Point

BODAWAY MESA

Nankoweap Rapid

Point Imperial

Kwagunt Rapid

PROPOSED ESCALADE RESORT PROJECT: Hotels, Shops, Tramway, Walkway, Restaurant

NORTH RIM LODGE

Confluence

GRAND CANYON NATIONAL PARK

Colorado River

Little Colorado River

0   10 Miles

15 Kilometers

Map by STEPHANIE SMITH

∿ Fedarko/McBride Traverse

☐ National Forest

— Highways and Roads

☐ Grand Canyon National Park

▨ Wilderness Areas

∿ River, Stream, or Wash

▨ Tribal Lands

⬚ National Recreation Areas

∿ River Rapids

▨ National Monuments

— State Boundary

CHAPTER 12

Dirty Business

"Dude . . . are you *okay?*" Pete murmurs as he kneels down beside me.

I can't muster a response.

"Is there anything I can *do?*"

I shake my head listlessly.

"Wanna take your pack off, at least?"

It's early evening, the sun is finally about to dip behind the rimrock off to the west, and I've marked the conclusion to the first day of our expedition—the delicious moment when it's finally time to stop walking, shed the weight strapped to my back, and start thinking about what's for supper—by pitching face-first into the dirt beside some bushes where we'll apparently be spending the night.

As Pete is trying to point out, however, I've skipped over the part that involves removing my pack.

"All right," he continues, sensing that there's no point in arguing with me. "Why don't we try to get some food in you?"

"*Mmf mm-mmf,*" I mumble.

"What's that?"

"Please fuck off."

There's a catch to my breath and my words quaver, as if they're afraid of tumbling to the ground and breaking into pieces.

"I can't absorb nutrients right now," I elaborate. "My body's too traumatized."

That may sound overblown, but it's true. Every part of me—feet, hips, neck, shoulders, legs—bears the weight of an ache that seems to cut through muscle, directly to bone. Also, the skin on my face feels as if someone held a blowtorch to it. Christ, even my hair feels burned.

I extend my arm and run my fingers over my scalp to confirm this last impression.

"Pete, my hair actually *hurts*."

"Weirdly, mine does, too."

"How is that even possible?"

"No clue. But given how today went, it kinda makes sense, doesn't it?"

*   *   *

Shortly after the rig truck had roared off, the road on which we'd been walking came to an end, and we shifted over to the sandy shoreline. Within a hundred yards or so the beach ended, too, leaving us to follow a faint fishermen's trail that ran parallel to the river while dipping though a series of dry washes festooned with cobbles and gravel. Meanwhile, the ground off to our right, away from the river, began to climb higher and higher until it had become a cliff.

We spent the better part of an hour clomping in single file, and around this point I began paying closer attention to my pack, which mysteriously appeared to be getting heavier by the minute, but seemed intent on creating other problems, too. The shoulder straps were cutting off the circulation in my arms, the waist belt was digging into my hips, and the chest strap seemed to be compressing my lungs, making breathing a chore.

The prospect of continuing under these conditions for the next seven hours felt ridiculous.

"Hey," I wheezed to Pete, who was directly in front of me and didn't appear to be faring much better, "how are you doing?"

We tottered another few steps in silence, which made me think that perhaps he hadn't heard me.

"How much longer . . . ," he finally said, the words emerging in staccato bursts between ragged gasps for air, "do you think it'll be . . . before these guys . . . stop for a snack?"

Just then, the trail made its way down to the edge of the river one last time, ventured tentatively toward a dense wall of brush, and stopped, as if throwing its hands in the air and concluding that there was no point in continuing farther. Directly ahead stood a tightly woven nest of tamarisk, an invasive species from North Africa and the Middle East that is capable of forming all but impenetrable hedges up to twenty feet high.

Clearly, an excellent spot for a snack.

Without breaking their stride, Rich and his crew dropped to the ground and started tunneling under the branches using their elbows and hips, like soldiers snaking beneath a lattice of barbed wire while machine-gun rounds tore through the air just above their heads. Having no better plan, Pete and I followed suit—and discovered that bushwhacking through a tamarisk thicket is its own form of combat.

As my backpack plowed into the brittle canopy of sticks hovering about a foot off the ground, a shower of dead leaves, broken twigs, and fragments of bark poured along the creases of my neck and down the length of my spine, where it mixed with my sweat to form a gritty ointment that caked to my back. Meanwhile, the weight of the pack was forcing my chest to furrow through the sand, much of which seemed to be funneling into the front of my shirt, and from there straight down my pants. Dirty business.

After several minutes, the brush thinned out just enough that I was able to get to my feet and determine that I was nowhere near the end of the thicket, but had merely broken into a pocket of clear ground. I'd also gotten separated from my companions, who, judging by the chorus of hoglike grunts, were somewhere off to my left. Listening to their thrashing, I was struck by the preposterousness of starting an epic journey by snuffling around in the underbrush like a pack of lost javelinas. I was also appalled by how unpleasant it was to have to make your own trail.

The next part of the thicket didn't offer any open space at ground level, so I opted for the only alternative: clambering straight into the mess by bracing my feet on the heavier branches, while parting the twigs and foliage with a breaststroke motion. Within a couple of steps, I lost my balance and crashed to the ground, creating a hole in the hedge as I fell.

That enabled me to stand up and go through the process again, and after repeating this several more times—snapping off just enough branches to open a space in which to stand up and point in the direction I needed to go before toppling over again—it seemed as if I was making some headway. This continued for what felt like another ten minutes, until I crashed through the far side of the grove, coated in grit and gasping for air, and glanced back to determine that the distance I'd covered amounted to about fifty feet. Meanwhile, just up ahead, Rich and his team, with Pete in tow, were already hurtling toward our next obstacle.

Directly in front of us was a steep slope covered in a field of boulders, each the size of a watermelon. Every piece of this rubble, known as talus, was balanced precariously on its neighbors, leaving the entire slope riddled with gaps, any of which could easily trap a foot or leg. When I stepped onto the leading edge of the first rock, it rolled with a hollow *ka-thunk*, spurring me to skitter onto the next stone, which also shifted just enough to throw me off-balance. Regaining my equilibrium would have been a simple matter had I not been strapped into a fifty-three-pound pack; now the only way to avoid toppling into the talus was to leap to another boulder while bracing for the possibility that it, too, might decide to roll.

That was my introduction to the technique for moving across an unstable talus slope: a demented form of hopscotch, paired with a desperate series of Swedish clog-dancing moves. Every jump harbored the possibility that an ankle or shin would catch between the boulders and snap like a breadstick. Each effort to restore balance—spastically flapping both arms while swiveling the hips—was so desperate and enervating that soon I was wishing I were back in the tamarisk, with my face in the dirt.

When we reached the end of the rubble field, this request was granted, thanks to a second fortress of brush even denser than the first. That was followed by yet another tumble of boulders, then more brush, and so on. On no stretch of ground could one foot be placed in front of the other without fierce effort and total concentration.

Pete and I did our best to keep up with Rich and his group, while falling ever farther behind them. Smeared with sand, legs trembling, I was shocked by the unrelenting toil of moving through the vegetation and the rocks, unaware that yet another challenge was about to materialize.

*   *   *

As the Colorado pushes south from Lee's Ferry, it carves into the bedrock at a rate of roughly eight feet per mile. At the same time, the ground begins lifting up at roughly eighty feet per mile. The combination of these opposing dynamics—a downward-drilling river cutting along the face of a steeply ascending plateau—exposes a suite of ancient rock strata that was buried deep underground hundreds of millions of years before the uplift ever took place. Within the first twenty-five miles of the river's passage through the canyon, no fewer than seven layers of stone climb roughly twenty-five hundred feet into the air, almost five times as tall as the Washington Monument. If you are traveling by boat, it's impressive to watch this geological pageant unfold. But on foot, you actually become part of the parade, meeting each new layer of rock as it emerges.

The first of these layers, the Kaibab Limestone, nosed out of the water less than a mile downstream from the Ferry, swiftly walling off both sides of the river inside a corridor. But within another mile and a half, its buff-colored cliffs had already shot more than three hundred feet into the air and given way to an even older stratum: a poorly cemented admixture of sandstone, shale, traces of gypsum, and even a bit of limestone known as the Toroweap Formation.

Together, these two layers now formed a thirty-foot cliff, which would have to be down-climbed. We took turns on the descent, in which each of us scrabbled blindly for notches on which to brace our feet. Looking down at Pete as he fumbled for a toehold, I noted that the skin on his neck had turned bright red, like an overripe tomato, and rivulets of sweat were running down the back of his shirt.

When he arrived at the bottom, it was my turn. I swiveled to face the rock, wrapped my fingers around a horn-shaped protrusion—and jerked my hand away so fast that I almost peeled off the wall. *Holy crap*, I thought to myself. *This place is turning into a furnace.*

By the time we finally halted for the snack that Pete had asked about several hours earlier, the ferocity of the heat had punched a serious dent into the arrogance and bravado of my morning.

I glanced over at the rest of our group. They didn't seem bothered by the heat or the grind.

"This is harder and hotter than I thought it would be," I confessed to Pete. "Do you think we can actually cut it?"

He weighed the question while guzzling half a liter of water.

"Totally," he said, less because he believed it and more because he knew that I needed some encouragement. "We're kicking some serious ass."

As we were about to discover, the real ass kicking had only just begun.

*   *   *

Back on our feet, we continued pushing across the Toroweap until yet another layer made its appearance. Known as the Coconino Sand-stone, its folds contain petrified dunes of windblown sand from an ancient, Sahara-like desert whose borders once covered most of northern Arizona. If you closely scan the dimples on the surface of the smooth, camel-colored rock, you can trace the humble comings and goings of the spiders and scorpions and millipedes that were part of that van-ished world.

With the emergence of the Coconino's leading ledge came yet another ramp that once again drew us up and away from the river, and as we ascended we found ourselves passing beneath the twin trusses of the Navajo Bridge, which soar more than 450 feet above the river.[*]

This is the last place a vehicle can cross the Colorado in four hundred miles, as well as our final glimpse of the outside world. Beyond this point, our stature and size would inexorably diminish, growing ever smaller until eventually we became as insignificant as spiders on a sea of sand.

As if to underscore that fact, a set of vertical cliffs directly to our right now rose more than two hundred feet to the canyon's lip, while off to our left, another set of cliffs plunged two hundred feet to the shoreline—which meant that for the moment we were cut off on a steep, narrow apron of talus perched between the rim and the river. This was our first direct contact with the no-man's-land running the length of the canyon's interior, a domain that would soon swell to include tier upon tier of ledges and cliffs, all stacked atop one another to form a kind of inverted wedding cake. We had entered the kingdom of the thru-hikers, the realm I'd been wondering about ever since my days rowing the *Jackass.*

As we picked our way across the steeply angled talus, Pete and I dropped far behind the rest of the group. It was well after 6:00 p.m., with the shadows more than halfway down the canyon walls, when we reached a break in the cliffs, descended to a section of sandy shoreline, and discovered that the day was finally over.

We arrived in camp to find everyone sitting cross-legged on their ground cloths, with their packs emptied and their gear arrayed neatly beside them. Dave and Chris were pouring boiling water onto their freeze-dried dinners, filling the air with the aroma of chicken broth, while Rich and Mike were inspecting their hiking shoes. During the afternoon, the ground had been so hot that the soles were now starting to peel back and delaminate. To keep them from coming apart completely, they would have to be cleaned and glued back together.

---

[*] When the first of the two spandrel-arch structures was built in the late 1920s, it was the third-highest bridge in America.

"Hey, everybody, guess what?" Rich exclaimed as we staggered up. "Pete and Kev are alive, and we're only a few miles behind schedule—congratulations!"

Chris and Mike stayed silent, evidently undecided over whether our survival was worth celebrating. Dave's face bore a look suggesting that, for the moment, Rich might no longer be one of his favorite people.

If anything else was said, it went straight over my head as I crumpled to the ground without bothering to fix dinner or write in my notebook. As for Pete, his efforts to revive me notwithstanding, he wasn't doing much better. His camera gear had spent most of the day in our packs, and he'd barely taken a single photo.

This is insane, I thought to myself as I closed my eyes. *How can we keep this up for another eleven days?*

*　　　*　　　*

An hour or so later, I was roused by the sound of something stirring nearby.

Peering into the night, I could see someone creeping through the darkness over to my pack, opening the top, and pulling out a massive telephoto lens that I was carrying for Pete, which weighed almost four pounds. Then the person returned to his sleeping pad and tucked the lens into the bottom of his pack.

It was Chris, lessening the load I'd have to carry the next day without making me feel badly about it.

Suffused with gratitude, I started to drift off again.

My last thought was that after such an unspeakably brutal induction, it only made sense for us to take a day off to rest and recover. We'd sleep in until ten o'clock, have a leisurely breakfast, and after that there would be plenty of time for the six of us to gather in a circle to share our feelings, explore our emotions, and discuss how to dial back the mileage and the pace to something more manageable.

I fell back to sleep nursing visions of late-morning coffee, and an afternoon bath in the river.

CHAPTER 13

The Godfather of
Grand Canyon Hiking

"Let's go, everybody—time to roll out!"

The moment I opened my eyes, I could tell that something was horribly wrong. It was 4:30 a.m., several hours prior to the earliest moment when it would be even marginally acceptable to start wrestling with the idea of getting out of bed. Yet there was Rich, moving from one sleeping pad to the next, rousing us from our sleeping bags.

Within seconds, everyone except for Pete and me had scrambled to his feet, flicked on his headlamp, and was rushing to do several things at once: get dressed, roll up his air mattress, fill water bottles from the river, cram cereal into his mouth, lace up his hiking shoes, and place everything else into his backpack in its proper order.[*]

All of this unfolded so swiftly that Pete and I had barely finished rubbing our eyes before the whole crew was standing in a circle, glaring at us.

---

[*] The final item on the checklist was answering the call of nature. Because we were all adhering to the rules of minimum-impact camping, we each had to find a private spot away from camp, dig a six-inch-deep hole to bury our waste, and clean our hands with disinfectant. Park rules prohibit the burning of toilet paper, so those of us who used it placed it in a special set of Ziploc bags.

"Okay, guys," said Rich sternly, "we need to get moving—right now."

The urgency in his voice made it seem as if we were already late for something important, a notion that left Pete and me befuddled.

"Why the rush? How come he's so tweaked?" I mumbled to myself in confusion as we started pulling ourselves together. "What the hell's his *problem?*"

We were about to learn. The hour preceding dawn signals the start of a race to break camp and be on the move by 5:30 to make the most of the evanescent portion of the day when the canyon's interior is wrapped in cool blue shadows, and the place doesn't feel like a total inferno.

This period of grace would end the moment the first rays of sunlight lasered into the depths, and the temperature started to soar. Between now and then, every second counted—so before Pete and I could register a protest, we found ourselves harnessed to our packs and stumbling beneath our loads as if we had never bothered to camp at all and had simply continued lurching through the night like the living dead.

Unfortunately, thanks to our sluggishness, the shadow hour was almost over by the time we finally broke camp. Ten minutes later, the sun crashed over the east rim, torching the walls just as we hit the next geological stratum, a layer called the Hermit Shale, whose rust-colored patina, Rich explained, derived from heavy concentrations of iron oxides embedded in the mud from which the shale had originally been formed, some 285 million years ago, when almost all of the exposed landforms on earth had merged to form a single, contiguous supercontinent known as Pangaea.

Yeah, whatever, I thought as I listened to Rich. I didn't give a hoot about the Hermit's chemical composition or its geomorphic pedigree because the only thing that mattered was its texture: so loose and crumbly that I sank to my ankles with each step, enabling dirt and grit to sluice over the tops of my shoes and work their way into my socks (a problem that would have been prevented had Pete and I bothered to bring gaiters).

Before long, we arrived at the mouth of the tributary that had been the objective of the previous day's march and began skirting along the edge of the canyon's first pocket of whitewater, an easy set of rapids known as Badger, which—oddly enough—was directly beneath the spot on the rim where Pete and I had met Rich's team and had staged our packing fiasco two nights earlier.

This felt like the opposite of progress.

As the day grew hotter, Pete and I found it impossible to keep pace with Chris, Dave, and Mike, who surged relentlessly ahead until we had all but lost sight of them. Rich, however, held back to keep an eye on us—a gesture of courtesy that subjected us to perhaps his most annoying trait, which was his disinterest in making any effort to curb or contain his passion for the canyon.

While Pete and I concentrated on the grim business of placing one foot in front of the other, Rich extolled the beauty of the rock, rhapsodized on the pleasures of moving across uneven terrain, and anticipated with delight the obstacles that lay ahead—all while delivering a mini-lecture on fossil variation within the thirteen different geomorphic reaches of the canyon. In the midst of this, he also spoke about himself: how he'd been drawn to the canyon, what it was about that first encounter that had left him transfixed, and why, instead of moving on to new ground, he'd kept coming back again and again.

I was in no mood to hear any of it. Regardless, that afternoon, we learned quite a bit not only about Rich himself, but also the subculture to which he belonged.

*　　　*　　　*

Like most people, he was initially hooked by the river. He'd grown up in Northern California, where his father farmed rice in a small agricultural town in the Sacramento Valley. Thanks to a keen interest in math and science, he sped through high school and college at an accelerated pace, and by his twentieth birthday he'd parlayed a degree in electrical engineering into a pair of defense-industry jobs, first in Los Angeles, then in Phoenix, helping to design guidance and tracking systems for F/A-18 fighter jets and Apache helicopters. The hours were so intense that shortly after moving to Arizona in 1988, his wife, Joanna, grew worried that he was working too hard and bought him and his favorite uncle seats on a Grand Canyon river trip in the hope that he'd take a break and relax.

The expedition, run by one of the canyon's motorized outfitters, included about twenty passengers and two guides aboard an enormous thirty-six-foot-long raft with an outboard engine. Like all mechanized trips, they moved fast, gunning thirty miles or more downstream each day—nearly twice the distance of oar boats, and covering the entire canyon in less than a week. There was little time to dawdle, but every now and then when they pulled over for lunch or set up camp for the night, they had a chance to take a brief hike up one of the side canyons.

On these excursions, Rich was struck by the allure of those tributaries: the sensation that just a few steps away from the river, a doorway opened onto another world. The keenness of his desire to go farther, to penetrate more deeply, would stay with him. When the river trip was finished, he couldn't stop thinking about those side canyons and resolved to return and get a firsthand look. The following summer he was back, this time with his brother-in-law Dale Diulus, on the first of what would become an increasingly ambitious series of hikes that entailed knocking off almost all the official trails in the canyon.

This felt like an immense undertaking—and during the five years it took for them to work their way through the list, the prospect of completion imparted a huge sense of accomplishment. But the more they hiked, the better they understood that the canyon's trail system barely scratched the surface of what was out there. So much more was waiting to be discovered for anyone willing to move beyond those pathways into the *true* backcountry.

By the mid-1990s, Rich realized that venturing into that zone would require not just homework, but also sleuthing. First, he read everything he could get his hands on at local libraries and small museums across northern Arizona—the antiquated maps, the defunct mining claims, the notebooks and journals of the government surveyors from the late 1800s, the letters hoarded by amateur canyon historians—and plumbed those documents for details. Then he tracked down the old-timers—the retired cattlemen, the forest rangers, and the half-crazed loners, anyone who might have knowledge about the terrain—and peppered them with questions.

During this research, he realized that, in one way or another, virtually every scrap of modern-day knowledge about moving through the canyon on foot traced back to just one person. An obsessive mathematician named Harvey Butchart had pieced together and codified such an astonishing number of routes that everyone who came after him was basically walking in his shadow.

*   *   *

As Rich explained to Pete and me, Butchart's initial bond with the canyon had been forged shortly after 1945, when he moved his family from the Midwest to take a job at a small college in Flagstaff that would eventually be known as Northern Arizona University. "Harvey was hired to run the math department while teaching algebra, trigonometry, integral calculus, and synthetic projective geometry," said Rich. "But in his free time, he found himself drawn into this immense wilderness just north of town."

Nowadays, the park hosts so many visitors that until quite recently only Great Smoky Mountains National Park, which features a highway corridor through the middle of it, draws more tourists. But back in Butchart's day, despite its fame, the place was still a bit of a backwater in terms of visitation. Only a few thousand tourists made it to the South Rim every year, and almost none of them ventured into the interior, unless it was in the safety of a guided mule train. Over the next several years, Butchart realized that this had created an anomaly:

"The canyon is less than a two-hour drive from Flagstaff, and yet the natural bridges, Indian ruins, caves, and rope-less climbs seem as little known as if they were in some remote area of Alaska," he would later write in an unpublished essay entitled "The Canyon Nobody Knows." "Although it was first seen by white men eighty years before the pilgrims landed from the *Mayflower*, and although prospectors swarmed over it for twenty years before 1900, for all practical purposes, it is still unknown territory."

It took several years for Butchart to fully grasp the implications of this; but when he did, it struck him like a kick from a mule. Deep inside the park lay hundreds of side canyons and tributary gorges that appeared to be largely untrammeled, and many of those recesses concealed tantalizing treasures—hidden waterfalls, secret gardens, prehistoric artifacts—that hadn't been seen or touched in hundreds of years, if ever. Those discoveries were available to anyone who was willing to just step off the trail, and there were enough of them, Butchart realized, to keep him occupied for the rest of his life.

By the early 1950s, he was devoting almost every weekend and holiday to increasingly ambitious hikes that took him far beyond the established trails. Those ventures taught him that cracking the code to the labyrinth required more than just physical stamina and a working knowledge of geology. At its essence, the canyon presented an interlocking series of math problems hinged on a keen understanding of geometry and topology, plus the ability to memorize highly complex details with near-photographic accuracy. "Thanks to the way Harvey's mind worked," said Rich, "he fit that bill almost perfectly."

*   *   *

Unfortunately, the combination of tenacity and single-mindedness that made Butchart so well suited for figuring out how the canyon was put together could also make him extremely challenging to deal with as a person.

When he wasn't out exploring by himself, Butchart was accompanied primarily by students who had joined the college's hiking club and submitted to his grueling fitness exam, the final phase of which included racing to the top of Mount Elden in seventy-five minutes or less. (This was the same trail on which I would later spot the mysterious snake while attempting to get in shape for my own foray into the canyon.)

Whoever passed the test was then invited to pile into Butchart's blue GMC Jimmy for a drive up to the canyon's rimlands, where the professor would rocket down dirt roads at speeds of up to eighty-five miles per hour, rooster-tailing through the turns and obliterating clumps of underbrush while turning to face passengers in the back seat to share details about the hike he had in mind. After an hour or two of having their heads slammed into the roof, anyone still clinging to the delusion that this would be a relaxing nature excursion arrived at the trailhead to discover that the real ordeal was just getting started.

Flinging on his pack and canteens, Butchart would set off at a merciless pace that his companions, most of whom were half his age, were expected to maintain for the next ten to twelve hours. He hiked this way all year, including through the triple-digit, brain-baking heat of midsummer, traversing distances in a single day that most people would not be able to cover in three. "'It was like the guy was made of piano wire,'" said Rich, quoting a line that one of those former students would later share with Butchart's biographer.

Like the Penitentes, the brotherhood of Catholic flagellants in the mountains of New Mexico who scourged themselves with tree branches while carrying crosses to atone for their sins, Butchart subordinated even the tiniest pleasures to a grander mission, in this case to cover as much unknown ground in the shortest time possible. To minimize minutes that might be wasted on tasks other than hiking, his meals were simple and astringent: prunes, sardines, and a daily ration of six sandwiches of Wonder bread slathered with margarine. He dispensed with a tent, preferring to sleep beneath the open sky, and when it rained, he wrapped himself up in a piece of plastic, like a burrito.

Because he was so straitlaced that he neither drank nor smoked—and because he possessed virtually no sense of humor—his camps boasted little in the way of entertainment. No music. Sparse laughter. Scant frivolities. And there were zero rest days in which to savor the pleasures of being in a place that had no analogue anywhere else on earth.

On the final day of the hike, when it was time to make the steep ascent back to the rim, Butchart would make no concession to the terrain. Even in his seventies, he could climb so fast and so relentlessly that for every excursion he led, it was said that he drove at least one student to vomit—if not within the canyon itself, then in the Jimmy during the drag race back to Flagstaff.[*]

In this manner, he burned through an extensive assortment of students and companions who couldn't keep up, but were also perceptive enough to discern that he took a measure of satisfaction in driving them into the ground. As a result, over his four-decade-long tenure in the canyon, he had almost no long-term hiking partners.

He also had more than his fair share of brushes with injury, and worse. Once he jumped from a boulder with a heavy backpack and landed so hard that his right heel bone split with an audible crack. On another occasion when he tripped and fell, the weight of his pack drove his chest into his canteen with enough force to snap several ribs. In the spring of 1964 when his pack caught on a protruding rock and threw him off-balance, he toppled over backward, caught his left hand between two rocks while attempting to brace the fall, and snapped his wrist at a double right angle. But his worst accident took place late in December of 1969, when he headed off on a one-day solo hike to explore a new route in the eastern part of the canyon without having bothered to tell anyone where he was going.

Toward evening he started clawing his way up a fixed rope that he'd set up earlier in the day on an eighty-foot overhang. He was using ascenders—a set of toothed mechanical devices that are thrust up the rope with one's hands, and which also have loops at the bottom for one's feet—when the rope began spinning so violently that he lost his grip on the ascenders, flipped upside down, and found himself hanging by his ankles with the loops cinched tightly around his feet.

This can be an exceptionally unpleasant way to die, and during the next forty minutes, Butchart got a taste of what that might feel like

---

[*] Despite his competitiveness, Butchart was often generous in sharing information with others. One of the many hikers who benefited from his advice was Colin Fletcher, whose thru-hike was essentially mapped out by Butchart—a service for which Butchart was given full credit in the pages of *The Man Who Walked Through Time*.

as he attempted to reach his feet and free himself from the loops, all the while becoming more exhausted and moving closer toward losing consciousness. By some miracle, right around dusk he pendulumed himself to the side, seized hold of a small tree with one hand, and hoisted himself high enough to free his feet with the other. Upon dropping to the ground, he then confronted the fact that, without warm clothes or matches (neither of which he was carrying), the only way for him to survive one of the longest nights of the year—a day from the winter solstice—was to find another route to the top, in pitch dark.

Thirty-one hours later, when he finally stumbled through the snowdrifts on the rim and reached his vehicle, he'd pulled off the most arduous forced march of his life. He was sixty-two years old.

*   *   *

Those mishaps did absolutely nothing to dampen Butchart's determination to become the first person in the modern era to reopen the lost world of the canyon's outback while building a list of accomplishments that others would find almost impossible to surpass. In the end, everything was secondary to those twin objectives—including, paradoxically, the integrity of the land itself. For Butchart, the canyon was an arena in which he could compete with others and through which he could inscribe his name in the history books. He never claimed to be especially moved by its beauty, and it's probably fair to say that he didn't give a hoot about conservation. He littered wherever and whenever convenient, often finishing up his lunch by tossing a sardine can over a cliff while braying, "No white man'll ever be down there." At least once, when completing the ascent of a remote butte, he carried a can of green paint and sprayed arrows onto the rocks so that he could find his way back down.

Although his reputation would be colored by these and many other compromises, his shortcomings coexist with a list of feats unlike anything else that had been amassed in the canyon since the time of the ancient peoples whose lingering presence had been such a source of fascination for Kenton Grua—and whose knowledge of the landscape included the places into which Butchart had been flinging those sardine cans.

By 1987, when Butchart completed the last of his 560 hikes below the rims, he had walked more than 12,000 miles, halfway around the circumference of the earth, and summited 83 of the 138 major peaks inside the canyon, including 28 ascents that had never before been recorded.

He also compiled more than seven thousand photographic slides, plus a meticulously detailed set of logbooks totaling 1,079 pages, a carefully annotated map, and thousands of pages of correspondence, the most comprehensive survey of the canyon's backcountry that has ever been assembled. Perhaps the only prize that eluded him was a continuous thru-hike like the one that Grua had pulled off—primarily because Butchart's singular compulsion was figuring out how to move up and down the canyon, as opposed to along its length.

"There's nobody else out there like Harvey—he's basically the god-father of Grand Canyon hiking," declared Rich. "And one of the unsung elements in his forty-three-year quest is what he left behind for people like me to stumble across."

"Which was what, exactly?" asked Pete, gasping for breath as we toiled through yet another talus field.

"Basically, it's an invitation to do what he did—to venture out of bounds, beyond the trails, and find out what's there."

During the many hours that Rich hung back with Pete and me as the three of us moved along some of the very same ground that Butchart had once covered, Rich's running commentary brought this distinguished deacon of the canyon to life. Many months later, Pete and I would come to appreciate what this meant. But right then, we were incapable of feeling gratitude for much of anything because we were faring no better than a pair of students struggling to keep pace with their professor, just before they started throwing up.

CHAPTER 14

Rock Bottom

Aroutine set in. Each morning at 4:30, Rich would wake us all up, triggering another mad scramble to dress, wrangle gear, and wolf down some food. He and his crew would then stand around waiting for Pete and me to finish packing; then nod with relief when we announced that we were ready to go; then sigh with exasperation when, thanks to our execrable pack discipline, one of us was forced to dump his belongings back onto the ground to find whatever he felt he needed in that moment—a Handi Wipe, a Snickers bar, a pen—and sigh again, this time with resignation, when we finally got moving.

For the next twelve hours, Rich and his companions would push forward as fast as possible while Pete and I desperately tried to keep up, draining our water bottles and sweating like donkeys, losing energy and speed by the minute, progressively retarding the pace of the entire group until darkness forced us to stop for the night. Then once camp was set, everyone would gather around to consult a visual reference that had been created several weeks prior to the start of the hike when Rich's wife, Joanna, had sat down in the living room of their home outside Phoenix, taken up a set of Magic Markers, and neatly inscribed on the outside of her husband's white backpack the location and date of every spot on the route where he and his crew intended to bed down each night, color coded by week.

Joanna's hope was that the itinerary would be an inspirational calendar for Rich and his team. Little did she realize that it would end up serving as an index to gauge how much further behind we were now falling, thanks to Pete and me, with every passing day.

After reviewing Joanna's timetable to find out where we were supposed to be, we would pull out our maps to determine where we actually were and how far we'd fallen short of that goal.* The endlessly widening gap between these two points would then provoke an animated discussion among Rich and his team, sometimes accompanied by spirited hand-waving, and eventually yielding an ambitious set of entirely new objectives for the following day in the hopes of getting us back on track.

Then everyone would eat dinner, go to sleep—and the cycle would start again.

*   *   *

The math was insidious, and as our mileage deficit increased, our location on any given day lost all connection to the schedule on Rich's pack. It also didn't help that for Pete and me, each of those miles not only stood as a rebuke of our performance, but also felt longer and harder than its predecessor—a trend that seemed to be linked to the expanding scale and complexity of the terrain as we encountered a line of irregular cliffs that made foot travel at the edge of the river almost impossible. Before long we were forced to climb several hundred feet above the Colorado, where we found ourselves picking along a series of narrow ledges with drop-offs so sheer that any loose stones we kicked over the edge would fall a full five seconds before plonking into the water below.

Although we had been on the move for only a few days, the toil and the heat had already taken a heavy toll on our gear. Despite assiduous

---

* In addition to paper maps, we were using an app called Trimble Outdoors, which enabled us to download U.S. Geological Survey topographical maps on our cell phones and geo-locate our position in real time, via our satellite link. Like Pete's digital cameras, all of this equipment was charged through our solar panels.

repair work each night in camp, the glue holding our footwear together continued to melt, and the soles kept peeling away. One of Mike's shoes now had a four-inch gash running along its bottom, and was all but split in half.

Our bodies were taking a beating, too—especially mine. Having decided at the end of our first day that I was too exhausted to properly treat the blisters on my feet with antiseptic and moleskin, and then having made things so much worse by encasing everything in duct tape, I could no longer deny that the skin was festering. The odor alone was impossible to ignore—a putrefying stench that wafted through the air whenever I removed my socks. But that paled in comparison to the pain. From the first stride I took in the morning to my last plodding lurch as I staggered into camp at night, my feet felt as if they were marinating in battery acid. All day long, my face was clenched in a grimace, a reflection of the effort I was making to suppress the impulse to tilt my head back and scream into the sky.

I certainly wasn't the only one with foot trouble. Rich had a few blisters forming on his toes, while Dave's left foot had developed a deep ache that refused to subside. One of Mike's ankles had turned purple and swollen after he accidentally bashed it against a rock. But none of those problems seemed to interfere with the team's capabilities, or their positive frame of mind. Dave, for example, refused to let his discomfort diminish the considerable pleasure he took in finding routes that would enable him to glide in and out of the washes, and across the boulder fields, in the smallest number of steps with the least possible expenditure of energy. Practicing this style of movement seemed to transport him into a Zen-like trance, as if navigating complex terrain with efficiency and elegance was its own form of meditation. Meanwhile, Chris and Rich, whose drive and enthusiasm appeared limitless—and who both seemed impervious to the heat—moved with the fluency of bobcats as they slid from one rock to the next without ever putting a foot wrong. But perhaps the most remarkable display of all came from Mike.

The start of the hike had been almost as hard on him as it was on Pete and me, and at the end of the first day, Mike's beet-red face and his thousand-yard stare had suggested that he, like us, might be teetering on the threshold of collapse. But since then, a change had come over him, and instead of progressively weakening, he'd been getting stronger. Within a day or two, if he wasn't surging to the front of the pack, he was either keeping pace with Chris and Rich or hiking close enough behind Dave to hop into his back pocket. Like them, he seemed to welcome and relish the challenges the canyon was laying in front of him.

Christ, I thought to myself, shocked by the realization, *these maniacs are actually* enjoying *this.*

*   *   *

As the route pulled us deeper into the Supai, yet another new layer of rock, we were offered a glimpse into the punishing detours imposed by tributary canyons, the extensive drainages snaking away from the main-stem canyon. We hit the first diversion late one morning when the ledge we were contouring along bent sharply to the right at the mouth of Rider Canyon, and as we completed the turn and began working our way into the tributary, the intensity of the heat became extraordinary, as if the walls had ignited and the air itself were on fire.

Up ahead, the rest of the group had already found a notch that enabled them to descend off the sun-blasted ledge and had lowered themselves into the shade along Rider's bottom, sixty feet below. When Pete and I finally arrived at the top of that notch, we could see Chris, Dave, and Mike lounging in the shadows next to a thin stream that ran between several pools of water. We were about to start making our way toward them when Pete halted in the midst of dropping off the lip, hauled himself back onto the ledge, and pulled back the front of his shirt to reveal the bizarre, rodent-like lump wriggling back and forth beneath the skin of his chest and belly.

Clearly we were dealing with something that went beyond simple misery and exhaustion. This was our first real crisis, and it arose from the peculiar dangers that manifest whenever one's baseline temperature climbs above 98.6°F, and the human body begins taking steps to prevent the cells in one's tissues from poaching like a frog in a simmering pot of water.*

Most people assume the greatest danger from prolonged exposure to extreme heat in the desert is running out of water—and for good reason. Water is critical to our primary defense against overheating, which involves lowering the surface temperature of the body through evaporating sweat. Running out of water triggers dehydration while cutting off your ability to sweat and leaving you vulnerable to heatstroke, which can be fatal. But not every heat-induced medical crisis in the backcountry unspools in this manner. Although it may sound bizarre, it's just as easy to die from drinking too much water as it is from too little—and the effects of this phenomenon were now playing out in Pete's body as he slumped on the ledge in Rider Canyon.

When you perspire heavily, especially under noxious heat and significant exertion, your sweat can flush up to half an ounce of electrolytes out of your body in a day, almost three teaspoons' worth. (Electrolytes are chemical compounds in the bloodstream—sodium, potassium, magnesium, chloride, and other minerals—that form ions capable of carrying electrical signals, and they matter enormously because those signals play a critical role in governing muscle contraction, nerve impulse transmission, and proper heartbeat.) If you attempt to *re*hydrate by imbibing copious amounts of water without taking care to replenish those lost salts and minerals, your electrolyte levels will become dangerously low.

This is known as hyponatremia. As the condition sets in, you'll experience fatigue and nausea while becoming combative. If you fail to correct the problem by, say, snacking on salty carbohydrates such as pretzels, potato chips, or pepperoni, painful muscle twitching and cramps will begin in the arms, legs, and torso. Left unchecked, the

---

* It's impossible to overstate the impact that a boost in core temperature can have on the body's organs, which begin shutting down at 106°F, a slide that becomes all but irreversible above 107. At 110, the membranes in one's cells will burst, and at 112, proteins denature and congeal as if one were boiling an egg.

electrolyte deficit will then induce swelling in the tissues of your brain followed by a drunken-like stupor, which accounts for hyponatremia's other name: water intoxication. This, in turn, will trigger fainting and convulsions.

*   *   *

None of this boded well for Pete as he leaned next to me on the ledge overlooking the floor of Rider. Evidently he'd committed a mistake that is all too common in the outback. After several days of profuse sweating and prolonged exertion, the delicate balance of electrolytes in his bloodstream had been thrown off. After he failed to correct that imbalance by moderating his water consumption while bumping up his salt intake, the disequilibrium was now playing havoc with the ion circuits controlling the large muscle groups girding his chest and abdomen.

Unsure what to do, I took a sip from my bottle, which felt like drinking straight from the spigot of a hot-water heater, and looked around. There was no sign of any birds or even insects—nothing but us was reckless enough to be out in the open. Nevertheless, despite the intensity of the sun, Pete needed to lie back for several minutes and allow the cramps to subside before he could descend.

"Let me hang out here for a few minutes and see if I feel better," he pleaded. "Go find some shade, and I'll catch up."

I wasn't sure this made sense, but lacking a better plan, I dropped into the crack and climbed down to a patch of shade on a small ledge— where I found Rich, crouched next to his pack and waiting for us. There, for the better part of the next thirty minutes, I listened as he launched into yet another Harvey Butchart anecdote while Pete, stretched out under the full sun, waited for his muscles to unclench.

Following two more aborted attempts to lower himself into the crack, Pete somehow willed his body to complete the descent and joined us on the ledge. From there, the three of us dropped the rest of the way down into the shady creek bed, linked up with our companions, and together made our way back to the river, where we set up camp along the shoreline.

That evening, we plied Pete with salty food, including the last of our beef jerky. That may have stopped things from getting worse, but it wasn't enough to correct the problem. Unlike dehydration, which can often be rectified by simply ingesting more water, rebalancing one's electrolytes and blood sodium levels is complicated and tricky. Without sustained rest under cooler conditions, it would be extremely difficult to properly restore his electrolyte quotas, and until that happened, the risk of his cramps morphing into convulsions would only grow.

Meanwhile, the pain in my feet had by now become so acute that nothing seemed to help. Even after I gobbled a dozen ibuprofen and sat next to the river immersing my duct-tape bootees for the better part of an hour, it still felt as if my ankles and toes were on fire.

That night, neither Pete nor I got a wink of sleep, and the following morning we were barely able to totter out of camp. By 10:30 a.m., we were in so much misery that Rich called a halt and rigged a shade tarp so that we could sit out the hottest part of the day.

We had barely covered two miles.

By 3:00 p.m., it was still scorching, but just downstream the shadows were beginning to angle down the canyon walls toward the river. Knowing that we were falling further behind schedule with each passing hour, Rich announced that it was time to gear up and ordered us to get ready for another push.

As we pulled ourselves to our feet, Pete and I knew that we couldn't endure this kind of punishment much longer, and that if we were to have any hope of continuing, we needed to catch a break.

Two hours later, we finally got one.

* * *

The sun was just about to dip below the rimrock when we arrived at a steep mound of rubble about twenty or thirty feet above the shoreline. I was far behind the rest of the group, and everyone had already disappeared over the far side by the time I ascended the crest and found myself gazing down on a beautiful crescent-shaped beach that I recognized from my river days as a spot where we had often pulled over for lunch. Along the shore was a pod of eight brightly colored rafts, each tied to an aluminum stake driven into the sand.

It took ten minutes for me to pick my way down to a cluster of tents and a circle of folding chairs, where my companions were surrounded by more than a dozen river runners. This eclectic group hailed from various parts of Colorado and Montana, and although a few of them seemed a bit taken aback by how ragged we looked—and probably by how bad we smelled—they had nevertheless rolled out the welcome mat. Each of my companions was clutching a cold beer in his hand and helping himself to a massive platter of hors d'oeuvres featuring crackers anointed with hummus, pesto, and fresh beets.

When I joined the group, we did our best to refrain from inhaling all the food at once and begging for seconds, focusing instead on politely answering the river runners' questions about how far we were going, how heavy our packs were, and why, instead of traveling by boat, we were floundering through the rocks like a band of deranged lunatics. But despite this heroic effort at self-control, within twenty minutes, we polished off the entire plate of appetizers while demolishing at least two beers apiece. Then, just as we were squaring up to the unwelcome prospect of hoisting our packs and shuffling off to spend another miserable night sleeping in the bushes, the boaters asked if we might do them the honor of staying for dinner.

Sirloin steaks were being laid on the grill, a batch of margaritas was about to be served, and for dessert a pineapple upside-down cake was already baking in the Dutch oven. Also, given that the sun had now set and the light was fading, maybe we'd like to spend the night with them, too?

This exceeded my wildest dreams. Dinner would be amazing on its own—especially the part about the pineapple upside-down cake. But the invitation to camp with these good people meant that instead of our having to get up at 4:30 and continue driving ourselves down-canyon

Among all the great natural wonders in the United States, the Grand Canyon stands as perhaps its most widely recognized landscape feature. It is the crown jewel and centerpiece of America's public lands, the standard against which all the rest are appraised. And yet the heart of the abyss is so remote and difficult to access that even to this day, there isn't a single trail that will take a person along the length of the entire chasm.

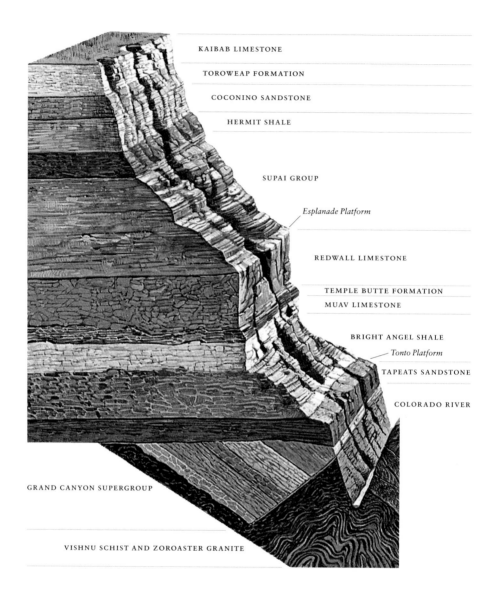

KAIBAB LIMESTONE

TOROWEAP FORMATION

COCONINO SANDSTONE

HERMIT SHALE

SUPAI GROUP

Esplanade Platform

REDWALL LIMESTONE

TEMPLE BUTTE FORMATION

MUAV LIMESTONE

BRIGHT ANGEL SHALE

Tonto Platform

TAPEATS SANDSTONE

COLORADO RIVER

GRAND CANYON SUPERGROUP

VISHNU SCHIST AND ZOROASTER GRANITE

Although the Colorado River spent roughly 6 million years carving out the canyon, the rock into which the chasm has been cut is far older. The mile-deep walls on both sides of the abyss comprise no fewer than twenty-seven formations whose lineages span eight separate geologic periods, during which nearly 40 percent of the planet's chronology was etched directly into the stone. By some measures, those walls showcase perhaps the finest cross-section of terrestrial time visible anywhere on the globe, a vertical concatenation of history stacked in horizontal strata, much like the pages of an immense book. Nowhere else has nature provided a more graphic display of its titanic indifference to the works and aspirations of humankind.

The distance from the highest points along the rims of the canyon to the Colorado River exceeds one vertical mile. Within the chasm, the mosaic of biology is so rich and varied that in a single day a hiker can pass through a spectrum of life zones equivalent to moving from the cool boreal forests of sub-Arctic Canada, thick with fir trees and great horned owls, to the Sonoran Desert of northern Mexico, an environment populated by scorpions, rattlesnakes, agaves, and toads. No other national park boasts a broader range of plants and animals wedged inside such a tightly compressed space.

"Wonderful and beautiful beyond description. . . . I could have sat and looked at it for days," Theodore Roosevelt wrote, following his first visit in May 1903, when he delivered a speech urging his fellow Americans to protect this superlative wonder of nature from extractive operations like the nineteenth-century copper mine in the photo below, located beneath the South Rim. The allure of the canyon was powerful enough that Roosevelt would later return to its depths on the back of a mule and hunt Mountain Lions on the North Rim. But thanks to fierce opposition from miners, loggers, and hydropower interests, his hopes of seeing the landscape elevated to the status of a national park would not reach fruition until 1919, a decade after the end of his presidency, and less than two months before he died.

$2.45 / V-852

The story of the first trip afoot through the Grand Canyon by the author of *The Complete Walker* *Colin Fletcher*

THE
MAN
WHO
WALKED
THROUGH
TIME

For my father (*top right*), who grew up in Pittsburgh, Pennsylvania, during an era when the city was so polluted that street-lights remained on during the daytime and not even the snow was white, the existence of a place like the Grand Canyon seemed like an impossible dream—which may have been why he handed me a copy of Colin Fletcher's classic hiking chronicle, *The Man Who Walked Through Time*. The image on the book's cover took hold of me and refused to let go, although more than four decades would pass before the opportunity to follow in Fletcher's footsteps presented itself.

When Pete McBride approached me with the idea that we walk the length of the canyon, he assured me that the hike would consist of an idyllic stroll along flat stretches of sand next to a cool green river, beneath a pink-and-tangerine tapestry of soaring rock walls. Unfortunately, only about a hundred yards of our journey (pictured above) conformed to this fantasy. The rest of the odyssey involved confronting a truth evoked by John Wesley Powell, the first white European to explore the canyon in the summer of 1869, when he declared that the landscape was "more difficult to traverse than the Alps or the Himalayas." (Unlike us, Powell opted to travel by boat.)

The topography of the canyon's interior, a vast and largely untrammeled zone between the edges of the river and the rims, can perhaps best be imagined as a range of mountains roughly the length of the Pyrenees, flipped upside down and countersunk below the horizon. Inside this three-dimensional labyrinth, every mile of lateral progress must be paid for with an additional two and a half miles of climbing, descending by rope, or detouring into and back out of some 740 tributaries branching off the mainstem canyon, extending the total distance to nearly 800 miles.

The depth of our delusion in believing that we could traverse the canyon "off the couch," with little preparation and virtually no experience, was etched in the expression on Pete's face on the morning after we began, as well as on the soles of our feet forty-eight hours later. In just six days, the immense physical demands of moving through stifling heat across all but impossible terrain had broken us to the point where we had collapsed. The following day, we ended our bid and headed for home, vowing never to return.

like a sweaty herd of cattle, we would be encouraged to stick around for coffee and breakfast. There would be bacon and sausage. There would be eggs cooked to order. There would be fresh fruit and orange juice. Jesus, there might even be *pancakes*.

None of this would bring an end to our torments. But a time-out, even for just a few hours, would offer Pete and me a chance to catch our breath and brace for the trials to come. Muttering a prayer of gratitude, I was turning toward Rich to suggest that we roll out our sleeping bags on the beach right next to the river so that we could take a refreshing bath before dinner when I heard him say something so unthinkable that at first I assumed I was hallucinating.

"We'd love to take you up on that offer," he said, casting a hard look downstream. "But we've got some more distance to cover before we stop for the night."

With that, he slung on his pack, waved goodbye, and started marching down the beach in the direction of the next talus field.

Within seconds, as Pete and I stared in disbelief, Dave, Chris, and Mike had shouldered their packs and followed suit.

"Thanks for the hospitality, you guys," Chris called out as they left. "Have a great trip!"

When Pete and I recovered our wits, we realized we had no choice but to follow them.

Upon arriving at the far end of the beach, just before heading into the talus, I looked back and saw the river runners raising their margarita glasses in a farewell toast. As I turned away, I could smell the steaks coming off the grill.

*   *   *

Pete and I spent the better part of the next two hours straggling far behind our companions as dusk faded to darkness, and our water bottles ran dry. The beers we'd guzzled didn't help our coordination, and somewhere in the middle of a boulder field, I fell twice, spraining both ankles—first the right, then the left.

On and on we trudged, until eventually the only thing guiding us forward was a faint stationary light, far in the distance, which signaled that Rich and his companions had finally stopped walking. When we reached the spot, we discovered that they had decided to camp on a bleak ledge littered with chips of limestone and sheep droppings.

After casting around fruitlessly for a patch of level ground, I used up my last teaspoon of energy to inflate my air mattress, then flung it onto a bed of sharp stones inside a tiny alcove whose contours, I realized only after lying down and discovering that I lacked the willpower to get back up, were about a foot shorter than me.

Just as I was about to drift off, something started rustling.

Switching on my headlamp, I trained the beam into the darkness. Less than a yard from my head, I spotted a creature that looked like a cross between a raccoon, a weasel, and an African lemur. Tufted ears. Long, bushy tail. Pointed nose and snout mounted beneath a pair of huge, brash, highly intelligent eyes that held not even a hint of embarrassment over having been caught rifling through a Ziploc bag containing my entire supply of Snickers bars.

This was a Ringtail, a nocturnal mammal that is described in the *Time/Life Guide to the Grand Canyon* as "beautiful, intelligent, playful, and sometimes even affectionate," a summary that conspicuously fails to mention its fondness for stealing anything that isn't nailed down. Lunging to the side, I grabbed a fist-size rock and heaved it at the critter's head, missing him by a yard. Instead of running away, he held his ground and scolded me with a series of menacing chitters that were accompanied by a strange hissing sound—until I realized that the hissing wasn't coming from the Ringtail, but from my air mattress, which had sprung a leak as I lunged for the rock and was now losing all its air.

As I deflated down onto the bed of stones, feeling the points poking into my back and hips, the Ringtail vanished into the darkness with the rest of my snacks, leaving me to ponder a quote that Rich had shared with me the previous afternoon, a comment made by a hiker recalling his state of mind at the end of an especially miserable day spent stumbling along this very section of the canyon.

"I remember thinking," the hiker had remarked, "that hell might well consist of hiking like this for eternity."

That was the last thought I remember before I blacked out.

*   *   *

Meanwhile, Rich and his team were convening their evening powwow.

By now, this had become a regular event. At each camp, just after Pete and I had collapsed, the rest of the group would quietly move off by themselves and gather in a circle to take stock of how badly we were doing, and how much further downhill things were likely to slide during the next twenty-four hours.

They began, as they always did, by tallying up our overall mileage deficit, and, after reviewing the terrain and the obstacles that lay ahead, devising a revised plan for the following day while wearily conceding that it would likely have to be tossed out the window as Pete and I plunged ever deeper into disarray. But that night, there was a new problem to wrestle with.

Somehow, despite all the extra weight that Pete and I were carrying, we hadn't brought enough of the things we truly needed. We were running low on gas for our cookstove. The batteries for our headlamps were almost dead. We'd burned through several key items in our med kit, such as alcohol swabs, antibacterial ointment, and ibuprofen. Plus, we were nearly out of Aquamira, the chlorine dioxide drops we were using to treat water we'd scooped from potholes or drawn from the river. (We had also brought along Pete's Steripen, which purifies drinking water with ultraviolet light, which he'd assured me was "bombproof," as he'd used it during an extended assignment in India on the Ganges, one of the world's most polluted rivers. But it had conked out within the first day.)

Having depleted our own supplies, we were constantly asking to "borrow" items from Rich and his crew. We were mooching food off them, too—especially salty tidbits such as pretzels and crackers, which were mostly gone. Now the entire group was running dangerously low on the stuff we needed to survive.

Seventeen miles downstream was a fully stocked supply cache. But at our current rate of progress, we might not make it there without rationing. That concern, however, took a back seat to an even bigger worry, because we were about to encounter a new and formidable band of rock.

The Redwall Limestone was laid down more than 340 million years in the past, when a series of oceans now long extinct rose to cover almost the entirety of present-day North America. But what matters most about this layer for anyone moving through the canyon on foot is that it forms a ring of cliffs whose height can exceed six hundred feet, a continuous set of vertical ramparts that snakes along both sides of the river, as well as into and out of almost every amphitheater and tributary canyon.

Along the Redwall's thousand-mile circumference, only a finite number of breaks in the wall enable a person to pass freely between the rims and the river. The quest to identify and map those breaches—many of which are remote and also quite dangerous, little more than crumbling stone ladders—had been a particular obsession of Harvey Butchart's. He called those passages "rare enough to be a collector's gem" and viewed the Redwall as the most imperious layer of rock in the entire canyon.*

It was also what Rich and his team feared might well end up killing Pete and me.

*   *   *

Just downstream from our camp, the Redwall would emerge from the river for the first time, and as it flared to its full height, we would be forced to climb onto the ledge that defined the tops of its cliffs. When we did so, the chances for us to descend to the Colorado would slowly begin to disappear. Initially, there would be a few spots where we could

---

* During his four-decade-long career, Butchart identified 164 Redwall breaks, most of which served as the crux of the 116 rim-to-river routes that he opened up.

pick our way back down if we needed to, but as the cliffs rose, those breaks would grow ever scarcer and farther apart. Eventually, escape would become extremely difficult if not impossible, and we'd be isolated from the river for an extended stretch of almost forty miles.

This represented the start of Rich's high route, and during our push through that first stretch, which was expected to take six days, we'd find water in only a handful of places—mostly in tiny pockets tucked into alcoves and recesses that were cloaked in shadow for much of the day. Rich knew where these were, having carefully scouted and mapped each of them; but they were separated by extensive sections of barren rock, some as long as ten miles.

Unless our entire group could sustain a fast pace during those forced marches between the water pockets, we might find ourselves trapped between them: unable to reach the next source, but too far away from the last one to get back. That's how people lost their lives up on the Redwall, and when they perished, it wasn't a coma brought on by acute hyponatremia that killed them. They died fully conscious, parched and prostrate in the dirt, with an empty water bottle clutched between their fingers.

Rich and his crew understood exactly how dangerous it was in that zone, and as Pete and I slept, they weighed the variables that would govern our survival—dwindling food and supplies, limited water, extended exposure to lethal temperatures—and tried to calculate how those variables would play out as our strength ebbed, our spirits waned, and our pace ground to a halt. The dilemma was no less stark than the stone itself. Without a chance for rest, Pete and I would not be able to continue and survive; but once we were on the Redwall, survival would dictate that there could be no rest at all.

"We just can't let these guys get any worse," declared Dave. "There's no margin for error up there."

CHAPTER 15

Snakebit

We got our first glimpse of the Redwall the following morning when a set of flagstones appeared in the shallows a few yards downstream from the spot where we had camped. The rock was as smooth as enamel, burnished by the sediments suspended in the river to a nacreous sheen amid the tremulous shadows that cue the break of day. But within a few hundred feet, the paving stones had risen above the shoreline to form cliffs on both sides of the river—and as the cliffs grew, extending high above the water, the rock began to change.

First, the surface turned rough, becoming less like glazed earthenware and more like the bark of a fire-hardened Ponderosa, encrusted in furrows, bristling with sharp edges. As the stone's pearl-white skin coarsened, its pigmentation shifted, too, as if a stream of colors was spilling down from the rims, or perhaps pouring from the sky—both of which were true.

Directly on top of the Redwall sat the orange-colored Supai Formation as well as the deep-red Hermit Shale, the band of crumbly siltstone and mudstone whose slopes had given us such trouble. Over many millennia, as sheets of rain and snowmelt had periodically slid down the faces of those layers, the water had taken up the tinting and smeared it over the surface of the limestone, creating something unique and marvelous. While the colors of the strata above were dark and bold, the Redwall's hues were subtle and delicate, a fusion of pastels—pink and vermilion, together with hints of peach and tangerine, coral and salmon—marking it as the one layer of the canyon that it's possible to imagine Monet having painted.

Under the right conditions, the complexion of the Redwall can leave one spellbound by its beauty. But as we ascended high above the river, Pete and I paid no attention to aesthetics. Along the tops of those cliffs, the walking was anything but easy. The ground was covered with extensive beds of cacti, and it was impossible to move more than a thousand yards without being forced to scramble into a deep wash and climb back out, or compelled to skirt around the branches of yet another tributary.

Throughout the rest of that morning we crawled like insects, inching along the terraces as the walls closed up and the river fell away. By late afternoon, we were cut off from the Colorado, with no option but to keep pressing forward deep into the evening hours until, just before dusk, we arrived at a shallow alcove where the rock was glossy and free of dirt. At the edge of the alcove was a crack in the cliff that Rich suspected might conceal a few potholes stocked with water, and when Chris scrambled down and confirmed this, he declared that we would camp there for the night.

It wasn't a bad spot, despite the fact that we were nowhere near the place Rich had hoped to reach. A smooth patio extended to the edge of the cliff, which fell three hundred feet, straight as a plumb bob, to the edge of the river. After shedding our packs, we spread out our things and tucked into the nest that each of us had arranged. The air began to cool while the stone retained a pleasant warmth, and after we had boiled our cooking water and poured it into our dinner bowls, the scent of rice and lentils and mushrooms tendriled through the evening air.

Our backs rested against an unscalable set of walls rising more than two thousand feet to the rim. Beyond the ends of our feet at the edge of the patio, we could hear the faint roar of the river. It felt as if we were a band of pigeons pinioned to the railing of a balcony on the side of a skyscraper.

By now the sun had set, but the walls on the far side of the canyon were facing almost directly west, enabling the stone to catch and hold the last of the light. Etched against the purple sky, the uppermost bands of rock turned a molten copper, while the torched reds of the Hermit Shale and the carrot-colored folds of the Supai looked alien enough to have been mined on a distant planet. But you only needed to lower your gaze a notch or two to realize that the Redwall stole the show.

The light spilling down the limestone turned the face of each cliff into forked rivers of fire. There were pink pools and riffles, eddies where the rose-tinted currents coiled and spun, and whirlpools the color of a freshly opened cantaloupe. This was light made liquid, as if someone had melted down the stained-glass windows of every cathedral in France and poured the emulsion over the stone. Even after the colors had fled from the sky, the Redwall retained its lantern glow, as if lit from within.

*   *   *

Although this day had been no less miserable than any of the days that preceded it, and although we were no less relieved to see it come to an end, the evening itself was different. Perhaps it was the splendor of the Redwall. Perhaps it was our awareness of just how cut off we were. Or maybe it was simply the way the canyon seemed to have gathered us gently in the palm of its hand. Whatever the reason, we did something that night that we hadn't done before: we leaned into the warmth of the stone and talked.

We'd chattered with one another on previous nights, but most of those conversations involved trading information about practical matters: repairing shoes, lancing blisters, patching holes in our socks. Tonight, for the first time, we did what the whitewater guides were surely doing at this same hour as they gathered around the decks of their boats on the river far below.

We told stories.

It was Chris, I think, who kicked things off by noting that when he'd knelt to fill up his water bottles from the pool at the edge of the alcove, the damp sand next to the water was marked with startlingly fresh hoofprints from a Bighorn Sheep that, perhaps only minutes earlier, had visited the pool. This reminded Pete that he'd recently spotted a video clip on YouTube of a Bighorn swimming across the Colorado somewhere inside the canyon—which instantly made everyone clamor for details about how fast the current was moving, and where the sheep had crossed, and how long it had taken to swim to the other side.

All of this prompted Mike to speculate that the Bighorns must be familiar with every pool and pothole up here on these ledges, which Dave confirmed—while adding that the sheep tend to get pushed around at night by the Mountain Lions, which make them restless and uneasy. And I suppose it was the image of a lion chasing its prey that spurred Rich to start talking about all the things *he* was chasing: the hidden routes he was hoping to explore, the mysterious side canyons that topped his wish list, the destinations he'd dreamed of visiting but hadn't yet found the time to. As he rattled off the names of these places, each elicited a chorus of approving murmurs from Dave and Chris and Mike.

As I lay back, listening to their words merging with the muted growling of the river, my thoughts returned to Harvey Butchart and the shape that his own obsession with this place had taken: not only the boldness of his ambition and the ferocity of his drive, but the aridity of his vision, too—his strange insistence on treating the canyon less as a crucible of wonder, and more as an arena in which to assert his supremacy over others.

Were Rich and his party driven by similar forces? To be sure, they were chasing a goal that fewer than a dozen people in recorded history had attained—a feat that not even Butchart himself had achieved—and they knew that if they pulled it off, their names would be added to a select list. But at the moment, what seemed to matter far more to them were our location and surroundings, as if their true goal lay not with the destination, but with the journey itself.

If there was a reward to their venture, perhaps a portion of it was being handed to them tonight as something ancient merged with the here and now: a cluster of humans, sitting in a circle, sharing stories beneath the canopy of the night. For a second or two, like glimpsing a shooting star from the corner of one's eye, I even thought I might have caught a trace of what drew and held them to this place.

Having worked among men and women who harbored the same feelings for the river at the canyon's bottom, I could understand how Rich and his companions felt, even though my brief stint as a hiker had offered little more than endless suffering. For the very first time, I felt truly connected to them—which surely would have made that night the most marvelous of the trip, were it not for what happened next.

*   *   *

After an hour or so, the conversation trailed away as everyone nodded off—except for Pete, who very much wanted to get some sleep, too, but who kept having to get up to pee, which he did four or five times. Then, finally, deep in the night, he arose one last time, dashed over to some bushes that were far enough away to be out of earshot, and succumbed to a titanic bout of diarrhea.

This depleted most of the water he'd ingested earlier that day, leaving him drained of energy and wrestling with a mounting panic. Hyponatremia has many symptoms, but diarrhea is not among them. What else was wrong with his body? he wondered. Heat exhaustion? Heatstroke? A stomach virus?

Squatting out there in the moonlight with his pants around his ankles, he wrestled with a concern that had been hounding him for days. For the first time ever, the McBride credo—the unshakable conviction that when things went off the rails, grit and determination would always see him through—seemed to be failing a critical test, and the shock of that realization left him feeling lost and alone.

Little did he know that less than a hundred feet away, I, too, was awake, and grappling with a different but no less vexing set of doubts.

Unlike Pete, I didn't have a brother who coached Olympic athletes and espoused fancy theories about transcending one's physical

limitations through mental resiliency. Nor did I have much faith in
the power of my own tenacity and grit. Instead, I was driven—and
tortured—by something quite a bit simpler and considerably less noble:
the corrosive power of shame.

For the past five days, I'd been racked with guilt over how poorly
Pete and I had prepared for this venture, and humiliated by our inability
to keep up with a group whose members were not only strong, proficient, and highly seasoned, but also extremely kind. Rich and his team
had never once complained or made fun of us, although God knows
they had ample justification. They had been unstinting in sharing their
knowledge, their gear, and their food, and starting with the gesture I
had witnessed on our very first night when Chris had quietly tucked
Pete's heaviest camera lens into his pack, they had done everything
they could to help pull us through.

In short, they'd been so much more decent than we had any right
to expect, and in light of their decency, it seemed self-evident that the
one thing that would be categorically unacceptable would be for Pete
and me to completely fall apart, because doing so would not simply
disrupt their schedule or deplete their supplies, but would decisively
end their trip and, with it, their dream.

I didn't want any part of that, which is why I'd been nursing a fierce
resolve to keep going. Yet now, thanks to Pete's worsening condition
and the ruinous state of my feet, it was no longer possible to deny
that Pete and I *had* fallen apart. We had deteriorated to the point that
our will to keep going had been overtaken by the realization that we
could no longer do so. Which, now that I thought about it, may have
been precisely what Andrew Holycross had been hinting at, on our first
morning back at Lee's Ferry, when he'd told us that we were about to
learn the difference between what we *wanted*, and what we *needed*.

So sometime in the middle of that night, Pete and I arrived separately
at a conclusion that we both recognized as inescapable. Although we
wanted to keep going, we needed to quit.

*   *   *

The following morning when we solemnly informed the rest of the group that we were too broken to continue, Rich gently broke the news that they had all known this for some time and had been patiently waiting for us to see this truth and accept the consequences. In the meantime, he explained, he'd already put in motion a plan that would bring an end to our nightmare.

Two days earlier, Rich had quietly taken out his DeLorme and sent a satellite text to a group of friends in Flagstaff alerting them that Pete and I would probably have to be extracted from South Canyon, a tributary drainage that offered an access route to the rim. Then the previous afternoon, he'd confirmed that a rescue would be necessary. By sunset, a truck had left Flagstaff, driven by a cheerful young river guide named Jean-Philippe Clark, who had already arrived at the rim last night, via a series of remote dirt roads, and was already working his way down to the Redwall with a heavy pack laden with seventy pounds of food and medical supplies, plus extra shoe glue and spare batteries. Our job right now, Rich explained, was to figure out how to get to the rendezvous point as quickly as possible without making Pete's condition any worse.

This wouldn't be easy. The distance we needed to cover included an enormous ravine that we would have to descend into and then climb back out of, and as we started making our way toward the ravine, Pete rapidly began to degrade. Within half an hour, the cramping spasms in his stomach and abdomen were forcing him to sit down every few minutes. When he stood back up, his legs wobbled and he complained of tunnel vision. He was also confused and slightly delirious, at one point raving over his sunglasses, which he was convinced he'd lost, until Rich pointed out that they were on top of his head.

Within an hour, his strength had so depleted that he could no longer handle the weight in his pack, although he refused to let us remove anything, forcing us to fish out the heaviest items, such as his water bottles and his cameras, when he wasn't looking. Eventually, as Chris, Dave, and Mike forged ahead to the rendezvous, Pete settled into a patch of shade next to a large boulder and refused to get up, mumbling that we needed to call for a helicopter evacuation.

While I pondered our next move, Rich dumped out his own pack and sifted through the contents in the hope of finding something he might have missed, which is how he located the packets of soy sauce that had been tucked at the bottom.

"This is pretty nasty," he said to Pete, holding up a fistful of packets. "But it's all we've got."

Wordlessly, Pete snatched the packets, tore them open, and sucked them dry one by one, then lay down in the dirt and closed his eyes. Within fifteen minutes, the salt in the soy sauce began to kick in, enabling him to roll over and pull himself to his feet.

Closing the gap to the meeting point took several additional pushes, each of which amounted to a forced march for Pete. The moment he stepped into the full sunlight, he would start to fade, and we would have to prod him to keep moving until we reached the next patch of shade.

After ninety minutes of stopping and starting, I spotted some movement in the distance and saw a figure cresting a low rise, trotting in our direction. It was Chris, and as he got closer, we could see that he had a walkie-talkie in his hand, which meant that he'd made contact with Clark.

"Guys, I've got 'em," he radioed back to the team when he reached us. "We're heading your way now."

In addition to the walkie-talkie, Chris was carrying several cans of potassium-rich coconut water. Pete downed an entire liter on the spot.

"We were starting to worry that you guys wouldn't make it," said Clark when we finally reached South Canyon, where he was waiting with the rest of the supplies.

"Us, too," said Rich.

Along with the coconut water, Clark had brought in a stash of salty foods that included precooked bacon and a hunk of salami. Pete ate his way through a good deal of this, then crawled into a patch of shade beneath a massive sandstone boulder and fell into a deep sleep.

Among the rest of the group, the mood was subdued. Rich and his crew, who were girding for the punishing and dangerous stretches along the Redwall that lay ahead, spent that evening combing through their gear in the hopes that if they could shed some excess weight, they might be able to make up some of the time that Pete and I had squandered.

Mike was especially ruthless, shaving a full six pounds by jettisoning his emergency shelter, his long underwear, a set of tent stakes, and his solar panels, which he had been using to recharge his cell phone. All of these items went into Clark's pack to be hauled out the next day.

The following morning, after bidding farewell, we watched Rich and his companions thread in single file along the Redwall ledge and, one by one, disappear. In two minutes, they were gone. Then, feeling whipped and humiliated, we turned to follow Clark as he started leading us on the twenty-two-hundred-foot climb to the rim.

*   *   *

Several hours later, having clawed our way up through the Supai, the Hermit Shale, the Coconino, and the Toroweap, Pete and I paused to catch our breath on an exposed piece of the Kaibab Limestone directly beneath the rim.

"So, when exactly was the canyon supposed to polish us into gemstones and turn us into hard-core hiking buffs?" I gasped, gazing into the cauldron of heat and misery through which we had toiled during the past five days.

"Not funny," Pete intoned wearily.

"Not joking," I barked back. "What the hell were we even thinking?!"

He shook his head in silence.

"Did we really imagine we could just go for it *off the couch*?"

"Maybe we're being taught some kind of a lesson," he replied. "Although I have no idea what we're supposed to be learning, aside from the fact that we totally suck."

Looking off to the northeast, I could spot the cliffs above Lee's Ferry, less than thirty miles away. It was stunning to see how little we'd achieved. We'd managed to cover eleven fewer miles than Kenton Grua had walked—alone and in moccasins—along this exact same stretch of river more than forty years earlier before he, too, had given up—an especially twisted irony, given that when we'd set out to walk in Grua's footsteps, we'd imagined retracing his triumph, not his failure. It was an impressive bungle, even by the standards we'd set on our previous debacles in the Himalayas, the Caucasus, and the Arctic.

In more ways than Pete or I cared to admit, we'd been treating the canyon exactly like I'd treated the snake that Holycross had quizzed me about back at Lee's Ferry.

I'd been unable to remember a single important detail because I hadn't bothered taking the snake seriously, and my failure to do so reflected a deeper deficiency in our entire approach to the world beneath the rims: our negligence, our foolishness, our reckless and perfunctory refusal to summon the respect that this place demanded.

By opting to take a shortcut, we had deliberately shirked the work and the preparation that were necessary not only for us to begin moving through the wild spaces of the canyon, but perhaps more important for the canyon's wildness to begin moving through us. As a result, we were unfit for the job—and our unfitness arose not merely from a brief and passing flirtation with bad judgment, poor discipline, or unpardonable cockiness, but from a sustained shortfall in our comportment and character.

For years, Pete and I had been cutting corners and flying by the seat of our pants while blowing past a series of increasingly dire warnings about the perils of fecklessness and hubris, and now we had finally stumbled into a landscape that had stripped away the illusions we'd been peddling of ourselves as a pair of badasses to reveal who we truly were, which was nothing more than a couple of jackasses.

Our accounts had now been settled by some richly deserved payback that we should have seen coming, and for which we had no one to blame but ourselves.

We had finally been bitten by the snake.

PART V

Rebooting

Walk on!

—The Buddha's last words to his disciples

CHAPTER 16

Acts of Contrition

ete and I returned to Flagstaff with our tails between our legs, feeling chastened and ashamed by the knowledge that word of our debacle had preceded our arrival, and that everyone in the community now knew had badly we had been spanked. To make matters worse, in the next forty-eight hours, one of us would have to summon the courage to pick up the phone, call our *National Geographic* editor in Washington, DC, and explain that we had fallen to pieces and would be unable to finish the job. The first order of business, however, was tending to our wounds.

The bottoms of my feet, which looked as if someone had fired a shotgun into them, required repeated soakings in warm water and Epsom salts. I couldn't hobble to the bathroom or the kitchen without leaving a trail of scarlet footprints across the floor.

Pete was worse. In addition to everything else that had befallen him, he'd stepped on a cactus on our way out of the canyon, and the tips of several spines were now working deep into the joint of his right ankle, requiring a visit to a surgeon. But the bigger concerns were his persistent grogginess and headaches, so the day after we got back, I phoned a physician who specialized in heat-related illnesses, who told us to come and see him immediately.

"Let's roll," I said to Pete. "We've got an appointment with someone who will know what's wrong with you."

Tom Myers had spent more than a quarter century at a small clinic on the South Rim that served as the nexus of medical care for nearly all the residents and visitors of the national park. It was the first stop for anybody who had been hurt or injured in the canyon, including patients who needed to be stabilized prior to being sent to a hospital in Flagstaff, Phoenix, or Las Vegas. As a result, Myers had deep experience with the havoc that excessive heat combined with insufficient water intake can inflict on the human body.

During those years, he had also been forced to deal with a wide range of deadly mishaps, from boatmen who had drowned in the river and hikers who had fallen to their deaths, to the victims of snakebites, flash floods, and falling rocks. When Myers realized that many of those incidents were entirely preventable, he and a coauthor named Michael Ghiglieri published a six-hundred-page book—the aforementioned *Over the Edge: Death in Grand Canyon*—in which they laid out the details behind each fatality that had taken place below the rims as far back as there were documented records, and explained how the majority of those tragedies could have been averted.

Meanwhile, during his free time, Myers found himself pulled into a series of increasingly ambitious hikes that exposed him to some of the same conditions he'd been treating in his patients, enabling him to conduct a number of informal experiments, not all of which were planned. Once he deliberately tried drinking muddy, untreated water from the Colorado (with predictably explosive results). On another occasion, he asked a friend to film him while being stung by a Bark Scorpion, reputed to be the most venomous scorpion in North America, just to see what it felt like. (His response was too profane to repeat here.)

It was in the midst of these misadventures that Myers first met Kenton Grua on a river trip, and in the years that followed, the two men grew close enough that they went on a number of day hikes together, as well as a backpacking trip. Those excursions fueled the doctor's growing fascination with the subculture of long-distance trekking below the rims, and in the early 2000s, he began putting together an article profiling the canyon's tiny community of thru-hikers, which featured the first published list of those who had completed a full traverse. Around the same time, Myers joined up with another coauthor, Elias Butler, and set to work on a second book project, a biography of someone who knew the canyon's interior better than anyone else.

When *Grand Obsession* was published in 2007, it offered the definitive portrait of Harvey Butchart—but the book's title could just as easily have applied to Myers himself. Indeed, if Butchart was the godfather of extreme hiking in the canyon, then Myers was in many ways its amanuensis, a witness and chronicler as omnipresent as the cactus mice and the canyon wrens.

*   *   *

"You were incredibly lucky," declared Myers, a trim man in his early fifties with a shock of brown hair that was starting to turn gray, after informing Pete that he'd suffered a severe bout of hyponatremia, compounded by overexertion in the excessive heat. "Given the symptoms you're describing on the day before you exited, you were about an hour or two away from a seizure."

Pete and I glanced at each other wordlessly.

"Okay, and what would have happened after that?" asked Pete.

"Typically, the convulsions would have lasted a minute or two before receding, but you'd likely remain unconscious because of swelling in your brain."

"And when would I regain consciousness?"

"Well, that would have been really unlikely without intravenous saline treatment in a hospital, possibly for several days, until the swelling receded. So without a helicopter evacuation and that kind of care"— Myers tossed up his hands and shrugged—"you could easily have died from a brain herniation."

We sat in silence, absorbing this.

"Look," continued Myers, "when it comes to human physiology, the canyon is essentially the biggest heat laboratory on the planet, especially during the summer months. Nowhere else, not even in the world of professional marathons and triathlons, is there as much data on what heat can do to the body, because no other place sees the cases that you see in the canyon."

We nodded in unison.

"So, you guys definitely need to get a better handle on what it takes to monitor your water consumption and avoid diluting your blood sodium when you go back down there. To help maintain your electrolyte balance, you'll need to start building in fifteen-minute recovery breaks for every hour that you're hiking so that you can rest, eat salty snacks, and, if necessary, pour water over yourselves to cool down. All those steps will be incredibly important as you move forward."

This took us by surprise, primarily because it was so at odds with a conclusion that each of us had arrived at during the previous few days—the conviction that the canyon was too big, too daunting, and too miserable for us to ever entertain the idea of going back.

What would be the point in continuing? we had been asking ourselves. *Haven't we learned our lesson?*

Myers must have read these thoughts because he now gave us a long stare. "Look, you two understand that you're not the first people to screw up their initial attempt to hike the canyon and then have to decide whether or not to return, right?"

"Yeah," Pete replied. "But we're pretty sure that none of those other folks messed up as badly as we did."

Myers cocked an eyebrow. "Well, then maybe you need to think a bit harder about the full story of Kenton Grua's thru-hike, because it reminds me of where you guys are right now."

For Myers, Grua was an inspiration and a hero not because he'd been victorious on his second attempt to complete his traverse—but because of how he'd handled the failure that preceded it.

"Kenton was a friend of mine, and he messed up on his first try," said Myers. "But he went back and tried again. Kenton didn't quit."

*　　*　　*

After Myers assured us that Pete's remaining symptoms would abate in a few days, the two of us returned to my house on Grand Canyon Avenue and plonked down in a pair of rocking chairs on the front porch to ruminate on the doctor's words.

"Look, even if you and I wanted to go back—which we *don't*—I don't see how it would be possible," said Pete. "Without somebody like Rich, how the hell would we be able to navigate all the technical challenges without getting totally lost?"

"We wouldn't," I conceded. "And even if there was a way to handle that, we'd still need to figure out how to draw up a whole set of backup plans for when things went wrong."

"Impossible."

We rocked back and forth, listening to the chairs creaking on the floorboards of the porch.

"Plus," Pete continued, "we'd have to redial every aspect of our gear and clothing program."

"Don't forget about our med kits and our meals," I added. "Those would all have to be redesigned, too."

The creaking sounds continued.

"Basically, we'd have to start over and rebuild everything from scratch," Pete said.

"And how would we do that?"

Now a long interval of silence ensued.

"I have absolutely no idea," he said.

Unbeknownst to either of us, the answers to those questions were about to present themselves, thanks to a sequence of events that had already been set in motion from deep inside the canyon.

*   *   *

Three days earlier, during the final evening we'd spent with Rich's crew, he had surreptitiously pulled his satellite tracker from his pack and tapped out a brief message that was transmitted in small fragments to several members of the hiking community in Flagstaff:

—HOWDY FOLKS FROM SOUTH CYN . . .

—PETE & KEVIN EXITING HERE TOMORROW . . .

—WOULD ANY OF YOU LIKE TO . . .

—HELP THEM . . .

—CONTINUE THEIR HIKE?

Among the recipients was Marieke Taney, a senior lecturer in outdoor leadership at Northern Arizona University. In addition to her academic credentials, she had spent fifteen seasons as a whitewater guide in the canyon, and nine seasons as a helicopter ski guide in Alaska. After taking some time to check in with the other recipients of Rich's message, Marieke reached out, and her text appeared on my phone while Pete and I were sitting on the porch: a request for us to come over to her house for dinner that night.

When we arrived, a group was waiting to meet us. Aaron Divine, Marieke's partner, was a field instructor at the National Outdoor Leadership School in Wyoming and had spent more than a decade working as an alpine mountain guide in Alaska's Denali National Park. Marieke's younger brother, Harlan, was a world-class kayaker who had completed more than 160 trips through the canyon as a river guide. Kelly McGrath guided the river, too, but she specialized in leading extended backcountry expeditions for veterans wounded in the wars of Iraq and Afghanistan. Her partner, Mathieu Brown, competed in extreme endurance events such as the Leadville Trail 100, and had also spent seven years at Prescott College in central Arizona teaching the Grand Canyon Semester, a program that exposed students to every branch of science connected with the park, from its botany and geology to its hydrologic and human history.

On the specifics of thru-hiking the canyon, these folks may not have matched the depth of experience that Rich's team commanded. But their résumés boasted a wider scope of knowledge, and they had all logged just as much if not more time in the field. If Rich and his crew qualified as the varsity squad, then these were the players you'd pick for the all-star team.

"So," Marieke said after everyone had grabbed a plate of food and settled in the living room, "we heard you guys might need some help climbing back in the saddle?"

There was a moment of awkward silence.

"Well, at this point, we're not sure we should actually be trying to get back on the horse," Pete told them. "As you probably heard, Kevin and I got bucked off pretty hard."

"We've all been spanked by the canyon, too," said Harlan. "And thanks to that, we've all had the chance to absorb the same lesson."

"What's that?" I asked.

"The canyon likes to start by tearing you down and destroying you," Mathieu explained. "So the first lesson it teaches is the importance of being humble."

"Clearly you've both had a hefty dose of that," interjected Kelly, "although I can see that you, Pete, may need another shot or two before it finally sinks in."

"And the second lesson," continued Mathieu, ignoring the aggrieved look that Pete was casting toward Kelly, "involves making better choices about what you bring and what you leave behind."

"Basically, it's about differentiating your wants from your needs," added Aaron.

"Look, we've heard all of this before," I told them, recalling what we'd been told back at Lee's Ferry.

"Well, you're about to hear a lot more of it," said Harlan.

"So have you guys unloaded your packs from your trip yet?" asked Kelly.

In unison, we shook our heads no.

"Good," said Mathieu. "Tomorrow morning, we want you to take those packs, dump everything on the floor, and then let me know you're ready for us to come over."

"When we get there, we're gonna start throwing stuff away," said Kelly, rubbing the palms of her hands together in anticipation.

"We've been through this once already," I repeated wearily, picturing Pete's powdered Gatorade flying through the air into the patch of cactus.

"That was tame compared to what we're gonna do tomorrow," said Mathieu, "because hiking in the canyon isn't just an exercise in reducing the weight of your pack to some arbitrary number."

"It's actually more like a philosophy," Aaron elaborated. "An attitude that helps shape your mindset as you move across the landscape."

"And starting tomorrow, both of you are about to undergo a serious attitude adjustment," said Kelly, looking pointedly at Pete. "Especially you, Mc*Brody*."

*　　*　　*

Pete and I spent most of the drive home in silence.

"Well," he finally observed, "it looks like we're going back in, whether we like it or not."

"Yep."

"So why do you suppose these guys are bending over backwards to help us?"

"No idea."

We drove for another minute or two.

"Okay, I want to ask you something," Pete announced in a persecuted tone that made it clear that something was bothering him even more than the group's mysterious motivations for preparing us to return to the canyon's demented inferno. "What's up with Kelly and the 'McBrody' thing?" he groused. "That's not even my *name*."

"Quit whining," I said, calling to mind Matt Brody, the lifeguard on *Baywatch* who wore Stars-and-Stripes Speedos, and whose motto was "There's no *I* in *team*—but there is a *me*." "She's totally got your number."

"Oh yeah?" Pete glared out the windshield into the night. "Well, she's probably got your number, too—Groover Boy."

*　　*　　*

The following morning, as promised, Kelly and Mathieu showed up and started flinging things away—and this time, Pete and I had no opportunity to sneak around in the dark reclaiming items from the reject pile. In less than two hours, they eliminated every item of clothing and equipment they deemed frivolous or unnecessary, reducing the core of our wardrobe to little more than a single pair of underwear and a pair of socks for each of us. Pete's belt went into the reject pile when Mathieu decided that the buckle was too heavy. Ditto my nine-bladed multi-tool, which Kelly called "a ridiculous pig."

Then they homed in on Pete's photography kit. When they were finished, his gear had been whittled down to a single camera with only two lenses, plus a solar panel to charge one set of batteries. He was allowed no backups, which meant that if anything was damaged, destroyed, or simply stopped working, he was out of luck. It was the only time in the fifteen years that I'd known Pete when he looked as if he might burst into tears.

That was just the start. Over the next several days we were subjected to a withering tutorial in the science and the subculture of ultralight backpacking, a discipline whose techniques and mindset boiled down to the baseline principle that nothing has a greater impact on the ease or difficulty with which one travels than weight. In essence, the less you carry, the farther and faster you will go.*

Under Mathieu and Kelly's remorseless supervision, Pete and I were forced to rid ourselves of everything that wasn't essential. Then, with great reluctance, they permitted us to add in a few items we'd failed to bring along during our first attempt, such as ankle gaiters and a lightweight ground cloth, that *were* essential. After that, they broke out the digital scale, started weighing everything, and recorded the results on a spreadsheet.

As Pete and I fell under the influence of their ideas, we were swiftly transformed into fanatics, adopting all the zealotry of the freshly converted. Before long, we knew that a medium-sized fuel canister weighed

---

* The data are irrefutable: a hiker schlepping a fifty-eight-pound pack will expend roughly the same energy over ten miles as a hiker carrying a ten-pound pack will expend in thirty miles. When it comes to load carrying, location matters, too: weight on the feet—say, boots—requires between four and six times more energy to move than the same weight on one's back.

thirteen ounces and could burn for one hundred minutes, boiling just enough water for forty-eight meals, which meant that we would need to carry only one canister, not two, if our next leg lasted no more than eight days. We knew that a wool T-shirt weighed six ounces, a synthetic T-shirt weighed four, a single razor blade, which replaced my four-ounce multi-tool, tipped the scales at 0.07 ounces, and the labels on our clothing weighed 0.02—which is why we used the razor blade to cut them off and discard them.

"Dude, what are you *doing*?" I asked one afternoon when I caught Pete weighing his wristwatch.

"Can you believe this thing is almost three ounces?" he exclaimed, incredulous. "I'm leaving this behind—you shouldn't have to carry that much weight just to know what time it is."

Meanwhile, Mathieu and Kelly decided that it was time to move on to Phase II of our makeover: nutrition and food.

*   *   *

Months earlier, Rich had warned us that inside the canyon, our bodies would be consuming up to five thousand calories a day, far above the average food intake for most people and the equivalent of eating between five and seven meals a day. When I first heard this number, I had dismissed it as absurd. Now that we knew the truth—that moving thousands of vertical feet up and down the walls of the canyon could burn all of that and more—we began retooling our food kits.

Because the average prepacked backpacker meal contains between three hundred and six hundred calories, purchasing a standard order of beef stroganoff, chicken, or spaghetti from REI—as we had done before—wouldn't be sufficient. So we repackaged all our meals, turbocharging them with dried vegetables, powdered cheese, powdered butter, and packages of ramen noodles to pump up the nutritional value as well as the caloric payload.

We also paid special attention to adding items such as peanut butter and olive oil that were especially dense in fat (which can carry up to nine calories per gram) as opposed to proteins and carbohydrates (which pack, on average, less than half that). On each meal packet, we noted down not only the total weight but also the number of calories, so that we could make good strategic decisions on whether to consume the heavier meals early in each segment of the hike—to help diminish the weight of our packs—or save those calorie-dense breakfasts and dinners for the most strenuous days on the most demanding terrain, when our bodies would truly need them.

All of this new data meant building new spreadsheets, which coincided with the move toward Phase III of the makeover. For this we broke out the topo maps, then sat down with the entire team to thoroughly reevaluate the route we'd be taking, based on their knowledge of the ground we'd have to cover.

Pete had originally envisioned breaking the canyon into three chunks: beginning, middle, and end. We hadn't even finished the opening phase, so completing that would be our first task. But after extensive discussion, we decided that our best strategy would be to split the middle and the end into two chunks each, which meant a total of five segments. One of those stretches would be short enough to allow us to carry all our food and supplies, while each of the remaining four segments would require a cache—so packing those buckets properly and organizing them for transport became our next priority.

Only later would it occur to me that none of this preparation included linking up with a fitness trainer, going to the gym, or racing to build up our muscles with protein shakes. The folks who were supervising us seemed to understand that there was simply no way for Pete and I to instantaneously acquire a new level of power or endurance. When it came to combating the heat, the aridity, and the endless detours of the side canyons, our success or failure, they knew, would hang on the strengths and weaknesses that we already possessed. In the desert, efficiency, discipline, and wiliness almost invariably win out over brute force. The key was understanding our limitations, then making the best possible decisions within those constraints.

The final task was to wait for the weather to improve (we'd been getting an unusual amount of rain), and then set a launch date. When we decided it would be October 26, the gravity of what was happening suddenly sank in.

Good Lord, I thought to myself as I was sitting on the front porch one night, staring up at the moon. *We're actually doing this again.*

*   *   *

The remainder of that month was a blur as we scrambled to absorb everything we were being taught. But as the days flew past, one concern continued to nag at me.

Although our mentors were sharing every trick they knew, no amount of coaching could make up for what Pete and I still lacked, the thing for which there was no substitute, which was the months and years of experience that we'd skipped over.

Are we really ready to go back in by ourselves? I wondered. *Is this truly something that the two of us can handle?*

While I never voiced those thoughts directly, Mathieu must have sensed them, because one morning as I was poring over the maps on the dining room table just a few days before we were due to leave, he looked over and told me to stop worrying.

"You guys are *way* too unqualified for us to let you try to do this on your own," he assured me.

"So then what's the plan?" I asked, half expecting him to suggest that we pull the plug and cancel everything.

"Kelly and I are going with you."

CHAPTER 17

Back Again, Wiser?

ack in my river days, the last trip of the season in late October was always the best because this was the finest time of year, when the days stayed warm, the nights turned crisp, and the angled light of late autumn painted the upper walls of the canyon the color of saffron while bathing the river in cool shadows. That was true then, and it felt no different now as we headed north on Highway 89, accompanied by a set of tightly organized backpacks that were a far cry from the heap of unopened boxes that had filled the back of the truck a month earlier.

A few miles past the old trading post of Cameron, Jean-Philippe Clark turned his truck off the main road and followed a series of tire tracks leading across the sharp limestone gravel through the bony scrub. Thanks to recent rainstorms, the air was cool and the ground was rinsed with the smell of fresh sagebrush and old juniper bark. Autumn had finally arrived in canyon country.

In the distance, skittish bands of horses whipped themselves into a gallop at the first sight of the truck, manes and tails flying as they raced for the far side of the nearest hillock. The tracks forked, skirting the occasional clump of banana yucca, then forked again before finally halting next to a small piñon tree. There, Pete and I shouldered our packs, waved farewell to Jean-Philippe, and followed Mathieu and Kelly down a shallow draw whose bed was tumbled with gray pebbles.

As the draw deepened, cliffs rose on either side, and the sky narrowed to a blue sash, bounded by bare stone. We spent the next several hours working down and down again, lowering ourselves over ledges and drop-offs, squeezing between large boulders, until the walls abruptly swung to the west—and there, framed inside a V-shaped notch, was the main canyon. The now familiar layers of rock were stacked neatly atop one another, just as we had left them, and far below at the base of those walls, three hundred feet beneath our feet, we could see the river, a thin band of green set against the orange sandstone.

For our point of entry, Mathieu and Kelly had selected a tributary known as 29-Mile Canyon, a name that derived from the distance separating it from Lee's Ferry. A short way downstream on the far side of the river lay South Canyon. Through an elegantly simple trick of land navigation, we were dropping in almost directly across from the very spot where Pete and I had spent the final night of our previous leg almost a month earlier.

We made our way down to the ledge that defined the top of the Redwall, then turned and continued moving down-canyon until the light faded, forcing us to stop for the night. As the sky turned lavender and the shadows crept up the canyon walls, Pete gave voice to a question that I, too, had been pondering:

"So where do you suppose Rich and his guys are camped tonight?"

"No way of knowing, except that they're somewhere off to the west," said Mathieu as he prepared to light the stove. "But wherever they're at, they'll spot the same constellations we do when it gets dark."

As he spoke, a thin screen of clouds was sliding across the sky. That night, we didn't see a single star.

*   *   *

For the better part of the next week, the ledge along the highest section of the Redwall became our catwalk. All day long, we treaded carefully in single file, eyes fixed directly in front of us, focusing intently on where to place our feet, while occasionally snatching glimpses of the dizzying drop-off directly to our right, where the limestone cliffs fell straight and true for more than five hundred feet to the bright river below.

During those days, we were always on the move, rarely stopping for more than a few minutes as we pressed along the arc of each morning and into the flaring light of late afternoon until, once again, the setting sun torched the tops of the distant buttes and mesas, making them glow like embers. This was our signal to find a pothole filled with clear water, set camp, and fix dinner amid the purple air of evening. Then, as twilight played on the surface of the Colorado, coruscating off its ripples and eddies, we would watch the moonbeams slide down the faces of the cliffs and extend across the broken plane of the river.

Our vantage atop those cliffs enabled us to monitor the progress of half a dozen river expeditions that were pushing downstream in tandem with us. In the early mornings, when the river was still bathed in shadow, we could hear the rattle of a spoon or the clatter of a pot lid as an early-rising boatman brewed the first batch of coffee. Then as the light came up and the day unspooled, we would move together with the brightly colored rafts and the occasional pod of dories until they disappeared and were replaced by the next group. Every now and then, we tried calling out and waving to them, but they never caught sight of us. From their perspective we were invisible, lost in the immense sweep of stone and sky.

Although Mathieu and Kelly had both taken part in plenty of river expeditions, they seemed to prefer being up high and on foot, despite the hardships it entailed.

"Carrying all your belongings and your food on your back, it makes me think about the sheer amount of crap those guys have with them down there," Kelly remarked one evening as we listened to the songs and laughter of a river party echo faintly from the depths. "The folding chairs, the coolers, the giant umbrellas—it's so much more than anybody really needs."

"It's nice to be up here without all that stuff," Mathieu agreed as he poured boiling water into our packets of freeze-dried dinner. "As much as we love our stuff, sometimes not having it opens you up to communicating with the landscape and truly being present, don't you think?"

"Maybe." Pete sounded doubtful. "But a cold beer would be pretty great."

"Or a gin and tonic," I chimed in.

This was followed by a moment of quasi-religious silence.

"With fresh lime, and ice," I added helpfully, setting off an earnest debate over which would be more refreshing on top of the Redwall right now, gin and tonics or margaritas.

From there, the discussion swiftly spilled (as cocktails naturally do) into talk of everyone's favorite dinners—salmon fillets, pork chops, or steaks with baked potatoes. Before we knew it, we were heedlessly plunging into the most excruciating topic for backpackers to torture themselves with, fresh vegetables.

"Tomatoes," said Kelly, closing her eyes.

"Cucumbers," purred Mathieu.

"Fresh beets," I murmured, provoking a chorus of howling moans.

"Right now, if we had some beets like the ones those rafters fed us back on that beach with Rich," wailed Pete, glaring into his bowl, "I wouldn't have to choke down this dehydrated goop."

"What exactly are you eating over there?" inquired Mathieu.

"It's supposed to be shepherd's pie with herb-infused potatoes," reported Pete, straining to read the label upside down. "But it tastes like somebody tore up a cereal box and poured ketchup on top. It's gonna give me horrible gas tonight."

"Beets would definitely help with the gas," said Kelly.

"Wait . . . really?" said Pete, for whom gas was always a concern.

"No." Kelly laughed. "I'm just messing with you."

*   *   *

Then late one morning, we heard a voice call out.

At first, I assumed that a boating party had finally spotted us, until I realized that the sound wasn't coming from below, but from a steep cone of talus high above us in the Supai. Scanning the slope, I spotted Harlan Taney, picking his way through the rocks while hauling a massive backpack with a two-hundred-foot rappelling rope, plus a set of inflatable boats, paddles, and life jackets, all of which we would need when it came time to cross the river.

A few minutes later, Jean-Philippe appeared, too, lugging another pack crammed with seventy-five pounds of additional food and provisions. Our mobile resupply cache had arrived.

The handoff was fast. Within minutes, Jean-Philippe was headed back up to the rim, where his truck was parked along a remote stretch of the Navajo Reservation. Meanwhile the rest of us, with Harlan in tow, dropped off the top of the Redwall into yet another geological fault. The descent was rough, and it took several hours to lower ourselves through a series of steep fissures and sharp drop-offs with the rope. But when we emerged at the bottom, we found ourselves standing beside the river.

The current was glissading past with a muscular hiss, like a snake writhing along the floor of a jungle, and lining the shore in both directions we could make out a series of crescent-shaped beaches. Each sickle of sand was fringed with an emerald collar of willows and reeds and sedges, and rising between the beaches were steep, muddy banks matted in a rich verdure of fern and watercress and moss.*

A new layer of rock was emerging, too—a stratum directly beneath the Redwall that was striated in thin flakes and folios, like the deckled edges of an illuminated manuscript from the Dark Ages. This was the Muav Limestone, and its peach-and-cream-colored cliffs now joined with the Redwall to form a set of vertical ramparts that soared almost a thousand feet above the river.

Weaving through the greenery along the base of the Muav, we spotted a set of faint trails speckled with Bighorn droppings. By following those coffee-bean-size pellets, we were able to continue pushing down-canyon

---

* It should come as no surprise to learn that nearly half of the eighteen hundred species of plants found in the canyon are located along the riparian corridor within about five hundred feet of the river.

for another couple of days, first on the south side of the river, then on the north side after we hitched a ride with a raucous band of river runners, who saved us the trouble of having to inflate our pack rafts and paddle across.

Somewhere along this section, we turned into the mouth of a massive tributary and hiked up the bed of a small stream purling through polished gravel beneath a line of cottonwood trees. For several miles, we walked beneath a lattice of gold and green light filtering through the cottonwood leaves, until Mathieu finally scrambled out of the streambed and began ascending a series of high-angled boulder fields studded with clumps of Prickly Pear cactus.

After a few hours of steady climbing, the boulder fields delivered us onto a moonscape of shaley dunes striated with strange colors: some were purple or green; others were mustard yellow or ash gray.

"It looks like another planet," observed Pete.

For the next two days, we were immersed in this strange new world as we worked our way into and back out of a trio of drainages—first Nankoweap, then Kwagunt, and finally Malgosa—that ran next to one another, like the splayed toes of a condor. As we made our way up the slopes of the first drainage and down into the second, we found ourselves slogging through tiny flakes of rock so loose and crumbly that with each step our shoes sank in well past the laces. This was so exhausting that late in the afternoon I found myself starting to wilt.

"You don't look so good," observed Mathieu after I complied with his order to sit down and drink half a liter of water. "How are you feeling?"

"Dizzy. It's like the sun is tapping on the top of my head with a ball-peen hammer."

Before I was permitted to stand back up, I was encouraged to eat a chocolate bar, followed by several handfuls of salted nuts and potato chips.

Meanwhile, Kelly opened the top of my pack and reached inside. "Let's lighten your load a bit," she said, plucking out several of the heaviest items, including the camp stove and our fuel canisters. "We don't want you coming apart at the seams like McBrody did at the start of your adventure, do we?"

Pete pretended to ignore that remark, but from the way he snorted and rolled his eyes, I could tell that he no longer minded being teased by Kelly. They were becoming friends.

*   *   *

Despite her fondness for pulling Pete's leg, Kelly, like the rest of us, could see how deeply he was immersing himself in his work as he sought to make up for the time he'd lost and the photos he'd failed to capture during the trials of our first leg. Each day, he would walk for hours holding his one-and-a-half-pound camera at arm's length to get footage of us on the move, and when we were traversing cliffs, he often shot with one hand while clinging to the rock with the other.

At times, I found this wildly irritating. If Pete wasn't blocking my path by stopping to take a photo or asking me for the eleventh time to take off my pack and fish out a lens or a filter he needed, then he was ordering me to go stand somewhere to provide a sense of scale for a video sequence he wanted to shoot. Nevertheless, by paying such close attention to his surroundings and being *present*, he was connecting deeply with the physical details of the landscape.

I was trying my best to do the same, although for me this mostly involved tagging closely behind Mathieu, whose knowledge of the canyon far exceeded my own, and listening to what he had to say. To walk in his shadow was to be continuously pelted with proof that, although I had spent years trying to master the canyon's nuances, I still had much to learn about the place.

He knew, for example, that a Bighorn Sheep's ability to conserve water, partly by retaining moisture from the droppings that we had been following, exceeds that of a camel. He knew that the Mourning Doves sipping from the potholes where we camped must sit on their eggs not to keep them warm, but to cool them by absorbing heat with their bodies; and that individual mesquite trees, whose bean pods he encouraged me to nibble on as we walked because they taste like molasses, can survive for more than nine hundred years—none of which I was aware of. He also knew (as I did not) that the stretch of the shoreline around Point Hansbrough, a long crest of Supai looming almost seventeen hundred feet above the Colorado that we had passed several days earlier, qualified as one of the most deeply incised river meanders on earth. And he knew that on the Redwall cliffs along that same section of the canyon were caves littered with the fossilized remains of extinct mammals, including the hair of woolly mountain goats and mammoths, the leg bones of dire wolves, and wing bones from a monstrous bird of prey known as a teratorn, which boasted a twelve-and-a-half-foot wingspan and was probably capable of devouring rabbits in a single gulp.

"Almost everywhere you look, with every step you take, the canyon seems intent on pulling you further into the past," Mathieu said one afternoon in reference to the relics in those limestone caverns, all of which belonged to prehistoric creatures that had inhabited the abyss prior to the end of the last ice age, between ten thousand and forty thousand years ago. "Everybody focuses on the ages of the rock layers, which are calibrated in tens of millions of years, but there are lots of other things that can add depth and richness to your understanding of how time works in this landscape."

Thanks to the flood of new data, I spent my days stumbling at Mathieu's heels, furiously trying to scribble these pieces of information down in my notebook to ensure I would remember them later. In the process, I often failed to note what was unfolding directly in front of me—a propensity that was demonstrated with special clarity one evening when, shortly after arriving in camp, I committed a blunder that brought me in direct contact with yet another temporal dimension to the world beneath the rims.

*   *   *

We had decided to spend the night at a spot where two washes came together, and when we arrived, it was already dark. One of the channels was as dry as an old boot; the other featured a runnel of water no wider than my pinkie dribbling along its bottom.

The rest of the group set up the stoves and unrolled their bedrolls along the empty wash. But after filling up my water bottles from the tiny stream, I was too lazy to lug my gear back to where they were and instead emptied my pack right there without bothering to take a close look at where I would be sleeping.

When I awoke the following morning, I discovered that the ground around me was littered with hundreds of potsherds, fragments of prehistoric earthenware—pieces of ancient water jars, serving bowls, and seed pots. Each was roughly the size of a small coin, and while some were a uniform shade of brown or maroon, a few bore jagged black-on-white lines. Thanks to my heedlessness, and in direct violation of the canyon's code of conduct, I had bedded down in the middle of an archaeological site.

One reason to avoid committing a blunder such as this, aside from its being enormously disrespectful, is that the precise spot where an artifact was originally deposited, its provenience, offers vital clues regarding its context and classification. Or to put it another way, altering position is akin to stealing—a theft that robs a thing of its story.

The people whose relics I had disturbed were part of a larger human drama of which I was dimly aware but had never confronted directly, until that moment. Their narrative is as much a part of this landscape as the annals of its rocks, or the records laid out in the teeth and hair of its prehistoric mammals and birds—an epic chronicle whose twists and turns are every bit as complex and confounding as any other part of the canyon's labyrinth.

The opening chapters of that saga unfolded long ago, and although many details are still obscure, the moment that the story itself first entered the consciousness of people who look and sound like me—white Americans of European descent—actually has a precise date and location.

It took place on the second Tuesday of August, in the summer of 1869, when members of the exploratory expedition led by Major John

Wesley Powell reached a remarkable place less than five miles from where we were now camped.

When they arrived, in much the same manner that I would experience almost 150 years later, they found themselves surrounded by evidence that the canyon was far more than just an empty stone vessel animated by desert plants, wild animals, and the workings of the wind.

CHAPTER 18

The Greater Unknown

The rainstorms that often erupt over northern Arizona in late July were especially heavy that summer, so the Colorado River was swollen and muddy when a group of nine oarsmen in three heavy wooden boats exited the main current and knifed their keels into the damp sand along the shoreline at the mouth of a stream that would later come to be called the Little Colorado. When they'd cast off several weeks earlier and many miles to the north on the journey that had delivered them to this point, there had been ten men in four boats, and by now the crew was wondering how many more might disappear before they fulfilled the quest set forth by the man who had led them into this mess—and who they were beginning to see as a desert version of Ahab.

Like the master of the *Pequod*, Powell was missing a limb, albeit an arm instead of a leg, lost to a Confederate minié ball during the first afternoon at the Battle of Shiloh. Also like Melville's mad captain, Powell was inflamed by a powerful obsession—although the forces that drove him had nothing to do with vengeance against a great white whale, and everything to do with penetrating the last great white space on the U.S. government's official survey map depicting the mysterious region where the Colorado River flowed through the Grand Canyon.

Mountain men and explorers alike had traded in the widespread belief that no one who ventured upon that river would emerge from

179

its deepest and least known canyon alive. In the absence of any hard evidence to refute it, a myth had taken root, at least in some circles, that although some native tribes were scattered across various points along the canyon's perimeter, the terrain at its bottom was far too harsh and inaccessible to support human settlement. If true, this suggested that the world the explorers were moving through was, and perhaps always had been, uninhabited—a theory that seemed to be holding up well over the first several days as Powell and his crew made their way down the canyon's initial sixty-one-mile stretch, from Lee's Ferry, where their records suggest that they saw little if any evidence of human habitation. Preoccupied with the back-breaking labor of lowering their boats on ropes through most of the major rapids and hauling the cargo along the shore by hand, it seems that they were unaware of how much evidence they were missing, until they arrived at the stream where they were now tying off their boats.

This stop would be important for a number of reasons, not the least of them being that it would anchor perhaps the most famous description in the report that Powell would later publish, which modern-day river guides would recite to their passengers at the very same spot more than a century later: "We are three-quarters of a mile in the depth of the earth, and the great river shrinks into insignificance as it dashes its angry waves against the walls and cliffs that rise to the world above. We have an unknown distance yet to run, an unknown river yet to explore."

Given Powell's ignorance of what lay ahead, he intended to linger for two full days so that his crew could repair the leaking boats, sift the last of their mildewed flour through a scrap of mosquito netting, boil their rancid bacon in the hopes of preventing it from rotting even further, and spread out the few pounds of dried apples they had left, now sodden with muddy river water, to let them soak up the sun. Meanwhile, Powell wanted to get a fix on their latitude and longitude, part of the trellis of data points for the map he was drafting in his head.

While the men busied themselves with their chores, Powell set off along the banks of the Little Colorado, intending to climb partway up a nearby cliff to survey the terrain—and there he stumbled across

THE GREATER UNKNOWN   181

something he hadn't expected. It was a trail made not by Bighorn Sheep or any other four-footed animal, but by human beings. "I can see no evidence of its having been travelled for a very long time," he would later write.

Clearly, people had been here before—a conclusion that was strengthened when he returned to camp to find his men puzzling over what appeared to be pieces of broken crockery scattered on the ground.

Who were those people? Powell and his men must have wondered. *What had brought them down here, and how long had they remained?*

*   *   *

In the days to come, as the explorers struggled to make their way through the heart of the canyon—contending with the challenges of vicious rapids, relentless rain, and dwindling food supplies—they found themselves repeatedly bumping up against archaeological sites offering clear evidence that people not only had passed through this place, but had actually lived here. Along the deltas at the mouths of some of the major side canyons, they found low dams and retaining walls built to help channel water onto fields, and even the remains of stone houses, some of which had more than one room, and on the rocks nearby, strange markings that Powell described as "etchings and hieroglyphics." Higher on the canyon walls, they spied small granaries in which corn had been stored for safekeeping—and in many cases, the dried mud that had been daubed between the masonry bore the whorled fingerprints of the hands that had placed those stones and smoothed the mortar.

The walls of most of the houses had long since collapsed. But inside the foundations Powell found pieces of earthenware pottery and even a metate, a hollowed-out stone used for grinding seeds and corn, which he described in his published report as "deeply worn, as if it had been much used." But perhaps the most memorable find took place on August 20 inside the remnants of a small building perched under an overhang on the right side of the river. One of the walls was still intact, and sitting on a rock extending from the wall to form a shelf was a woven basket.

It was rounded like a globe and large enough, Powell guessed, to have contained perhaps a third of a bushel of seeds or corn, although it was now empty and far too fragile to hold anything but air. He took it in his hands, but it came apart, and as the pieces fell to the floor, he noticed something else. "There are many beautiful flint chips," he later wrote, "as if this had been the home of an old arrow-maker."

In that moment, Powell must have felt as if he were being invited to step across a threshold into an earlier time. The crumbling walls and doorway as well as the implements inside were links to a prehistoric past that was richer and more complex than most European people dared to imagine. Each relic was a kind of trapdoor through which one could descend into an older America, ancient and venerable enough to turn the notion of "the New World" completely on its head.

Amid those insights lay another revelation, too, because if the spectacle of the canyon's geology—its Quaternary faults, its crinoid fossils, its igneous intrusions—could leave one in awe, Powell realized, then the mysteries of its human past, when glimpsed through the portal of artifacts such as these, were no less powerful. He had no idea who these people might have been, or that their fingerprints and belongings were speaking to him across the arc of almost a full millennium. The only thing he felt he could say with certainty was that they and their descendants seemed to have vanished—until several days farther downstream, when he and his crew were met with yet another surprise.

By now they were growing desperate: their boats were leaking, their clothing was in tatters, their food all but gone, and still there was no sign of the canyon coming to an end. So it came as an absolute shock when, late on the morning of August 26, they rounded a bend, glanced over at the far shoreline, and found themselves staring across the current at somebody's garden.

The little patch of vegetables, which had been planted on the right side of the river, was irrigated with water flowing from a small spring at the base of a nearby cliff. The plot was filled with corn, melons, and squash, and although the corn wasn't yet ready for harvest and the melons were still too green to eat, the squash were ripe and plump and far too tempting to pass up.

Pulling to shore, the men raced around snatching up a dozen or so of the juiciest-looking fruits, then leaped back in their boats and scurried off before anyone could confront them. When they'd rowed far enough downstream to avoid being followed, they pulled over again, put the kettle on the fire, and concocted a batch of squash stew, which they feasted on, twice—first for lunch and then again that night for supper.

"Never was fruit so sweet as these stolen squashes," Powell would later write. But no less satisfying, at least for the nascent branches of science devoted to the study of human beings and their cultures, was the revelation imparted by that garden.

Although the canyon had certainly been occupied a long time ago, a number of those people were apparently *still here*.

*　　　*　　　*

During that first expedition, Powell would record eight separate sites along the river that were strewn with prehistoric relics, thereby becoming the first white person to take note of the artifacts belonging to the people of the canyon. What he uncovered were clues to a story so intricate and tangled that his successors in the emerging fields of Southwestern archaeology and anthropology would spend the next 150 years attempting to unravel the particulars, a project that continues to this day.

In the decades to follow, the number of sites discovered would expand from those eight original plots—slowly at first, but later in a wild rush as a series of archaeological surveys flushed out more and more sites during the final decades of the twentieth century. The total, which now exceeds 4,300, offers a vivid index of the extent to which the people who left behind these artifacts were able not only to move through the canyon's vast recesses on foot, but also to embrace it as home.

Judging by the evidence, they seem to have been everywhere: along the rims, across the plateaus, and throughout the canyon's central corridor, as well as in its extensive network of tributaries. They had even scaled many of the isolated buttes and summits of the interior, places whites wouldn't ascend for the first time until the 1960s and '70s. There was, it seemed, almost no place that they had failed to penetrate and explore, and the data that has emerged reveals, among other startling truths, that for much of the past ten thousand years, the canyon has cradled a rich medley of human cultures, as successive waves of prehistoric peoples surged and ebbed through its recesses, one after another, like tidal currents washing into and back out of a sea cave.

Although all of these migrants left some type of imprint, the marks of those who are believed to have arrived first are breathtakingly faint. Aside from what Western scholars can glean from a single pair of spearpoints—a partial Folsom projectile point found near the river and a fragment of a Clovis point located by a bird-watcher on the South Rim—we know almost nothing about the roving bands of Paleo-Indians who may, according to one perspective, have been among the earliest humans to move across this region during the twilight of the Pleistocene, some eleven thousand to thirteen thousand years ago. They arrived during a time when their counterparts out on the Great Plains were using Clovis-tipped spears to slaughter mammoths and giant ground sloths while fending off attacks by short-faced bears, saber-toothed cats, and perhaps some of the dire wolves whose leg bones were lodged in the cliffs beneath the ridgeline that would later come to be called Point Hansbrough.

Nor do scholars know much about the bands of nomadic hunters who came next, who are now referred to as the Archaic people, and who seem to have left behind almost nothing, aside from a handful of campsites scattered along the river corridor, a few dozen remarkable pieces of rock art, and hundreds of tiny figurines resembling Bighorn Sheep fashioned from willow twigs, which they deposited on the floors of caves in the Redwall Limestone.

During a span of time stretching from 8000 BC—when the cultivation of wheat and barley spread from the shores of the Tigris and

Euphrates rivers in Mesopotamia into what is now Turkey and Greece—to the completion of Stonehenge sometime around 2000 BC, the people who were migrating into and out of the Grand Canyon seem to have made little impact. Only around 1000 BC—a century or two before Homer is believed to have composed the *Iliad* and *Odyssey*—does a more detailed picture emerge with the appearance of the people whom we currently refer to as the Ancestral Puebloans.

Their arrival followed the introduction of agriculture to the Southwest from Mesoamerica with the "three sisters" of corn, beans, and squash. Moving into the canyon in sporadic waves starting around 500 BC, they were drawn by access to wild game, and edible wild plants such as agave and mesquite, as well as an extended growing season and water for their crops.

By AD 800 they were well versed in making pottery and irrigating gardens, and with the arrival of the eleventh century, roughly around the time that the Normans were launching their invasion of England, the Puebloans were building multiroom homes resembling the structure whose remnants sheltered the metate that Powell would later spot. Eventually, they began growing cotton for use in textiles, making their own ceramic pottery, and erecting large kivas—circular underground chambers used for religious rites.

Aided by some unusually wet and fertile years, their population increased until it crested around 1130, when a prolonged drought began forcing them back out of the canyon and up onto the surrounding plateaus. There, they would eventually fold themselves into a series of pueblos stretching from the high mesas of Arizona's Painted Desert to the fertile bottomlands of New Mexico's Rio Grande Valley.*

Meanwhile, a final influx of newcomers approached from several directions, each according to a different timetable. By the 1300s, at least five bands of the Paiute tribe were moving in from the northwest and laying claim not only to the plateaus along the North Rim, but

* To this day, the people who belong to a number of these Pueblo communities—in particular the Hopi and Zuni tribes—retain powerful ties that link them directly to the canyon.

also to many of the major tributaries along that side of the Colorado. At roughly the same time, the ancestors of what would become the Hualapai, the Havasupai, and the Yavapai tribes were pushing their way up from the southwest, each settling or foraging along a different section of the South Rim.

Finally, sometime in the sixteenth century, the Navajo would move down from the northeast. Although only a small number of them would ever live directly inside the canyon, they would hover close enough to its eastern edge that they would come to consider its interior a critical part of their homeland, as well as a place of refuge during crises.*

*   *   *

In all, the ancestral lands of at least eleven prehistoric tribes either abutted or lay directly inside the canyon, and the story they inscribed during the years prior to the arrival of Powell's first expedition was so intricately layered that in many ways it seems to mirror the land itself. Today, more than a century and a half later, the human history of this place—much like its geology and ecology—is perhaps best understood as an interlocked series of strata that dip into and merge with one another.

Within that constellation of tribes are diverse histories, asymmetrical technologies, and unique points of view. Some nations, such as the Zuni and the Hopi, were largely sedentary, rooted to permanent villages where they depended heavily on agriculture and coaxed as many as fifteen varieties of corn from fields composed mainly of sand. Others, such as the various bands of Paiute, were highly mobile, almost continuously on the move as they foraged with the seasons. Their survival as hunters, gatherers, and opportunistic planters hinged on a comprehensive understanding of the ever-shifting currents of seeds

---

* As we'll see shortly, a number of tribes vehemently reject this chronology and present a compelling case that they have been a part of the landscape forever.

and nuts, roots and flowers, insects and rodents, that ebbed and surged within the canyon's diverse microenvironments.

Despite the many differences among these nations, however, today they all hold in common a number of key elements, beginning with the conviction that the canyon forms part of the core of their identities, and that the place itself helps to anchor each of them as a distinctive people whose ethos, much like the roots of a juniper tree, is wrapped around the rock itself at many important locations both above and below the rims.

Some of these spots, such as the travertine spire beneath a hundred-foot waterfall known as *Chimik'yana'kya dey'a*, which is where the Zuni believe they first emerged, are shrines that bind the members of a tribe to a particular point by affirming where they come from. Other sites harbor resources that can be found nowhere else, such as the hidden overhang beneath the South Rim where the Havasupai gather hematite, the reddish mineral used for body painting and as a commodity to trade with other tribes, who employ it for ceremonial purposes. Still other places serve as markers that are described in precise detail and then linked together—each butte and pillar, each turning of the canyon walls—in a repertoire of songs, poems, and chants that essentially function as oral maps.

All of this means that every facet of the land is alive and responsive, like the strings of an instrument, to a set of harmonics that include—but also expand far beyond—human needs and hopes and longings. Without exception, each tribe regards the canyon as a place of reverence, a kind of open-air cathedral whose interior is consecrated by memory and stories and the weight of time. For all of these societies, the chasm is hallowed ground, an aboriginal holy land.

*   *   *

To travel through the canyon as Powell did in the summer of 1869 was tantamount to traversing the sacred spaces of people who were exquisitely attuned to every grade and nuance of their habitat—far more so than the white settlers who were contemporaries of the one-armed explorer, and who began rapidly moving onto the surrounding rimlands during the 1870s. Men who couldn't survive for more than a few days without gunpowder and cast iron, paraffin and bacon—but who nevertheless conceived themselves as discovering the land and ferreting out its secrets for the first time.

Spurred by a set of mining and homesteading laws that offered virtually free access to any public land for mineral prospecting, cattle grazing, or agriculture, the newcomers repeatedly found themselves coming into contact with the indigenous peoples of the region. During those encounters, the interlopers rarely concluded that they were coming face-to-face with communities worthy of anything other than mystification or contempt. Regardless of who the prior occupants of the country might be, whatever language they might speak, or where their territory might lie, none was regarded as having a legitimate claim on the land. The only proper response was to push them aside.

The pattern for what was now about to unfold, an era of intense and violent dislocation for the tribes, had already been established directly to the east of the canyon five years before Powell arrived, when the U.S. Army embarked on a scorched-earth campaign across the Navajo Nation, confiscating their sheep and horses, burning their homes, and cutting down every peach tree in their central sanctuary of Canyon de Chelly. When the holdouts were left with no choice but to surrender, virtually the entire tribe, more than eighty-five hundred people, was forced to march some four hundred miles to a desolate camp in eastern New Mexico, an exodus known as the Long Walk. More than two hundred died along the way, and hundreds more perished from disease and malnutrition once they arrived.

By the early 1880s, most of the canyon's other tribes were being stripped of their lands and resources in similar fashion: without legal warrant, and often at the behest of the federal government, which had adopted a strategy of attempting to break the tribes' connection to their ancestral territories by confining them to reservations and by setting up a system of boarding schools, where their children were separated from their language and their culture in the hopes of turning them into white people. The Hopi and Zuni were assigned to reservations far from the canyon, cutting them off from some of their most sacred places, while the Havasupai were deprived of almost the entirety of their home ground.

As for the Navajo, they were eventually permitted to return to areas that were a fraction of the size of their ancestral lands, although these would later grow. Around the same time, in a reprise of the mass deportation to which the Navajo had been subjected, the Yavapai were hunted by army troops as "wild animals"—in the words of one general—until they surrendered and were forced onto one reservation, then uprooted again and marched 180 miles to a second reservation that was even hotter, drier, and smaller than the first.

Meanwhile, off in the west, every member of the Hualapai tribe, which had launched a series of skirmishes in defense of their lands, was rounded up in the same manner and driven into exile, more than a hundred miles to the south. But perhaps the harshest treatment of all was reserved for the Southern Paiute. Decades after separating various bands of the tribe from almost all of their aboriginal lands and herding them onto a handful of scattered reservations on marginal patches of turf that effectively ratified their dispossession, the federal government passed legislation terminating their status as a separate people. They would later win partial reinstatement in a fight that is still ongoing, but their legal annulment pointedly symbolizes the despair and the dislocation that all of the tribes endured as their links to the canyon were systematically severed.

*   *   *

Although none of this history is a secret, many of the specific details, as well as the larger story of how they unfolded, are unfamiliar to the general public today. Most people who come to the canyon tend to arrive, as Pete and I had, with little appreciation for the fact that the place they are setting out to explore—a landscape that appears to be pristine and untouched—was once part of a complex mosaic of native desert cultures, each an entity unto itself, whose connections to the land ran far deeper than many modern Americans can even begin to imagine.

Few of these visitors understand that the cliffs they gaze at, the trails they venture down, and the springs from which they drink all belonged, in the fullest sense of that word, to people who were a part of this landscape long before the arrival of Europeans. Like Powell himself, almost none of these modern sightseers is able to grasp—at least initially—that in ways both large and small, those people still belong to this place. And much like me when I discovered that I had unwittingly spent the night atop a trove of potsherds, many tourists are too oblivious to fathom the implications of evidence that is all around until they finally realize that each and every artifact has a story to share—and that after you have begun to absorb the larger narrative, nothing in the canyon will ever be the same again.

CHAPTER 19

Where Water
Comes Together

The potsherds were everywhere, scattered for twenty yards in every direction, each fragment part of a shattered mirror reflecting the lives of the people who had once called this place home. Scanning the ground, I imagined that they had probably picked this spot for the same reasons that had drawn us: it was protected, it was beautiful, and it offered two sources of water, although only one was flowing at the moment.

As I tried to look at the place through their eyes, it seemed as if past and present were sliding together in a way that, for a brief and intoxicating moment, made it impossible to distinguish one from the other. And during that interval, I found myself confronting, perhaps for the first time, the notion that any understanding of this landscape that fails to embrace the story of these people and their descendants is fundamentally incomplete.

After I had collected my belongings and sheepishly tiptoed out of the little patch of potsherds—some of which I later learned dated from the eleventh century—we spent the rest of the day descending a long series of gulches that eventually delivered us back to the edge of the Colorado, where we turned and resumed working our way downstream. Just before sunset, we arrived at a sandy beach covered with large boulders where the river bent to the right before vanishing into evening shadows. Beyond the middle of the current was a small island, sitting low in the water, and on the far side of the island was a stream whose waters were a brilliant shade of turquoise.

This was the Little Colorado River, where Powell and his crew had glimpsed the prehistoric trail. It is the largest tributary inside the canyon, a gorge that extends nearly sixty miles to the east before merging with the rim, and it drains almost twenty-seven thousand square miles of the Painted Desert, an area larger than Massachusetts, Vermont, and Connecticut put together. When storms fill its branches with brown waves of sediment-rich floodwaters, its volume can rival that of the Colorado itself.

Later that night, I found a smooth boulder a few yards from the edge of the river to lean against, and watched the rounded urn of the moon rise above the highest cliffs on the far side of the river and pour itself into the canyon, generating a peculiar effect. On the near side of the river, where we were camped, the moonlight cast every feature—the faces of the cliffs, the current along the shore, the boulder field next to our camp—in a milky glow that was powerful enough to throw off its own shadows. But on the far side of the Colorado, the light was streaming down at an angle that permitted it to touch only the highest bands of rock, leaving the lower sections of the canyon walls, and the stretch of shoreline below them, lost in darkness.

Somewhere out there on the half-black, half-silver millrace, the waters of the two rivers mingled and joined at a point known as the Confluence. This was the spot that Pete and I had been aiming toward back in late September during the first leg of our journey. It was also the place that Mathieu, Kelly, and Harlan had committed to seeing that we reached.

Given where things had stood almost six weeks earlier, this felt like quite an accomplishment: the end of the first and, presumably, the harshest segment of the transect. If someone had handed me a cocktail right then, I would have toasted our pluck and perseverance.

I had no way of knowing that everything we had undergone to this point was, in essence, preparation and training. A prelude and foundation for the core purpose of our journey, which would begin revealing itself the following day for the very first time.

*   *   *

The Confluence

At dawn, we inflated our pod of pack rafts, ferried ourselves across the chilly currents of the river, then followed Mathieu down a well-marked trail along the north bank of the Little Colorado. Ten minutes later, he stopped and peered up at an immense field of talus that rose to the base of a set of high cliffs, which shot straight to the canyon's cream-colored caprock, etched with razored clarity against a cobalt skyline. To my eye, the entire expanse looked impregnable, a chaos of steep and precariously balanced rubble, topped with a stack of unscalable escarpments soaring for more than three thousand vertical feet—eighteen Niagara Falls, stacked one atop the other.

"Okay, I think this'll work," Mathieu announced. With that, he started working his way up the first of a long series of zigzags that would take us back and forth as we ascended through the Muav, the Redwall, and the Supai.

By the time we made it to the crumbling slopes of the Hermit Shale, nearly two thousand vertical feet above the river, our pace had slowed to a grind. But still we kept plodding, climbing steadily from one hour to the next, inching ever farther away from the river, ever closer to the battlements that formed the final barrier to the rim.

During the ascent, Mathieu paused briefly to catch his breath on a shallow ledge of sandstone.

"The places that are most worth visiting—they're never easy to get into or back out of, are they?" he said.

I was too winded—bent at the waist, hands clutching my knees, gasping for air—to say anything in response.

"In addition to its mysteries and its beauty," he continued, "I think suffering is at the center of what it means to be in the canyon."

Who could argue with that? I thought while nodding in agreement. *I just wish somebody would put an elevator in here.*

An hour or so later, we reached the base of the highest cliffs, squeezed our bodies into a type of corner known as a dihedral, and began clawing upward by jamming our fingers and toes into cracks in the stone. At several points, we were forced to remove our packs and pass them from one person to the next so that we could free-climb without being thrown off-balance and sent plummeting onto the last cone of talus, now several hundred feet below. By late afternoon, we'd clambered through the final set of moves, seized the upper lip of the Kaibab Limestone, and popped out to find ourselves awash in the scent of sage.

The ground on which we stood was rolling, treeless, and almost empty but for a band of horses galloping in the near distance through the sagebrush and the blond bunchgrasses, beneath an immense sky. Off against the horizon to the north hovered the orange escarpments of the cliffs that loom above Lee's Ferry. And far to the south, sixty miles away, we could make out the tops of the San Francisco Peaks, just outside Flagstaff, glistening with fresh snow.

It's difficult to overstate the impact of stepping, in the span of a heartbeat, from the vertical world of the canyon onto the flat domain of the rim country. It felt as if we were a family of trolls who had scrabbled up from the underworld—which was probably the impression we conveyed to Jean-Philippe Clark and his father, Roger, who by prior arrangement were waiting at the top of the cliffs, and who gave us all bear hugs, without making any mention of how badly we must have smelled.

"Hop in and let's go," Roger said, opening the door to his son's truck. "There's somebody waiting to meet you just across the way."

Minutes later, we pulled to a stop along the near side of a low outcropping of limestone. On the far side stood a Navajo woman clad in a red velveteen dress, facing the canyon. Her hair was long and gray, on her feet she wore low-cut moccasins with buttons fashioned from coins, and her hands were gathered around a long walking stick made from the dried stalk of a yucca.

Even with her back to us, something about the figure she cut, especially the way her hair spilled over her shoulders and fell toward her waist, made it seem as if every inch of her belonged to the canyon. But to fully understand just how deep her connection truly ran, you have to know a few things about who she was, and how she had come to be standing on that spot.

*   *   *

The Navajo Nation, whose western border we had crossed during our ascent from the edge of the river, is the largest Native American reservation in the United States—twenty-five thousand square miles, a landmass roughly the size of West Virginia that stretches across the Four Corners region, where the borders of Arizona, New Mexico, Colorado, and Utah come together. But even by the standards of emptiness and isolation unique to *Diné Bikéyah*, the Navajos' name for their homeland, the northwestern corner of this territory along the edge of the Grand Canyon is singular.

It was here, amid the maze of tributary drainages extending away from the Colorado, that small groups of Navajo evaded capture by U.S. Army soldiers in the winter of 1864, some of the only members of the tribe who were never forced into exile during the Long Walk. Even today, this area is still viewed as a kind of stronghold by the now-aging descendants of those resisters, many of whom have kept faith with the old ways, living along the rimlands in widely scattered hogans—rounded one-room dwellings made of logs and earth—while tending their sheep and grazing their horses.

Those elders and the traditions they maintain offered a remedy for the kind of malady that a young mother named Dee Yellowhorse found herself confronting back in 1967, not long after she'd moved beyond the reservation to find a job and build a future, only to realize that her child, an eight-year-old daughter named Renae, was losing her ability to speak Navajo—and with it the most important link to her culture. That summer, Renae's mother first drove her to the rimlands from their home in Tuba City, the largest town on the western end of the reservation, and dropped her off at the home of her grandparents, Mae and Joe, who lived with their extended family less than a mile from the edge of the canyon.

Over the next several months, the eight-year-old girl completed what she would later call the most important phase of her education. In between learning to tend the animals and help with the chores, she received language lessons from her aunties and cousins, who tutored her with enough patience and discipline that by midsummer her Navajo was starting to come back.

As her language strengthened, so, too, did her connection to the land, especially the section of the rim from which it was possible to look down and see the Confluence, where the turquoise waters of *Tólchíʼíkooh*, the Little Colorado, met the olive-colored current of *Bitsʼíís Nínééʼézi*, the Colorado.

From the point where they converged, the two streams flowed side by side, each separate and distinct. Then gradually they began mixing, and within less than a quarter of a mile the waters merged to become something that was neither wholly one or the other, but a hybrid, seamless and new.

The nexus where the waters came together, her relatives explained, was one of the most important shrines in all of *Diné Bikéyah*, the place where life began, as well as the site to which the spirits of the dead returned. It was infused with so much spiritual power that not only would clans all across the Navajo Nation make pilgrimages to this sector of the rim to perform ceremonies and make offerings, but so, too, would members of the Hopi and the Zuni nations, who also considered the Confluence sacred ground.*

Even the Havasupai, the Paiute, and the Hualapai could recite stories about this place, and to hear those stories told was to grasp that the Confluence was not simply a juncture where two desert rivers joined, but an axis point along which many different streams of culture and spirituality braided to become one.

That summer was one of the most memorable of the young girl's life, and when it was over, she kept coming back. Even after graduating from college and starting a family of her own, she continued delivering food and supplies to her grandmother and her aunties on the weekends, helping out during lambing and shearing seasons, and celebrating birthdays and attending reunions throughout the year.

Eventually, she began to imagine that perhaps the lands overlooking the Confluence could one day offer the kind of anchor and lodestone for her own children that it had once given to her—until the spring of 2012, when she caught wind of events that had the potential to change the place forever.

---

* Just a short distance upstream from the Confluence, for example, was a hollow mound of travertine known as the *Sipapuni*, through which the Hopi believed that their ancestors emerged into this world before embarking on a series of migrations that eventually brought them to the cluster of villages perched along a set of high mesas some seventy miles east of the canyon, where they remain to this day.

*   *   *

A group of investors from Phoenix and Scottsdale, men with experience in real-estate development, hotel marketing, and theme-park ventures, had announced their intention to build a resort on the rim overlooking where the Colorado and the Little Colorado Rivers come together. The so-called Escalade project would spread across 420 acres and was estimated to cost somewhere between $500 million and $1.1 billion. It would include a complex of hotels, restaurants, and a movie theater as well as gift shops, a health spa, and many other attractions. But the centerpiece of it all would be a cable-driven tramway whose eight-passenger gondolas would carry as many as ten thousand visitors a day down the cliffs, and deposit them next to the Confluence.

The leader of this project, a developer named Lamar Whitmer, had already advised a number of Arizona tribes looking to invest in resorts and other forms of entertainment. He took it as a given that the National Park Service would be horrified by his proposal, but he also knew that the land along the rim belonged to the Navajo, and as a sovereign nation they had the right to do whatever they pleased with it. The primary challenge, he reckoned, would be to win over those members of the tribe who lived along the rimlands by convincing them that the resort would bring modernization, economic growth, and some much-needed jobs to one of the poorest corners of the reservation (while, not incidentally, making a pile of money for himself and his partners).

"We're going to employ an awful lot of people in an impoverished area and help them save their culture," Whitmer declared. "What's better than that?"

The first two efforts to sell the project to residents of the area were decisively voted down. But in the autumn of 2012, after convincing a number of Navajo families that they would benefit from the investment, Whitmer and his partners convened a meeting among the local stakeholders—including Renae Yellowhorse—with less than forty-eight hours' notice.

Amid cries of "It's illegal" and "That's not fair" and "Who are *you*?" a third vote on a resolution to move forward with the development passed, 59–52. This opened the door for the investors to submit a formal proposal directly to the Navajo nation's legislative council at the tribe's capital in the town of Window Rock, 150 miles east of the canyon, near the New Mexico border.

Afterward, Yellowhorse wondered what had just happened. A margin of only *seven* votes, cast amid a tumultuous and hastily convened meeting? That hardly seemed like a resounding victory, much less a clear mandate to move forward with a scheme that was so divisive and controversial. In her view, the vote wasn't a license to push ahead, but a testament to how far the developers were willing to go to manipulate tribal politics and exploit economic hardship to get what they wanted.

Yellowhorse wasn't the only one who felt that way. A few days later she learned that one of her grandparents' neighbors, Dolores Wilson-Aguirre, whose family had a sheep camp less than three miles from the Confluence overlook, was so outraged that she had joined forces with a number of other locals who also felt that they were being railroaded. They called themselves Save the Confluence, and they had been convening once or twice a month at the Denny's restaurant in Tuba City in hopes of finding a strategy to solicit opposition to the Escalade project and take the fight to the developers.

To say the odds were not in their favor was an understatement commensurate with the size of the canyon itself. There were only around two dozen of them, almost all of whom were women, and at the time they had few connections, little experience with tribal politics, and almost no financial resources. Nevertheless, Yellowhorse agreed to join the group and began attending their meetings—and within a few months she said yes when they asked her to become the organization's spokesperson.

In that capacity, she was eager to speak to anyone and everyone who was willing to listen to what she had to say—including, it now appeared, Pete and me.

*   *   *

The location was impressive, to say the least. Unlike most overlooks, instead of one's staring into or across the canyon, it was possible to gaze directly *along* it. To the south, less than eight miles away, soared the Palisades of the Desert, the dramatic two-thousand-foot-high rock faces that form the canyon's southeastern wall, shimmering in the rich coppery light. On the far side of the river directly west of the Palisades rose Vishnu Temple, arguably the most famous of the canyon's 147 named peaks, whose summit glinted like a lantern in the topmost window of a castle tower, nearly four thousand feet above its base. Far below, at the bottom of the ascent we had just completed, we could see the Confluence itself.

The sweeping grandeur all but took our breath away—and I understood why the developers had locked onto this spot. There was nothing even remotely like it.

For a long moment, we all stood in silence, staring out at the castellated expanse of buttes and pinnacles and promontories, taking in the wonder of it all, and then Yellowhorse turned to face us.

"You know, there's a myth that we left this landscape—but we never did," she said. "Native peoples have never stopped using these lands, and being a part of these lands."

"You continue to use this place right here?" asked Pete.

She nodded. "This is a special place, a holy place without a roof, because it's the place where people's spirits return after they've passed on." She gestured down toward the Confluence. "My father is here and my mother, my uncles, my father's parents, and my mother's mother, who I never met. Even though their earthly remains are in their graves in Tuba City, this is where their spirits are, and when I come out here, I can hear them, the people who have come before me."

Now Yellowhorse drew our attention to a notch in the rim about a hundred yards in front of her. "That's where the tramway would start." She sketched out how the one-and-a-half-mile-long system of pylons and cables would thread through the notch, descending two thousand vertical feet to the first set of cliffs on the top of the Redwall, and from there dropping another thousand feet to a terminal building perched just above the banks of the Colorado, where an elevated steel walkway would extend more than a hundred yards along the shoreline to an amphitheater, an observation deck, and a restaurant looming directly above the Confluence.

I was familiar with the general details of the project, but this was the first chance I'd been given to visualize it directly, and in the midst of Yellowhorse's explanation, it dawned on me that the route we had just taken to get out of the canyon was no accident. Mathieu and his team had led us up through those cliffs on a line running roughly parallel to that of the proposed cableway to give us an on-the-ground view of what the same journey would look like from the inside of a gondola.

"Up to ten thousand people a day going in and out of there—can you imagine?" Yellowhorse said, interrupting my thoughts. "The size of the bathroom down there will be four thousand square feet, and they'll have to haul all the sewage they collect each day back to the rim every night, probably by using the tramway."

While Pete and I tried to conceive how *that* would work, Yellowhorse sighed and shook her head. "Realistically, we're not against economic development. We just don't want to see it happening at one of our most sacred places."

Then after taking a deep breath, she burst into tears.

It took a few minutes for Yellowhorse to compose herself, and when she resumed speaking, the first thing she did was apologize.

"It's been more than two years, and it still gets to me," she said, drying her eyes on the hem of her skirt, "because I know that if that tramway comes through here, it will dig into the heart of the earth, and I will never be able to come here again to feel the spirits of my family and my ancestors. That's why we're fighting so hard to keep this place pristine. Otherwise it will never be the same for our children, and for their children."

Had the developers made any gestures that might indicate a recognition of what this space meant to her people? I asked.

They had.

Yellowhorse explained that along the section of the rim overlooking the Confluence—not far from where we were standing—Whitmer and his team had pledged to set aside an acre of ground that would be walled off on three sides as a protected zone, inside of which Native Americans would be permitted to conduct prayers and make offerings. In addition, any Navajo tribal elders who wished to visit the Confluence for additional prayers would be allowed to hitch a ride on the tramway, for free.

"They're also planning on building something called a Navajoland Discovery Center," added Yellowhorse, "that will tell the stories of the Navajo and the other tribes' relationships to the canyon. They're saying it will be a chance for visitors to learn about Native cultures and their creation stories."

Did those gestures carry any weight? I asked. Had they softened her objections?

"No." She shook her head. "Absolutely not."

"Why not?" asked Pete.

"Because we don't want to be the Disneyland on the edge of the Grand Canyon. That's not how we want our stories told—we are not 'Pocahontas on the Rim.'"

After I took a moment to think about that, one final question popped into my mind. "So if Lamar Whitmer were here right now and you could speak to him directly, what would you want to say to him?"

"I would just basically want to ask *why*. Why can't you listen to people when we say that this is where we pray, and this is where we place our offerings—not only the Navajo but the Hopi and the Zuni and the Paiute, every tribe that holds the canyon as a sacred space? Why can you not be mindful of that and heed that? Why can you not hear our voices—really *hear* them?"

*   *   *

It was a long ride back to Flagstaff that night, and I spent much of it thinking about Yellowhorse: how her story dovetailed with a wider narrative of all the tribes of the canyon, past and present—and about how little I'd known or cared about any of those stories, up until now.

During the drive, it occurred to me that Pete's and my odyssey might have a reason behind it that was a bit more complicated and challenging than simply celebrating the hundredth anniversary of the National Park System by assaying the finest of its jewels. Although I still wasn't sure exactly what this larger objective might entail, clearly it seemed to be tied to the story of the land's original inhabitants—and to the fact that, as Powell himself had realized, their descendants were still a vital part of the landscape.

Mostly, though, I thought about a trio of lines by the poet and short-story writer Raymond Carver, who understood sadness and loss in the lives of ordinary people, and who wrote with the kind of brevity and precision that stones would employ, if they cared to talk:

> *The places where water comes together*
> *with other water. Those places stand out*
> *in my mind like holy places.*

Those words stayed with me for the rest of the drive as we skirted along the western edge of the Navajo nation, allowing the night to carry us home.

PART VI

The Sudden Poetry of Springs

Every pilgrimage to the desert is a pilgrimage to the self.

There is no place to hide and so we are found.

—Terry Tempest Williams

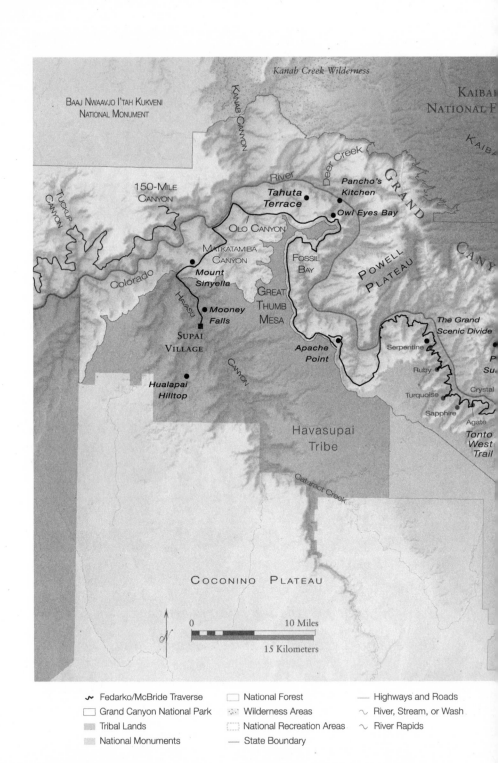

KANAB CANYON

Kanab Creek Wilderness

BAAJ NWAAVJO I'TAH KUKVENI
NATIONAL MONUMENT

KAIBA[

NATIONAL F[

KAIBA

150-MILE
CANYON

River

Deer Creek

Tahuta
Terrace

Pancho's
Kitchen

GRAND

TUCKUP
CANYON

OLO CANYON

Owl Eyes Bay

Colorado

MATKATAMIBA
CANYON

FOSSIL
BAY

POWELL
PLATEAU

CANY

Mount
Sinyella

HAVASU

GREAT

Mooney
Falls

THUMB

MESA

The Grand
Scenic Divide

SUPAI
VILLAGE

CANYON

Apache
Point

Serpentine

P

Su

Ruby

Hualapai
Hilltop

Turquoise

Crystal

Sapphire

Agate

Havasupai
Tribe

Tonto
West
Trail

Cataract Creek

COCONINO   PLATEAU

0   10 Miles

N

15 Kilometers

〰 Fedarko/McBride Traverse   ☐ National Forest   —— Highways and Roads
☐ Grand Canyon National Park   ⠿ Wilderness Areas   ∿ River, Stream, or Wash
▦ Tribal Lands   ⬚ National Recreation Areas   ∿ River Rapids
▦ National Monuments   — State Boundary

Central Grand Canyon

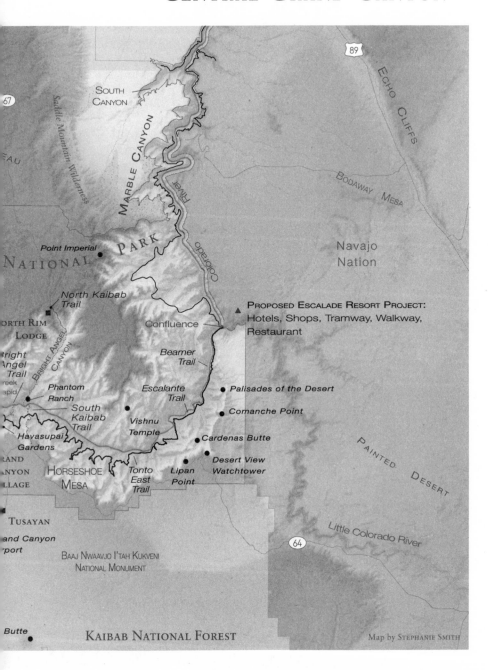

89

ECHO CLIFFS

SOUTH CANYON

67

MARBLE CANYON

Saddle Mountain Wilderness

River

BODAWAY MESA

EAU

Point Imperial

PARK

NATIONAL

North Kaibab Trail

Navajo Nation

ORTH RIM LODGE

Confluence

PROPOSED ESCALADE RESORT PROJECT: Hotels, Shops, Tramway, Walkway, Restaurant

right Angel Trail

BRIGHT ANGEL CANYON

Beamer Trail

Colorado

reek apid

Phantom Ranch

Escalante Trail

Palisades of the Desert

South Kaibab Trail

Comanche Point

Havasupai Gardens

Vishnu Temple

Cardenas Butte

PAINTED DESERT

RAND NYON LLAGE

HORSESHOE MESA

Tonto East Trail

Lipan Point

Desert View Watchtower

TUSAYAN

and Canyon rport

Little Colorado River

64

Baaj Nwaavjo I'tah Kukveni National Monument

Butte

KAIBAB NATIONAL FOREST

Map by STEPHANIE SMITH

CHAPTER 20

The Return of
the Hiking King

If Pete and I had embarked on our venture as two of the most unfit and least worthy wanderers in the history of the canyon, it was also true that we had been trying our best to atone for our sins. Thanks to that effort, we were now returning to Flagstaff in better shape than before, having found some new allies and picked up a few skills. More important, however, we had acquired a new level of respect for the canyon—and armed with this perspective, we understood how imperative it was for us to keep moving.

"We should leave right away," declared Pete, who wanted to return without delay so that we could push through the central section of the canyon—the segment running beneath the most heavily touristed parts of the South Rim—during the coolest months of the year. "We can't afford to waste any time."

He was right. Moving swiftly would enable us to build and maintain the momentum we would need to cross the hottest and driest part of the canyon—the far west—before the temperatures started to soar in late spring. It was compelling logic, undermined only by something that mattered even more than the changing seasons or the distance separating us from the Grand Wash Cliffs.

Back home in Pennsylvania, the person who had first enabled me to find my way to the canyon by handing me a copy of Colin Fletcher's book almost forty years earlier—and who had taught me to hike as a young boy by leading my brother and me through the spilly piles in the strip mine behind my grandparents' house—was dying.

My father was now seventy-six, and he had been successfully battling prostate cancer for the better part of a decade. But during the past year, the disease had come roaring back, extending its tentacles deep into his bones, and just before Pete and I got back to Flagstaff, he had completed several rounds of chemotherapy. The treatments had not gone well, and the side effects had been brutal. When I spoke with my mom on the phone, I was gutted by the realization my family needed me, and that regardless of what our canyon plans might require, I had to fly back to Pittsburgh immediately.

*   *   *

After some discussion, Pete and I agreed that the best path forward was to do something we'd never done in all the years that we'd spent working together: we would have to split up. While I headed off on what would prove to be the first of a series of trips back East, he would restock his provisions, clean his gear, and return to the canyon to keep the project on track by pressing our line forward.

In light of how much trouble we'd gotten ourselves into on the first leg of our journey, I thought it might have been wise to send Pete off in the company of Mathieu or Harlan. They were comfortable letting him go alone, however, because they planned to monitor his progress through his satellite tracker. "If anything goes wrong, we'll know exactly where he is and how to get to him," Mathieu assured me.

They also knew that the section Pete would be tackling was by far the shortest, easiest, and most straightforward segment of the entire journey because it featured something that had been missing up to this point: a trail.

It was actually three trails linked together in a sequence that started at the mouth of the Little Colorado and extended along the south side of the canyon, winding into and out of one tributary drainage after another for the better part of twenty-five river miles until it intersected with Bright Angel Trail, the canyon's most popular rim-to-river tourist path, which led directly to the South Rim. Known as the Tonto East Trail system, it was part of the longest and most assiduously maintained path in the entire park. Its smooth surface, which resembled the kind of buffed single-track favored by mountain bikers, made it easy to walk and virtually impossible to get lost on, the opposite of the kind of bushwhacking we'd been doing ever since leaving Lee's Ferry.

Neither of us liked the idea of separating, not least because it meant that if we made it all the way to the Grand Wash Cliffs, I would have to find a way to circle back and polish off that portion of the Tonto on my own. But there didn't seem to be a better alternative. So in the middle of November, Pete grabbed his pack, hitched a ride back to the same area along the east rim where we'd met Renae Yellowhorse, and dropped back into the canyon by himself.

If all went well, he'd be back in Flagstaff well before the end of the month. Meanwhile, I headed for the airport and caught a flight to Pennsylvania.

*   *   *

Anybody who has ever watched a loved one endure multiple rounds of chemotherapy is familiar with the havoc it can inflict. This was the first time I had witnessed such a thing firsthand, however, and the sight of my father when I walked into the house where I'd grown up left me stunned and reeling.

He was sitting in his armchair surrounded by a stack of books and multiple pairs of reading glasses, and even though there was a fire in the woodstove, he was wearing a wool knit cap. When he removed the hat, I could see that almost all of his hair was gone.

My mother had prepared me for this, so I wasn't completely shocked by the sight of his bald head or the absence of the mustache he'd worn for as long as I could remember. But what took me aback was that the poisons had stripped him of his eyebrows and even his eyelashes, which left him looking confused and helpless, like a baby bird that had been blown out of its nest by a windstorm and dropped on the floor of the forest.

The chemo had ravaged the rest of him, too. His hands and arms were covered in bruises, and his fingers looked thin and brittle, as if the bones were on the verge of breaking. The only part of him that seemed to have been spared were a few wisps of hair at the very top of his head that formed a kind of white corona, like cottonwood duff.

"You can touch it if you want," he said softly.

When I hesitated, he repeated the invitation. "It's okay. Go ahead."

As I touched the fluff, the tips of my fingers brushed his scalp. The skin felt as dry and delicate as the frond of a dead fern, and the sensation left me with the chilling realization that along with his eyebrows and his eyelashes, something else had been taken from him, too.

My dad had never been the kind of man who had worn his strength on his sleeve, but in the years before he had met my mother and started a family, he had been a marine, and that part of him had always been evident in the way he carried himself. You could see it in the rigidity of his back, the straightness of his neck, and the squareness of his shoulders. Now the marine was gone, replaced by a frail old man who had stepped over the threshold demarcating the end of the autumn of his life, and was in the process of moving toward whatever lay beyond.

I was in Pittsburgh for only a few days, and during that time, I later realized, I underwent a transition of my own, a turning point in how I saw my father. I had arrived with the memory of the vigorous and energetic person he had once been, and I left with the image of a man I barely recognized, a shadow of the person I had known.

When my parents dropped me at the airport, I did something I'd never done before. Instead of grabbing my bags and hustling straight inside after a quick goodbye, I lingered on the curb and waved as they drove off, my mom at the wheel, my dad glancing back at me from the passenger seat. After they had disappeared, I kept waving, not knowing if this would be my last farewell.

When I finally turned to enter the terminal, I felt as if I were being pulled in two directions, torn between his journey and mine.

*   *   *

At sunset on the final Friday before Thanksgiving, a day after I'd returned to Arizona, a tempest began tearing through downtown Flagstaff with the apparent aim of stripping the last remaining bits of foliage from the branches of every tree along Grand Canyon Avenue. With each renewed gust, the backs of the two rocking chairs on my porch thumped furiously against the front of the house. Amid all the commotion, I failed to register a knock at the door until it swung open and Pete walked in, looking as if he'd been sleeping in a pile of dead leaves.

"What's for dinner?" he demanded. "And don't tell me it's freeze-dried shepherd's pie."

Chicken and dumplings, made from a recipe my dad had given me before I left, had been simmering in a Dutch oven for hours. As I ladled him a bowl, he pulled a stool next to the stove and launched into an account of his solo excursion on the Tonto: the smooth progress he'd made, thanks to the trail; the cooler temperatures he'd enjoyed, now that late fall had arrived; and how he'd seen almost no other hikers, which meant he'd had no one to talk to—and how lonely that had felt. But mostly he talked about the brooding November light that had enabled him to take some unusual photographs, including one image that seemed to excite him more than any of the others.

He'd taken the shot several miles downstream from the Confluence when his gaze was pulled up toward Coronado Butte, one of the most distinctive features in that part of the canyon, whose square-headed summit dominated the skyline. A storm was moving in off the desert rangelands of the Mojave, more than a hundred miles to the west, and as the clouds poured over the walls, they created a show of light and shadow unlike anything else he'd ever witnessed either above or below the rims. In the foreground, sunbeams were refracting through sheens of mist hanging from the cliffs like curtains, and behind that light show loomed the wall of the storm itself.

The drama had lasted for less than thirty seconds before the clouds closed in, turning everything gray. But during that interval, Pete had just enough time to snap off a single frame.

"What do you think?" he asked as he dialed up the image in the viewfinder and handed me his camera.

The ragged scrim of mist imparted a disconcerting sense that the canyon went on forever, bounded by neither space nor time, and that if you gazed into it long enough, you might disappear into that vortex and never emerge.

"Whoa," I murmured, stunned by its spectral moodiness.

The clouds were as gauzy as the strands of hair on my dad's head, as bruised looking as the marks on his skin, and as I took in those details, I marveled at the realization that Pete's image, shot from deep within the canyon, somehow conjured what it had felt like to witness my father being swallowed up by the arrival of winter.

Absorbed by the photograph, I failed to hear a set of knocks coming from the front porch and allowed the pounding to continue until the door suddenly swung open to reveal a figure far more disheveled than Pete. A man so haggard and drawn, wearing a beard so bushy and clothing so tattered, that at first I took him for some sort of vagabond or drifter. Then I peered more closely at his face, and recognized someone I had last seen almost two months earlier.

Rich Rudow was back.

He wasn't alone. Almost a dozen other people spilled in behind him, including Kelly, Harlan, and Dave Nally. Once inside, everybody headed straight for the kitchen so that Rich, who bore a look that blended deep weariness with ravenous hunger, could get to the food.

He collapsed onto the same stool by the stove where Pete had been sitting and barely said a word as he shoveled dumplings into his mouth, moaning with pleasure.

Halfway through his third bowl, he finally put down his spoon and took a deep breath. "We just got out of the canyon this afternoon," he said with a sigh. "I don't even know where to begin."

"That's easy," I said. "Start when you said goodbye to us back in October after Peter and I bailed on our first leg, just before you guys disappeared into the Redwall."

*   *   *

From the second they were rid of Pete and me, Rich and his team began racing across the top of the Redwall like a pack of unleashed deerhounds. They spent the next several days scampering from one pothole to the next as they clawed their way into and out of a series of immense side canyons that dropped off the North Rim. Even during the steepest climbs, they refused to slacken their pace, and soon they were doubling the distance they'd covered each day with Pete and me in tow.

Right off the bat, they caught a break with the weather when the heat wave that had dogged us from Lee's Ferry finally broke, and the temperatures dropped into the eighties. That marked the start of a marvelous one-week stretch in which the hike became everything they'd dreamed it might be: a strong, well-oiled team, moving fast over glorious rock through crisp dawns, demanding afternoons, and nights drenched in starlight. Each day glided smoothly into the next, and before they knew it, they'd all but made up the time they'd lost. But just as they were poised to tie back into their original plan—the schedule designed to deliver them to the Grand Wash Cliffs before the first snowfall—autumn's crystalline clarity clouded over, and to everyone's astonishment it started to rain.

The first shower struck as they were side-hilling across a talus field a hundred feet above the river. As they ran for higher ground, a thin waterfall spouted from the lip of the Kaibab Limestone, more than four thousand feet above their heads. Ten minutes later, a slurry of brown water brimming with gravel, rocks the size of cannonballs, and shattered tree limbs filled up the bed of the wash not fifty feet from their position, then roared downslope over the next set of cliffs toward the Colorado.

That night, crackling flashes of lightning lit up the inner canyon all the way from the river to the rimrock while the walls echoed with rolling booms of thunder and the air was swept by sheets of rain. The wind blew with enough force to bend the pair of trekking poles that served as the main support for the mid, their emergency tent, making them vibrate like the mast of a ship under too much sail. Rich, who lay adjacent to the poles, clasped them between his arms and chest until daybreak to ensure they held.

An isolated autumn storm or two isn't unusual in the Southwest. But this marked the start of a fall unlike any other in more than three decades, stretching all the way back to the storms in the winter of 1983 that had powered Kenton Grua's speed run in the *Emerald Mile*. In a five-week onslaught, the canyon was hammered by an almost unbroken series of heavy storms that rode the jet stream in a phalanx, with only a few days separating each from the next.

Exposed to the full fury of the weather, Rich and his crew spent entire days battling the wind and the rain while black clouds from three or four separate cells circled in confusion above them. To stay ahead of the flash floods triggered by each storm—and thereby avoid being cut off from their caches and running out of food—they were forced into a series of back-to-back races. They forded drainages where the water rose to their knees and sometimes past their thighs, staggering under the weight of their packs to keep from losing their balance, bracing with their trekking poles, terrified by the knowledge that if a flood materialized, they would be swept to their deaths amid a churning cauldron of mud and debris.*

Soon their clothing, their packs, and the tent were soaked. Each evening, crammed inside the mid, they spent hours scraping mud from their shoes and applying glue to the soles to keep them going another day. On some nights, they slept only a few hours before waking, breaking down the wet tent and hastening through the darkness to get across another big side canyon before the next storm arrived.

*   *   *

In the midst of confronting these challenges, they saw things that few hikers ever witness. The biggest storms generated scores of waterfalls, and they could look up and spot them pouring simultaneously from every set of ledges. Some were chocolate brown, others russet red or bright orange. Each was laden with broken bits of gravel, small pebbles, and every now and then an impossibly huge boulder sailing atop the debris like a doomed ship with a storm-severed anchor chain. Together,

---

* Among those hikers who have been overtaken by a flash flood in the canyon, almost all have perished. The bodies of many were stripped of clothing and so broken that it was almost impossible to recognize their features; others disappeared entirely after being wedged beneath tons of debris. Among the handful who survived was a man from Chicago named John McCue, who sought refuge behind a large boulder in the bed of a narrow side canyon with his sister and brother-in-law, as they were engulfed in a chest-high slurry of water and debris. McCue's companions drowned and their bodies were swept through the side canyon into the Colorado, where they were discovered several weeks later, thirty and forty-six miles downstream. McCue somehow pulled himself from the floodwaters after being tumbled for more than a mile. He emerged from the maelstrom battered, covered in mud, and crying brown tears because the force of the water had peeled open his eyelids, forcing silt into the tear ducts.

these sights presented a breathtaking spectacle of beauty laced with menace, a demonstration of how the world inside the canyon is dismantled and reassembled with each new weather event.

These images and many others—the rounded bellies of clouds scudding far above, as if they were a school of pearl-colored fish glimpsed from the floor of the ocean; the golden pillars of light that occasionally pierced the sky to touch the tops of distant mesas, like columns supporting the weight of heaven itself—would lodge firmly in their memories and remain there for the rest of their lives. But all of that was reserved for later. For now, they were beaten and weary, worn past the point of recovery, and one by one they began to drop out.

Mike St. Pierre, whose knees ached so badly that he was having trouble sleeping at night, was the first to go. As originally planned, he left the company when they reached Phantom Ranch, but in far worse shape than he'd anticipated and in the company of the ever-reliable Jean-Philippe Clark, who came down to retrieve him.

Shortly after that, Dave suffered his first big setback one evening when he sat down on a rock and accidentally tipped backward into a Prickly Pear cactus, driving more than a hundred spines through his shirt and into his back. Rich and Chris extracted around sixty of them, but even with tweezers they were unable to pull out the tiniest spines, hairlike needles known as glochids that are notorious for working their way beneath the skin.

Dave had already been feeling ill enough that he was forced to pause every few steps to catch his breath. He suspected he had developed some sort of infection, possibly in his lungs, and might need to see a doctor. Whatever the cause, the cumulative demands on his body—the endless hours, the relentless pace, the agony of an already-heavy pack made even heavier by waterlogged gear—were now made worse by the cactus quills embedded up and down his spine.

"Oh, my aching back and bones!" he scrawled in his journal one night.

Seven days after Mike exited, Dave was finally forced to call it quits. He hiked out on a little-used trail to the North Rim that marked the exact halfway point of the trek, in the company of his three daughters, whom he had alerted via satellite text.

Although he would later insist this wasn't true, the delays that Pete and I had imposed during the earliest part of the hike, and the strain of trying to make up the time that we had squandered, had probably cost Dave his thru-hike.

Meanwhile, in keeping with the pact they had made, Rich and Chris kept pushing.

*   *   *

In late October, a respite finally arrived—the same pocket of bright, clear weather that had enabled Pete and me to return to the canyon with Matthieu, Kelly, and Harlan and make our way to the Little Colorado with so few problems. Although the weather held for more than a week, Chris now had a pronounced limp, thanks to a dull pain in his right foot that refused to subside. (X-rays would later reveal that he was hiking on a stress fracture in the fifth metatarsal.) And for the first time, Rich was in trouble, too.

He was feeling weak, and despite his intake of more than five thousand calories a day, he was rapidly losing weight. Then he started suffering from bouts of nausea, followed by severe diarrhea. By the time they reached a campground on the North Rim known as Toroweap, on the forty-first day of their journey, Rich could barely walk.

In desperation, he sent a satellite text to Dr. Tom Myers back in Flagstaff, who diagnosed the problem as an intestinal infection from giardia, a parasite Rich had probably picked up by drinking untreated water at a place called Dragon Creek, thanks to a small colony of beavers that inhabited the lower reaches of the drainage.

Myers immediately prescribed antibiotics, and the medication was flown by small plane into a remote ranch on the North Rim called the Bar 10, which boasted its own airstrip. A ranch hand then drove an ATV eight miles through a chain of volcanic fields to Rich and Chris's camp, where the package was handed off.

Over the next few days, Rich slowly regained his strength as he and Chris shuffled across a massive set of benches and promontories that extend through the far-western part of the park. But to their dismay, the weather again took a turn for the worse, and as they pushed into the middle weeks of November, an additional set of storms came at them, one after another: dark anvil-headed cloud banks suspended thousands of feet in the sky, each connected to the ground by a thick gray stanchion of heavy rain, studded with hail.

Once again, they endured soaked gear, nights spent shivering in the tent, and frigid dawns with everything coated in rime. Once again, too, their intended routes through the side canyons were systematically cut off by flash floods, forcing them to revise their plans and then modify those amended options with even less attractive alternatives.

Eventually, they fell back on a series of daring lines that drew on all the knowledge they had mustered from the years of preparation they had poured into this venture: bold shortcuts across crumbling Supai ledges and dicey scrambles through half-remembered breaks in the Redwall to reach their last caches—the ones containing their final resupplies of food, plus critically important stashes of cold-weather gear.

The meticulously laid blueprint of the final leg of their journey had to be torn up and redrawn several times before they outfoxed the very last flood and got across a drainage called Surprise Canyon. A few days later, they descended to the river just upstream from the Grand Wash Cliffs, where they broke out their pack rafts and crossed the Colorado to a sandy beach.

Standing on the shore to cheer their arrival and shuttle them back to Flagstaff was a group that included Dave, plus a number of the friends and well-wishers who had seen them off from Lee's Ferry back in September.

*   *   *

On the drive back, they tallied up the numbers. The continuous traverse that Rich had first envisioned more than five years earlier had taken fifty-seven days, one day longer than planned. During that time they had covered a linear distance of roughly seven hundred miles while completing almost three hundred thousand vertical feet of climbing, equivalent to ascending from Base Camp to the summit of Mount Everest twenty-six times. But the most remarkable figures were those connected to the weather.

At the start of their venture, they'd anticipated having to set up their emergency shelter no more than four or five nights during the entire hike. Thanks to the storms, however, they'd been forced to deploy the mid twenty-one times, while witnessing thirteen separate flash floods.*

By any of those metrics, theirs was an astounding achievement. But perhaps the most graphic calibration of the toll exacted by the ordeal was that Rich, who was in superb physical condition at the outset of the hike with an exceptionally low body-fat percentage, had shed more than twenty pounds, almost 15 percent of his body weight.

"That was the hardest thing I've ever done in my life," he croaked as he laid into his fourth bowl of food while shaking his head at what he and Chris had pulled off.

By now, the party was in full swing. With the exception of Mike, who was back in Maine, and Chris—who had wisely made a beeline for home to see his fiancée—almost everyone else who was part of Rich's expedition and ours was inside the house. Harlan's sister Marieke was there, too, along with her partner, Aaron. Even Dr. Myers had shown up.

Later that evening, I glanced over at Rich, who still hadn't moved from his perch next to the stove, and was struck by the thought that this man had just returned from leading perhaps the most experienced and best-prepared team ever to attempt a thru-hike of the canyon—and that despite all of their preparation and knowledge, one member of the squad had been physically shattered, and the other two had barely made it through.

---

* For comparison, consider George Steck, a contemporary of Harvey Butchart's who spent more than twenty-five years hiking the canyon. During that time, the total number of flash floods that Steck encountered was five.

The profile of his body—gaunt, drained, a shell of what it had been just two months earlier—offered a harbinger of the challenges that lay in store for Pete and me in the weeks and months ahead as we set out to tackle the central portion of our own journey during the coldest, darkest season of the year.

"You and Pete really need to think about moving soon," Rich advised, catching my eye as he reached for another bowl of dumplings. "It's shaping up to be one hell of a winter in the canyon."

CHAPTER 21

Gems

"How about you stop monitoring your Instagram feed for, like, five seconds and pay attention to the road, huh?" I snarled as I clutched the wheel of my truck in both hands while scanning the forest on either side of the highway. "I'm trying to spot the elk on the road."

"Relax," said Pete, glancing up briefly from the passenger seat before returning to his cell phone. "They get out of the way most of the time."

"Yeah, and when they don't, you mow through their legs and the rest of them comes flying through the front windshield. It's even less appealing than freezing to death in the canyon, which is apparently what we're about to do."

"Always so *negative*," Pete muttered. "Do you have to look on the dark side of *everything*?"

In truth, we were both on edge. Although we had hoped to follow Rich's counsel and launch our next push as soon as possible, the holidays had intervened, as did several additional trips back East to see my father—who had been in the hospital twice, thanks to infections that his immune system could no longer fend off—and we'd lost the entire month of December. Now it was mid-January, and conditions were frigid enough that elk were drifting down from the snow-draped flanks of the San Francisco Peaks as we made our way north through the wintry night.

Two hours later, we rolled past park headquarters, whose buildings were buttoned-up and whose windows were shuttered, into an empty parking lot dusted with spindrift that rose in the air, curling like cold smoke. There we hoisted our packs, each of which was stuffed with more than forty-five pounds of warm clothing and heavy winter gear, and walked beneath the branches of the piñons to the edge of the canyon's vast atrium, cast in the ghostly blue glow that precedes sunrise, filled with a silence as immense and heavy as the stone itself.

During the peak part of the summer, thousands of people flocked here each day, but at this hour in the middle of the offseason, the place was deserted. Nothing stirred as each of us strapped on a set of MICROspikes, traction devices resembling lightweight crampons, and began clomping down the steep switchbacks along the upper portion of the Bright Angel Trail, which Pete had ascended just before Thanksgiving—and which, despite its popularity, I had never once hiked during all my years as a boatman.

For the first mile and a half, the trail was coated in four inches of ice, and the only sound was the clink and crunch of the spikes beneath our feet as we shuffled along, moving deeper into the rock. Before long, the ice had given way to snow, followed by frozen mud, which turned squishy as the switchbacks delivered us to the base of the Redwall, just over three thousand vertical feet below the rim.

Up ahead, a line of massive Fremont Cottonwoods formed a canopy arching over a little creek whose waters ran amber in the morning light. We had arrived at Indian Garden,* the most heavily visited oasis inside the canyon. From early spring through late autumn, when the banks of the creek are covered in flowers and the foliage in the trees is alive with birds, the place teems with day hikers and campers. Now there was no one.

We hustled past the darkened ranger station with its broad front porch, through an empty campground, and beyond a set of wooden

---

* The name of this place has since been changed, and we will get to the reasons why in good time.

benches to the far end of the trees, where we emerged beneath an open sky. The shoulders of the Redwall and Muav cliffs that enveloped the garden on three sides had now swung open like a set of castle gates, eight hundred feet tall.

Directly in front of us, a footpath cut across a tableland from east to west. This was the Tonto Trail, and back in November Pete had traversed its eastern section. Now we would follow the trail's western arm until it came to an end at a tributary called Bass Canyon.

"Look familiar?" I asked Pete.

"Feels like I came through just yesterday," he said, nodding. "It's not something you easily forget."

*   *   *

The Tonto Platform is a broad bench roughly thirty-five miles long and almost a quarter mile wide that dominates the central reaches of the canyon's interior on both sides of the Colorado. The surface of the platform, overlaid with a dull purple-and-greenish layer of rock known as the Bright Angel Shale and almost entirely devoid of trees, is dotted with clumps of blackbrush and turpentine broom that grudgingly surrender to the odd agave or Prickly Pear cactus. Scattered randomly amid the brush are blocks of limestone the size of washing machines or refrigerators that appear to have been cast off by the nearby cliffs with the disdain of a motorist flinging litter out the window of a passing car.

Initially, to my eye, the Tonto appeared monotonous and flat, but as we began making our way along the first segment, I could see that the trail continuously swerved back and forth as it followed a series of promontories, each extending out like a finger toward the centerline of the canyon. As we worked our way toward the tip of the first spur, the brush gradually tapered off until we found ourselves standing on a promontory covered with sharp bits of gravel. There, the ground gave way and I found myself gazing down through almost a thousand feet of air to take in a feature that I had seen many times from the bottom during my years on the river, but never from above.

This was the Inner Granite Gorge, a dramatic V-shaped cleft that forms a canyon within the canyon. Within this narrow world, all but invisible from most points along the rim, the river looks nothing like it does upstream. There are no wide sand beaches, no lush bands of foliage lining the banks, and as the width of the canyon tightens, the constriction amps the river's fury, as if charging it with electricity. Some of the biggest rapids in the West are down there, vicious cauldrons such as Hermit and Granite and Horn Creek that can flip a two-ton motor raft upside down in the blink of an eye. But the most impressive thing about the gorge is its walls, which plummet directly into the water, as if arrowing straight for the center of the earth.

The tops of those walls are composed of chocolate-colored Tapeats Sandstone, formed more than 500 million years ago. Directly underneath is an unconformity, a line of contact between two layers, where at least ten vertical miles of stone representing more than 1.2 billion years—a span of time greater than the age of all the other strata combined—has been worn away and is now missing. Beneath that gap lay the unfathomably thick recesses of the darkest, densest rock in the entire canyon, the anchor and cornerstone for everything else.

Each layer in the canyon is imposing in its own way, but none is stranger or more otherworldly than the Vishnu Formation, an ancient form of metamorphic schist, blacker than obsidian and marbled with veins of pinkish granite and alabaster quartz, that looks as if it were forged from an ore mined on some other galaxy. It belongs to a murkier and more enigmatic period in the planet's past, an era that extends back almost a full 2 billion years to a time predating the arrival of the first animals, the first plants, even the earliest fungi, when life on earth had not progressed beyond single-celled bacteria.

"Do you think this is what geologists have in mind when they refer to deep time?" wondered Pete, peering over the edge to study the schist.

"Well, it's definitely the craton," I said.

"What's a craton?"

"The nucleus of the continent. We're basically looking at the geologic bedrock of North America."

*   *   *

As the Tonto Trail wanders west, it keeps more or less to the same level, weaving into and back out of a series of tributary canyons of greatly varying size, much like a section of coastline that is broken up between projecting headlands and their corresponding inlets or bays. In the days to come, as we worked our way from one embayment to the next, it became clear that we were being offered a glimpse into some of the smallest and brightest of the canyon's hidden treasures—glittering little jewels created by rainfall or snowmelt on the rimlands high above. In a journey that can take days, years, even centuries, depending on the pathway, moisture seeps into the thin soil, percolating through a complex network of fractures and faults in the underlying layers of rock until the groundwaters eventually emerge in the form of what the writer Wallace Stegner once called "the sudden poetry of springs."

Those springs are referred to as "native waters," in contrast with the "exotic waters" of the river far below, which derive in large part from snow deposited hundreds of miles away in the Rocky Mountains of Wyoming and Colorado. Except in a handful of places such as Indian Garden, where the flow of groundwater is sufficient to drive a robust stream, most springs in the canyon are tiny. In a landscape as arid as this, however, the thinnest trickle is sufficient to incite a riot of greenery and movement. A spring-fed pool no wider than a hubcap can support a luxuriant garden of reeds and bulrushes shrouded in lime-colored curtains of Maidenhair Fern, along with clusters of cattails and horsetails tucked amid beds of watercress so verdant they seem to glow from within.*

Along this section of the Tonto lie nearly a dozen of these springs, many of which, fittingly, are named after a semiprecious stone—Crystal, Agate, Sapphire, Turquoise, Emerald, Ruby, and Serpentine—no two

---

* According to Larry Stevens, who runs the Springs Stewardship Institute in Flagstaff, the collective acreage covered by seeps and springs amounts to less than 0.01 percent of the canyon's total surface area—yet each site supports a density of plant species one hundred to five hundred times greater than that of the surrounding desert.

of which are exactly alike. While some smear themselves across the face of a cliff to form what are called hanging gardens, others inveigle their way through the rocky debris of a talus slope, dribbling along the ground for only a short distance before they either dry up entirely or disappear back into the earth.

They can also be inscrutably fickle—here one day, gone the next, vanishing altogether for weeks or months, only to return according to timetables known solely to themselves. A few are so isolated that they foster species that evolve entirely in isolation, plants and insects that are endemic to a single water feature. (A pair of springs just below the South Rim in the Monument Creek drainage, for example, are home to a unique cluster of redbud trees that produce white rather than purple blossoms, while seeps in other parts of the canyon host rare or one-of-a-kind populations of millipedes, water bugs, and riparian beetles, many of which can be found nowhere else.)

Regardless of its size or rate of flow, each of these springs amounts to a pocket-size miracle: an act of defiance against the encircling desert where the air thrums with insects, the foliage resounds with birdsong, and if there is sand, it is damp enough to record the comings and goings of the nimble-footed night creatures that pay a visit to the pools between sunset and sunrise: the deer and the sheep, the skunks and the bobcats, the lions and the pocket mice, each dropping by, regular as clockwork, for a few sips of water.

For the better part of the next week, Pete and I spent every day moving from one of these gems to the next. As we passed through the head of each alcove, we entered another cloister of greenery so exotic and vibrant that it felt as if we were stepping into a procession of hobbit dens carpeted with moss and wreathed in noonday shade. Then the trail would draw us away from the warrens and recesses of that particular side canyon and beckon us back onto yet another headland with yet another breathtaking view of the inner gorge, where once again we could hear the roar of the river and gaze down upon its roiling lines of current while taking in the sweep and roll of the wide terraces beneath an even wider sky.

Sometimes we opted to spend the night far out on those points, seduced by the sweeping views and the sense of unfettered wildness. But just as often we allowed ourselves to be pulled into a protective niche and camp next to the whiskey-colored pools set in the shadow-polished slickrock, where we would be sung to sleep by the metronome of moving water.

During those days and nights, I fell so thoroughly under the spell of the Tonto that every plane and angle of the landscape seemed to shimmer with fresh radiance. The gorgeous texture of the plum-colored gravel strewn over the ground. The waxy crimson fruit of the Prickly Pear cactus and the brittle mint-green leaves of the rabbitbrush. The steely-blue casing of the sky.

On we went, each successive swing leading us farther west. The days were just warm enough for us to welcome the touch of the sun, but never hot enough that we broke into a sweat. The nights were crisp and chilled, and in the mornings when we awoke, the skins of our sleeping bags crackled with frost.

*   *   *

In the evenings when we halted, my thoughts often turned toward my father and the debts I owed to him that I had never repaid. Surrounded by the beauty of the Tonto, I was struck by how deeply I'd been permitted to drink from the canyon's cup of wonder, and how stingy I'd been about sharing those gifts with the person who had first pointed me toward this place, many years ago.

In all the time that I'd devoted to this landscape, first on the river and now along the ramparts of rock, I had never once bothered to reach out and invite him to experience it for himself.

"Hey, Dad," I could have said anytime in the past fifteen years, "let's make a plan to get you out here so that you can see something bigger than the spilly piles back home."

"Thank you for asking," he would have replied. "When do you want me to come?"

I was having this imaginary conversation with him for perhaps the fifth or sixth time one night while Pete and I sat together, quietly sharing a cup of hot chocolate, when our camp was flooded with the white glow of the moon, which had just risen over the rimrock. Looking at the cliffs above, I found myself wondering why the upper walls had suddenly come alive with tiny flashes, as if a host of fireflies had invaded the canyon.

The most recent storm had blanketed the highest ledges and terraces in a layer of fresh snow whose crystals were now shimmering in the moonlight in a way that made it look as if the air itself was twinkling. It was strange and wondrous, the kind of vision that can make one's heart skip a beat.

"Do you wish your dad could have seen this?" asked Pete, who knew me well enough that he could sometimes read my thoughts.

"Yeah."

"And are you feeling like you should have spent more time with him, and now it's too late?"

"Maybe."

"Do you feel guilty because you're out here instead of back there with him?"

"I think I like it better when we talk less," I said. "How about we do that now?"

"So do you think it's possible," he continued, ignoring my request, "that part of what we're doing out here right now might involve a dream that's not just yours, but his, too?"

"I have no idea."

"I think you do. And I think that if he could see the way the snow is glittering up there in the dark, he would probably tell you that you need to keep going and drink it all in."

*   *   *

Talks such as this were always brief because on most evenings neither Peter nor I could stay awake for more than a few minutes. We were on the move from dawn to twilight, rarely stopping for a break. The trail enabled us to cover distances that would have been unthinkable during the fall—up to twenty miles each day—and by the end of that week, we were rapidly approaching a transition point where the canyon undergoes a dramatic change.

Not far from a place called Elves Chasm, the Tonto Platform would abruptly vanish beneath a wall of travertine limestone. The platform wouldn't reemerge for another ninety miles downstream and would never again display the breadth or expansiveness it achieved in the central part of the canyon. Beyond that point, we had been told, things turn wild. Out there, the terrain would be harsher, riskier, more remote, than anything we'd yet faced. But before we could tackle those challenges, we had some business to take care of.

First, we needed to replenish our supplies by climbing back up to the rim to rendezvous with Harlan Taney, who would shuttle us back to park headquarters to assemble the heaviest loads of the entire traverse—more than fifty pounds of food, ropes, helmets, harnesses, slings, ascenders, carabiners, and other climbing gear. In addition to that, we also had an appointment with a woman from another Native tribe who, like Renae Yellowhorse, was hoping to speak with us about her people's ties to the canyon.

On our final day on the Tonto, we arrived at Bass Canyon, turned into its drainage, and began climbing, moving fast to get as close as possible to the rim before we ran out of daylight. By evening, having ascended both the Redwall and the Supai, we bedded down for a few hours on a patch of dirt beneath the bare branches of a dead piñon tree. When we awoke at 3:00 a.m., tiny pellets of ice were coming down hard, pelting us as we resumed our race through the frigid darkness to the top.

Timing was critical. To reach us, Harlan and his crew would be traversing eight miles on an unpaved road of frozen mud topped with a thin coating of snow. After retrieving us, they'd have to make it back to the highway no later than 9:30 a.m., when the snow would melt and the mud would turn to impassable goop. If we forced them to wait, their vehicles would bog down, and we would all be stranded on the plateau.

We hit the snow line a few minutes after leaving camp and spent the next several hours breaking through the frozen crust. We topped out on the rim just before dawn, and there we watched the first rays of sunlight spill into the canyon, turning every east-facing facet of rock pink.

Within fifteen minutes, we heard the sound of engines and turned as three vehicles—two Polaris ATVs and a Jeep—lurched through the junipers and skidded to a stop. The drivers on both ATVs were bundled in Carhartt overalls, wool hats, ski goggles, and bright blue rubber kitchen gloves with cuffs that went halfway up the elbows.

"What's up with all the clothing?" I asked, shouting to be heard over the sound of the motor.

"You'll see," snapped Harlan. "Climb in—we're on a clock."

They drove as fast as the road permitted, accelerating on the straight stretches and drifting madly through the turns, and as the sun rose and the air warmed, the mud began to soften. Soon one of the Polarises bogged down and had to be winched free. Then it refused to start, so we had to cable it to the back of the Jeep and pull it like a toboggan.

By the time we finally hit pavement, the road had turned to soup, and when we rolled into park headquarters at midmorning, everyone was slathered with mud.

CHAPTER 22

The Woman in the White Deerskin Dress

We spent the rest of that day and a good chunk of the following morning cleaning gear, gathering provisions, and trying to figure out how to stuff everything we needed for the next segment of the hike into our packs. In the midst of those preparations, we received word that the woman who wanted to meet with us was waiting at the head of the Bright Angel Trail.

She was sitting on a stone wall in the bright winter sun, just a few feet from where we'd started our previous leg, and she looked to be about sixty. She had warm brown eyes and long black hair streaked with gray, and she had arrived in some of her finest clothing, which included brown leggings, a bright red shawl, and a pair of red moccasins. She had also painted her face with streaks of hematite, but what stood out above everything else was her dress.

It was fashioned from soft deerskin and held together with a white belt studded with silver and turquoise, but its most salient feature was its color, which was bone white. Clad in its folds, she looked immaculate and regal, like an empress of the desert.

"My name is Dianna Sue White Dove Uqualla," she said, "although in the place where my people live, which you'll be passing through in a few weeks, everybody just calls me Baby Sue."

Then she reached into her pocket. "Here—I've brought something for each of you."

In her hand, she held a pair of tiny brown pouches made of the same leather as her moccasins, each with its own little drawstring. She told us they were filled with tobacco and instructed us to tie them around our necks and wear them under our shirts for the duration of our journey.

"Every morning when you get up, crumple some sage leaves in your hand and rub them over your faces—that way the land will come to know that you are there," she told us. "And whenever you reach a spring, open these pouches and sprinkle some of your tobacco to express your thanks. This will be your armor and your protection."

Although we were touched by the gifts, her words left us slightly confused. We might not be veterans of the canyon just yet, but we no longer felt like complete rookies, either. Was it truly necessary to protect ourselves by tossing around bits of tobacco, and did we really need to inform the land of our presence with sage leaves?

"Oh, yes, absolutely," she said as she read the expression on my face and sensed my skepticism. "This is our *home* that you will be walking through."

If her home has a central axis, it is a bright creek lined with cottonwoods and willows nestled deep inside a side canyon more than thirty miles to the west of where Ms. Uqualla now sat. For the better part of a millennium, this small haven has stood as perhaps the closest thing that North America has ever had to a Shangri-la, as well as the anchor and lodestar of the Havasupai, a tribe whose story is as closely tied to the landscape as the native waters that run through the springs on the canyon's walls.

*   *   *

Western scholars have wrangled vehemently over exactly where the tribe originally came from, and when they first arrived in the canyon. Some experts contend that the Havasupai, whose name translates as "People of the Blue-Green Waters," migrated from the lowlands to the south as early as AD 600, while others insist they hail from the scrublands of the Great Basin in present-day Nevada, and that they didn't arrive until sometime around 1350. But the white researchers all seem to agree that the tribe's dialect belongs to an ancient family of languages—one of the oldest in North America—whose footprint extends from western Arizona all the way to Baja California.

As for the Havasupai themselves, however, they say that it is impossible for them to have come from anywhere else or to have arrived in the canyon by any particular date. In their view, they have inhabited this part of the world since time immemorial, which means that regardless of whatever theories the experts might claim to have teased forth, there has never been a time when the Havasupai identity wasn't tied directly to *Havsuwa*, known to outsiders as Havasu Canyon. It was here that they gained a sense of themselves as a distinctive society whom neighboring tribes would come to honor as the "guardians of the Grand Canyon," a people whose understanding of the chasm's interior ran deeper than anyone else's.

Although the Havasupai's traditional knowledge embraced such diverse matters as the terrain, the animals, and the weather, in no area were they more qualified than in the field of phytology, the study of the plants and their secrets. Like the Paiute, their seminomadic neighbors on the north side of the canyon, and the Hualapai, directly to the west, the Havasupai possessed such a comprehensive grasp of botany that each leaf, seed, stem, and root had a name, a timetable, and a specific set of uses. In addition to their knowing what to eat and when to gather it—agave hearts in the spring, Prickly Pear fruits in late summer, mesquite beans and piñon nuts in the fall—their expertise ran deep enough that a stroll through the brush could yield medicines, tools, and even beauty products such as the roots of the Narrow Leaf yucca (which yields a lather for shampooing one's hair).

They were more than just expert gatherers, however. Like their Hopi and Navajo neighbors to the east, they were also farmers, and their knack for tilling and cultivation enabled them to coax far more than the standard array of corn, beans, squash, melons, and pumpkins from the fertile bottomlands along Havasu Creek. The trees in their orchards were heavy with a mix of both indigenous and non-native fruits that included apricots and plums, apples and pears, pomegranates and peaches, plus two types of fig, black and green.

Each spring, members of the tribe would reopen the network of irrigation canals that ran for miles along the banks of the creek to freshen the fields before planting began at the first flight of the cotton-wood seeds in March. Then they would carefully tend their gardens throughout the summer until the final corn crop signaled the arrival of the Peach Festival in August, which drew not only the Navajo, the Hualapai, and the Hopis, but even members of the distant Zuni nation, almost 250 miles to the southeast.

In addition to feasting and celebration, a lively exchange of goods took place in which the Havasupai traded hematite, soft white buck-skins, and beautifully crafted baskets for turquoise from other parts of the Colorado Plateau, seashells from the Pacific, and scarlet macaw feathers from the jungles of Mexico. When the festivities concluded and the guests departed, the tribe then packed up and prepared to embark on a migration whose itinerary, in a reversal of the birds that move up and down the canyon walls with the seasons, would take them from the canyon's depths to its rimlands.*

In October, as weather cooled and the days grew short, families made their way up to the South Rim and spread out across the Coconino Plateau, which could appear barren and harsh to anyone not familiar with it. At an altitude of more than six thousand feet, the rim country was dotted with low junipers and piñon pines, but devoid of a single peren-nial creek or stream. (According to one account, in the central portion of the Coconino Plateau bordering the South Rim, only eleven springs and shallow sinkholes are reliable sources of water. Each is tiny and separated from its nearest neighbors by distances of forty or fifty miles.)

---

* Inside the canyon, an assortment of flickers, nutcrackers, and solitaires opt to forgo flying south during the fall and instead simply pop down to the warmer reaches along the river, where the climate feels more like Mexico's.

To the Havasupai, this was another kind of paradise. The plateau was teeming with rabbits, turkeys, and porcupines as well as deer and pronghorn, and during the winter everything was easier to track in the snow. The game furnished as much as 70 percent of the protein in their diet, and the land offered an endless supply of a resource conspicuously lacking in their summer home: firewood, which kept them warm until the end of February, when the thaw arrived and it was time to return and prepare their fields for spring planting.

This cycle—spending the warmest part of the year in the stifling depths of the canyon and the coldest months on the exposed rimlands—might have struck an outsider as counterintuitive. But for the Havasupai, it worked superbly, reinforcing their sense of themselves as a people of movement, rather than stasis—a tribe whose true home had always been in neither one place nor the other, but both—until the years immediately following the American Civil War, when their world changed forever as white settlers began pouring into the territory for the first time in large numbers.

By the early 1870s, cattlemen were swarming onto the Havasupai's winter range, laying claim to the grass and the springs for the exclusive use of their stock. Around the same time, prospectors began staking claims around promising deposits of lead, zinc, and silver deep inside Havasu Canyon, and driving ore-laden mules through the middle of the village. The resulting friction convinced federal officials of the need to protect the tribe from further encroachment by establishing a reservation—a move that might have done some good, had the government not set aside only 518 acres of the tribe's summer fields next to the creek along the floor of the canyon, and none of the rimlands on which they depended during the winter.

When the boundaries were ratified in the spring of 1882, the Havasupai's reservation was one of the smallest allotted to any tribe in the United States, less than a single square mile. This was clearly inadequate, even for a community numbering no more than three hundred members, and soon the first in a series of petitions was submitted on their behalf to the Bureau of Indian Affairs urging that the boundaries be enlarged immediately. Unfortunately, however, these requests were about to collide with a larger story of conservation that was already unfolding on the national stage.

*   *   *

Over the next decade, three successive attempts by U.S. senator Benjamin Harrison to designate the Grand Canyon as a national park failed to gain traction in Congress. But in 1893, Harrison, who was by then in the White House, issued a presidential proclamation establishing a forest reserve in the hopes of preventing almost 2 million acres of the canyon and its rimlands from being ravaged by settlers, miners, and timber companies. In the years to follow, forest rangers who encountered any Havasupai inside this reserve, which encompassed vast stretches of the tribe's winter rangelands, would treat them as interlopers and order them to return to their meager enclave, where their problems mounted with each passing winter.

From November to March, the sun would clear the canyon walls only after 10:00 a.m. and by 3:00 p.m. had disappeared again. Game was scarce, and firewood was so precious that the tribal council was forced to assign ownership of each cottonwood tree to an individual family. Residents crammed into tiny houses to keep warm, aiding the spread of illnesses such as smallpox, measles, and influenza, for which the tribe had no natural immunity. Women were especially vulnerable, and deaths to mothers during childbirth soared. By 1905, the tribe's population had plummeted to just 115, a 60 percent drop over five years. By the following year, there were three men for every two women.*

Efforts to address these problems by expanding the reservation were repeatedly blocked as the canyon and its rimlands underwent a series of additional designations that culminated in February of 1919 with

---

* When the pandemic of 1918 reached Havasu Canyon, and influenza spread among the overcrowded houses, nearly half of the tribe succumbed to the disease. The toll was especially dreadful among the young. Several families lost all of their children. At the village's only school, not a single girl survived.

Woodrow Wilson affixing his signature to a bill establishing Grand Canyon National Park as a public space "for the benefit and enjoyment of the people." Thanks to ferocious resistance on the part of northern Arizona's ranchers, miners, and timbermen, the park was woefully undersized, encompassing less than half of the actual canyon. But very much in keeping with the laws establishing the dozen national parks that had preceded it—including Yellowstone, Yosemite, Glacier, and others that had been carved directly from the homelands of indigenous people—Grand Canyon's enacting legislation made no mention of the Havasupai, or any of the ten other tribes whose ancestral lands abutted or lay inside the canyon.

In the eyes of park administrators, if those tribes had a place in the canyon, it was part of a colorful and exotic past. Indigenous people had no direct claims on the land even though it had been stolen from them, and little if any role to play in the present or the future, an attitude borne out by the earliest visitors' guides and interpretive exhibits, which highlighted the major points of geological and biological interest in the park while barely mentioning anything about the Native Americans' presence.

Later, when funding became available for a small anthropology museum, a placard in one of the display cases aired a belief held by the Mormon Church that Native Americans belonged to one of the lost tribes of Israel. Another placard mentioned that the canyon's earliest peoples may have descended from refugees who fled the submerged city of Atlantis.

*   *   *

From the moment of the park's inception, the Havasupai were regarded by members of the Park Service as the least sophisticated and "most primitive" of the canyon tribes, an attitude that was bluntly summarized by Polly Mead Patraw, who worked as a naturalist during the early years and was married to the park's assistant superintendent. "The Hopis were the smart ones, and the Havasupai were the dumb ones, and the Navajos were kind of in between," Patraw would declare decades later in an astonishingly candid oral history interview. "The Havasupai were sort of scorned there on the rim of the canyon, you know—they were kind of scummy people, we looked down our noses to them."

As is often the case, sentiments and policy went hand in hand. Park rangers who encountered members of the tribe hunting deer or gathering piñon nuts on the rimlands during the winter would demand that they return to their reservation, then destroy their camps. And in 1928, just as administrators were preparing to celebrate the ten-year anniversary of the park's founding, rangers forcibly removed two elderly Havasupai—a man who was known to the whites as Billy Burro, and his wife, Tsoojva—from their wickiup next to the creek at Indian Garden, the oasis three thousand feet below the South Rim and visible from the head of the Bright Angel Trail, where they had been living for many years. Burro, who was seventy-nine, died within a year.

In the years immediately following that eviction, the "guardians of the Grand Canyon" were viewed as little better than squatters and deadbeats with no role to play other than as a source of manual labor for low-paying construction jobs or as bellhops, washerwomen, and salad girls in the lobbies, laundry rooms, and kitchens of the tourist hotels. As an index of how poorly they were faring, each Havasupai adult was making, on average, $53 a year—enough to pay for two weeks of groceries, a single pair of work shoes, a visit to the dentist, and a ballpoint pen. In the tribe's estimation, however, their greatest problem was the persistent hostility among park administrators not only toward their culture, but also for the notion that they might have a legitimate claim on the canyon—an attitude neatly encapsulated in an incident that took place in 1962, when officials at the South Rim authorized the construction of a public campground in a part of Havasu Canyon where the tribe had traditionally burned the bodies of their deceased. When the work was complete, visitors had no idea they were pitching their tents in a crematorium, and sleeping among the dead.

All of this underscores an unsettling truth from the perspective of the Havasupai. In effect if not intent, the designation of Grand Canyon

National Park was leveraged not only to prevent a natural wonder from being destroyed by private developers while establishing a stunning tourist destination, but also to wrench the landscape away from its original inhabitants—with particular emphasis given to the tribe that was considered the canyon's stewards and protectors.

Those details still have yet to be fully incorporated into the popular story of the park, and even today this history receives too little attention. Which was precisely why the woman in the white deerskin dress had come to speak with Pete and me at the head of the Bright Angel Trail.

*   *   *

From her perch on the low stone wall, Dianna Uqualla gazed down toward the tops of the cottonwoods surrounding the creek at Indian Garden, the sanctuary from which her ancestors had been permanently evicted shortly after the park's inception. As she took in the view, she said something I was barely able to catch, perhaps because she was conducting this part of the conversation primarily with herself.

"I am amazed to see such beauty still left in the world," she murmured. "Everything down there has remained pure because the land moves. The land *always* moves."

Then without any warning—and in a way that reminded me of what had happened with Renae Yellowhorse two months earlier—her shoulders began to shake as she placed her face in her hands and started to weep.

Stunned by this display of grief, Pete and I took a step back to give her a moment to compose herself. But unlike Yellowhorse, she made no effort to contain her emotions. Instead, she leaned into her pain and wailed, emitting a series of sharp cries that seemed to come from deep in her belly, followed by a keening sound.

"My people are very much a part of this place, but we were forced to leave this area, which was our home—and for many years my elders before me have fought against that, to say *no*," she said. "We have already been pushed too far. We have already been punished too much.

We are real. We are not just a name. We are *humans*—and we are a part of this world, right here, because this is our home."

Only when the keening subsided did she wipe away her tears, which had already smeared the hematite paint on her face, and resume speaking.

"I'm sorry to be so emotional—it is the tears I cry for my people." She continued to wipe her cheeks with one hand while rearranging her shawl around her shoulders with the other. Then she delivered the final portion of the message she wanted to convey to us.

"This is a very powerful journey you are on, and by the time you have finished, you will realize that something in you has changed. But to really see the canyon—to touch and feel and hear everything about this place—you will have to pay attention."

She gave us—me, especially, it seemed—a look whose intensity reminded me of Andrew Holycross when he'd grilled me about the snake back at Lee's Ferry.

"Slow down. *Listen.* And take time to observe—especially the little things, like a lizard in the rocks, or maybe some birds flying by in the morning. Because all the creatures you will meet? They are trying to tell you something."

She paused, as if underscoring the importance of our remembering what came next.

"Everything down there—all of it—is alive."

PART VII

In the House of Tumbled Stones

Everything here is bone.

—Craig Childs

CHAPTER 23

The Great Thumb

Not far beyond the end of the Tonto Trail, the Colorado River is compelled to detour around an enormous impediment jutting out from the South Rim. Turning sharply, the river heads north for ten miles before wheeling and returning south, taking more than twenty miles to cover terrain that a raven could glide across in just a few minutes. When viewed from above, this protrusion is so conspicuous that it sticks out like a sore thumb—an impression that wasn't lost on a member of the U.S. Board on Geographic Names who glimpsed this feature from the window of a plane in 1932 and christened it the Great Thumb Mesa.

The Thumb sits in a class by itself. Although there are many isolated spots along the South Rim, no other appendage extends so far (almost twenty miles), is quite so slender—roughly a thousand yards wide at its narrowest point—or soars so high (almost forty-five hundred vertical feet) above the river. Also, nothing else comes close to presenting thru-hikers with a more seductive temptation to cheat.

For anyone moving along the south side of the river on foot, the smartest way to get around this obstacle is to climb to the rim, cross over the narrow strip of headland at the base of the Thumb—about three miles of walking on mostly flat ground—and drop back into the canyon on the far side. This neat trick offers a simple solution to a complicated problem. But in addition to its being illegal because it entails crossing into a restricted area beyond the border of the park, it's considered a violation of a different set of rules by the long-distance backpacking community, whose members frown on thru-hikers who leave a gap in their line or log miles above the rim, regardless of how short the distance.

The only alternative is to circumnavigate the Thumb by moving out to its northernmost tip and then back again on a daring route that includes some of the canyon's most treacherous terrain, and where breaks in the Redwall that might enable passage between the rim and the river are almost nonexistent. Along three-quarters of that perimeter, there is just one rim-to-river route that does not require ropes—an extremely sketchy Ancestral Puebloan line that Harvey Butchart rediscovered only after many years of searching. There is only a single system of ledges suitable for walking, part of a larger network of terraces known as the Esplanade, which is perched atop the Supai and is so contorted—weaving continuously into and out of a series of deep and highly complex bays—that its total length stretches to almost a hundred miles. Finally, in all that distance there is only one reliable year-round spring, and just a handful of routes by which one can climb to the top of the mesa, which is also devoid of water.

To pull off a trip around the Thumb on the Esplanade, you are entirely dependent on potholes that usually evaporate within a week or ten days of the last storm. Hence, not only are timing and speed critical, but commitment must be total because you soon lose the option of stopping to rest or turn back (even if water is available, you will run out of food and starve). Beyond a certain point, the only way out is through.

For all of these reasons, the next phase of our journey would require some adjustments, starting with the lineup. Our team of supervisors back in Flagstaff had been comfortable allowing Pete and me to waltz along the Tonto Trail by ourselves. But the Great Thumb was far too dangerous for that kind of looseness.

For the time being, our days of traveling without a chaperone were over.

*　　　*　　　*

Two hours before dawn on the morning after our meeting with Dianna Uqualla, Pete and I once again found ourselves hurtling down the frozen dirt track in a convoy of ATVs led by Harlan Taney. After they deposited us at the same spot where they'd picked us up two days earlier, we hoisted our packs, grimacing under the weight of eight days of food and considerably more gear than we were used to carrying, cinched our hip belts, and set off after the woman who had volunteered to lead us on the initial approach to the Thumb.

Even by the standards of the canyon veterans who were overseeing our journey, Amy Martin's connection to the world below the rims ran especially deep. Her mother had carried her into this place for the first time in the autumn of 1978, four months before she was even born, and she'd been coming back ever since, first for recreation and adventure on a series of family trips as a young girl, then later to work as a park ranger and a river guide as well as a professional photographer.

With Amy's help, our first task was to find a route that would carry us past the end of the Tonto Trail and enable us to rendezvous with Kelly McGrath, who would be dropping off the rim in forty-eight hours to provide additional backup. Until we linked up with Kelly, Amy would be hauling, in addition to her own gear, eleven pounds of Pete's camera equipment that I simply wasn't strong enough to carry, given the weight of our packs.

We descended back through the upper layers of rock, moving swiftly down to the top of the Supai in the frost-chilled air, then began pushing west along the start of the Esplanade. Without the boulevard of the Tonto Trail, it felt like a return to the unforgiving conditions that had defined the first part of our trek: terrain where you have to make your own path instead of following someone else's, where each step matters, and where mistakes can be costly.

We spent the next two days weaving among cactus and yucca, or thrashing through the thickets of dwarf piñon that grew at these colder, north-facing heights—all while moving over ground that was more cracked and broken than perhaps anything we had yet seen. The top of the Supai was heavily incised with innumerable ravines and drainage channels that came in every size and shape. Some of these we simply climbed into and scrambled back out of, which was efficient but exhausting. Others were too steep and had to be rounded by working back along their branches and nodes, which was inefficient *and* exhausting.

While Pete and I stumbled and grumbled, Amy glided smoothly forward, never slowing down. Long stretches were covered with a thin layer of snow that was crisp and brittle, and it crunched in a way that made it hard to hear one another, so we walked in silence. We spent every hour of daylight moving through long cold shadows and brief patches of warm sunlight. In the evenings when we stopped, all three of us vanished into our sleeping bags while still swallowing the last bite of dinner—although Pete and I were never too tired to tell jokes to each other before falling asleep.

"You two are obviously able to entertain yourselves," Amy remarked one night from her tent after listening to us cackling like hyenas. "I feel like I don't even need to be here."

As we hustled to keep pace with Amy, Pete and I did our best to follow Dianna Uqualla's instructions. On most mornings (but not all), we rubbed our faces with sage, and at the edges of most (but not all) of the springs we encountered, we scattered bits of tobacco. Performing these rituals felt a bit odd, if only because they didn't come naturally to us. But this reluctance was balanced by a respect for the gifts we had been given—even though we didn't fully understand what they represented just yet—and the conviction that it would be exceedingly foolish to ignore the counsel of the woman in the white deerskin dress.

On the morning of our third day, when Amy paused on a low hill to scan the terrain ahead for our meeting point with Kelly, I looked up and saw what looked like the hull of an immense stone ship whose bow was pointing directly north. The structure was so vast, blocking out the entire horizon while pulling most of the light in the sky down onto itself, that it took a moment or two before I could tear my eyes away from this first glimpse of the Great Thumb and follow Amy's gaze along a fin of sandstone in front of us toward a tent that was pitched on a flat patch of dirt.

In front of the tent, Kelly was standing next to a man who looked suspiciously like someone I'd last seen back in November, when he was perched on a stool next to the stove in my kitchen.

"We figured you were done with us, Rich!" exclaimed Pete when we reached their campsite.

"What can I say?" He shrugged, winking at Amy and Kelly. "I knew you and Kev were gonna need as much help as you could get, so here I am."

*   *   *

Despite our making light of his presence, Rich's decision to join us underscored the challenges that lay ahead. Although Pete and I didn't know it yet, he possessed a deeper understanding than almost anyone else of just how dangerous that looming monolith of rock could be, and the consequences that even a single misstep can carry out on the farthest reaches of the Thumb.

Our plan was simple if not easy—to follow the terraces atop the Supai into and out of a series of niches and embayments until we arrived at the very tip of the Thumb, then to keep moving around the far side. Over the next few days as we worked toward that goal, the Esplanade seemed to welcome us into its embrace as its platform slowly widened and became slightly less broken. Soon we found ourselves pushing across long stretches of slickrock graced with soft curves and gentle undulations that seemed to mirror the shape of moving water.

The color of that rock was deeply pleasing to the eye, a honeyed brown with a hint of toasted orange that suggested what might happen to sunlight if it were barreled and aged. Along the patios were thin patches of soil anchoring the trunks of ancient juniper trees whose green needles scratched at the glassy blue sky, and at the base of those trees were tufts of coarse yellow grass and clumps of sagebrush, whose scent lay heavy on the still winter air.

The Esplanade was bracketed by two parallel sets of cliffs. On the inside of the terrace, the stacked layers of Hermit, Coconino, Toroweap, and Kaibab soared fifteen hundred feet all the way up to the rim. Meanwhile, the outer edge of the platform was marked by the lip of the Supai, whose cliff faces dropped to meet the Redwall far below, which plummeted even farther into the Muav, an almost unbroken fall of twenty-two hundred feet to the bottom of the canyon.

Before long, we began hearing and seeing some of the animals that Dianna Uqualla had mentioned. Early one morning, a deer exploded out of an arroyo directly in front of us, clearing a hundred-yard slope of gravel in a series of stiff-legged bounds. Later, while crossing a gully, we stumbled on the skull of a Bighorn Sheep whose jaw cavity and brainpan were tightly packed with pebbles and mud. That evening, after we had set camp along a precipice, a tiny bat fluttered in from the ocean of open air beyond the outer edge of the Esplanade, emitting a scarcely audible burst of squeaks and chirps while completing a wobbly circle just above our heads, then disappeared back over the canyon. None of us had known that a bat could warble like a songbird, but the creature kept looping back again and again, and each time it returned, we were treated to another aria.

We never glimpsed a Mountain Lion, although we spent three days following the tracks of one whose pawprints were bigger than the palm of Rich's hand—until Pete finally pointed out that it wasn't really clear who was following whom. The animals seemed to be everywhere and nowhere. Even when they were invisible, we could sense their presence in a way that made the terrain come alive—and as they made themselves known to us, the land opened up in other ways, too.

*   *   *

The women in our little group proved to be more observant than the men. Amy and Kelly were both exceptionally good at finding water, which was often hidden in narrow potholes deep inside the drainages. But they noticed many other things, too.

Several dozen times a day, Rich, Pete, or I would march across a section of the ground, then turn to see that one of the women had stopped to pluck something out of the dirt—often an object lying no more than an inch or two from one of our footprints. When we padded back to where the women were standing, they would hand over a small arrowhead or a broken piece of pottery, which would be passed from one person to the next so that we could all share in the discovery.

The first time this happened, I was the last person to handle the item—a triangular-shaped potsherd with black-on-white lines—and when I was finished looking at it, mindful of the lesson I'd learned the previous autumn about the importance of provenience after cluelessly spending the night in the field of potsherds near the Little Colorado, I flicked the little piece of pottery in the general direction of where I thought it had been lying. As I resumed walking, however, something made me turn around, and I caught sight of Kelly as she stooped to retrieve the artifact and carefully returned it to the exact spot and at precisely the same angle where it was found.

As we pressed toward the tip of the Thumb, Amy and Kelly continued to spot other artifacts that the rest of us missed. Late one morning, Amy crouched down and plucked from the dirt a three-inch-long biface, a prehistoric cutting tool knapped from a piece of chert, that could have been used for many purposes, including harvesting the hearts of agave plants, which can be roasted and eaten. The biface had been shaped like the point of a spear, and its scalloped facets gleamed white and gold, as if a fire were smoldering somewhere inside the stone.

That wasn't the only thing on the Esplanade filled with a light that continued to burn. One afternoon as we were taking a break for lunch on the side of a shallow gully whose surface was littered with dozens of potsherds, Amy picked up a curved piece of tan pottery and held it up to the light. After a moment, she reached out to pick up a second piece lying a yard away, tilted her head in thought, then rotated each piece and gently fit them together. Then Kelly rose, walked a few paces down the gully, and returned with two more pieces, which joined perfectly with the first two.

Within a few minutes, they had assembled almost the entire top to a clay pot featuring a high neck and a thick, flared rim. As Rich, Pete, and I silently watched the jar come together, we felt as if we were witnessing a temporary reawakening, a faint quickening of the ground from which the pot had once been shaped and molded by human hands, and to which it was now returning.

Kelly and Amy could find only about half the pieces, but even this partial reassembly had the power to bend time back upon itself, pulling us from the present deep into the past. As we finished eating, we gazed in wonder at the half skeleton of the pot. When the lunch break was over, the women gathered up the pieces and enacted the ritual of placing each where it belonged. Then we resumed our march.

By now it was clear from the potsherds and the other artifacts that although the Great Thumb may have looked and felt terribly remote, people had once been all over this part of the Esplanade. We spotted overhangs where belongings had been stored, niches in which campfires were built, and shallow pits surrounded by doughnut-shaped mounds of fire-cracked rock where agave hearts had been buried and cooked. One afternoon as we circled a hump of orange slickrock that rose to perhaps forty feet, Kelly's eye was drawn toward a shallow cave tucked beneath an overhang. Curious, she took off her pack, got down on her knees, and scooted inside—then beckoned the rest of us to follow.

On the floor inside, atop a thinly compacted layer of windblown dirt, an array of small arrowheads and coin-size pieces of broken pottery lay scattered amid bits of charcoal. Off to one side was a neatly stacked pile of desiccated juniper twigs, glossy with time and the color of old, rubbed silver. Tucked all the way toward the back, in a corner where the ceiling angled into the floor, lay a tiny mat, no bigger than the palm of one's hand. The mat had been threaded into a checkerboard pattern using strips of dried plant material—perhaps yucca or agave. From the way the ends of the fibers protruded from the edges, it was clearly intended to form the bottom center of what would have been a handwoven basket had its maker, almost certainly a woman, not set the material aside and, for reasons as mysterious and unfathomable as any of the canyon's many other riddles, failed to return.

The space inside that shelter was low, little more than a yard in height, but the entrance was long, extending for more than thirty feet, and as we crouched in the dirt, leaning on our elbows and taking care to avoid disturbing anything, it occurred to me that although we knew almost nothing about the last group of people to occupy this space— how many of them there had been, when they'd arrived and how long they'd stayed, or the reasons they'd left without coming back—we did know a thing or two about how they spent their time.

They must have been working constantly with their hands— knapping arrowheads and skinning rabbits, tanning hides or repairing sandals—because the things that enabled them to survive weren't sealed in a plastic bucket waiting for them in the bushes at the bottom of the canyon. Every morsel of food they consumed, every tool they used and piece of clothing they wore, had been gathered directly from the land. I couldn't imagine the skills they'd mastered and the knowledge they'd drawn upon, knowledge regarding not only the terrain and the weather, but also the communities of plants and animals that lived inside this place. I knew that we wouldn't have lasted more than seventy-two hours in the world that these people had, in one fashion or another, occupied for millennia.

*   *   *

That evening, a few minutes after sunset, we moved onto a fin of sandstone that was cantilevered twenty or thirty feet off the lip of the Esplanade, and set our camp there, suspended over the chasm. Far below, amid the shadows pooling on the canyon's bottom, the thin wire of the river gleamed briefly, like a filament in a light bulb just as it's flicked off.

More than half a million acres of rock were out there, and aside from the five of us, not a single human was visible in any of it.

As we gathered in a circle to fix our dinner, the last of the light melted away, the first of the stars stippled the sky with icy pinpoints of light, and the flame of our stove seemed to illuminate our aloneness: a tiny cluster of men and women, gathered around a single blue bar of burning butane, surrounded by a sea of stone. It marvels me, as I recall now how it felt that night, to say that we weren't shocked into silence, but simply did what people have done since the dawn of time. We told stories.

It started when Amy remembered how, years earlier while working in the central part of the canyon, she had stumbled across the body of a dead hawk lying on the ground, its beak covered in blood, and how baffled she was by the scene—until several feet away she discovered the mangled body of a rattlesnake that had evidently been snatched into the air by the hawk, but had somehow managed to sink its fangs into the breast of its captor in midflight, killing them both.

From there, talk turned to the roasting pits that we'd passed, along with the question of just how long it took to cook the heart of an agave, and whether any of us had ever eaten one, and if so, what it tasted like.

"I think they take about three days to bake," said Rich, "and they're packed with all sorts of sugars, so they're supposed to be incredibly tasty."

"Some of them taste like potatoes," added Amy, who had sampled several during a river trip for members of the Hualapai tribe. "But there are sweeter varieties that are almost like molasses or pineapple."

Things continued in this vein until just before bed, when Rich pulled out his satellite tracker and shared a weather report that had arrived from his brother-in-law, Dale Diulus, in Phoenix. A massive storm was pushing down from Alaska, and unlike the autumn squalls that had drenched Rich and his crew back in October and November, this was a full-on winter juggernaut freighted with sleet and snow—the kind of frontal system that could drive the temperature far below freezing, like a hammer sinking a nail into a board.

The storm was still a long way off, Dale reported, lumbering out over the Pacific. All sorts of things might happen over the next several days to weaken or deflect it. But if it held to its current course, he warned, sometime in the next few days the Great Thumb might find itself directly in the path of something big.

Later that night, an owl filled the darkness with its hooting, but Rich and Pete and I didn't learn about it until the following morning. The women were the only ones who heard its call.

CHAPTER 24

The Storm

S unrise the following morning brought bleached-blue skies, high cirrus clouds known as mares' tails, and a fresh weather report from Dale indicating that the storm had strengthened overnight and appeared to be heading straight in our direction. Winds with gusts as high as forty miles an hour were running ahead of the front and set to strike us within the next twenty-four hours. When the main body of the storm hit, chances were 60 percent that it would deposit snow all the way down to the elevation of the Esplanade.

None of this was good news. Snow would make it extremely dangerous to move, especially when the route forced us to traverse the outer lip of the Supai or along the edges of the steep-sided bays. On top of that, together with a loss of visibility, the strong winds would prevent the park's helitack team, which was responsible for search-and-rescue missions, from penetrating the airspace anywhere beneath the rims. If we suffered a mishap or injury, we'd be cut off from an air rescue until conditions improved.

When we were packed and ready to go, Amy and Rich moved toward the top of a sandstone bench on the far side of camp, while Kelly and I held back so that Pete could photograph a chunk of Kaibab Limestone the size of a delivery van that had tumbled from the cliffs above and come to rest on the brink of the Esplanade. It was tilted at such an extreme angle that it looked as if it would take nothing more than a touch of birdsong to send the block plummeting into the chasm.

When Pete had finished composing his shot, we lingered for a moment, each of us pondering how long it might be before the stone gave way. Then we cinched our belts and headed off, walking three abreast toward the top of the rise, beyond which the others had disappeared.

A minute or two later, we were brought to a halt by a high-pitched cry that sounded vaguely like the little singing bat from a few nights earlier. It was so faint that I wondered if my ears were playing tricks on me.

"Did you hear that?" I asked Kelly. "Any idea what it was?"

"Not sure," she said. "What about you, Pete?"

Pete was in the midst of shaking his head no when the cry was repeated—louder and more distinct, and this time it left no doubt in our minds. It was the sound of someone screaming.

Exchanging looks of horror, we dropped our poles and packs, sprinting for the top of the bench.

When we popped over the crest, we found ourselves gazing down on the kind of scene that every canyon hiker dreads. Rich was kneeling next to Amy, who was lying on the ground, face up and motionless.

*   *   *

More than thirty years earlier, when Amy was only eight years old and walking across a boat dock, her leg had gone through a gap between the planks, and as she twisted free and toppled into the water, her left kneecap had popped out of position. In the decades since, the tendons around the patella had weakened, making it susceptible to repeated dislocations. This tended to occur when she made a sudden change in direction while her left foot was planted on the ground, which is exactly what she'd done when she'd taken off her backpack on the far side of the bench to retrieve something, then swung the pack back over her shoulders.

She'd screamed once when the patella had pulled free, rotating all the way around to the far side of the joint into the pocket at the back of her knee, dropping her to the dirt. Then she'd screamed a second time when she took a deep breath, seized the kneecap in both hands, and wrenched it back where it belonged.

After we rushed down and gathered next to Rich, she sat up and examined her knee.

"I am so sorry, you guys—I can't believe I did something this dumb."

The rest of us were appalled. In addition to intense pain and swelling, the ligaments around a pulled patella are easily torn, and sometimes fragments of cartilage or bone can tear away, too. People who suffer a dislocation are often unable to walk for hours, while others require surgery. Almost everyone needs a day or two of total immobilization, followed by physical therapy, before fully recovering.

Given the nature of Amy's injury, the smartest thing to do, it seemed to me, was to contact the park's emergency dispatch center, explain where we were and what had happened, and request an immediate helicopter extraction. Whether Amy qualified for such a rescue—and, if so, what priority her case was assigned—would depend on the search-and-rescue shift manager, who was typically tasked with prioritizing at least six daily distress calls inside the canyon from backpackers, whitewater boaters, rock climbers, and other visitors who found themselves in trouble. To set that process in motion, all we needed to do was to sound the alarm—except that Amy was having none of it.

"No way," she announced. "We are *not* calling this in."

I didn't know then just how many calls the park receives each day from people demanding rescue, many of whom, like me, give little thought to the cost of these operations or the fact that each mission puts the lives of the flight crew at risk. Amy did, however—and she wanted no part of it. The problem was hers to bear, and ours to solve.

Nevertheless, the idea that we might simply resume our hike didn't seem wise. Moving on an injured knee into the teeth of a monster storm along one of the most dangerous stretches of ground in the canyon seemed beyond reckless. If her knee blew out completely, we'd be trapped far out on the Thumb with little food, no access to the river, and no way of getting her to safety.

As the least experienced member of the team, this wasn't my call. And to be fair, at the time I had no idea just how tough and resilient Amy was—although Rich did.

"If you don't think that knee is going to hold, our only option is to get you out," he said to her.

"It's good," Amy assured him as she stood and took several hesitant steps.

"If you have any doubts, this is the time to back out," Rich continued. "You sure you're up for doing this?"

"Absolutely." She leveled a flat look at him that conveyed her resolve.

"Okay, then let's get the knee wrapped and stabilized," he said. "We need to get moving—now."

*   *   *

As we resumed our push, the terrain once again turned rough. The stretches of slickrock were now studded with heavily weathered boulders the size of trash cans, which we were constantly forced to squeeze through or clamber over. Soon the ravines reappeared, each of which had to be threaded, one after the other.

The air was calm, and because we refrained from talking—each of us concentrating on pressing forward while keeping a close eye on Amy—we were enveloped in the sounds of our own movement. The crunch of boots on soil. The tap and click of trekking poles against stone. The crisp snap of a broken sagebrush twig or a dead juniper branch, interspersed with the grunts of people shouldering heavy loads.

Amy kept up, but she walked with gritted teeth and a pronounced hitch in her step. Every half hour, we paused for a few minutes to give her a chance to massage the knee and rewrap the Ace bandage that was helping to stabilize the joint. By midmorning, we had reached the mouth of the largest side drainage on the eastern arm of the Thumb, a tributary known as Fossil Canyon, which was so vast that we spent the better part of the next six hours just getting to its head, which we rounded shortly before dusk.

We stopped at the base of an overhanging monolith of loose shale that was roughly the size of a two-story town house, where we spent thirty minutes gathering large rocks to help anchor the tiny tent that Pete and I were using, plus the larger mid that sheltered Rich, Amy, and Kelly. As we were finishing dinner—which ended as quickly as it began, now that we were on half rations and voraciously hungry—Rich pulled up a message from Dale, which contained a summary of the latest weather details.

The Four Corners of the Southwest was about to get clobbered. Sometime in the next twenty-four to forty-eight hours, temperatures would plummet into the teens during the day and fall as low as 5°F at night. Sixteen inches of snow were expected to fall in Flagstaff, while the southern parts of Utah and Colorado were predicted to receive two feet. No mention was made of how much might accumulate inside the canyon, but the chances of the storm hitting us directly were now 100 percent.

Later, Pete and I lay awake inside our tent listening to the conversation next door as Rich, Amy, and Kelly speculated on how many inches of snow the Esplanade would receive (maybe a foot), how much it would slow us down (a lot), how many days of food we had left (barely three), how many days it would take us to reach our next supply cache under normal conditions (at least four), how many additional days we'd need to travel that same distance while breaking through fresh snow (unknown), and how much weight their emergency shelter could withstand before the only thing holding it up—two trekking poles lashed together—would fail, which was also anybody's guess.

From all of this, one thing seemed clear to each of them: if the storm pinned us down or if Amy's knee gave way and it became impossible for her to walk, we'd be on our own, with nothing in reserve.

*   *   *

That night, the air turned dead still and the temperature shot up almost fifteen degrees. Then just after midnight, the wind began pummeling the walls of the tents. By dawn it felt as if the gusts were kicking well past thirty-five miles an hour.

We left at sunrise under a sky that was mostly clear, but rapidly filling with fat clouds whose edges were torn by wind, and whose sunken underbellies were the color of wet cement. From the get-go, Pete walked with a limp almost as bad as Amy's—although he hadn't bothered telling anybody about it, he'd twisted his left ankle the day before and the tendons were now so swollen that they squeaked with each step he took.

Nevertheless, we made good time getting out of Fossil, punching through a section of rolling benchlands whose surface was covered with grayish gravel and blue-green brush, out of which the twisted skeletons of a few dead piñon trees arose like watchmen, with their fingers pointed toward the sky. As if to underscore the barrenness of this district, the patches of potsherds that had littered the ground everywhere else seemed to drop off and disappear.

Within a few hours, we were free of Fossil and once more pushing toward the far end of the Thumb on the Esplanade's main scaffold. We broke for lunch on a horn-shaped promontory whose tip featured three round potholes, each the size of a small bathtub and filled with at least two feet of clear, icy water. As we ate, Amy unwrapped her knee and immersed it until she could no longer feel anything. Meanwhile, Pete removed his shoe and sock to expose his ankle, which was now swollen up like a boiled sausage, and plunged it into the pool next to Amy's while munching on ibuprofen pills as if they were Tic Tacs.

Our team was falling apart.

Minutes later, Rich looked up at the sky, now the color of a rifle barrel, walked off into the brush, and picked up the hollow stalk of a dead agave whose diameter was as thick as his wrist. As we resumed walking, he squared off the ends of the stalk with his knife to create a sturdy brown spar that measured about five feet long. Instead of using it as a hiking stick, however, he simply carried it in his hand, which left me wondering what he was planning to do with the thing.

The Esplanade was now starting to narrow, pinching from an ample bench to the width of a window ledge that in places was no more than a few feet across. As we shuffled along this constricted surface, the cliffs fell away into the open air, making us tremendously exposed and vulnerable, like a family of mice slinking across the throne room of Valhalla.

Three hours later, as we approached a steep bay on the outermost point of the Thumb, one of the most isolated and exposed pieces of real estate anywhere in the canyon, the storm finally hit.

*   *   *

Because this section of the Thumb bends back on itself slightly, the recess where we were standing faced southeast, affording an unobstructed view of a forty-mile stretch of the South Rim and an unbroken chain of thunderheads that now loomed just beyond the rim. They filled the horizon, a phalanx of coal-black clouds that seemed to grow darker and heavier and more menacing by the minute, with blue-black columns of mist streaming from their undersides.

They advanced in a line, as if pulled by the mass of frigid air running directly in front of them, and when they reached the edge of the canyon, they struck the piñon and juniper trees along its lip like a locomotive plowing through a picket fence. Then the entire cloud train spilled its freight directly into the chasm, engulfing the towers, spires, and high ridgelines in a glistening shroud of moisture, while shafts of low-angle sunlight flared briefly against the fastness of the stone before they were snuffed out.

The display was spectacular and stupefying. In less than thirty seconds, the clouds had closed in completely, cutting off the light and cooling the air with the abruptness of someone slamming the door to a cellar. Then the first squall of freezing rain mixed with bits of hail began pelting the slickrock.

As nuggets of ice bounced around our feet, we recovered our wits and belatedly began racing in search of a flat spot where our tents might not only be protected from the wind, but could also stand clear of the water that suddenly seemed to be everywhere at once. Dozens of streams and waterfalls were now streaking across the face of the Esplanade, sluicing over each ledge and protrusion in a mad rush to drain into the abyss.

Within minutes, as we dashed from one overhang to another, scrambling to find some semblance of shelter, our clothing and packs were soaked. We searched the terrace, but found nothing—which is when it finally dawned on us that this was why the potsherds that had been strewn so generously inside the protected inlets and bays along the Thumb's inner arm had vanished earlier that morning. Dianna Uqualla's forebears, and the Ancestral Puebloans who had preceded them, had all known better than to congregate out here on the extreme end of the promontory, where every nook and corner not only was exposed to the full fury of the elements, but doubled as a discharge conduit for running water.

Eventually, we found a sliver of level ground that didn't seem to be serving as a storm drain and pitched our shelters. With darkness closing in, we anchored the smaller tent with ten heavy boulders, then secured the edges of the mid with two dozen more. When everything was in place, Rich ducked inside the mid, seized the two trekking poles that provided the structure's only support, and doubled their strength by wrapping the dead agave stalk to the poles with several rounds of duct tape.

*   *   *

The night was black and wet and devoid of stars. For hours, the sleet hammered down like bullets, until finally, around 11:00 p.m., everything turned to snow. There was nothing soft or fluffy about those flakes—they were gritty, and they landed like fistfuls of gravel on the tent in which Pete and I were huddled.

For the rest of the night, the wind punched the side of the tent facing the edge of the chasm, each blow pressing the walls almost halfway over while slapping the wet fabric into the side of my face as I lay awake, wondering if the poles could bear the weight of the snow and the force of the wind. As I tried to imagine what was unfolding in the darkness outside, I felt the night lift me back to my childhood and was reminded, for the first time in many years, what it had once felt like, as a small boy, to be truly scared of the weather.

When dawn arrived, muted and gray and stingingly cold, I carefully unzipped the door and poked my head out to confront a scene that felt alien and menacing.

We were wrapped in scudding clouds that obscured almost everything, except for a few holes torn open by the wind. Through those openings, I caught fleeting glimpses of the surrounding canyon, as if I were gazing through the portal of a moving ship or the window of an airplane. Each feature appeared abruptly—an isolated patch on the face of a cliff, a distant escarpment of rock—and lingered for only a second or two before vanishing behind the veil as another hole shredded open to expose something else.

The effect was eerie and bewildering, but it was the ground around us that sent a cold shudder slicing through my chest and belly. We were suspended thousands of feet in the air on a catwalk of sandstone, every square inch of which was now smothered in almost a foot of fresh-fallen snow.

CHAPTER 25

Beneath the Eyes of the Owl

There's nothing unique about a heavy winter storm over the canyon. At least two or three times every winter, the South Rim is covered in twelve to eighteen inches of snow, while between November and May the highest points along the North Rim can receive more than a hundred. However, it's rare to see any significant accumulation below the top of the Supai, where the snow generally turns to rain while it's still in the air or melts as it hits the ground. It's almost unheard of for nine inches to blanket the Esplanade—and in the tent next to ours, Pete and I could hear an animated discussion about what this meant.

Apparently, Amy's sleeping bag had been protruding from under the wall of the mid for most of the night, so now Kelly and Amy were remarking about how nice it would be to just stay in their sleeping bags and huddle inside the tent for the rest of the day—if only Amy's bag wasn't soaked through. Their laughter was hesitant and muted.

Meanwhile, Rich untied the flap of the tent, popped his head outside, and took in the scene.

"Good God," he muttered, as the snow continued to fall. "This shows no signs of stopping."

By now, the rest of us were emerging and stamping our feet as we took down the tents and crammed the wet fabric into our packs. Rich reported that the temperature was 31°F, and that we had to cover as much ground as we possibly could during the next several hours.

"It may be a bad idea to move in this weather—we might not be able to see where we're going, and the terrain will be tough in this snow—but the one thing we *cannot* do is to stay here," he said, knowing that we didn't have enough food and supplies to wait for the weather to clear.

Somewhere up ahead, the Esplanade was about to hook around the tip of the Thumb, and just beyond that point, the top of the Supai would widen out dramatically. If we could reach the transition point by nightfall, we would be on safe ground, free from having to skirt along the edges of the cliffs. But if we fell short of that goal and the temperature rose by only a degree or two, the snow would soften during the day, then freeze overnight. By tomorrow morning, the tip of the Thumb would be lacquered in ice.

As we raced to get ready, Rich reached into his pack, pulled out a handful of Ziploc baggies and black trash bags, and passed them around. "We'll line the inside of our shoes with these, so our socks and feet stay dry," he explained, "and then we'll put on our spikes."

*   *   *

Within minutes, we found ourselves moving across a landscape whose signature features had been redrawn into a kind of cartoon. The barbed circle of leaves at the base of each yucca was now a fluffy white snowball. The spines of the cacti were lollipopped with dollops of alabaster, and every boulder, large and small alike, wore a white bowler hat. But if the desert appeared more benign, even comical, it was filled with fresh menace.

As unsettling as it could be to tread the bare slickrock along the sharp edge of a six-hundred-foot precipice, easing one's way through a snowfield whose outer lip was obscured in mist was flat-out terrifying. Especially when Rich warned us about what happens to the Esplanade Sandstone when it becomes saturated with moisture.

"The stone here is brittle and highly friable," he cautioned. "When this stuff gets wet, pieces of it tend to break off without any warning, so be super-careful with your footing."

"What do you suppose the animals are doing?" I wondered aloud as Rich peered into the mist.

"Unlike us, they're being smart," he said. "They're bedded down under the junipers, keeping low and waiting it out."

As if to underscore the folly of ignoring this wisdom, our movements were clumsy and our progress was halted by frequent slips. Every few minutes, Kelly was forced to stop because the trash bags wrapped around her calves and ankles were shredding to pieces and beginning to entangle her feet. While she attempted to retie the bags, Amy and I pounded our trekking poles on our spikes, where clumps of ice were building up. Meanwhile Pete, who had somehow lost one of his gloves, was now forced to walk with his right hand exposed, although he occasionally tucked it in his pocket to keep his fingers from freezing.*

There was no sign of the sun, and in its absence, we found ourselves swathed in an endlessly shifting morass of gray and white fog. Unable to read the terrain ahead, we burned energy we couldn't afford to lose, and time we didn't have.

Still the snow continued to fall. As it came down, I reflected on how truly precarious our position had become, and how dependent we were on one another. Never before had I felt so tiny, so cut off, so vulnerable— or so completely reliant on the people I was with. How, I wondered, could we have imagined we could pull off something as audacious as a midwinter circumnavigation of this immense mesa without anticipating that something terrible might cast its shadow over the benches of the Esplanade, like a hawk snatching a rattlesnake in its talons?

And then, just before 2:00 p.m., we rounded a turn and found ourselves staring at the place we'd been struggling to reach.

---

* Remarkably, Pete carried his camera in his other hand throughout the entire day and never stopped shooting.

* * *

On the northernmost point of the Thumb, I could see the walls flaring open into a horseshoe-shaped amphitheater that resembled a kind of vault. The upper layers of this chamber were composed of soaring vertical cliffs perched atop a steep slope of Hermit Shale, and at the base of that formation, the thin ledge of the Esplanade all but vanished, like a section of roof without a gutter.

The only way to get through the amphitheater was to traverse the slope of loose, shaley material, knowing that a single misstep could easily send us skittering down the incline, then kick us over the edge and into space. It was a four-hundred-foot plummet to the first ledge, a narrow band of Supai, and if you ricocheted off that, you'd plunge another six hundred feet before hitting the top of the Redwall—a prospect whose dreadfulness was intensified by the features that gave this recess its name.

Set high into the cliffs, smack in the middle of the alcove, was a pair of indentations, each vaguely resembling the socket of an eye. The diameter of those cavities spanned more than two hundred feet, large enough that they could readily be spotted eight miles away along the North Rim, or even from a passing aircraft. From those distances the eye sockets, when paired together with a beak-like pro- trusion of rock extending a hundred feet below, resembled the face of a predatory bird.

To stand anywhere inside that space is to feel the unblinking gaze of those enormous hollowed-out orbs, which seem to track one's every move. Perhaps for that reason, no spot anywhere else in the canyon can fully match the spookiness and menace of Owl Eyes Bay.[*]

As we surveyed the amphitheater, however, we spotted something encouraging. At the far end of the horseshoe, roughly a mile away, the Esplanade reappeared as a broad platform, known as Tahuta Terrace. It looked as wide and flat as the deck of an aircraft carrier—safe ground.

---

[*] The name by which the Havasupai know this bay, Hyu Yuu, means the same thing: Owl Eyes.

To get there, we would have to force a line directly across the Hermit Shale, staying high enough on the slope that if any of us lost our footing and started to slip, we'd have only a few seconds to arrest our slide before being catapulted off the lip of the Supai. We'd need to proceed with extreme care—but we'd also have to move fast enough to cross the entire alcove before darkness set in, because spending the night perched in the middle of Owl Eyes would be unthinkable.

We had less than three hours of daylight to pull this off.

Before setting out, Rich took a moment to make sure everyone understood the consequences of a mistake. "You have to concentrate on every step that you put down," he said, staring hard at each of us. "If you hit ice and you slip anywhere inside this bay, you're gone—you're dead."

With that, we took off.

*   *   *

Rich went first, probing the steeply angled snowfield with his trekking poles, followed by Amy and Kelly, then me, with Pete bringing up the rear. The snow was extremely slippery, and so, too, was the soil beneath it. But the most treacherous features were tilted slabs of stone lurking under the snow, whose slick surfaces threatened to send us rocketing toward the edge, so each person carefully stepped into the line of tracks laid down by Rich.

Amy fumbled once or twice but maintained her equilibrium, despite her rickety knee, while Kelly struggled to stay upright, wobbling on the clumps of ice encasing the bottoms of her spikes, which robbed her of traction and balance. Within five minutes, one of her aluminum trekking poles snapped in half. She cursed once, then went silent, pouring every dram of energy and concentration into the grim business of staying on her feet.

I was faring even worse. Every few minutes I would lose my footing, crash to the ground, and strangle the nearest bush or clump of frozen grass in a desperate bid to halt my skid before it became unstoppable.

Pete, who was forced to witness all of this without being able to lend a hand for fear of going down himself, was horrified at the prospect of watching me whoosh over the precipice and disappear.

We moved in fits and starts, creeping beneath the flinty stare of the eye sockets in the cliff high above. The air seemed to grow colder, and the angle of the terrain never let up, but sometime late in the afternoon—nobody was keeping track of the time—it looked as if the storm might be starting to lift. As the snow tapered off, the mist thinned and the cloud cover began to break up, permitting shafts of late-afternoon sunlight to glissade in from the west and igniting the bands of yellow sandstone high above the bay.

As we inched forward, we drew closer to what seemed to be the only spot of relief on the entire slope, the beak-like promontory extending out from the middle of the U-shaped bay. It was less than eighty feet wide and protruded no more than forty yards before hooking into a sharp drop-off.

When we finally reached this landmark after more than two hours of struggle and clambered on top of it, we discovered a pair of bare-branched redbud trees anchored at the near end, flanked by a gnarled, ancient-looking juniper. Beyond them, out at the point of the beak, stood something even more singular. A cairn of flat rocks had carefully been stacked to a height of roughly four feet to form a miniature watchtower, along the lines of something that the Ancestral Puebloans might once have built.

After we followed Rich out to the cairn, I allowed my eyes to travel along the rest of the bay to where the Esplanade reappeared at Tahuta Terrace.

It was just over half a mile away, and I wanted nothing more than for us to keep plodding so that we could reach it before the light faded and night fell over the canyon. But when I turned to look at Rich, who was standing with his back to us, I could see that something was wrong. From the manner in which his shoulders shook and his torso heaved, it was clear that he was sobbing.

*   *   *

The rest of us stood in silence and stared at one another, astonished and confused, until Rich wiped the tears from his eyes and turned to face us.

"It's still here," he said, gently stroking the side of the cairn with the palm of his hand.

Then he told us the story of the woman in whose memory it was built, and whose passion for the canyon ran as deep as the drop-off on the far side of the little monument.

CHAPTER 26

Casa de Piatra

Her name was Ioana Elise Hociota, and she had fallen under the spell of the canyon not long after emigrating to the United States from Romania with her parents and sister in the autumn of 2002. She was brilliant, brash, and filled with an irrepressible exuberance—a prodigy who spoke four languages and enjoyed running marathons almost as much as she loved taking selfies.

After earning dual degrees in math and biology at Arizona State University in Phoenix, she was intent on securing admission into a PhD program in pure mathematics, which she considered the true language of the universe. But in the midst of those plans, she had somehow found the time to fall in love with renowned snake expert Andrew Holycross, the man who had promised Pete and me back at the start of our venture that "the toughest hike in America" would teach us the difference between what we wanted and what we needed.

Among the couple's many shared interests, perhaps the greatest were their fondness for desert hiking and their passion for preserving wild places. Within a year of their meeting each other, Holycross had taken Hociota (pronounced *hoe-chi-OTTA*) on the first of what would become dozens of backpacking trips in the canyon. Many of those excursions took place along exceptionally remote reaches south of the river, which eventually drew the pair into discussing the possibility of an ambitious thru-hike on the north side of the chasm with their friend Rich, who was always eager to discuss maps and routes.

In the summer of 2011, Holycross and Hociota were married on the North Rim at a place called Marble Viewpoint, the highest observation point in the entire park, which opens to a vista that extends all the way from the Vermilion Cliffs and the House Rock Valley to the gorge of the Little Colorado River. After vows were exchanged, the bride's family greeted the newlyweds with the words *casa de piatra*, which means "house of stone," a Romanian wedding benediction for a strong and lasting union.

"We thought it so apropos—Grand Canyon was our house of stone," Holycross would later recall. "As a couple, that was where Ioana and I were at our very best. We were like peas in a pod down there."

By then their obsession with the world beneath the rims had inspired so many hikes that they were well on their way to assembling all the pieces of a sectional traverse along the south side of the Colorado— although each had a handful of gaps that still needed to be filled. For Hociota, only two segments remained, one of which included the portion of the Esplanade along Owl Eyes Bay, which she intended to complete in February 2012.

Holycross was unable to join her on that leg because of his teaching responsibilities, so instead she invited Matthias Kawski, a mathematics professor who had accompanied the couple on many of their excursions in the canyon. The route was roughly twenty-two miles, which they intended to complete in three days.

* * *

The morning of February 25 was one of those gorgeous intervals that occur only in midwinter: crisp, windless, and flooded with light. The ground was dry, the temperature was in the high sixties, and the terrain felt safe—well within their abilities—when they rounded the bend into Owl Eyes and began working across, moving cautiously but making excellent time. By noon they had reached the beak in the middle of the alcove—the very place we were now standing—and took a break to have lunch and bask in the sun.

After they'd finished eating, they resumed their traverse, each taking a slightly different angle. Kawski worked his way farther up into the slopes above the Supai bench, while Hociota stayed low, contouring about fifty feet from the lip. They were out of each other's line of sight when Hociota lost her footing and started skidding down a hidden feature, a long chute lined with dirt and gravel that funneled toward the cliff edge.

From above, Kawski heard the clatter of some loose rocks, and a brief cry. "A muted scream maybe one or two seconds long," he would later recall. "It was very short, almost like a bird." Then a beat or two later, there was a dull thump, followed by silence.

Scrambling back to where he'd last seen his companion, Kawski screamed her name repeatedly, getting no response. Knowing that it was impossible for him to descend the cliff whose edge she had tumbled over, it was clear that his only option was to make his way to their exit point as fast as possible to seek help. (Although they were carrying a satellite phone, which they had borrowed from Rich, it was stowed in Hociota's backpack.)

Within ten minutes, he was on his way, racing for a break in the Coconino and Kaibab cliffs that would enable him to ascend to the rim. He paused only once, after reaching a point in the horseshoe-shaped amphitheater that enabled him to see the base of the cliffs from which Hociota had fallen. He stopped just long enough to take dozens of photos using his telephoto lens, then resumed moving.

*   *   *

By 6:00, Kawski had run out of light and was forced to bivouac for the night, bedding down beneath a set of ledges at the base of the exit route. Meanwhile, Holycross was in Flagstaff waiting for a check-in call from his wife on the sat phone, and beginning to wonder if something had gone wrong.

Shortly after sunset, he reached out to Rich and told him he had a bad feeling. Within thirty minutes, both men were in their vehicles heading toward the South Rim, and from there onto a series of dirt roads that runs across the top of the Great Thumb Mesa.

They didn't reach the top of the route where Kawski and Hociota were expected to emerge until after 3:00 a.m. When they arrived, they parked their rigs a short distance apart, then each man crawled into his bag and fell fast asleep. As he was drifting off, Rich was briefly roused by what he thought was the sound of Hociota's voice, calling out her husband's name from somewhere in the canyon below—

Andrewwwwww!

He heard it just the one time, and he wasn't sure whether the cry was part of a dream. But as he fell back asleep, he wondered if she'd topped out with Kawski and rejoined Holycross.

*　　　*　　　*

The following morning, there were no signs of the hikers.

By 10:00 a.m., having waited anxiously since sunrise, the two men decided to drive to a section of the mesa overlooking Owl Eyes to see if they could spot anything. Scanning the bay with binoculars, they caught sight of some footprints in the soil, perhaps fourteen hundred feet below and a quarter mile away, but weren't sure what to make of them. So once more, they headed back to the exit point—and there Holycross finally heard Kawski calling out, some three hundred yards below as he clawed his way toward the top.

"Where's Ioana?" yelled Holycross, cupping his hands around his mouth.

"*She's down!*" Kawski cried.

"*What do you mean?*"

It took a moment for Kawski to respond, but there was no mistaking his reply:

"*She fell—below Owl Eyes.*"

"*Is she alive?!*" Holycross screamed.

"I don't know . . . probably not."

Standing at the edge of the rim with the binoculars, Rich watched helplessly as Holycross crumpled to the ground, broken in grief; then he scuttered down to Kawski—who had collapsed in exhaustion, having expended all his energy to reach this point—to obtain the coordinates of the spot where Hociota had fallen.

While Rich relayed that information by satellite text to his brother-in-law in Phoenix, along with a request to alert the park's emergency dispatcher, Holycross drove his FJ Cruiser to a spot that had cell phone reception and called in the same information from the roof of the vehicle. Within the hour, a helicopter was scanning the ledges below Owl Eyes, and the pilot spotted Hociota's body.

Ninety minutes later, the chopper returned with a ranger named Debbie Brenchley. Suspended from a hundred-foot rope anchored to the belly of the helicopter's fuselage as the pilot hovered above, Brenchley gently retrieved Hociota, along with her backpack.

She had fallen almost four hundred feet to her death, bouncing off the cliff band at least once before coming to rest on a talus slope in the Supai.

Hociota was only twenty-four years old, and she had hiked more than a thousand miles in the world beneath the rims, almost all of it off-trail. Had she been able to finish the few remaining miles of her journey, she would have been the youngest woman ever to hike the length of the Grand Canyon.

*   *   *

Eleven weeks later, on a Sunday in May, Holycross and Kawski returned to Owl Eyes along with Rich and a few other close friends, and together they made their way across the slopes to the promontory in the middle of the bay. They brought with them a four-hundred-foot climbing rope, and after anchoring it to a small tree just above the slab where Hociota had lost her footing, Rich and Holycross rappelled down to the base of the cliffs to retrieve the items that Brenchley had missed: Hociota's trekking pole, a small satchel, and her camera, which may have been the most important item for Holycross, because it contained the last selfies she had taken.

When they'd gathered her things and ascended back up the rope, they discovered that Kawski and their other two friends had built the cairn that would serve as Ioana's memorial.

"Nice job, Matthias," said Rich. "I don't know when I'll be back here, but when I am, I hope it's still standing."

"Oh, don't worry—I did the math on the base," assured the professor of differential geometry. "This thing is going to be here whenever you return."

*   *   *

"I'll be damned if Matthias wasn't right," said Rich, surveying the cairn in the icy-blue light as the sun began to slide beyond the distant buttes and towers off to the west, turning the clouds above us into copper-bottomed frigates sailing toward the darkening sky in the east. "It's good to see that this is surviving the test of time."

Then he looked at where we were standing. "This is the spot where they had lunch just before she fell. You can see why they stopped here, right? It's a terrific location—a special place."

As the rest of the group admired Kawski's handiwork, I looked again to my left in the direction of Tahuta Terrace, trying to gauge how much light we had left.

It was now well past five o'clock. Purple shadows were creeping across the face of the cliffs all along the North Rim, and evening was preparing to fling its frigid cloak over the inside of the bay. But out beyond the far end of the alcove, half a mile from where we stood, the terrace was still glinting in the dying light, and although there was less of it with each passing minute, I couldn't help but wonder if it might still be possible to reach the safety of that patio, if only we could muster the will to strap on our packs, gather our courage, and start *running*.

As if he'd read my thoughts, Rich pulled his attention away from the cairn and gave voice to what he and the rest of the group already knew. At the rate we'd been going, it would take at least another hour or two for us to traverse that slope, and if we resumed moving, we would find ourselves benighted on impossible ground.

Even though it cut against the impulse that we all shared to escape from this spooky place by getting to that terrace as fast as possible, the best choice—the *only* choice—was to do what none of us wanted, which was to stay right here.

"Look, we didn't plan it this way, but this is really the only spot to spend the night—and Ioana would have known that," said Rich. "She would have been glad to know that we took shelter in this place and set our camp here. If you knew her like I did, you'd know that she would have been thrilled by that."

He was right, and everyone nodded in agreement—except me.

I didn't think it was a good idea at all to spend the next thirteen hours inside this frozen chamber of death, hoping that the soft snow on the far side of the nose wouldn't turn to solid ice overnight, and then, when morning arrived and the light returned, to set off across those slopes while praying that Kelly's crampons stayed on her feet and that Amy's knee didn't give out and that nothing else happened that might cause one of us to lose our footing and plummet to our death in the same manner as the vivacious young woman who had once viewed mathematics as the purest language of the universe.

But what could I do?

Sooner or later, every difficult journey collides against a moment that crystallizes the imperative of accepting that the outcome of any ambitious undertaking can neither be ordained nor engineered by its participants, and that the heart of an odyssey is reached—and its deeper truths begin to reveal themselves—only after the illusion of control is permitted to fall away and disappear into the gathering night, like a loose pebble over a cliff.

So, dropping my pack on the snow, I pitched in to help set up camp.

*   *   *

We staked our tents next to the pair of redbud trees and the gnarled juniper, and when we were finished, it was far too cold to stand around outside, so the five of us retreated into our respective shelters to melt snow and boil water and heat our dinners. After Pete and I had eaten, we donned every piece of clothing we carried, including our rain parkas, and sealed ourselves up in our sleeping bags with our water bottles tucked under our arms and beneath our feet to keep them from freezing.

As I lay back in the darkness, my thoughts turned toward something that Rich had told us earlier about Holycross, and what had happened to him after he lost his wife.

In the days immediately following Hociota's death, he had formed an intense hatred toward the canyon for having taken her from him—a feeling that festered for weeks, until eventually, despite his best efforts, its grip slowly began to loosen. Eventually, with the passage of time, somewhere inside his heart a space opened in which he was able to revisit the memories of the times they had spent and the things they had done together in the world beneath the rims. And as his love for the landscape returned to him, with it came the possibility that he might consider allowing himself to return to the land.

Hociota was no quitter. So in the autumn of the year of her death, Holycross resolved to finish the remainder of her sectional traverse along the south side of the canyon. To honor her as well as the life they had shared, he carried her backpack the whole way, along with a lock of her hair.

Then a year after that, still feeling the pull of their unfulfilled dream, he set off on the nonstop, continuous traverse along the north side of the canyon that he and Hociota had originally envisioned doing together with Rich. This second effort took sixty-five days to complete, and when it was over, he became one of only three people to have completed transects along both sides of the river.

As I reclined in the tent pondering those achievements, I recalled the first day of our hike back at Lee's Ferry, when Holycross had fixed me with that incredulous, mystifying stare as he realized how casually Pete and I were entering this landscape: how poorly we'd prepared, and how ignorant we were of the toll this place can levy on those who love it.

No wonder he looked at us that way, I thought.

Given what I now knew, I was astonished that the man had bothered speaking to me at all.

PART VIII

Beneath the Ramparts of Time

Wildness is out there.

—Jack Turner

CHAPTER 27

The Godscape

"Heads up, dude!" exclaimed Pete. "Your shoelaces are on fire."

It was a few minutes before sunrise and I was in a foul mood: huddled in the vestibule of the tent, shivering uncontrollably as I held my shoes—which had turned into blocks of ice overnight—over the flame of our camp stove in the hopes of thawing them just enough to ram my feet inside.

The interior of the tent was a jumbled mess: clothing and gear everywhere—pants and T-shirts and dirty dishes, all glazed in a crackling layer of frost. Anything that had been liquid last night—the contents of our water bottles, the chili from dinner that had spilled onto the floor—was now as solid as my shoes. And there in the middle of this clutter lay Pete, warmly cocooned into his sleeping bag like a croissant in the oven, amusing himself by making lame jokes at my expense.

"Not funny," I said. "Instead of clowning around, why don't you think about getting out of your—?"

"*Your goddamn shoe is on fire!*"

Pete wasn't kidding. I furiously pounded one of my Adidas into the snow to snuff out the flames, then studied the partially blackened toe box and realized, with dismay, that it was still too frozen to get a foot into. Meanwhile, Pete was flinging our backpacks through the doorway and extracting himself from the tent so that we could take stock of what the morning had delivered.

The temperature was ten degrees, and the bay was still draped in darkness. But sometime during the night the storm had passed, and the first rays of sunshine were starting to touch the alcoves and cliffs on the far side of the canyon, turning the snow and rock and even the air itself golden.

We could now see a series of side canyons spilling down from the North Rim that had been obscured by clouds the day before, and I recognized exactly where we were because I knew the section of the river below us well, thanks to my summers with the dories. Back then, I would have scoffed if someone had suggested I might one day find myself standing in my socks more than three thousand feet above the shoreline in the middle of winter, struggling to figure out how to force my feet into a pair of frosted bricks.

A minute or two later, our companions popped out of their shelter with a solution to the problem. Taking mugs of snow they had melted over their camp stove, they poured the boiling water directly over the footwear. After the shoes were doused, we were told to put them on right away so that they could refreeze around our feet. With that, it was time to pack up and get underway.

The terrain seemed even steeper than it had the day before, but the sandstone terraces that lay just beyond the end of the bay, bathed in morning light, drew closer with each step. It took almost three hours, and the second half of the passage unfolded in full sun, which softened the snow and loosened the soil beneath, making everything even more slippery.

We cleared the bay just before noon. When Pete finally reached safe ground, ten minutes after Rich, we all paused to take a long look back at our camp and realized that the spot where Hociota had slipped, which had been hidden from view, was now visible.

We could see the slab beside which she had lost her footing, the channel that had funneled her over the edge, and the face of the cliff down which she had been hurled. We could even see the cone of talus on the ledge where she had landed. It felt as if we had passed over a piece of haunted ground, and we were grateful for the tiny place where her memorial stood, a toehold that had enabled us to survive the night.

The light was bright and the air was still, and although the temperature was still only thirty-two degrees, we celebrated our arrival by upending our packs, spreading our gear out on the sun-warm slickrock, and waiting for it all to dry. Then we got up and gathered our things and resumed our journey, feeling like new people.

*   *   *

We pushed west through a set of low hills and shallow ravines whose flanks were coated in red dirt and dotted with blackbrush and sagebrush and dull-green clumps of Mormon Tea. Fresh hoofprints were all around, proof that deer and wild horses were moving just beyond the horizon, and every now and then a quail would explode from the base of one of the rectangular blocks of limestone that had tumbled down from the ridges above. There were hundreds of those blocks, each the size of a shipping container, and a number of them stood upright, leaning away at moody angles, like the stone heads on Easter Island.

The wild horses had made a faint trail that we followed, now losing the track, then finding it again, until we climbed onto a saddle between two hills and found ourselves gazing out across a vast plain of sandstone, acre upon acre, all of it stained to a dense shade of terra-cotta orange.

The surface of that stone was dimpled with shallow craters. Each was roughly the size of a birdbath, filled with snowmelt and coated in a thin sheet of ice that glittered like blue glass. Hundreds of frozen pools were out there, and together they formed a glittering mosaic of sharded light, as if the sky had somehow slid away from its moorings, run aground, and shattered itself to pieces on the red reef of the Esplanade.

None of us had ever seen anything quite like this, and for several minutes we were unable to do more than simply stand and stare, overpowered by the vision that was laid before us.

"Welcome to the far side of the canyon," said Rich. He explained that although the Esplanade had first emerged as a geologic feature more than thirty miles behind us, it achieved its flaming fullness only out here on the far side of the Great Thumb, where these immense terraces become the dominant and defining element of the canyon's western reaches.

"Very few people get to see this wonderland because it's so remote and so hard to reach," he continued. "There's nothing else like it any-where—and maybe that's why the folks who have spent time out here have another name for this place."

"And what would that be?" asked Pete.

"They call it the Godscape."

The name alone might well have been sufficient reason for us to linger and ponder its shades of meaning, were it not that each of our packs now contained only about a day's rations, and that somewhere out there in that three-hundred-square-mile expanse of slickrock lay a narrow opening—a kind of doorway—that would enable us to descend to the bottom of the canyon, where our next supply cache had been tucked behind some bushes next to the river.

Only Rich knew exactly where that opening lay, how far it was, and the terrain we needed to cross to get there. But we all understood that if we didn't keep moving, we were going to run out of food.

*   *   *

We dropped off the saddle onto the edge of the stony plain, and as we began weaving among the frozen puddles, we discovered that the surface of the Esplanade here was more complicated than it initially appeared. The slickrock was studded with strange-looking humps and domes, some shaped like the backs of turtles, others resembling the caps of mushrooms, all of them worn and polished by the grit-laden winds that sweep in from the west.

As we made our way across the expanse, bathed in crisp air and basking beneath the weak winter sun, we found ourselves awash in a curious exhilaration, a kind of exuberance that seemed to draw not only from the openness of the Esplanade but also from the fact that the walking was actually pleasant. Now that we were no longer floundering through nine inches of snow while focused on the ground at our feet to avoid stepping off the edge of a cliff, we were finally able to take the full measure of our surroundings.

Every few minutes, something unexpected would announce itself. Signs of the Ancestral Puebloans slowly returned—potsherds and arrowheads peeking through the dirt, or the stacked-stone walls of tiny granaries tucked beneath the overhangs. Off in the distance, Amy spotted a band of wild horses just before they disappeared into one of the many arroyos that cut across the sandstone. Even farther out, the lines of cliffs that defined the rims of the canyon spilled down from both sides, each tier receding into the next until, out against the farthest horizon, they formed a purple notch set against a light blue sky.

We spent the rest of the day pushing west until, somewhere out in that spectacular country, Rich found the wide seam in the rock—a wedge-shaped fissure, less than thirty yards wide—that would enable us to complete the first stage of our descent to the river. Upon entering its trough, we crept down a ramp studded with shattered boulders that took us all the way down to the Redwall, where we set camp. Famished, we gobbled the last half ration of our dehydrated dinners and tried to pretend we weren't desperate for more.

Early the following morning, we moved along the top of the Redwall until we arrived at the edge of a deep fissure. The opening was extremely narrow, no more than fifteen feet across, while the walls were smooth and absolutely vertical. Somewhere in the shadows far below were the faint sounds of moving water.

As I knelt and peered into the top of the crack, Rich, Amy, and Kelly dropped their packs and began digging out heavy pieces of gear. Each item—plastic helmets, aluminum carabiners, a 135-foot coil of eight-millimeter rope—landed at the lip of the crack with a clatter or a thump. Soon there was a substantial mound of equipment, especially after Pete and I had retrieved the half-forgotten items we'd been instructed to add to our own packs.

When everything was laid out, each of us donned a helmet and a climbing harness, and selected a set of nylon loops known as slings. Then an exchange took place involving some technical rock-climbing lingo that I found baffling, having done this only once before in a climbing gym.

"The rope's super slick," observed Amy, "so we can use two carabiners on our ATCs."

"Just put a bight through your descender, lock it, and you're good to go," advised Rich as he slung some webbing around a boulder and anchored the climbing rope to it.

Then Kelly stepped to the edge and flung the rope directly into the fissure. It cut through the air with a high-pitched whipping sound, slapping against the walls as it fell into the darkness.

*   *   *

To say that I knew nothing about what we were about to do would be an understatement. In addition to my ignorance about rappelling and rock climbing—the techniques, the terminology, and the safety protocols we'd need to employ as we lowered ourselves down that rope—I had no idea that the fissure itself was part of a hidden world that had a fascinating story to tell, in part because Rich himself had played a leading role in its discovery and exploration almost a decade earlier.

The world inside of that crack was the topographic equivalent of a strongbox whose secrets and treasures could be accessed only if one had a key. And the key, Rich had figured out, was a willingness to follow the water wherever it wanted to go.

CHAPTER 28

Drenched in Wonder

I t's almost impossible to overstate the single-mindedness of rain in the canyon. Anytime a thunderstorm is unleashed, every drop of water that falls seeks out the fastest and most direct route to the Colorado River—often in the form of a flash flood or a debris flow. As these torrents sluice over the softer, less impervious strata of rock, they continue the work of widening out the tributaries along both sides of the river. But when the runoff strikes the harder layers—especially the limestones—it can create one of the most remarkable landscape features of the Southwest.

Churning with abrasive loads of cobblestones and boulders, a flash flood that encounters an imperfection in the Redwall or the Muav often opens an incision and, over time, cuts into the stone like a surgical knife. Thanks to the density and resistance of limestone, some of these cracks are exceptionally narrow, with depths greatly exceeding their widths. In many places, they span less than seven feet at the base—just wide enough to run one's fingertips along adjacent walls that soar hundreds of feet from bottom to top. These crevices are known as slot canyons, and they have long been regarded as places to be avoided at all costs by everyone who ventures into the canyon on foot.

For good reason. It's not unusual for an isolated cloudburst dozens of miles away to send a deluge of water and mud crashing through a

slot whose walls block out all but a thin strip of sky, obliterating everything in its path—which is why experienced hikers have traditionally
made every effort to steer clear of these traps, especially during the
monsoon season in late summer when heavy afternoon rain showers
pay sporadic visits to the canyon. Even Harvey Butchart, who is said
to have left no stone unturned during his quest to explore the canyon,
recoiled from the slots, deeming them far too intimidating and dangerous to gamble with.

As a result, virtually everything about these features—how many
there were, how deep they ran, what they might contain, and whether
it was even possible for a person to wriggle through them—was a
tantalizing mystery back in the early 2000s, when Rich first stumbled
across Butchart's records. But after combing through the math professor's old logbooks and studying the topographic map upon which
he had carefully inscribed each of his hikes, Rich had an intriguing
realization. The logbooks and the map offered not only a comprehensive guide to all the places Butchart had explored during his four-
decade-long quest, but also a blueprint of the areas that he had done
his best to *avoid*.

It didn't take long to figure out that many of the spots Butchart's
routes had steered clear of were entry points to uncharted slots, many
of which didn't even have names. If Rich wanted to probe the last of
the canyon's great unknown, all he had to do was follow the map and
walk through those doorways.

*   *   *

To join him in this effort, Rich recruited Todd Martin, an electrical
engineer and veteran backcountry enthusiast from Phoenix who ran a
quirky website called ToddsHikingGuide.com. Their first project was
a slot known as Buck Farm, forty miles downstream from Lee's Ferry,
into which they descended with a two-hundred-foot climbing rope in
the spring of 2008. When they found the passage blocked by a chockstone, a massive boulder wedged between the walls like a cork in a

bottle, they were treated to a crash course in one of the most terrifying aspects of slot-canyon descents.

On the far side of the chockstone, the slot's horizontal floor gave way to a vertical drop of more than thirty-five feet, framed by walls too smooth to offer any handholds. Their first challenge was to establish a rappel anchor by looping the rope through a pinch point between the chockstone and the wall of the slot, then lower themselves into the shadowy reaches below. But the most unsettling part of the business unfolded only after they had both completed the descent and confronted the fact that, having brought only one rope, they needed to bring it with them for whatever lay ahead.*

After taking a deep breath, they pulled on the rope until its free end snaked through the anchor, fell through the air, and dropped at their feet with a muffled thud, cutting off any possibility of retreat. From this point forward, the only way out was down. They would either surmount every other challenge or be trapped inside the slot, screaming for help until they perished.

Over the next several hours as Rich and Todd wormed deeper into the recesses of the slot, they rappelled four additional times. The longest of these was 160 vertical feet, almost half the height of the Statue of Liberty. At multiple points between those drops they were also forced to brace themselves against the polished walls using their elbows, their knees, and the seats of their pants—anything that might create enough friction to prevent them from sliding to their deaths—before they finally reached the bottom.

They had picked Buck Farm for their first project because it was one of a handful of Grand Canyon slots that had already been descended by others, which meant they had at least a vague idea of what they were getting into. But six months later when they ventured into an unexplored slot called Saddle, eight miles farther downstream, they encountered something every bit as frightening as pulling their rope through an anchor and closing off their retreat.

---

* Hauling multiple ropes is heavy and impractical; leaving them behind is expensive.

The men's preparation and research had made clear to them that even the best topographic maps and the most refined satellite imagery couldn't shed much light on critical details inside an unknown slot canyon. Yes, the vertical distance between the top of a slot and the bottom of the canyon could be gauged; but the number of individual drops and the height of each was an enigma, because the walls were simply too high, the space inside too narrow, and the shadows too deep for any of that information to escape. So the only way to find out what lay inside an uncharted crevice such as Saddle was to make an educated guess as to how much rope might be needed and then rappel in, hoping for the best and praying that everything would work out okay.

In this case, it didn't. In what they assumed would be an overabundance of caution, they actually brought *two* ropes, including a four-hundred-foot-long monster that weighed almost twenty pounds. This proved more than sufficient for every drop they encountered until, deep inside the slot, Rich lowered himself off a massive chockstone, rappelled all the way down to the sharp end of the rope—and found himself stranded on a ledge no more than nine inches wide, with another sixty feet of drop, the height of a five-story building, still yawning beneath his heels.

His only choice was to pull out an emergency bolt kit that he was astute enough to have brought along, auger into the limestone with a hand drill, and place an anchor in the face of the rock. Next, he called for Todd and two friends (who had unwisely joined them) to rappel down one by one to the ledge, where all four men clipped off to the same anchor while balanced on their toes. Then they pulled the rope down on their heads—along with a shower of small pebbles—tied the rope off to the new anchor, and completed the final phase of the rappel.*

---

* Although bolting is regarded as inappropriate in wilderness areas and thus discouraged in many parts of national parks, it is sometimes critical for safety. Whenever possible, however, climbers in the canyon build their anchors with natural materials—using the pinch points of boulders, the trunks of trees, or piling heavy rocks into a stack known (somewhat disconcertingly) as a "deadman"—to which they can tie off their ropes.

This was far more drama than any of them had bargained for. But twelve hours later, when they finally arrived at the river, they had completed the first descent in recorded history of Saddle Canyon— an achievement that, despite the terror it had induced, whetted their appetite for more.

*   *   *

Soon, Rich and Todd were scouring Butchart's old map to identify auspicious-looking prospects, then heading back into the canyon, where they found themselves grappling with a host of new challenges, many of them posed by water. Thanks to the fractures in the surrounding limestone, slots into which they descended were often filled with robust streams and waterfalls, all of which had to be waded through or rappelled into. But the most daunting element they faced, by far, was the giant potholes.

Unlike the shallow dimples up on the Esplanade, these were deep, bowl-shaped cavities hollowed out by countless floods. The largest of them could extend ten yards across, reaching depths of fifteen or even twenty feet. Sometimes the lip was so high, and the surface of the stone so slippery—seven or eight feet of vertical, unblemished slickrock— that if you and your partner dropped in together, you could both wind up treading water and scrabbling desperately at the sides, until you drowned. (In 2005, two students from Brigham Young University perished in precisely this manner inside a deep pothole in Utah's Choprock Canyon.)

These were known as keeper potholes, and the prospect of becoming ensnared in one was perhaps even more horrifying than having your retreat cut off or running out of rope in the middle of a rappel. What's more, the danger wasn't restricted only to humans. Sometime in 2006, a mother bear and her cubs became trapped in a keeper on Arizona's Mogollon Rim. Six months later when Rich descended into the same hole during a practice trip for the Grand Canyon, he found that the pool was filled with a kind of rotting goulash that he described as "bear soup."

As awful as the possibility of dying in a keeper pothole may have been, a hundred other mistakes could kill you just as easily—and as the pace of their exploration picked up, Rich and Todd began to understand how even the tiniest slipup or the most innocuous oversight could carry irrevocable consequences, especially given that the absence of a satellite signal anywhere inside a slot prevented them from summoning help.

As they began to grasp how shockingly *dangerous* these places were, their exploratory ventures were infused with an edginess that persisted even after they had popped out like a pair of wet sewer rats at the bottom of a slot, where they would pull out their pack rafts, cradle their backpacks on their laps, and launch down the Colorado—knowing full well that if they were tipped upside down or became entangled in their gear amid the river's eddies, whirlpools, or monster standing waves, they'd be pulled to the bottom and drowned.

Between those pockets of turbulence, however, lay long, dreamy stretches of calm water where they could simply relax, lie back, and drift, gazing up while silently watching the walls scroll past until, invariably, one of them spotted something intriguing—perhaps a tiny alcove tucked high in the limestone, or a narrow crack terminating in a pour-over perched three hundred feet above the river. Often those features were visible for no more than a few seconds before the current ferried them past, but that was more than enough time to glimpse the irresistible possibility of something new.

"Hey, what's that?" one of them would call out, pointing up. "Ya think it goes all the way to the top of the Redwall?"

"Dunno," the other would reply. "Only one way to find out."

Which was the signal for them both to exclaim in unison:

"Let's add it to the list!"

*   *   *

By 2009, Rich and Todd were spending every moment of their free time inside the canyon, and excursions that had started as quick, single-hit weekend strikes were now mushrooming into full-blown, weeklong expeditions linking four or five slots together. As their ambitions expanded, so, too, did their respect for the paramount truth about slot-canyon exploration: the number of ways you could die far exceeded the number of tools and gadgets you could stuff inside your pack—and, therefore, one's life depended on getting that balance exactly right. But even after they had pared things down to bring only what they truly needed, the loads they were forced to carry could still be crushing.

As a result, each excursion was brutish and grinding: the labor it demanded; the misery and anxiety it inflicted; the sheer amount of donkeywork necessary to get to the other end alive. But there was something marvelous about this obsession of theirs, too.

On the finest days, when they were so in sync that each move slid flawlessly into the next, as spare as stone and as fluid as water, a single slot could serve up a smorgasbord of satisfactions unmatched by almost anything else. No other sport or hobby seemed to corral so many different subdisciplines—climbing and caving, orienteering and backpacking, swimming and river running—under the umbrella of a larger pursuit while demanding absolute mastery of each. No other job or line of work offered such an immensely rewarding set of puzzles—mechanical, cognitive, navigational—that needed to be resolved. As Todd was fond of pointing out, no specialty subjected its practitioners to a more variegated breadth of terrain harboring such a colorful and distinctive range of perils with a greater potential for injury or death—all within the same afternoon.

The completion of each new project inspired half a dozen others, and sometimes it seemed as if there were no limit to the number of unexplored slots still hidden deep in the canyon, untouched and beckoning. And if the men's inability to resist the summons of those mysteries qualified as a kind of sickness or fever, then they wanted no part of any cure that might have dulled their desire to find out where those features led, or blunted their fascination with the treasures awaiting them inside—marvels unlike anything that could be found anywhere else.

Over the ages, each slot had been sculpted into a work of astonishing symmetry and elegance by the gritty torrents that had repeatedly funneled through it. Countless floods had cambered their flanks with graceful curves while sanding their walls to a clean, silken finish. After each surge subsided, the crystalline waters from the springs, and the muted light filtering into the undulating crevices, had nursed the return of the secret gardens that flourished deep amid the recesses, like orchids taking root at the bottom of a vase.

No two slots were exactly alike, each extraordinary in its own way. One might be studded with a stair-step chain of tumbling waterfalls, while another was necklaced with a string of terraced basins the size of bathtubs, each pouring into the next, and a third could feature an overhang where water percolated through so many tiny fractures in the ceiling that if you sat beneath it, you would find yourself in a continuous shower emanating from clouds of moss.

The walls of one slot they discovered were spanned by a limestone arch as elegant as any bridge in Amsterdam, while the floor of another was carpeted for more than a thousand yards with Scarlet Monkey Flowers and Maidenhair Ferns. There was even a slot whose final drop delivered you into the branches of a redbud tree beside the Colorado— and if you made the descent in March, when the tree was in bloom, you would find yourself standing on the shore caught in a brief burst of magenta-colored flower petals.

Some slots left them speechless, while others seemed to call out for names. Sidewinder curved back and forth like the body of the serpent. The Sistine Chapel featured overhangs stained in a tapestry of color. Twist and Shout boasted a ballroom-size alcove in which the two engineers, unable to restrain their exuberance, broke into a dance. Even the slots that were destined to remain nameless had features worthy of commemoration, especially when it came to the bell-shaped chambers along the outer curves and bends. The sides of the Heart Room were crimson, while those of the Wine Room looked like merlot. Inside the Corkscrew Room, the walls rotated through one 140-degree turn, dropped twenty feet, completed another 140-degree turn, then dropped again into a keeper hole that you had to swim across.

At the bottom of a slot called Climax was a pair of oval-shaped pot-holes called the Eyes, and the water in those pools glowed with a yellow light reflecting down from the upper walls. Whenever a cloud passed over the narrow strip of sky above the top of the slot, a blue shadow would slide sleepily across the surface of the water, making it seem as if the eyes were blinking, evoking the unnerving possibility that the slot might be a living entity—which, in a very real sense, they all were.

*   *   *

Every now and then, Rich and Todd would rappel into a slot that was dull and featureless, but for the most part they found themselves drenched in wonder. Inside grottoes veiled behind dripping curtains of fern, they encountered frogs and tadpoles, rattlesnakes, Bighorn Sheep, and even a handful of Spotted Owls. For these and many other shy creatures, the slots offered a refugium, a web of shadow-cooled sanctuaries where they were safe from scrutiny and pursuit, shielded from the harshness of the more open and exposed world above. And yet, the longer that the two men lingered inside these worlds, the better they came to understand just how illusory those protections could be.

Many slots were too gorgeous to visit only once, and as they returned again and again, they were struck by the changes they observed. A slot whose gracefully fluted walls transfixed them when they first laid eyes on it in November might be plastered in mud by the following October. A pristine catch basin ringed with watercress one summer could be choked with gravel the following spring. It was astonishing what could happen in just a few months. Bushes and trees ripped out by their roots. Delicate water features demolished. Oases buried beneath enough sand and scree to fill the belly of an ore freighter.

If the floods that wrought this destruction were sporadic and random, they occurred with considerably greater frequency than anyone had previously assumed. Although a slot might remain untouched for a hundred years, it was equally likely, depending on the alignment of storm cells and cloudbursts, for that same slot to be scoured down to bedrock once every three years. As Rich and Todd took note of these changes, they began to see that the beauty of these transitory worlds was a blade whose edge was sharpened by the awareness of its evanescence—the haunted knowledge that the elements that made these places so lovely were destined to be obliterated, in the blink of an eye.

And there was something else, too. Thanks to the years Rich had spent in the backcountry, he had a solid grasp of how thoroughly the canyon's ancient peoples had taken its measure and unraveled its riddles prior to the arrival of whites. Better than most experts, he understood that among their many other talents, the Ancestral Puebloans were remarkable rock climbers, capable of amazing feats that had enabled them to reach deep into places that most whites deemed inaccessible. But despite his and Todd's best efforts, the two men could find no evidence in the crevices they were exploring to suggest that anyone had ever been there before them, thereby raising the rather remarkable possibility—at least until other proof came to light—that they may have been the first people in all of human history to see those slots.

In this day and age, it's exceedingly rare for anyone to open up a piece of terrain where human beings have never set foot. To have done so in the heart of an iconic national park that hosts roughly 5 million visitors each year—and that has been mapped, surveyed, photographed, and analyzed as extensively as the Grand Canyon—is virtually without precedent. Yet, that's what Rich, Todd, and a handful of their friends seemed to have pulled off.

In four years, they spent more than 200 nights below the rim dropping into 165 separate slot canyons, more than 100 of which are believed to have been first descents.[*]

*   *   *

[*] By Rich and Todd's best reckoning, this represents roughly two-thirds of the total number of slots in the canyon, which means that there may still be a hundred unexplored crevices left—although this number diminishes with every passing year.

In 2011, Todd pulled together much of the knowledge that he and Rich had acquired over the previous five years and published the first-ever guidebook to the technical slots inside the Grand Canyon. Then shortly after the book's debut, he turned away from the canyon to focus on a set of new adventures, including motorized parachuting. Meanwhile, Rich adopted the opposite approach and took his obsession to the next level, based on one final epiphany regarding the features that they had explored.

The more he thought about it, the more he began to see the slots not just as a series of individual challenges, but as an interlocking network of passages. Properly linked, they might enable a person to move back and forth between different ledge systems inside the chasm, much like a game of Chutes and Ladders.

From this insight, it was but a small step to the idea that would serve as the key to his thru-hike. If he could use the slot canyons as both a source of drinking water *and* as a means of reaching food stashes that had been placed either next to the river or on otherwise inaccessible terraces, then he could chart a route along the highest and cleanest lines in the canyon.

Four years later, he had brought that vision to fruition and celebrated its consummation while sitting on a stool next to the stove in my kitchen in Flagstaff. Now he was about to show Pete, Amy, Kelly, and me how the principle worked by taking us into one of the most exquisite of all the slots that he and Todd had discovered.

It was known as Olo, and if all went well, it would enable us to conclude our circumnavigation of the Great Thumb Mesa by escaping the Esplanade, descending to the bottom of the canyon, and reaching our resupply cache before we ran out of food.

CHAPTER 29

Olo

"I t's probably best not to look down right now," advised Pete.

Ignoring this excellent counsel, I turned my head, glanced beneath my feet, and promptly felt a queasy sensation in my stomach. The only thing preventing me from plummeting 110 feet and spattering on the rocks below was my right hand, which was clenched around the long trail of rope from which I dangled in midair as I slowly lowered myself toward the ground with the aid of the rappel device fastened to the front of my climbing harness.

For a moment, I was sickened by the length of the drop, the slenderness of the rope, and the irrational thought that my hand might somehow decide, all on its own, to simply *let go*. But as I inched downward, the weight of my pack gently pulled my upper body away from the rope, sending me into a sluggish, clockwise spin, and all of those concerns vanished as I took stock of the world I was entering.

The space between the walls, which was tight and tapered toward the top, gently ballooned outward as I lowered myself deeper into the chamber, as if I were a spider on a thread dropping down the neck of a wine bottle. It was quiet, too—a tomb-like hush pierced only by a faint crunch when my toes finally touched the ground, which was covered with small shards of creamy-white gravel.

Kelly and Amy were already there, and after Rich and Pete had completed their descents, we pulled the rope, cutting off our exit, and set off walking in single file along the gently sloping floor of the slot. As we walked, the space between the walls flared like the bell end of a trumpet, yawning as wide as 150 feet for a hundred yards or more before pinching back to where we could run the tips of our fingers against both sides simultaneously. In each of these atria, the walls caught and amplified the sounds of our passing—the clomp of our feet, the rustle of the gravel, the clink of the metal carabiners clipped to our climbing harnesses.

As my eyes adjusted to the dimness, I could see that the walls were coarsely polished and graced with complex curves, as if they had been sculpted from something more supple and elastic than stone. The flanks of the slot cambered back and forth in a series of sinuous, interlocking bends, while high above, the thin strip of daylight continued to narrow until the upper sections of the walls, now soaring more than three hundred feet above us, arched back upon themselves and pinched off the sky completely.

Deep inside the vault, the air should have felt murky and dark. Instead, it was awash in a lustrous radiance, lit with a soft sheen that appeared to emanate from several different places at once. Although the sky itself had vanished, sunlight was still pouring into the top of the slot, and long, gleaming fingers of gold extended far down the walls, filling the interior with an effulgence so delicate, elusive, and gorgeous that we lowered our voices and spoke in whispers, as if we had stepped into a place of worship.

"I feel like this is what people are trying to create when they build *actual* cathedrals," murmured Amy, staring up as she stood in a patch of sunshine no bigger than a manhole cover. "The light is so warm and comforting you want to scoop it up and bottle it so you can preserve the way it makes you feel—and then you realize that not only can't you capture it, you can't even *name* it."

*   *   *

Soon we hit the next rappel, and after that they started coming fast, one after another. Each was more complicated than the last and separated from the next by a stretch of relatively easy walking. During these intervals, we began to encounter little islands of vegetation. First came the pods of scraggly acacia trees, some clinging to the edges of the walls while others defiantly sprouted from the middle of the floor. Next came tiny groves of redbuds, vibrant and green, followed by clusters of Coyote Willow, whose narrow leaves and reddish-brown bark filled the air with the faint but distinctively clean aroma that heralded the presence of moisture.

Shortly after that, we arrived at the edge of a pothole whose bottom was peppered with black-and-white bits of gravel, each piece as sharp as a hand-knapped arrowhead. This was the first in a chain of stair-step pools ringed with foliage that included springy garlands of moss, moist beds of watercress, and quivering locks of Maidenhair Fern.

Some of these pools were ovular, others shaped like teardrops, and still others formed perfect cylinders. Many were shallow, harboring no more than a few inches of water, although a bright handful plunged five or even six feet down. Each was fed by its upstream neighbor and spilled into its downstream companion by means of a fluted channel no more than a few inches wide, hewn into the bedrock.

From there, the stream funneled into a chain of waterfalls, dropping from one basin into the next, each feeder flowing at its own rate, and striking with a different timbre and frequency so that the sounds merged to form a kind of fluid melody and the walls resounded with the music of moving water. Transfixed, we stood listening to this rhapsody until it was interrupted by a harsh rattle of loose stones, and we glanced down just in time to spot a trio of Bighorns, a mother with a pair of baby lambs, scampering down the trough of slickrock.

"I'm pretty sure they come in here to have their babies," whispered Rich. "This place is very protected—it has everything they need."

God only knew how they had found their way into Olo, or by what impossible-to-follow route the mother was now making their escape. But there they were: clattering across the terraces and splashing through the channel of water before—*poof!*—disappearing around the next downstream bend, leaving us stunned by the encounter and wondering if they might have materialized from the catacombs of our imagination, a vivid embodiment of Olo's magic.

*   *   *

By now, we had penetrated to the bottom of the Redwall, where we encountered an entirely new layer of rock, a stratum of limestone known as the Temple Butte Formation, which is present only in certain sections of the canyon, and whose lineage extends back more than 375 million years. In addition to its unusual coloration—an alluring blend of purple, gray, and cream—the Temple Butte is distinctive for its tendency to break away in large chunks. As the floor of the slot drew us deeper into the layer, we could see that dozens of enormous boulders, each the size of a bread truck, were wedged into the narrowest spaces between the walls, now less than thirty feet apart, directly above our heads.

It was spooky, to say the least, to pass beneath the bellies of these monsters while wondering how precariously they were anchored, and whether some tiny alteration in the forces holding Olo together—a faint shift of air currents, or the sound of a stone kicked into a pool— might bring one of those behemoths down on our heads, squashing us like bugs. Something about the gnarled purple whorls contorting their undersides seemed to underscore not only how small we were, but also how far we had descended—and how lost we would be if anything went wrong inside this crypt.

"How high do you think the walls are here?" asked Pete, craning his neck in the hopes of spotting a sliver of the sky.

"Well, the Redwall in this part of the canyon is about five hundred feet thick, and they say the Temple Butte can extend to seven hundred, so we're probably looking up at almost twelve hundred feet of rock," replied Rich.

That seemed absurd for such a narrow space, yet the floor con- tinued to drop through two more rappels, the first sending us down a forty-foot waterfall, the second corkscrewing through a channel so tight that we were forced to remove our packs and lower them on a zip line, which took almost an hour for us to rig. After that, we went deeper still.

Around 4:00 p.m., we hit the base of the Temple Butte and entered the Muav Limestone. There we encountered a sequence of pools lined with rock the color of chalk, each deeper than the one before it. This was followed by another three rappels, the last of which finally deposited us on a small, crescent-shaped spit of sand featuring a slender cottonwood tree whose branches and leaves framed the slow, brown churn of the Colorado River. We had reached the bottom.

After Pete had pulled our rope through the final anchor, Kelly and Amy plunged into a nearby clump of willows, rummaged around for a few minutes, and emerged with a pair of plastic five-gallon buckets, each weighing thirty-five pounds, that had been hidden a few weeks earlier by Jean-Philippe Clark.

"Nothing ever goes exactly according to plan, and we're a perfect example of that," observed Rich as he pried the lid from one of the resupply caches and began pulling out chocolate bars, beef jerky, and packets of ramen noodles, all of which we eyed ravenously. "We got hammered by an epic storm and had to wallow through nine inches of snow around Owl Eyes—which is probably the first time anybody's ever been crazy enough to do that—but at least we didn't run out of food."

"Oh, really?" said Pete, holding up a Ziploc bag containing the last of his provisions. "Would you say that four jelly beans isn't running out of food?"

"Nope!" replied Rich, who, like the rest of us, had nothing even remotely edible left anywhere in his pack. "But, by God, we cut it pretty damn close."*

*   *   *

* As with all of our caches, the buckets were later retrieved either by us or by our friends.

Early the following morning when the stars were still twinkling in the blue-dark sky, we broke camp and began pushing down-canyon. Despite our fully loaded packs, we moved swiftly, following a set of steeply tilted ledges along the shore for almost two miles before arriving at a side canyon called Matkatamiba. There we turned into the mouth, ascended the bed of a small stream until the water slowed to a trickle before disappearing altogether, then kept on climbing.

Although this part of Matkat, as the boatmen call it, wasn't quite narrow enough to qualify as a true slot—at the spot we entered, the floor spanned the width of a two-lane street—it had nevertheless been sculpted by forces similar to those that had shaped Olo. Before long, we encountered the first sign of these events when we arrived at the base of a giant pile of boulders wedged tightly between the walls of the tributary, rising to a height of eighty or ninety feet.

The stones were immense, hunks of rock the size of coal barges, and they were jumbled together haphazardly, as if they'd been dumped directly from the sky. They were jackstrawed like timbers in a logjam— an apt comparison, given the number of dead trees whose branches and trunks were bristling from the spaces between the boulders. Together, they offered stark evidence of the size and ferocity of the floods that had hurtled through this drainage, snatching up these leviathans and tumbling them together like pebbles in a cement mixer.

"Kinda makes you want to barf when you think about what it took to move all this stuff," remarked Kelly, shaking her head as she surveyed the mound. "Can you imagine us trying to outrun something like that?"

Fortunately, we only needed to hoist ourselves into the mess, scrambling up through the cracks and wormholes between the stones, clawing with our fingers and toes, bracing with elbows and knees and shoulders and butts as we grunted and cursed and heaved our way to the top of the pile. There, another wide and gently ascending boulevard beckoned us toward the base of yet another arrested avalanche, a pattern that would repeat itself almost a dozen times during the remainder of the morning and all through the afternoon.

On we went, up one obstacle and onto the next, straight through the guts of the drainage—through the Muav and the Temple Butte, the Redwall and the Supai—an ascent that seems as remarkable to me now as it did to me then, for the simple fact that we never paused, not even for a moment, until, just before sunset, we punched through the final section of the climb and found ourselves back on the seared red terraces of the Esplanade, with the Colorado once again lost in the depths far below.

We emerged less than a mile away from a sentinel of sandstone that shot more than a thousand feet into the air from its base—a chimney-shaped column of straight-sided Coconino Sandstone girded at its pedestal with an angled apron of Hermit Shale, and capped at the summit with a pyramid of Toroweap Formation. This was Mount Sinyella, a pillar whose symmetry and boldness were unmatched by anything else on the Esplanade, which is surely why it is sacred to the Havasupai, whose home village lay somewhere off to the southwest, on the far side of the monolith.

Out beyond Sinyella's silhouette, a ring of cliffs extended in all directions to the canyon's rims, and for a long moment we stood and took in the view without anyone saying a word. Then Rich spun in a slow circle, and as he pivoted, he summoned the names of the promontories and embayments along the rimlands in a low, rhythmic murmur, as if he were reciting a kind of free-verse poem:

> Beaver Canyon. Little Coyote Canyon. Cork Spring Canyon.
> Tuwago Point. Yumtheska Point. Kanab Point.
> Fishtail Mesa and Flatiron Butte.
> The Kangaroo Headland.
> And, oh my gosh—
> there's the Tenderfoot Rim.

Each feature in the litany was a separate compass point on the map of Rich's wanderings during the years he'd spent exploring, and invoking their names seemed to remind him of what he loved most about this place.

"You know, to me, this is the essence of the canyon, right here," he remarked. "It's amazing, in this day and age, that you can go out on the Esplanade, under the shadow of the Great Thumb Mesa, and not see another soul."

"Who else comes out here?" asked Pete.

"Well, almost nobody—this is really remote." Rich's look suggested this answer was self-evident. "We've been on this route for, what? Almost two weeks? It took us eleven days of enormously hard travel to get here."

"I get that," said Pete, "but how many people do you think would stand on this spot in a given year?"

"Only a few."

"Give us an actual number," I pressed.

"Less than a dozen."

No one said anything as we thought about that.

"But there are some years where you have only one or two people out here," Rich added. "And there are other years where there's nobody at all. Sometimes it's just zero."

*   *   *

We set camp on a rounded hump of orange slickrock just as the evening sky was filling with clouds tinted pink and gold by the setting sun. Framed in the middle of it all stood Sinyella, singular in its magnificence, and when I crouched next to a pothole to gather water, the reflection of the monolith on the surface of the pool quivered in the ripples set off by the touch of my bottle.

Perhaps it was the tremulous image of the Havasupai's soaring icon that returned my thoughts to Dianna Uqualla and the instructions she had given to Pete and me that we pay special attention to the animals and listen to what they were trying to tell us. By now, I understood that she wasn't simply asking us to attend to the comings and goings of the canyon wrens and the cactus mice and the lizards.

Those details were important, to be sure. But so, too, were the human stories of the land—in particular, the story of her people. A community whose past amounted, perhaps more than anything else, to its own kind of slot canyon. A living entity that was deeply hidden, filled with beauty, and punctuated by cataclysms like the one that had descended on them back during the years of her girlhood, when they were forced to hurl themselves into one final battle to avoid being wiped off the map entirely.

CHAPTER 30

In Sinyella's Shadow

B y the beginning of the 1970s, the Havasupai's prospects were as grim as those of a family of bears trapped in a keeper hole. Almost half of the adult population had no job, and among those between the ages of eighteen and twenty-four, the unemployment rate was 73 percent. Life expectancy was just forty-four years, a quarter-century less than that of other Americans, while the suicide rate was four times the national average. Members had taken to calling themselves "the forgotten tribe" because aside from the limited number of tourists who were willing to make the trek into their village, few outsiders seemed to know they even existed, much less to care about the unresolved grievance that lay at the root of their problems.

For almost seventy years, the tribe and its supporters had repeatedly been petitioning to enlarge the borders of their miniature reservation. So far, all of those entreaties had fallen on deaf ears—including their most recent effort, in 1967, when the tribal council declared that it was an "immoral act" for the U.S. Forest Service and the National Park Service to keep them confined to less than one square mile while depriving them of their lands along the South Rim.

On the heels of this latest plea—which, like its six predecessors, was denied—the Indian Claims Commission had proposed paying the Havasupai $1,240,000 to compensate them for the loss of the bulk of their ancestral territory, which came out to fifty-four cents an acre for real estate that they had never wanted to sell in the first place. The tribe initially tried to refuse the money, but were advised by their attorney, whose compensation would amount to 10 percent of the settlement, that they should accept the offer.*

When the deal was finally signed, the numbers on the balance sheet were shocking. As author Stephen Hirst notes in *I Am the Grand Canyon*, after subtracting their attorney's commission and setting aside 75 percent of the settlement to be held in trust by the Bureau of Indian Affairs, each adult among the 425 recorded members of the tribe would receive $651.37 for the loss of their birthright. At the time, that was almost enough money to purchase a color TV and a pair of tickets to a Rolling Stones concert. Meanwhile, the Park Service continued pressing its decades-long campaign to fold the 518-acre reservation into the park and pack the remaining Havasupai off to the Hualapai Reservation, directly to the west.

In the face of these challenges, another tribe might have folded its tents and given up. Instead, the Havasupai decided to double down by throwing everything they had into one last fight in their fifty-year war with the Park Service to see if their homelands could be restored to them.

*   *   *

By this point, more than half a century had passed since the establishment of Grand Canyon National Park, and despite many changes, one constant was the conviction among conservationists that the park's boundaries needed to be dramatically broadened. Thanks to some important advancements in scientists' understanding of biology and

---

* The Indian Claims Commission was set up to provide compensation for indigenous lands that had been unjustly expropriated by the United States. In the hopes of resolving their grievances with the federal government, every tribe in the country was encouraged to file a suit putting forth their claims, and after the suits had been adjudicated, plaintiffs would receive a financial settlement. The process unfolded at a glacial pace, and there was no provision for handing back what tribes wanted most, which was the land itself.

wildlife management, the arguments in favor of such an expansion now extended considerably beyond the already troubling fact that in defiance of geology, hydrography, and topography, the narrow ribbon of parkland that Colin Fletcher had traversed in the spring of 1963 embraced only about a third of the actual canyon.

Experts could now demonstrate that the park's footprint was too small to protect the habitats of native plants or to accommodate the seasonal movement of important animals. These concerns enabled park officials to argue that it was impossible for their agency to fulfill its mandate to protect the landscape and to shelter the species that depended upon it—a problem they proposed to resolve with a new master plan that would consolidate the extensive patchwork of federal landholdings abutting the canyon into a significantly larger park.

To no one's surprise, when word of the plan was released in 1971, it triggered objections from the usual cast of opponents: ranchers, rural libertarians incensed by any form of federal oversight, and politicians catering to those interests—people whose predecessors had so fiercely resisted the establishment of the park a few generations earlier. By now, the park also had some brand-new adversaries in the mining community, thanks to the discovery of several high-grade uranium deposits in and around the canyon. But as these groups were about to discover, shifts in the political landscape had placed some powerful new tools in the hands of conservationists.

Thanks to a key piece of legislation, the National Environmental Policy Act, profound changes were unfolding in how decisions were made with respect to federal lands. Transparency and full public participation as well as rigorous scientific analysis were now mandated by law, and conservationists used these requirements to push for expanded park borders that would come far closer to embracing the entire canyon. Around this shared vision, a coalition emerged among an unlikely set of groups who under normal circumstances could barely stand to be in the same room with one another, much less agree to cooperate.

Foremost among these, perhaps, was Barry Goldwater, Arizona's right-wing Republican senator who had voted against the 1964 Civil

Rights Act, and who despised conservationists almost as much as he loathed environmental regulations and taxes. Despite his hostility to anything that bore the whiff of a liberal agenda, however, Goldwater cared deeply about the canyon—which he'd floated through on a river trip in 1940—and was willing to throw his support behind a pair of bills that would enable Grand Canyon National Park to extend all the way from Lee's Ferry to the Grand Wash Cliffs while folding in many of the major side canyons on the surrounding plateaus.

Although this was remarkable enough, the added twist was that Goldwater had also been persuaded to care about the Havasupai after meeting them for the first time in January of 1973, and the bill that he introduced in the U.S. Senate later that same year included a proposal to restore a substantial portion of their tribe's ancestral lands on the rims. In his introductory remarks, Goldwater acknowledged that a number of the Havasupai's Native American neighbors viewed them as the "keepers" of the canyon and its sacred places. The senator also warned that the tribe "may pass into extinction" if some portion of its economic land base was not restored to them. "They are natives of the Grand Canyon," he declared, "and surely any bill relating to the ecology of the canyon should include protection of the human beings who live there."

In light of the arch-conservative principles that formed the bedrock of Goldwater's beliefs, perhaps the only thing more remarkable than the proposal itself was the ferocity of the response it triggered within the environmental community.

*　　　*　　　*

It was no surprise to anyone that Park Service officials were against the idea of returning territory to the tribe from the get-go. But it came as something of a shock when the Sierra Club, which feared that the Havasupai could not be trusted to protect their own land from developers, publicly alleged that if the rimlands were given back, the tribe intended to create an Indian version of "Disneyland on the plateau"—a baseless claim that was deliberately intended to provoke outrage.

The Havasupai were having none of it. The community prepared to muster its resources, hire new lawyers, and fling itself into a fight that would unfold not on the South Rim of the canyon, but inside the congressional committee rooms and offices of Washington, DC. From the moment the first set of hearings kicked off in the Senate in the spring of 1973, members of Congress saw the tribe's fury and resolve on full display.

"We live in a Park Service zoo," declared Augustine Hanna, a military veteran and one of the tribal council's youngest members, in his opening remarks to the politicians on the dais above him. "Remember— we used to own the whole place."

If any member of the Senate committee harbored lingering questions regarding the alleged plans to turn the plateau lands into a theme park or resort, Hanna addressed those concerns by calling the rumors started by the Sierra Club "just crazy." He added that the tribe had no interest in "some big business operation" that would turn them into white people. "We like our way of life," he announced defiantly. "We think it is *better* than yours."

Those statements were buttressed by an extensive dossier laying out the injustices that had been committed against the Havasupai during the previous ninety years, and providing hard evidence that their reservation was too small to allow them to survive. They presented maps, letters, and correspondence dating back as far as 1885, plus a copy of the offer they had submitted, upon learning that they had been misled by their own lawyer, to return the money they had been paid by the Indian Claims Commission as part of their land-claims settlement.

*   *   *

Along with Hanna, the tribe had sent almost a dozen of its members to Washington. They spent the better part of that year working sixteen-hour days in a sustained effort to press their case to politicians, administration officials, and any reporter who would listen to them. By the spring of 1974, when the *Washington Post* published an editorial urging Congress to return a portion of their homeland, there were signs that things were beginning to swing in their favor.

It took another eight months for the House and Senate to debate and then pass the bill. But on January 3, 1975, ten days after it was sent to the White House, President Gerald Ford affixed his signature to Public Law 93-620, otherwise known as the Grand Canyon National Park Enlargement Act.

The new law came close to doubling the size of the park, expanding it from 673,575 acres to roughly 1.2 million. Over the objections of the Sierra Club, the law also returned title to 185,000 acres of federal land on the rim of the canyon to the Havasupai and gave the tribe the right to use an additional 95,300 acres inside the park for traditional practices such as hunting and gathering wild plants, while prohibiting them from engaging in commercial timber or mining operations.

In the end, both sides gained something significant. The park finally encompassed the canyon for which it was named; and even though administrators would now be forced to share more than 10 percent of the expanded terrain with the Havasupai, the tribe developed an environmentally sensitive plan for using that land. Meanwhile, the territory that was repatriated to the Havasupai included a significant portion of their winter range on the plateau, an area roughly the size of all five boroughs of New York City. This was still well short of the 3 million acres of their traditional homeland; yet it was enough, in the eyes of the tribe, to enable them to begin making themselves whole. Like the ceramic pot that Kelly and Amy had temporarily reassembled, significant parts of their domain were still missing. But enough of the original vessel was restored to provide a glimpse of what it had once been—and might one day become again.

To this day, the Havasupai land restoration remains one of the largest pieces of real estate that the federal government has given back to a single tribe in the history of the United States.

*   *   *

Parts of this story were on my mind when the first rays of sunlight struck the pointed capstone on Mount Sinyella's summit on the morning after Rich informed us how few outsiders actually get to see this part of the canyon in any given year. As the light chased the shadows down the tapered flanks of the great pedestal, then spilled across the section of slickrock on which we had erected our tents, it revealed something I'd failed to notice the night before.

The terraces surrounding Sinyella were dotted with hundreds of the Utah variety of century plants, a species of agave characterized by dozens of leathery blue-green leaves that form a rosette at ground level. Each leaf in the circle, which can grow up to twenty inches long, features a vicious needlelike spike at its tip and curved thorns along its edges—and when the first rays of light swept the terraces, the spikes and thorns on every rosette flickered like candlewicks touched by a single matchstick.

By now, we had all emerged from our tents and were standing together, each of us holding a steaming cup of coffee, as we took in the spectacle of hundreds of agaves, all flaring to life in the same instant.

"You know, there *ought* to be some places left like this, where you can get out and see how it once was—how it looked a thousand years ago, or a thousand years before that," declared Rich, echoing his remarks from the previous evening. "It's so important that these places remain unspoiled."

This may well have been true. But in that moment, I was struck by the difference between imagining that we were being offered a glimpse of what this place looked like a millennium ago, and how it might feel to know that your ancestors had been firmly tied to the landscape for that entire time. How would it feel, I wondered, to be part of an unbroken human lineage that anchored you to this ground as deeply as a field of century plants—and by virtue of those roots, to know that the land belonged to you, and you belonged to the land, in a way that white visitors such as us could only dimly perceive?

CHAPTER 31

The People of the Blue-Green Water

Within thirty minutes, we were packed and on the move.

It took the better part of an hour to circle the flanks of Sinyella, which has a small spring at its base where the Havasupai sometimes leave offerings, and reach a point on the far side of the monolith where the Esplanade fell away into the depths of a massive tributary canyon. The cliffs seemed to offer no way down, but Rich ushered us through a series of four rappels. At the bottom of each drop, a steep talus slope led to the top of the next rappel. The talus was so brittle that everything we touched seemed to break into pieces, dislodging chunks of stone and forcing us to yell, *"Rock!—rock!—rock!,"* to warn those below as the missiles hurtled toward them.

Two hours later, when we had completed the final rappel and reached the bottom of the tributary, I looked back up at the cliffs, trying in vain to pick out the notch at the edge of the Esplanade where we had begun our descent. The walls now appeared seamless, as if someone up there had shut a door behind us. Then I turned and saw that we had arrived at the edge of a turbulent stream whose waters were a breathtaking shade of blue-green. After fourteen days, ninety miles, and more than fourteen thousand feet of climbing and descending, we had finally made it to Havasu Creek.

Without needing to exchange a word, we turned to the left and began making our way upstream, following a trail along the shoreline while enveloped by the sound of rushing water as the path wove through a dense tapestry of exotic greenery that included thickets of wild grape, patches of long-stemmed grass that looked like alfalfa, and thick beds of dandelions and monkeyflowers carpeting the ground beneath a canopy of cottonwood and willow trees. Because the sunlight had not yet reached the bottom of the drainage, it felt as if the day's clock had been turned back, returning us to the indigo hour bracketing the break of dawn. The tumbling creek and the teeming jungle along its banks were still cloaked in shadow, creating the sensation that we were moving through a fairy kingdom, dappled with both mystery and revelation.

The sun returned just as we arrived at a place where the current was rushing over a series of low ledges, each forming a tiny waterfall, no more than a foot or two high, with its own little pool. Mist hovered above the surface of the creek, scattering beams of light as they passed through the grapevines, and tinting the bottom of the gorge with a soft but vivid mix of tones: turquoise water, green vines, crimson rock—and above it all, a sky of Kingfisher blue.

As the trail beckoned us farther up the side canyon, the stream split into forks, and between the forks were small islands covered with clover and studded with groves of cottonwoods whose branches were backlit by the soaring walls of stone. On one of the islands, a lone Bighorn ram whose horns appeared to be twice the size of his head grazed contentedly. As we rounded the bend, he glanced up with a mouthful of grass between his teeth, chewed twice, and calmly ambled off into the trees.

Farther on, the path wove through clumps of cactus thrumming with hundreds of powder-blue dragonflies that made the air shimmer as they arose in a cloud, surrounding us as we walked. Shortly after that, we came upon a pair of ducks preening their feathers and nuzzling each other's neck as they paddled slowly around a pool at the foot of a ledge. They seemed indifferent to our presence, showing neither interest nor alarm as we shuffled past.

Then all of a sudden, we stepped into a clearing and found our-selves standing at the edge of a half-acre pool into which a thunderous column containing all of Havasu Creek was plummeting from the top of a waterfall whose lip was more than two hundred feet above our heads, greater than the height of Niagara.

*   *   *

The waterfall was created by a cliff of travertine whose face conveyed the impression of a liquid mudflow that had congealed. Embedded within the travertine were twigs and branches and even entire tree trunks that had been swept through the canyon by storm-driven floods and were now petrified in calcium carbonate, a snapshot of the tumult and chaos of a flash flood, frozen in stone.

Along the back side of the waterfall, the surface of the travertine was coated in brilliant green moss and clumps of Maidenhair Fern whose leaves quivered in the breeze created by the main column of the cascade. Inside that column, four or five plumes of water were undulating back and forth in a liquid helix, braiding together and coming apart three or four times before jackhammering into the surface of the pool with enough fury to create a spray whose droplets, rising into the sunlight, glinted like tiny shards of stained glass.

We followed the trail around the right side of the pool to a set of crude stairs hacked into the travertine that led up the cliff to the mouth of a tunnel. Inside the tunnel, which was originally excavated by a party of nineteenth-century lead and silver miners, the light faded and then disappeared, forcing us to fumble with our hands as we climbed through a series of steep twists and turns until we emerged at the top of the falls.

From there, a bumpy trail skirted the bank of the creek through an empty campground, past a line of picnic tables and a row of composting toilets, eventually drawing us into an amphitheater of relatively flat ground divided into a grid of green fields ringed by soaring ramparts of red sandstone. The fields were dotted with small houses, and next to some of the houses was a fenced corral with a horse or two standing inside.

The trail now widened into a dirt road that meandered through the center of the village, passing a row of structures that included a school, a tourist lodge, a small grocery store, a café, a post office, and the tribal headquarters building. A large stretch of open ground that served as an occasional volleyball court was surrounded by cottonwoods and a chain-link fence, and along this stretch, amid the aroma of fry bread and the sound of barking dogs, we encountered Dianna Uqualla's people.

Several were sitting on benches in front of the buildings or puttering past on ATVs, but most were simply strolling up and down the road. There were mothers and fathers with young children, old men and women, and groups of teenagers. Like the ducks and the ram and the dragonflies along the creek beneath the waterfall, none seemed to have much interest in us—and perhaps for good reason.

Each year, roughly thirty thousand outsiders converge on Supai Village to hike the trails and stay in the lodge or camp next to the creek. There is still no road to the outside world, so aside from a relatively small number of river runners who make their way up from the Colorado, the rest descend on foot, by horseback, or in one of the multiple helicopter flights that are available several days a week. Although those visitors provide a vital source of income for the tribe, few are familiar with the story of the Havasupai, or possess a context for understanding what has unfolded here in the years that followed the tribe's land-restoration victory.

*   *   *

Shortly after their homelands on the rim were restored to them in the winter of 1975, the tribe launched a sustained effort to rebuild what had been lost. Over the next several years, they designed and erected a new school so that their children could remain at home through the eighth grade before heading off to boarding school programs beyond the reservation. They wrote primers and textbooks that incorporated their history, drew up a revised map of their homeland in which the labels assigned by government surveyors were replaced with their original names, and they codified a written version of their language by assembling the tribe's first dictionary. Thanks to those efforts, many members of the community now speak Havasupai as their first language.

They also began interviewing elders to record their memories and catalog their knowledge of native plants and animals. They set out to revive ancient skills such as pottery- and basketmaking. In an effort to benefit from small-scale tourism, the only industry to which they had access, they built a modest twenty-five-room lodge inside the village as well as the café and general store, and began offering guided hikes and mule-packing services to visitors.

Many of these efforts resulted in positive change, but in other respects the tribe's welfare remained static. Despite the introduction of power lines and generators as well as water- and sewage-treatment facilities, the reservation during those years was still without basic services such as garbage collection, affordable groceries, or a fire department, and the cumulative effects of the tribe's hundred-year struggle were manifest in a range of stubborn afflictions.

By the mid-1990s, in addition to ongoing struggles with alcoholism, depression, and suicide, the community was reeling from addiction and crime driven by crystal meth, and nearly all the adults in the village suffered from type 2 diabetes. As a result, members of the tribe now find themselves enjoying the fruits of an astonishing moral and cultural victory, while continuing to wrestle with a host of unresolved practical challenges and a future that remains precarious.

* * *

Thanks to the delays imposed by the snowstorm that we had weathered while rounding the Great Thumb Mesa, we were now two days behind schedule, which meant that no one was waiting to meet us on the canyon's rim to drive us home—and although we could have arranged for a pickup, we had neither the provisions nor the permits to stay in the campground just below the village. Our best option, said Rich, was to purchase tickets and exit on one of the helicopter flights that enable tribal members to shuttle back and forth for errands or personal business.

The open area in the center of the village doubled as a helipad, and we arrived shortly before the last sortie of the day. When our flight circled overhead and landed, the pilot opened the door and a group of mothers and their children who had evidently been doing their shopping got out carrying bags of groceries, cartons of paper towels, and a collection of plastic toys. Then we clambered aboard with our packs and trekking poles.

As the chopper lifted off and climbed toward the rim, we could see the trail that accesses Havasu Canyon ascending in a series of steep switchbacks through the canyon's upper suite of rock layers. Looking back, we caught a brief glimpse of the thin ribbon of the creek tumbling through the village and past the fields on its way to the waterfall and the travertine terraces. Then the creek was swallowed up by the surrounding cliffs, and almost before we knew it we were above the vastness of the Coconino Plateau, the winter range that the Havasupai had regained more than forty years earlier.

"Look at that!" exclaimed Pete, who was sitting up front next to the pilot, and whose voice came in through the headsets that we all were wearing. "Kev—can you believe we've covered all that distance since September?"

Far to the east, high above the jumbled chaos of turrets and spires and buttes inside the chasm, I could just make out the hazy, rose-colored escarpments of the Vermilion Cliffs looming over Lee's Ferry. They looked fantastically distant, and the idea that—with the exception of this one helicopter ride—we had covered every inch of that ground on foot felt like quite an achievement, worthy of a high five from Rich. But when I turned toward him, I could see that his face was pressed to the opposite window, and that he was gazing west, out across the maze of rock that we still needed to cover to reach the Grand Wash Cliffs, whose profile still lay beyond the horizon.

I couldn't see the expression on Rich's face, but he was shaking his head as the mike on his headset caught a remark that he probably meant to keep to himself:

"You guys still have a long way to go."

PART IX

Boneland
and Bedrock

You were made and set here

to give voice to this,

your own astonishment.

—Annie Dillard

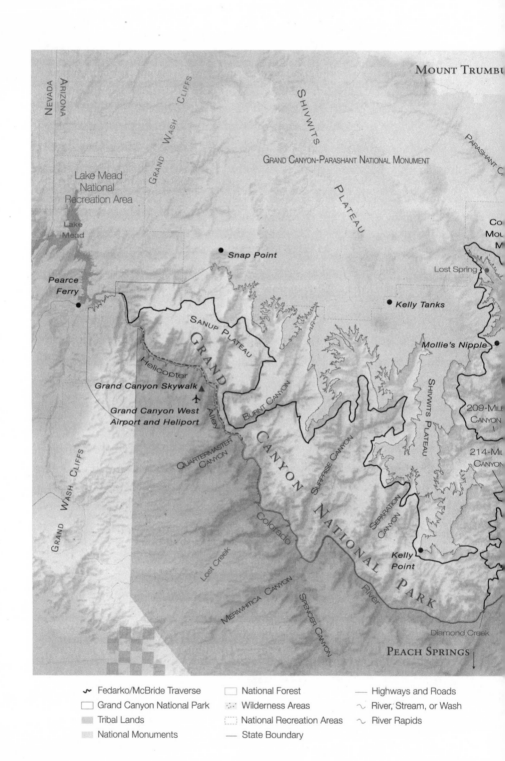

MOUNT TRUMBU

NEVADA

ARIZONA

GRAND WASH CLIFFS

SHIVWITS

GRAND CANYON-PARASHANT NATIONAL MONUMENT

PLATEAU

PARASHANT C

Lake Mead
National
Recreation Area

Lake
Mead

Snap Point

CO
MOL
M

Lost Spring

Pearce
Ferry

Kelly Tanks

SANUP PLATEAU

GRAND

Mollie's Nipple

Helicopter

Grand Canyon Skywalk

Grand Canyon West
Airport and Heliport

Alley

BURNT CANYON

SHIVWITS PLATEAU

209-MILE
CANYON

214-MILE
CANYON

QUARTERMASTER
CANYON

CANYON

SURPRISE CANYON

NATIONAL

SEPARATION
CANYON

Lost Creek

Colorado

Kelly
Point

GRAND WASH CLIFFS

River

PARK

MERIWHITICA CANYON

SPENCER CANYON

Diamond Creek

PEACH SPRINGS

Legend

- ∿ Fedarko/McBride Traverse
- ☐ Grand Canyon National Park
- ▨ Tribal Lands
- ▨ National Monuments
- ☐ National Forest
- ⠿ Wilderness Areas
- ⠇⠇ National Recreation Areas
- — State Boundary
- — Highways and Roads
- ∿ River, Stream, or Wash
- ∿ River Rapids

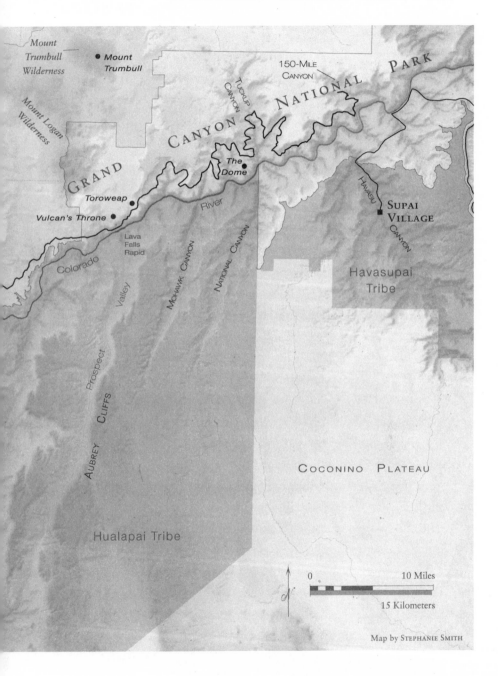

Mount Trumbull Wilderness

Mount Logan Wilderness

Mount Trumbull

150-MILE CANYON

TUCKUP CANYON

GRAND CANYON NATIONAL PARK

The Dome

HAVASU CANYON

SUPAI VILLAGE

Toroweap

River

Vulcan's Throne

Lava Falls Rapid

Colorado

Valley

MOHAWK CANYON

NATIONAL CANYON

Havasupai Tribe

Prospect

AUBREY CLIFFS

COCONINO PLATEAU

Hualapai Tribe

0   10 Miles

N

15 Kilometers

Map by STEPHANIE SMITH

CHAPTER 32

All In

ack in Flagstaff, the first call I made was to my father, who had just completed his final round of chemotherapy. He reported that he was still feeling weak and nauseous, but his body seemed to be responding well to the treatment. His doctors appeared to have bought him some time, although it was unclear exactly how much.

"I'll book a flight home right away," I told him.

"Don't," he said. "You and Pete need to keep going."

"Are you sure?"

"Keep going," he repeated, then unwittingly confirmed what Pete had already anticipated he would say. "Drink everything in."

With that, Pete and I turned our attention to preparations for our next segment, which would unfold along the cliffs and terraces on the north side of the canyon—the terrain where Rich had built the crux of his high route. But that wasn't the only change.

When Rich and the rest of our crew met to discuss our performance out on the Great Thumb Mesa, they concluded, somewhat to our astonishment, that Pete and I were finally ready to venture into the trackless reaches of the canyon's interior without direct supervision. The team would still help plan our route and would monitor our progress via satellite tracking. They would also assist with shuttling, setting up food caches, and other logistics. But we had apparently demonstrated just enough competency for them to allow us to head off on our own without the benefit of a trail.

Pete was thrilled by this news, but I was wary, given that the part of the chasm we would be heading into was, in many respects, even more cut off than where we had already been. Merely reaching the *start* of the next segment entailed a 250-mile drive into the heart of a remote bight of sagebrush and broken mesas tucked just below the Utah border. Featuring almost eight thousand square miles of mostly empty rangeland where one can sometimes drive for days without seeing another person, it is known as the Arizona Strip—or, to some of those who know it well, "America's Tibet."

*   *   *

The drive out to the Strip took more than six hours, and the final forty miles involved navigating a network of unpaved and mostly unmarked Forest Service roads across a rugged expanse of juniper and piñon trees on the far side of the Kaibab Plateau, the loftiest point on the North Rim. Without Harlan Taney at the wheel, we would have gotten hopelessly lost.

He delivered us exactly where we needed to be a few minutes before sunset, giving us just enough time to peer over the edge of the canyon and take our bearings from a feature that seemed both oddly familiar and strangely new, because now we were seeing it from a completely different angle. Directly beneath us, the ground fell away through the topmost layers of rock, plunging almost two thousand feet to the vast boulevard of the Esplanade. It extended as far to the east and west as the eye could see—bloodred in the dying light and neatly bisected by a thin, horizontal shadow delineating where the walls of the canyon's inner gorge dropped to the hidden waters of the Colorado.

The following morning, Pete and I waved goodbye to Harlan, stepped over a broken strand of barbed wire spiraling between a pair of half-rotted fence posts, and followed the remnants of a cattle trail down a steep tributary filled with sand and tumbled stones that plunged through the Kaibab, Toroweap, and Coconino in a series of sharp twists and bends before opening onto a broad fantail of Hermit Shale. When we reached the base of the shale, we turned right and headed into a part of the canyon with a unique past and a troubled history.

The location that Rich and the rest of the team had selected for our point of reentry sat almost directly opposite Havasu Canyon, ensuring that there would be no gap in our transect. Known as 150-Mile Canyon, this tributary lay just outside the western boundary of the national park when it was first established in 1919—which meant that the remainder of our trek would now unfold on terrain that had not been protected until the original borders of the park were enlarged by Congress in 1975. Prior to that year, almost all this ground had been open to mineral prospectors, mining companies, and, most important, to a group of die-hard cattlemen who had created one of the most colorful and cantankerous strongholds of hardline ranching in the Southwest.

Starting in the 1920s, a small band of intrepid stockmen in search of open rangeland had drifted onto this part of the Arizona Strip with their families, and discovered that it offered an unusual opportunity to graze cattle *inside* the canyon. Each autumn, they drove their animals down a handful of tributaries to the broad benches of the Esplanade—which the ranchers called the Sandrock—then fenced off the routes back to the rim to prevent the stock from escaping.

Unable to climb out or descend farther, the cattle would spend the winter months roaming the Esplanade, nosing among the sparse desert grasses in search of forage while slurping from a scattering of tiny springs. Then sometime in April, the stockmen would return and lead the cows back up to the high country, completing one of the most picaresque cattle drives in the history of the American West.

The ranchers who depended on this part of the canyon were ferociously tough, even by the astringent standards of the high desert, and a measure of that toughness was evident in the disdain they reserved for anything that might restrict their use of public lands. When the Sandrock and its rim country were finally brought under the aegis of the National Park Service after 1975, that spirit of independence curdled into a contempt for federal land agencies that persists to this day. Even now, a number of those ranchers continue to believe the land belongs to them because their forebears arrived here when it was still "empty," and they regard their claim on the canyon as deeper than anyone else's, despite evidence all around—often directly at their feet—that this simply isn't true.*

*   *   *

Our plan was to head west across the Esplanade along the base of the Hermit Shale in much the same way that a herd of cattle might follow a drift fence: keeping the high cliffs off our right shoulder, slaking our thirst from the seeps and potholes, and stopping for the night wherever darkness overtook us. Along the way, we had been advised to keep our eyes open because this stretch of the canyon was rumored to harbor an especially rich trove of historical sites. And sure enough, before long, we stumbled across a set of artifacts unlike anything we had encountered before.

Late in the afternoon of that first day, we arrived at a massive over-hanging slab of sandstone less than a hundred yards from a shallow spring trickling from a crack in the rock. Beneath the slab was an alcove, and when our eyes adjusted to the shadows inside, we could see that the space had once sheltered an encampment stocked with tools and provisions. In the center of the chamber was a set of vintage mattress springs and a metal bed frame. Stacked neatly along the back wall was an array of battered-looking picks and shovels, and piled next to the tools were bridles and other pieces of horse tack. There was also a stack of wooden crates filled with horseshoes, cast-iron cookware, and buckles of every shape and size, plus a crude shelf with a tin coffee cup and an assortment of jars with their contents neatly labeled in

* It's no coincidence that one of the most prominent ranching clans along the far-western end of the Arizona Strip is the Bundys, a number of whom have participated in armed uprisings against the Bureau of Land Management in Nevada and the U.S. Fish and Wildlife Service in Oregon.

After Pete and I fell to pieces during our first attempt, a team of all-stars from the community who care most deeply about the canyon came to our aid, led by Rich Rudow (*top, second from left*), one of the foremost experts on long-distance hiking beneath the rims. Kelly McGrath (*lower left, brandishing a can of Spam*) specialized in leading backcountry expeditions for wounded veterans, while her partner, Mathieu Brown (standing next to Kelly), competed in some of the toughest endurance races in the west, such as the Leadville Trail 100. But no one's connection to the landscape ran deeper than that of Amy Martin (*lower right*), a former park ranger and guide whose mother had first brought her into the canyon when she was pregnant, four months before Amy was born.

In a vertical desert where there is no trail, perhaps the only thing more important than land-navigation skills involving the use of a compass combined with both topographic and geologic maps is the ability to locate water. On the remote system of terraces known as the Esplanade that is perched more than two thousand feet above the river, our lives depended on ephemeral pools of rainwater or snowmelt known as potholes. They were our lifeline and salvation.

In addition to the misery of moving through dense forests of cholla cactus, whose spines cling to the skin like Velcro, or the pain of losing one's balance and breaking one's fall by plunging an arm into a barrel cactus, we also contended with a nutrition deficit. Although we were ingesting more than five thousand calories a day, we were burning more energy than we could put into our bodies. By early spring, each of us had lost almost 15 percent of his body weight, and we were both looking emaciated.

Perhaps the most secret and remarkable of the canyon's many gems are the narrow crevices carved by exceptionally violent flash floods whose vertical walls soar hundreds of feet high, and whose width often amounts to less than twenty feet. Accessible only by rope, every square inch of stone inside these slot canyons is saturated in the lustrous tones—almond and rose, chestnut and salmon, chocolate and peach, coffee and eggplant and plum—of rock that has been permitted to marinate and mellow in the urn of time.

In addition to its biological richness and its geologic treasures, the canyon is filled with evidence that for thousands of years prior to the arrival of white Europeans, this place was home to successive waves of indigenous people whose connection with and understanding of the land ran deep. Nearly everywhere one ventures, it's possible to find artifacts in the form of hand-knapped stone tools that were employed for hunting, or fragments of pots that were used for carrying water or seeds (see next page). Most remarkable of all, however, are sections of the canyon walls emblazoned with petroglyphs or pictographs, which are among the most ancient forms of art in the Southwest.

13

14

15

16

Most people who come to the canyon tend to arrive, as Pete and I had, with no idea that the terrain they traverse is home to eleven different tribes whose ancestral lands either abut or lie directly inside what is now the national park. Today, these cultures are still vibrant, and their members are as much a part of the landscape as their ancestors were—including women like Renae Yellowhorse (above left), a member of the Navajo Nation, and Dianna Sue White Dove Uqualla, an elder of the Havasupai tribe.

17

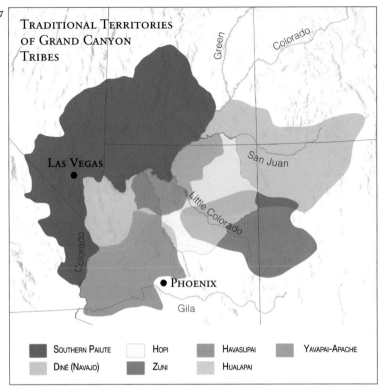

Traditional Territories of Grand Canyon Tribes

Green
Colorado
● LAS VEGAS
San Juan
Little Colorado
Colorado
● PHOENIX
Gila

	Southern Paiute		Hopi		Havasupai		Yavapai-Apache
	Diné (Navajo)		Zuni		Hualapai		

18

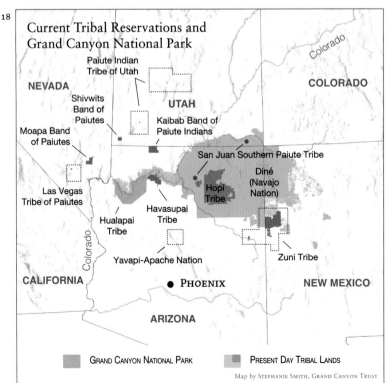

Current Tribal Reservations and Grand Canyon National Park

Paiute Indian
Tribe of Utah

NEVADA

COLORADO

Shivwits
Band of
Paiutes

UTAH

Moapa Band
of Paiutes

Kaibab Band of
Paiute Indians

San Juan Southern Paiute Tribe

Diné
(Navajo
Nation)

Hopi
Tribe

Las Vegas
Tribe of Paiutes

Havasupai
Tribe

Hualapai
Tribe

Colorado

Zuni Tribe

Yavapi-Apache Nation

CALIFORNIA

● PHOENIX

NEW MEXICO

ARIZONA

	Grand Canyon National Park		Present Day Tribal Lands

Map by Stephanie Smith, Grand Canyon Trust

Each of the tribes of the canyon has a different understanding of its rights and responsibilities when it comes to the land. In the western part of the chasm, the Hualapai have achieved a level of economic pros-perity denied to them in the past by flooding the skies above their reservation with hundreds of air tours each day that enable tourists to fly beneath the rims and land next to the river, unaware of the damage they are inflict-ing on the soundscape. The density of traffic is captured in this photo montage (*top*), which merges all of the flights passing through one section of Helicopter Alley during an eight-hour period into a single image. Only after sunset, when the last chopper has departed and the stars drench the heavens, are the silence and stillness that stand as signature elements of this place able to return.

22

23

24

The western border of the park is so remote that the only thing demarcating it are three metal fence posts driven into the sagebrush. Reaching this milestone represented the completion of an odyssey that had taken more than a year to finish. After passing through that boundary, however, Pete and I came to understand that the rewards for our effort lay not in the act of completion, but in the gifts that had already been handed to us along the way: the wonders we had witnessed, the hardships we endured, and the bond of friendship that was sealed by both.

old-fashioned cursive script: baking powder, tartar sauce, maple syrup. There was even a handmade deck of playing cards.

For a fleeting moment, it felt as if we had been dropped into the pages of a Zane Grey novel, a scene suffused so deeply with the tang and texture of the Old West that neither of us would have been surprised to hear a horse snort and turn to see a wrangler ride up to deliver the news that there would be beans again for supper tonight. Each item felt like a part of the distant past—until my eyes adjusted to the shadows and I spotted something far older lying on the dirt floor.

Getting down on my hands and knees, I could pick out dozens of potsherds similar to those we had seen on the Great Thumb Mesa and, prior to that, in the side canyons upstream from the Confluence of the Little Colorado. Some were orange or red, while others bore a stark black-on-white pattern. Mixed among those dime-size pieces of shattered clay were scores of even smaller articles—distinctive, scale-shaped chips of rock left behind from the knapping of prehistoric stone tools and weapons.

As I scanned the alcove, something on the wall that had escaped my notice earlier—perhaps because it was partially obscured by a cluster of axe handles—now caught my eye. It was the profile of a Bighorn Sheep, with four legs and a set of horns curving backward from the top of its head. The image, which had been pecked directly into the face of the rock, was a type of prehistoric carving known as a petroglyph. Directly beneath the sheep's belly was a smaller figure, identical in every detail except for the horns, and after a moment of confusion, Pete and I realized that it was a lamb, suckling at the udder of its mother.

I assumed that the etchings on the wall as well as the artifacts on the ground were the handiwork of one of the five bands of the Southern Paiute tribe, who may have begun migrating into the plateaus along the North Rim sometime in the fourteenth century—a time frame that roughly coincided with the latest possible arrival of Dianna Uqualla's Havasupai ancestors on the opposite side of the canyon. But later I would come to learn that the alcove's lineage was quite a bit more complicated.

While some of the potsherds may have derived from Paiute pottery, other fragments clearly belonged to earthenware fashioned by the Ancestral Puebloans who had occupied the canyon for hundreds of years prior to the influx of the Paiute. As for the petroglyph of the mother and the baby sheep, that may have been the work of the nomadic bands of hunters and gatherers who predated even the Puebloans.

Hence, here on the floor and walls of a single rock shelter, the convoluted saga of the canyon's early human history was laid out in a manner not unlike the strata of its stone walls, a narrative whose secrets were extensively layered and highly nuanced. Overlaid on those prehistoric objects were implements used by white stockmen who had arrived around the time of the Great Depression, and who had been drawn to this alcove because it offered them the same amenities it had furnished to the tribal people who had been here long before them: shelter from the elements, proximity to good water, and an opening that faced southeast, which promised warm sun in the winter and cool shadows in the summer.

Over the next several days, as Pete and I encountered one site after another, the pattern that we observed inside that first camp would repeat over and over. The details of the prehistoric artifacts would vary, especially the artistic representations on the rock walls. Some petroglyphs were easily recognizable—reptiles or snakes or deer—while others were abstract shapes: miniature labyrinths, mysterious squiggles, and spirals that seemed to collapse on themselves. At a number of locations, those images coexisted with the names of whites whose families had moved into the landscape in the early part of the twentieth century, along with specific dates—1922, 1932, 1933. In some cases, the newer markings had been chiseled directly over the originals, as if to obliterate whatever meaning or significance those older inscriptions might have held.

Regardless of the intentions behind this graffiti, the results were the same. As Pete and I moved west, we were continuously reminded that we were covering ground upon which each succeeding wave of human culture had affixed its signature to create a kind of desert palimpsest: a manuscript that had been effaced by successive layers of later writing, even as traces of the original narrative remained—lines that were faint and challenging to discern, but indelibly present.

*   *   *

Meanwhile, winter was beginning to release its grip, and everywhere we saw signs that a change in season was imminent. The nights were still long and the hours before dawn remained frigid; but the sun was spilling its light over the easternmost rock a few minutes earlier each morning, and the days were starting to warm. Then one afternoon toward the tail end of February as we were shuffling across a patch of bare dirt in a recess on the slickrock, I spotted the tip of something green poking through the soil. Spring was on its way.

While we were curious about what sorts of desert flowers might be on the verge of blooming, we never permitted our thoughts to stray too far from the mundane but critical details of moving through a place that, despite our growing confidence, still afforded no margin for error. We spent the better part of each day wrestling with a hundred different questions concerning where we were, how far we had come, which obstacles lay ahead, and how much distance we still needed to cover. Among those preoccupations and concerns, nothing focused our minds more acutely than where to find water.

This section of the Esplanade had no tributary drainages that offered easy access to the bottom of the canyon. Without ropes and without Rich's deep knowledge of slots, we had no way to reach the Colorado, twenty-four hundred feet below, even though we could often hear the dull rush of its rapids emanating from the depths—a sound that felt oddly disconcerting. We were walking within earshot of the largest and most dependable source of water in the entire Southwest, with no means of accessing it.

Likewise, there were only a handful of breaks that might enable us to climb through the upper cliffs to the North Rim, and those were of little use because this section of the rim was almost entirely dry. For the time being, we were just as dependent on the potholes of the

Esplanade, which out here are also known as *tinajas*, as we had been on the Great Thumb—with the added twist that as the weather stabilized, the storms faded, and the temperatures rose, the pools of water were beginning to disappear.

Like everything else that happens in the desert during the spring, there was nothing gradual about this. One day, it seemed as if every acre of slickrock held a dozen puddles brimming with water, some to a depth of a foot or more. Twenty-four hours later, two-thirds of those pools had evaporated—and a day after that, we were venturing deep into the side drainages or far out on the promontories in the hopes of finding pockets of moisture.

We were helped by a series of Rich's GPS points that guided us to the potholes he had found to be the most reliable. But in many of these places the water was so shallow—no more than an inch or two deep—that it was impossible to fill our bottles by tilting them on their sides. Had our friends not warned us about this, we would have been forced to sop up the contents of the *tinajas* with our filthy shirts and squeeze the liquid into the bottles. Thanks to their advice, we had brought along a pair of plastic syringes.

This method of extracting water was tedious and time-consuming: sometimes it could take ninety minutes or more to fill all our bottles. But the syringes enabled us to extract as much water as we were willing to carry—up to seven or eight liters apiece—and although this could add fifteen or more pounds to the thirty-five pounds that we were already hauling in each of our packs, those reserves sustained us when we were forced to spend the night at a dry camp. On those evenings, we recalled a final warning that Rich had shared with us just before we left:

"Remember that you're never moving toward water—you are always moving *away* from it."

Now we began to fully understand the wisdom of that dictum, which underscored the imperative of resisting any impulse to push beyond the point where it was impossible to return to the last known source of water. As the puddles dried out and the distances between those that remained grew longer, the *tinajas* offered a glimpse of just how harsh the Esplanade could be, and what it took to survive out on those stone reaches for creatures who, unlike us, actually belonged here.

*   *   *

In many of the remaining potholes, the water was teeming with tiny plants and animals that had been granted an astonishingly brief interval in which to mature and reproduce. Each time a storm refilled a depleted puddle, the moisture would trigger a miniature burst of algae, and a day or so later, dozens of tadpoles with bulging eyes and flickering tails would materialize from the mud at the bottom of the puddle, swimming furiously around the pool as they fed on the algae, and, in some cases, one another.

Within another few days, the surviving tadpoles had matured into Spadefoot Toads. They were capable of living as long as a decade, most of which would be spent buried underground, except when they emerged once each year to mate—a demonstration of hardiness and resiliency that was surpassed only by a hermaphroditic species of the Long-Tailed Tadpole Shrimp, which appeared in the potholes around roughly the same time as the toads. The shrimp, which looked like minute Horseshoe Crabs and were no more than an inch and a half long, would grow to maturity in just eight days, when they would reproduce by laying eggs that could remain dormant for a century or more, abiding invisibly just beneath the surface, patiently awaiting a return of conditions that would enable them, too, to venture into the light.*

During the fleeting interregnum between the frigid weeks of winter and the inferno of the summer, each pothole on the Esplanade was a world unto itself, bustling with creatures locked in a mad dance to consummate an entire cycle of life before the pool in which they swam vanished into thin air.

* In 2014, eggs of the Long-Tailed Tadpole Shrimp that were taken to the International Space Station and exposed to the frigid vacuum of outer space managed to hatch without a problem after being returned to earth.

Thanks to that dance, the water that Pete and I collected in our bottles was often alive, squirming with shrimp larvae, minuscule tadpoles, and floating bits of algae. As the weather warmed and the moisture dissipated, we didn't bother trying to distinguish one thing from another. Instead, we closed our eyes and swallowed hard, imbibing everything.

We were all in.

CHAPTER 33

Ghosts of a Former World

As we pressed on through the end of February, a cadence emerged in the unfurling of our days and nights. We awoke each morning in the predawn, broke camp beneath the last of the stars, and were on our way before the first rays of light began laying purple shadows across the Esplanade.

From early morning through late afternoon, the sky was hot and clear, and as we shuffled through the streaming light, it seemed to both of us that we were doing something rather old and fine, which amounted to nothing more than two friends moving across a wilderness of stone, carrying their possessions on their backs, looking for water.

All day we glided across slickrock so close-grained that it felt like fine sandpaper, so smooth we could have walked barefoot as we threaded through the extended arms of the arroyos spilling down from the cliffs just to the north. As we pushed into the shadowed recesses of each bay and then returned to the sunlight, it felt as if we were shifting back and forth between the languorous glow of late afternoon and the vestigial lavender haze of early evening.

"Do you feel like stopping?" one of us would ask.

"Not really," the other would reply. "There's still some light left—let's go on a bit longer."

So we kept moving, pressing on until dusk forced us to search out a hollow spot on the sandstone just big enough for our sleeping bags and our camp stove, where we would drop our packs, take off our shoes, and fix our supper. After that, we would sit cross-legged beneath the first of the stars, sip our steaming mugs of tea, and work—Pete backing up and indexing the day's photos; me scribbling in my notebook beneath the glow of my headlamp—until our chins dropped to our chests, and we succumbed to a sleep as dense and dreamless as the stone on which we lay.

*   *   *

During those weeks the routine remained the same, but other things began to change, especially our bodies. By now, the months of walking had whipped us into a level of fitness that neither of us had even approached in years. We were so accustomed to our packs that we no longer minded or even registered their weight and felt strangely naked without them, and we had the stamina to move without pause or strain from sunrise to sunset.

This would have been unthinkable two months earlier, but we no longer looked or felt as we had then. Each of us was leaner and thinner—Pete had lost more than thirty pounds, while I had shed almost fifteen—and as the flab burned away, the muscles in our shoulders and stomachs, and especially our legs, turned taut and strong. But perhaps the most striking change was in the color of our skin.

At odd moments, in the midst of performing a simple task such as, say, filling a water bottle or lighting the stove or buckling the harness on my pack, I would glance down and note that my fingers and wrists as well as the backs of my hands had so darkened that they resembled strips of beef jerky. Then I would examine my forearms, turning them this way and that, and observe the same change.

At first, I assumed that this was the work of the sun. But then I noticed the reddish-brown tones creeping across my chest and torso, areas protected by clothing from the elements. Pete observed a similar change with his skin, and gradually it dawned on us that this was no suntan. Instead, it was dirt: a veneer of dust and grit and sand from all the different layers of rock in the canyon—red and brown, black and pink, orange and tan—that was coating every inch of our bodies. And not just the surface, either, because the dirt was also working its way behind our fingernails, around the lines at the corners of our eyes, and into whorled grooves at the tips of our fingers.

Eventually, we realized that as the days bled into weeks, the dirt was bleeding into us. Through our hair and teeth, down our throats into our lungs, perhaps even into our blood, and from there suffusing the chambers of our hearts, until it began to feel as if, in taking on the texture of the land, we had become moving, breathing embodiments of the canyon itself.

"I don't think I've ever been this dirty before," I remarked one afternoon.

"Me, neither—I've never gone this long without a bath," Pete said. "But what's weird is that I don't *feel* dirty. Is that crazy?"

"Probably. But I feel the same way."

As I look back now, this makes sense to me in a way that it did not at the time. Although we were encrusted in dirt, the land was so pure and polished—bathed in bright air, scrubbed by the hard desert light—that moving across its surface cleansed and purified us.

With each passing day this feeling intensified until finally, late one morning, we arrived at a tributary so massive that Rich had warned us it would take a full two days for us to navigate its interior. In ancient times, he had also explained, this side canyon had served as a thruway connecting the Havasupai on the south side of the canyon with several bands of Paiute that lived to the north, and the stories told by both tribes—ancient stories that were recited only during the longest nights of the winter—spoke of how this route was marked by artifacts, burial sites, and rock art that could be found nowhere else in the canyon.

Turning into the mouth of the side canyon, we spent several hours working our way down to the bottom of the drainage and retrieved a supply cache that had been placed there for us several weeks earlier by our friend Jean-Philippe Clark. Then we continued up the dry creek bed until we reached a section of cliff that leaned out to form an overhang—and there, to our astonishment, we found ourselves passing through an invisible portal to what can only be described as another dimension of time and mind.

*   *   *

Emblazoned on the face of the sandstone was an array of images unlike any I had ever imagined. Although there were a number of animals—a cluster of Bighorns, a bird or two, perhaps a snake, and even a worm—most of the figures were human, albeit with impossibly thin bodies, stunted feet and legs, and oval-shaped heads whose faces were devoid of eyes or mouths, noses or ears.

They were more than two dozen of these forms, which are known to scholars as anthropomorphs, and they were arranged neatly in a line, each touching the next, all staring directly at us with a spooky blankness. The largest were more than six feet tall, with elongated torsos that appeared to be divided into segments or cavities, like the thoraxes of insects. Several were raising their arms in mute supplication, and their outstretched hands displayed varying numbers of digits—some boasting five or six fingers, others claiming only two or three, a few with none at all.

Together, the group looked vaguely familiar and manifestly alien at once, as if they embodied a ghostly fusion in which human, animal, and supernatural blended together, twisting and braiding in a way that conveyed the dreamlike impression that they were moving: undulating gently from left to right like a field of kelp rooted to the seafloor, swaying amid invisible currents within the ocean of time.

Unlike the prehistoric petroglyphs we had already encountered along the Esplanade, these images had neither been etched nor pecked into the rock using stone tools. Instead, they belonged to an older genre of expression created by brushing the surface of the rock in colors obtained from plant or mineral dyes: black and white, green and blue, yellow and red. Known as polychrome pictographs—essentially stone paintings—they were gorgeous, vibrant, and far more detailed than their distant petroglyph cousins.

The age of those images is believed to exceed four thousand years—roughly concurrent with the Neolithic circles at Stonehenge, the first Mayan temples in the jungles of the Yucatán, and the Great Pyramid of Giza. This was art in a category of its own, perhaps the wildest and most exquisitely detailed set of polychrome pictographs in the entire Southwest. A vision so spectral that to permit one's eyes to run along its vivid and confounding features is to feel oneself pulled toward the oldest and deepest period of human history anywhere in the canyon—an era whose lineage extends long past the brief tenure of the nineteenth-century cattlemen, far beyond the distant autumn of 1540 when the soldiers of Spain had gazed into the abyss for the first time, and arrows directly into the heart of a mystic and aboriginal dreamtime.

*   *   *

The prehistoric nomads who fashioned those images are known to us as the Archaic people, already mentioned in chapter 18, who are believed to have entered the Colorado Plateau some nine thousand years ago, and who spent the better part of the next six millennia hunting and gathering in and around the chasm. Aside from an assortment of tiny split-twig figurines in the shape of Bighorn Sheep that they placed inside various caves, a few campsites that are now buried beneath sand from the river, and a handful of pictographs like these, they seem to have left behind little evidence as a testament to their presence. Almost every other detail regarding their daily lives—how they clothed their bodies, assembled their shelters, or memorialized their dead; whether they sewed their garments and footwear with needles fashioned from deer antlers or cactus spines—all of it remains a total enigma.

In keeping with that mystery, whatever meanings and messages might reside in the painted pictographs have also been lost—although experts have formulated some intriguing theories about what the images might represent. Perhaps the most compelling of these posits that the

panels were the work of religious seers who may have altered their
state of consciousness through rituals that included fasting, dancing,
and perhaps even the use of natural hallucinogens such as datura, a
flowering perennial laden with psychoactive chemicals that is common
throughout the canyon.*

According to this theory, the trances enabled the clairvoyants to
communicate with the spirits of animals, plants, and their own ancestors—and the paintings are a record of those vision journeys, as well as
a depiction of the phantasmal beings whom the shamans encountered
along the way.

Although this hypothesis is both provocative and plausible, the
experts have yet to conceive of a viable way to test it. Instead, we are
left to contemplate the few things that are certain: that those faceless
apparitions have been staring out from the side of this cobblestone
drainage, watching the days flick past, the moon move through its
phases, and the stars wheel into view, for thousands of years—and
that we have absolutely no idea who they are or what they have to
say. We also know that those figures wield the power of things that
have endured for a very long time, and that they guard the door to
an ancient America—a place where the belief may have prevailed that
humans, animals, and plants could not only communicate in a common
language, but could even move fluidly from one form to another.

As Pete and I stood in silence, contemplating these and other matters, I took note of the peculiar sense that the figures on the wall were
neither static nor frozen, but instead appeared to be oscillating in tune
with some invisible current, as if an almost imperceptible shiver of
energy were passing through them.

The more we stared, the more they moved, and although at first it
seemed as if this may have been an optical trick, the more I thought

---

* Also known as Jimsonweed, datura belongs to the nightshade family. Its alkaloids, found
in all parts of the plant, induce hallucinations when taken in small quantities; in larger doses,
the chemicals can disrupt cardiac as well as diaphragm muscles, triggering a rapid death by
heart attack and suffocation. Also, touching any part of the plant and then rubbing one's eyes
can dilate the pupils and temporarily blur one's vision.

about it, the less satisfying I found this explanation. Eventually, I was left with the only idea that made any sense, even though it also made no sense at all, which was the possibility that the figures themselves and perhaps even the rock upon which they had been painted might, in some way that I could neither accept nor comprehend, actually be alive.

Pete and I spent almost three hours gazing at the panels until the sun finally slipped beyond the top of the narrow tributary, and the boulders on which we were sitting began to grow cool. Then we gathered our things and left.

*   *   *

That night, we set our camp next to a small pothole out at the tip of a sandstone promontory, where the uppermost edge of the Supai fell almost a thousand feet to a ledge at the top of the Redwall, then fell again for another sixteen hundred feet to the river, now invisible in the evening shadows. At twilight, the wind picked up and blew hard for thirty minutes before dropping off abruptly, as if someone had pulled the plug on a fan, and amid the ensuing stillness, the heavens surrendered to a darkness more pure and more absolute than anything else we had yet encountered.

By now we had ventured far beyond where even the faintest glimmer of artificial illumination crept into the sky from the hotels and gas stations on the South Rim, while the lights of Las Vegas were still too far to the west to register on the horizon. This left us enveloped in something singular, because aside from the deserts of eastern Oregon, the badlands of southern Utah, and a few isolated pockets in places such as Death Valley, no other part of the country can match the darkness that looms over this section of the canyon on a calm, moonless night just before the stars emerge.

The first of those stars, the ones trailing the last of the twilight and riding the leading edge of night, were little more than timid specks, trickling thinly from the headwaters of the heavens in isolated pairs and trios. But as they grew in number, they coalesced to form a celestial current that slowly built into a torrent of light as the constellations started winking open one by one—the soaring cross of Cygnus, the hot blue cluster of the Pleiades, Cassiopeia's bright and jagged arc—until, abruptly and without warning, the great rushing surge of the Milky Way shimmered into view, and the entire sky condensed into an ocean speckled with silver.

Astronomers will tell you that in the right place and under ideal conditions—no breeze to stir up the dust, no clouds to obscure the sky—the human eye can discern no more than twenty-five hundred stars at night. But based on what Pete and I witnessed that night, this figure is absurdly low, because the stars that appeared above our heads were beyond counting, and as they tumbled down to the horizon on every point of the compass, we took note of something else, too.

Although each tiny fleck seemed to glitter like an iridescent jewel— some emerald, others sapphire or turquoise—their fire was anything but uniform. A few burned with a sharpness that made them seem close at hand, while others flared faintly, their luster dimmed by distance. This merging of proximity and remoteness imbued the heavens with not only radiance, but also with dimensionality and depth, transforming the sky into a vast, inverted cauldron whose base was closely fitted to the horizon, whose sides curved upward into the inky lacquer of space, and whose interior was now filled with wraithlike tendrils of starlight that twisted and coiled, pulsing with a stately languor whose undulations were as subtle and as imperious as the shimmering forms on the painted panel we had seen that afternoon.

This is what astronomers call celestial vaulting, the revelatory effect produced by the rushing awareness of two opposing impressions: the sudden apprehension of the vastness and the depth of the heavens, combined with the arrival of a moment of understanding that transmits, in a single burst, the tininess and the insignificance of earth as well as everything that moves or breathes upon its surface.

This wasn't anything like the kind of night that van Gogh had once painted, a candelabra of stars looming protectively over a sleepy cluster of tapering church spires, neatly planted fields, and sturdy farmhouses whose windows gleam with lamplight. This was a sky belonging to a time that no longer exists—a sky that has never been seen, or even imagined, by most people living in such places as Boston or Dallas or Los Angeles. A sky whose wildness can call forth and amplify the wildness of the land—and perhaps, too, the wildness within oneself—by offering up a glimpse of the darkness that our earliest ancestors once knew, back when humans must have lived in almost continuous humility and awe, transfixed by the inescapable sense of just how small and unimportant they were—little more than Tadpole Shrimp or Spadefoot Toads, creatures unburdened by delusions that the world could be sculpted to suit their ambitions and needs.

The kind of sky, the kind of darkness, that will enable you to fully grasp for the very first time the true meaning of the word *nightfall*.

*　　*　　*

Pete and I talked of many things that night. We were curious why the ancient artists who had painted those stone panels didn't seem to have worried much about the correct number of fingers and toes of the human forms. We speculated on how old the illustrations might be and how they had survived for so long out in the open. But mostly, we wondered if there was any connection between those images and the things that Dianna Uqualla had said to us back at the head of the Bright Angel Trail, a stage of our journey that felt so distant that Pete asked me to pull out my notebook and read her words out loud.

"'Everything down there has remained pure because the land moves,'" I recited. "'The land *always* moves.'"

"What did she mean by that?" Pete mused.

"I'm not sure. But the figures in those paintings seemed to shimmer, like there was a tremor of energy running through them. We both saw it."

"What did she say about the lizards and the birds?"

"'All the creatures you will meet—they are trying to tell you something.'"

"Do you think she was urging us to listen to the animals? Or was she telling us to listen to the stories of her people?"

In truth, I suspected it might be both. In the end, weren't they one and the same?

Whatever the answer might be, it was interrupted by the sight of a meteor flashing across the fretwork of stars—a trace of burning silver that was snuffed out almost as quickly as it appeared.

"Did you see that?" Pete exclaimed.

"Yep. And I think maybe I heard it, too."

"Dude, that's just your imagination."

"Maybe, but there it is again. Can't you hear it?"

Now he could—although at this point we both realized that the noise wasn't coming from the heavens above, but the canyon below, somewhere out beyond the edge of the promontory where we were perched. The sound was faint and tremulous, but when we stood up and padded in our stockinged feet to the lip of the precipice, taking extreme care to avoid stepping over the edge, we could hear it clearly:

Ba-haaaaaaa.

A herd of Bighorn Sheep, clustered far beneath us on the top of the Redwall, was bleating in the darkness.

We knelt quietly, waiting for them to call out again. But now the sheep went quiet, perhaps sensing that we were above them.

Then Pete cupped his palms around his mouth and tried out a quavering imitation:

Ba-ha-ha-ha-ha.

This was followed by a long silence—until a series of tentative responses burbled up from of the depths.

Ba-aaaa?

Ba-haaaaaaa . . .

Ba-ha-ha-ha-haaaaaaa!

For a heartbeat or two, it seemed to me that we might be witnessing an electrifying moment of interspecies communication—although it wasn't exactly clear what kind of message the Bighorns hoped to convey.

Were they warning us about a Mountain Lion? Were they inquiring about a lost lamb? Did they simply want others of their kind to know that they were out there, huddled against the night?

"What do you think they're trying to tell us?" Pete whispered.

"I don't know."

As the final reply faded away, we conceded that we didn't have the faintest idea what the hell the sheep were attempting to say. Like the ghostly forms on the pictographs, they were speaking to us in a language that was beyond our comprehension.

All we could do was to acknowledge that they were out there—and recognize that their presence imbued the canyon with yet another layer of wonder, one that both assuaged and amplified our aloneness.

CHAPTER 34

Smelling the Barn

Over the next several days, Pete and I found ourselves infused with a vigor and a drive unlike any we had yet known—a kind of euphoria that seemed to arise, at least in part, from the growing awareness of just how far we had come. Since September, we had traversed almost five hundred miles; and although we still had nearly three hundred left to go, we were closer to the end than either of us had ever dreamed possible.

Regardless of its source, that well of energy now triggered a kind of madness in the form of something that neither of us would have considered doing six months earlier. Late one afternoon, without bothering to discuss the matter, we cinched the shoulder straps on our packs, tightened our hip belts and chest harnesses, and started running.

The temperature was in the low nineties, and each of us was carrying almost thirty-five pounds of gear, plus four quarts of water apiece, but none of that mattered. For the better part of the next three hours, we continued trotting together, side by side along the slickrock, in an unspoken celebration of the distance separating the clueless chowderheads that we had been at the start of this venture from the hardened desert legionnaires whom we were convinced we had become.

The following day, we were still feeling magnificent when the Esplanade delivered us to a tiny campground on the North Rim at a place called Toroweap, which sits at the end of a sixty-mile-long dirt road and is supervised by the most remote ranger station in the entire canyon. There, we caught a ride back to Flagstaff and flung ourselves into an intensive week of restocking provisions and repairing gear, preparing to circle straight back to Toroweap to polish off the remainder of the hike by combining our final two segments into one massive 260-mile push that would carry us all the way through to the Grand Wash Cliffs.

From Toroweap, we would need at least three days of hard travel to reach one of the most formidable geographic obstacles in the entire canyon, a twenty-eight-mile-long peninsula known as the Shivwits Plateau, which juts off the North Rim in the same manner as the Great Thumb Mesa, but extends in the opposite direction. It would take an entire week to round the southern tip of that headland, plus an additional week after that to work our way from the far side of the Shivwits across the immense benches in the far western part of the park leading to the Grand Wash Cliffs.

In terms of both linear distance and scarcity of water, this would be bigger and more ambitious than anything we had yet attempted. But in our view, the circumstances called for a measure of audacity. The western Grand Canyon is part of the Mojave, the hottest and driest of North America's four deserts, and sometime in the middle of March the door to the hiking season would begin to close. By April, the temperatures would be searing, and almost every pocket of open water on the high route would be gone. If we failed to reach the Grand Wash Cliffs before then, we'd be forced to postpone the rest of the journey for another six months, sitting out the entire summer until cooler weather returned in late autumn.

It was a bold plan, to say the least. But as we pointed out to Rich—who took some convincing before he was willing to sign off on it—there could be no better way to finish our project. An odyssey that began with failure and ignominy would conclude in triumph.

Before setting off on a venture as risky and daring as this, a wiser and more experienced pair of hikers might well have paused to sniff the air and ask if it was possible to detect a trace of the cockiness and hubris for which they had already been thoroughly spanked.

They might also have devoted a moment or two to dwell on the merits of being humble in the face of the powerful and mysterious forces they had just witnessed. And then maybe they would have thought about dialing it back a notch or two.

But not us.

Like a couple of mules in a pack train completing the final steps of their climb up the Bright Angel Trail to the South Rim, we had no interest in doing anything other than raising our tails and charging ahead full tilt, convinced that we could smell the barn.

All I can say now, looking back on that moment, is that we should have known better. Despite the many lessons we'd been taught, especially about the perils of hubris, Pete and I still had a thing or two to learn.

CHAPTER 35

Badlands

On March 9, the sky was clear and the air was crisp as we took in one of the most dramatic vistas in the canyon. At the edge of the parking area at Toroweap, the sandstone cliffs fell in an almost unbroken sweep to the Colorado, which cut along the canyon's bottom toward the base of the Shivwits Plateau, an indigo-colored promontory hovering directly to the west, and extending across the entire horizon from north to south.

Although we had been gone for less than a week, the season was already changing with bewildering speed. The spring rush of migratory songbirds had kicked off just a few days earlier with the appearance of the first meadowlarks. The next two weeks would bring a host of other arrivals, with at least half a dozen species showing up every few days, and as we shouldered our packs, we were greeted by one of the most flamboyant newcomers, a Broad-Tailed Hummingbird that whizzed past us, sounding like a multirotor drone, then circled back to hover over a scarlet penstemon, just one of the many wildflowers that had begun to bloom.

All around us, petals of every shape and size were popping up in patches of dirt: little pink mariposa lilies, golden desert dandelions, and tiny lavender clusters of storksbill. Soon they would be followed by purple four-o'clocks, lemon-colored fiddle-necks, and, most dramatic of all, the flaming-orange blossoms atop the twenty-foot-long branches of the ocotillo, a shrub whose early budding cycles have evolved to coincide with the peak arrival of at least four different species of hummingbird.

The interval in which these flowers and birds all came together was incredibly brief. Within two or three weeks, most of the male hummers would have departed for the wildflower meadows up on the Kaibab Plateau, while the leaves of the ocotillo and the brittlebush either withered in place or dropped to the ground, leaving their branches looking desiccated and dead. But for the moment, as the desert bathed in spring's benedictory gleam, it felt as if there could be no finer place on earth than the western reaches of the canyon.

Just west of the Toroweap overlook, the terrain underwent a dramatic change, thanks to a chain of ancient volcanic eruptions that had taken place some eight hundred thousand years ago, which was practically the day before yesterday on the scale of geological time. On at least seventeen occasions, waves of lava had poured over the rim, streaming down the walls of the canyon and choking off the river. Some of those basalt barriers had approached two thousand feet in height, creating a series of lakes that may have extended, in one instance, more than four hundred miles upstream, well beyond present-day Lee's Ferry.*

Within minutes of setting off, we encountered the first remnants of this dramatic era as we sidestepped across the slopes of a six-hundred-foot-high cone of cinder known as Vulcan's Throne, one of more than two hundred volcanic vents arising like warts from the rimlands beyond Toroweap. We spent the next nine hours picking through fields of black basalt dotted with Creosote Bush, whose branches were adorned with tiny yellow flowers. The longer we walked, the hotter it got and the more water we guzzled until, almost before we realized it, we had drained every last bottle.

---

* At least five of those dams failed catastrophically as the reservoirs behind them overtopped their parapets. The water was released in hours or days, generating floods so immense that boulders the size of one-story houses were hurled high onto the cliff bands, in some cases six hundred feet above the canyon bottom.

By now, it was early afternoon, and the air temperature was 96°F, although the surface of the basalt was probably approaching 170°F. As the hours ground on, I felt myself growing lightheaded, the insides of my mouth turned dry, and it became difficult to swallow. Although we'd gotten low on water at several points, this was the first time we'd ever run out completely, and it was terrifying to realize how swiftly our bodies began to shut down. By late afternoon, I lost the ability to make saliva or spit, then noticed something even more alarming when I stopped to urinate.

"Pete, my pee is the color of carrot juice," I announced in a panicky voice several registers above normal.

"Mine, too," he confirmed from several feet away, where he was irrigating a Creosote Bush. "But it hasn't turned brown or black yet, which is good news."

"Thanks. Now I feel so much better."

Just before sunset, we located an anemic pothole coated with a thin film of brackish water and called it quits. We'd walked twenty-four miles, the longest distance we'd ever covered in a single day. Our legs and ankles were throbbing, and the skin on the bottoms of our feet was starting to blister—something we hadn't seen since the previous September.

*   *   *

That set the tone for the following morning, when we spent hours bushwhacking through thickets of creosote, then were forced to draw water from a pothole ringed with a toupee of diseased-looking algae. This kept us going until early evening, when we began scrambling up a steep, narrow cleft whose floor was pitted with a stair-step series of potholes.

At first, we were delighted by the chance to replace the pond-scum smoothies in our bottles with clean water. But the cleft itself was no place to spend the night—especially with a thick bank of clouds gathering in the sky at sunset—and as the light faded and darkness fell, navigating through the potholes became progressively trickier, even with our headlamps. Before long, I slipped and plunged face-first into one of the pools.

The water was only a couple of feet deep, but the weight of my pack drove my face and chest into a rock on the bottom with enough force to knock the wind out of me. Then while climbing back out, I twisted one of my fingers so badly it felt as if it had popped out of its socket.

Meanwhile, Pete had clambered up to the edge of the next pool, a monster extending well beyond the reach of his headlamp. With no other choice, he dropped his pack on the ledge, waded into the pool until the water went past his chin, and dog-paddled for another ten yards until he reached the far side, where he waited for me to swim across in two separate trips with our packs.

So it went, ascending from one pitch-black pool to the next for the better part of two hours, until we finally emerged onto a small patio of polished limestone that seemed like a terrific spot to spread out our sodden gear, collapse on top of our soaked sleeping pads, and drift into a deep and much-needed slumber—until just before 2:00 a.m., when the clouds we'd spotted earlier opened up, and it started to rain.

At first, we tried telling ourselves it was just a sprinkle that would subside in a few minutes. But soon an inch of water was sluicing across the limestone deck, snatching up our belongings with the obvious aim of washing everything straight back down the cleft that we had just climbed out of. We spent the next thirty minutes dashing around grabbing everything we could find and flinging it under some large boulders next to the patio while frantically searching for some dry ground where we could lie down.

Eventually, Pete found a corner-shaped ledge protecting a triangular patch of dirt, at the back end of which was a jumble of sharp twigs and spines.

"Watch out for that cactus," I warned as we prepared to bed down for the rest of the night. "It looks nasty."

"It's a pack-rat nest, not a cactus," Pete corrected me. "It's actually called a midden, and they build them by gathering up sharp objects to make a little fortress."

"Did I ask for a nighttime lecture on the nesting habits of the local rodent population?" I asked, conducting a one-way conversation with myself. "No, I did not."

"And they cement everything together with their own urine."

*   *   *

By morning, the rain had stopped, enabling us to dry our belongings in the sun. But the fogbank of moodiness that had descended on us refused to lift as we resumed our push up the drainage, where we encountered something new. For the first time, the canyon was about to turn ugly.

As we approached the head of an enormous tributary called Parashant Canyon, we stumbled upon the opening to a tunnel that had been sunk into the side of a steep slope covered with reddish dirt. This was the Copper Mountain Mine, a body of ore that was tapped as a source of lead, zinc, and high-grade copper at the start of the twentieth century, and that was later discovered to contain uranium.

After the site was subsumed by the park, a gate with heavy steel bars was erected at the entrance to the shaft, and a yellow-and-black sign was affixed to the front, along with a placard stating DANGER: HIGH RADIATION AREA. It is one of almost a dozen such sites inside the canyon or along its perimeter that have been contaminated by radiation.*

Apart from the sign itself, the place looked abandoned, but wreckage was everywhere. For hundreds of yards in all directions, the ground was covered with panels of sheet metal, broken sections of pipe, rusted wheels, metal gratings, and steel cables, plus a derrick and two massive engines that must have been responsible for powering the operation.

---

* There is also an ongoing operation on the South Rim known as the Pinyon Plain Mine, which sits less than eight miles east of the park's main entrance, where uranium ore is currently being extracted. The mine, which is owned and operated by Energy Fuels Resources, a company based in Canada, has drawn fierce opposition from the Havasupai, who make a compelling argument that given the risk of contamination, uranium extraction on public lands along the periphery of the canyon is both inappropriate and unsafe.

For a surreal moment, I felt myself transported back to the junk-strewn slopes of the spilly piles in the strip mine behind my grandparents' house in western Pennsylvania. The scene offered a glimpse of an alternative reality: a vision of what many other parts of the canyon might now look like without the protection that the park, despite its many flaws and imperfections, had provided during the past century.

Just beyond the entrance to the mine, we arrived at a dirt road strewn with the carcasses of junked trucks and automobiles. Then a mile or two beyond the last vehicle, we moved off the road and into a tributary called Andrus Canyon, at the head of which was a place known as Lost Spring, where we were hoping to make camp.

Before long, we caught the odor of livestock, and soon we found ourselves tiptoeing past a dozen or so cranky-looking cows nibbling on saltbush, part of a herd belonging to one of the ranching families who continue to maintain grazing rights along the rimlands. Judging by the huffing and stamping, the cows didn't appreciate having their lunch interrupted by a pair of dirtbag hikers. Although they weren't to blame for what happened next, I prefer to think it was entirely their fault when I failed to pay attention to where I was putting my feet, stepped on a loose rock, and went crashing to the ground.

Unlike the previous evening, there was no pool of water to cushion my landing. Instead, I plunged directly onto a sturdy Barrel Cactus the size of a fire hydrant and broke my fall by driving dozens of its inch-long spines directly into my right forearm. The next thing I knew, I was lying on my back next to the base of the uprooted cactus and clutching my arm, which felt as if it had been shot through with a nail gun, while trying to stop the bleeding.

Pete, who had heard the fall and raced back in my direction, initially thought I had suffered a compound fracture. After wiping off the blood with some swabs from our med kit, we agreed that it wasn't quite as bad as it looked. The skin had been pierced in more than forty places, and at the point of each puncture, an angry welt about the size of a jelly bean was now pulsing blood and throbbing with pain. No bones were broken, however, and none of the cactus spikes seemed to have cut into a major blood vessel.

Given that we were once again out of water, we decided that the best thing to do was to get ourselves to Lost Spring, where I could properly clean and disinfect my wounds. So after Pete transferred some of the heaviest items in my pack over to his, we spent the remainder of the day pushing toward the head of Andrus while I held my arm away from my body like the handle of a broom to prevent it from touching my grubby shirt.

Just before sunset, we spotted a cluster of cottonwoods in the distance whose acid-green leaves, which were just beginning to bud, marked the location of the spring. But as we drew closer, we discovered that the ground was coated in dollops of cow manure, and when we finally reached the edge of the grove, we were dismayed to find that a group of cattle—probably the same nasty-tempered bunch we'd encountered earlier in the day—had churned the entire seep into brown goop, which meant that every drop of water bubbling out of the ground was contaminated with cow feces.

*   *   *

Stunned by the damage that such a tiny herd could inflict on a desert spring, we spent the next half hour inspecting every inch of ground beneath the trees in the hopes of ferreting out a pocket of untainted water. When nothing materialized, we pulled out our syringes, headed farther down the drainage, and feverishly dug through the sand with our hands as darkness descended, looking for moisture and squirting whatever water we found into our bottles, half a teaspoon at a time.

Almost two hours later, each of us had filled only half a bottle from the sand pockets. Demoralized, we headed back to the trees, where Pete gathered another liter from the bovine cesspool at the head of the spring, which he repeatedly bombarded with ultraviolet light from our Steripen, followed by a triple dose of bleach. Meanwhile, I cast around with my headlamp to find a patch of ground that wasn't covered in cow pies where we could unfurl our bedrolls.

"I don't think it's a good idea to try to clean my arm with that water," I told Pete when he returned. "Do we have any antiseptic in the med kit?"

"None left," he reported after rummaging earnestly through the kit. "But try some of this."

He handed over a slimy-looking tube of ointment that appeared to have one or two squeezes left inside.

"What is it?" I asked while unrolling the tube to scan the label, which was barely legible. "'Antifungal jelly for treatment of athlete's foot, ringworm, and other skin conditions.' Are you serious?"

"Somebody gave it to me for a rash on my crotch back in November, and it was super effective. I think it's got, like, pretty much the same ingredients as Neosporin."

"Wait . . . so you want me to disinfect my arm with the same lube that you've been smearing all over your—?"

"Forget it!" he barked, sounding hurt. "Just trying to be helpful."

"Not helping, McBrody," I snapped as I gingerly inserted my air mattress between a Prickly Pear Cactus on one side and a Beavertail Cactus on the other.

"Oh, you want some *help*, Groover Boy? All right, how about helping yourself to some cow shit and slathering *that* on your arm, huh?"

"Cow shit, crotch cream—same difference," I muttered, angrily punching my pack into a pillow and lying back on my air mattress. "Why don't you take that tube and shove it up—"

"Wha-*fuck*!" I shrieked, shooting to my feet and clapping both hands to my backside, which felt as if it had been struck with an electric cattle prod.

"What's wrong—are you okay?" Pete cried, dropping his irritation as I snatched my air mattress off a tiny Hedgehog Cactus I had just lain on top of, then stared in dismay as the mattress deflated the same way it had six months earlier when I'd hurled a rock at the Ringtail that had stolen my Snickers bars.

"I can't believe this is happening *again*," I wailed.

With no better option, I dejectedly dragged my gear off to another spot, spread out the drooping airless mattress—now nothing more than a second ground tarp—and did my best to extract the hedgehog spines from my backside.

"Dude, I'm sorry for yelling at you," Pete said mournfully from inside his cactus thicket a few yards away. "This is almost as bad as when we started, isn't it?"

"Maybe worse."

This was followed by a long silence as I lay back and glared at the stars through the nest of cactus branches above my head.

"I'm sorry I yelled at you, too," I finally said.

"Let me know if you change your mind on the crotch ointment."

"You suck."

"So do you."

*   *   *

The pain in my arm made it impossible to sleep for the first part of the night. Eventually, I drifted into a stuporous slumber that extended well past 2:00 a.m., when I was roused by a mysterious odor that was pungent enough to penetrate my dreams and awaken me to the disturbing possibility that something had crawled into the middle of our camp and died.

After fumbling for my headlamp and scanning the darkness without finding anything amiss, I concluded that the source of the fetor was Pete, who was snoring away like a band saw.

Repulsed by his poor hygiene and general nastiness, I yanked the hood of my sleeping bag over my head and gagged helplessly as the stench intensified, a miasma of filthy underwear, sweat-caked skin and hair, and the noxious flatulence produced by dehydrated backpacker meals and too much beef jerky. It was enough to make my eyes water.

I wasn't smelling Pete, and I sure as hell wasn't smelling the barn.

I was smelling *myself*.

CHAPTER 36

Rock Bottom, Again

B y some miracle, my arm didn't get infected, and over the next several days, the punctures began to heal—aided, perhaps, by the fact that I changed my mind and reluctantly agreed to use the remainder of Pete's crotch ointment. It was a lucky break, but apparently it depleted our entire allotment of good fortune. From this point forward, it felt as if the journey had turned into a two-man death march.

We were up at dawn and out of camp half an hour later, charging forward with the single-minded aim of covering as much ground as possible, scenery be damned. We burned through seventeen miles on the average days, twenty on the good ones, and in the midst of these marathons, we grimly ticked off one side canyon after another, barely registering any details beyond their names on the map.

The mornings were hot and long and physically draining. The afternoons were infernos. We stopped wherever darkness found us, and we set our camps without giving a thought to comfort or views, bedding down on patches of cobblestones, piles of deadfall, or random plots of dirt. During the fleeting intervals between dinner and sleep, we focused on the mathematics of how-far-have-we-come and when-will-this-end. The pleasures and gratifications of discovery had now vanished, and along with this loss, we forfeited two things that had sustained us throughout every other part of the traverse, including the worst stretches of all: our camaraderie and the sense of humor that had always bound us together.

Was it possible, I speculated, that the deepest essence of the canyon's character might be grounded in neither beauty nor wonder, but capriciousness and cruelty? Was this the sort of place that beats you senseless in the beginning, and then permits you to partake in a bit of its wild witchery as you move through its heart—only to snatch all the magic back by beating you up all over again as you approach the end, leaving you with nothing?

"Do you think that maybe the best parts of this are behind us now—and that the only thing left is more suffering?" I asked Pete one evening as he lanced another blister on his foot, hoping that he might say something cheerful and uplifting.

"Definitely," he replied. "I'm not sure I even see the point in continuing. Do you?"

Our gloominess was further aggravated by a new ritual, a practice we adopted partly, I suspect, because we had grown weary of talking and begun to get on each other's nerves. It began at roughly the same time each night, just after we'd zippered ourselves into our sleeping bags and were preparing to go to sleep. As we lay back staring up at the stars, Pete would pull out his cell phone and call up an audio version of *Desert Solitaire*, Edward Abbey's beloved homage to the canyon country of the Southwest.

In the eyes of some, Abbey's writing and his views have not aged well, especially when it comes to women and Native Americans. But despite these problems, we, like many others, were nevertheless drawn to his flair for capturing the precarity of the natural world—its tenuousness, its fragility, its exquisite vulnerability to human intrusion—all of which is showcased in the book's introduction when the author warns his readers not to jump into their vehicles in the hopes of seeing some of the splendors he plans to call forth in the pages that follow:

In the first place, you can't see anything from a car; you've got to get out of the goddamned contraption and walk, better yet crawl, on hands and knees, over the sandstone and through the thornbush and cactus. When traces of blood begin to mark your trail, you'll see something, maybe. Probably not.

It's a measure of how long and hard our own odyssey had been that Pete and I were never able to keep awake beyond the end of that paragraph. And so each night, we would restart the recording from the beginning and listen all over again to the same ill-tempered admonishment in the hopes of getting to the inspiring parts that lay beyond—the images of blue mesas, endless stone, and bright desert air—only to once more close our eyes and fall asleep with Abbey's dark and melancholy pessimism reinforcing the promise that when the sun leered drunkenly over the rimrock the following morning, blaring the arrival of another day, it would be even more miserable than the one that preceded it.

*   *   *

One afternoon, out on a nameless terrace somewhere beneath the Shivwits Plateau, we stumbled across a dirt road used by cattle ranchers and heard a rumbling sound in the distance. A pair of ATVs had just topped a low hill, and both drivers were now speeding in our direction.

The two men, who turned out to be from Flagstaff and were out riding for recreation, peeled to a stop directly in front of us and flipped up their goggles, which is when I realized that I knew one of them. John O'Brien, an old friend from my river days and one of the finest guides on the Colorado, had grown up in Tuba City among the Hopi and the Navajo, including some of Renae Yellowhorse's people.

"Are you guys *all right*?" exclaimed John, who didn't recognize me at first. "Are you *injured*?"

When we confirmed that we were mostly okay, and that we didn't really need anything (except for maybe a ride to the Grand Wash Cliffs), they were visibly relieved.

"When we spotted you two as we crested that ridge back there, we figured you guys needed medical assistance," John told us. "We thought you were survivors from a plane crash."

At first, we thought he must be joking and chuckled awkwardly. But their expressions made it evident that they were serious, which induced us to take a closer look at each other for the first time in days—and in that moment we understood how we must have appeared through the eyes of others.

Our skin was peeling with sunburn, our faces were unshaven, our trekking poles were broken, and our hair looked as if there might be birds nesting in it. As for our clothing, our shirts were ragged and filled with holes, our pants were falling from our hips, and our shoes, which were coming apart in several directions at once, were held together with duct tape.

No wonder these men had feared the worst. We looked like a pair of hoboes who had fallen out of the sky after being tossed from the back of a cargo plane.

After handing us some candy bars (sadly, they weren't carrying any hard liquor or hallucinogenic drugs), they wished us well, revved their engines, and spun off. We stood watching them until they faded into the distance. Then we stood and watched their cloud of dust until that, too, disappeared.

"You know what?" said Pete as he hoisted his pack with a weary grunt. "I really miss the rest of our crew—Rich and Amy and Kelly and Mathieu and Harlan and Jean-Philippe. No matter how tough it got out here, things always felt better with those guys around, didn't they?"

"I know. I miss them, too."

*   *   *

A few days later, we left the Esplanade behind and dropped into a tributary known as 209-Mile Canyon, tracing its winding bed for hours until it finally delivered us to the edge of the Colorado, whose current

perfectly mirrored our mental state: dull green, torpid, shoveling slug-
gishly along the shore. Once again, we were back on the Tonto, the shelf
on top of the Tapeats Sandstone, which we'd last seen in late January
when we began our trip around the Great Thumb Mesa.

Over the next several days as we moved downstream, the river cut
deeper, and before long the Tonto had formed a catwalk running along
the top of what is called the Lower Granite Gorge, whose walls fell
for almost a thousand feet, directly into the river.* Along this stretch,
the number of breaks where one could clamber down to the shoreline
were limited, which meant that our lives still depended on pockets of
water in the rock, most of which now tasted briny and foul, as if drawn
from the radiator of an overheated truck and mixed with a scoop of
borax. It never fully quenched our thirst, and like cough medicine, we
had to choke it down in gulps.

Late one morning, we entered a zone where the potholes all but
disappeared, and the surface of the Tonto was almost bereft of anything green or living, with one notable exception: a type of succulent
that seemed to thrive on dreariness and heat. It looked like a stunted
tree, rising to a height of three or four feet, with a trunk as thick as a
man's arm and more than a dozen fleshy green branches encased in a
matting of stiff, hairlike needles so dense that the entire plant appeared
to be coated in fur.

This was a Golden Cholla Cactus (pronounced CHOY-a), and it
displayed a weird and menacing beauty, especially when bathed in direct
sunshine, which glinted off the spines in a way that made it seem as if
every fork and stem was sheathed in a silvery corona of light. At the
slightest tremor, however, densely needled segments on the branches,
each no more than a few inches long, would detach and Velcro themselves to the skin or hair of any passing creature, earning the plant an
evocative nickname: the "jumping cactus." Even a faint brush against
one of those lobes could feel like seizing a pincushion.

---

* This is the last of the three gorges—Upper, Middle, and Lower—that form the subbasement
of the canyon.

Soon we found ourselves moving through groves of cholla so thick that it became impossible to squeeze between individual trees without grazing against them and getting drilled by hundreds of spines. The pain was incandescent, akin to ramming one's finger into a light socket.

Before long, pieces of cholla were sticking from our legs, our shoulders, our bums, even our hair—although for once Pete seemed to be getting it worse than me. Delirious with pain from a cluster of spines lodged in his calf, he staggered two steps back and lurched into an entire cluster of trees, windmilling his arms and roaring like a bear while tearing wildly at the air with his hands.

"Ow—ow—ow!" he yelped.

"Dude, stop," I exclaimed. "You're making it worse."

"You're the one making it worse."

"Will you just hold still so I can pull it out?" I pleaded while trying to pry off a spiny wad the size of a sea urchin.

He flinched at the pain. "Get away from me, you dick!"

"Jesus—you just stuck me in the hand."

"Good—now you know what it feels like."

In this manner, we blundered from one section of the cactus forest to another, rabid with frustration and rage. Occasionally we'd hit a small clearing, only to plunge back into the thicket for another round. This continued until early evening, when we arrived at the end of a promontory and found ourselves facing yet another problem.

More than seven hundred feet below us was a patch of shoreline next to the river covered in a tangle of thick green brush. Somewhere inside that thicket was our last supply cache: a pair of buckets stuffed with enough food and additional provisions to propel us to the Grand Wash Cliffs.

After peering over the edge from several different angles and failing to spot an obvious way to descend the walls, we realized we had to choose between spending the night amid the cholla up on the Tonto without any food or water—both of which were now gone—or dropping over the rim and hoping that we could find a route down to the river before darkness arrived and left us stranded on the middle of the cliffs.

"What do you want to do?" I asked.

"Anything is better than this fricking cactus forest. Let's go for it."

Pete led off, lowering himself down a series of vertical cracks while doing his best to avoid sticking his hands into the cholla clinging to the sides of the cliff. At the bottom of each crack, he moved along a thin, crumbling ledge to the top of another crack. In this manner, he worked his way down the face of the cliff, making steady progress over the next hour as I fumbled for handholds in the rapidly fading light and attempted to follow his coaching from below.

"Okay—there's a great hold just to the right of that knob. . . .

"Good—now bring your left toe down six inches, and there's a pocket to stand on. . . ."

Halfway down, I paid him for his service by kicking loose a rectangular-shaped rock about the size of a microwave oven.

"I *told* you not to step on that rock!" he squawked as the boulder, which easily weighed several hundred pounds, missed his head by three or four inches, swiping the outside of his pack before crashing to the base of the cliff with a sickening thud.

"Sorry," I mumbled. "It's so dark, I can't tell one rock from the next."

"Figure it out," he snapped. "If you wind up killing me, you'll never get down off this wall on your own."

*   *   *

The descent took more than two hours, and we were still sixty feet above the bottom when the light failed completely, forcing us to navigate the final set of moves by feel—which set me up to ram the palm of my hand into one last cholla before we arrived at the base. When we finally reached the ground, we retrieved our headlamps from our packs—a move that was far too dicey to pull off during the climb—and began thrashing through the brush toward the Colorado.

It's testament to how thick the vegetation was that even with headlamps, we only located the river by tripping over the edge of its five-foot-high bank. Clutching on to each other for balance, we toppled off the lip like a pair of deranged bolero dancers.

Fortunately the water was only thigh-deep, but the bank was too muddy and steep to claw our way back up, so we were forced to thrash along the shoreline, stumbling and falling onto all fours, until we had worked our way into a little cove and were able to pull ourselves back onto dry ground. From there, it took another twenty minutes of bushwhacking before we found our cache, lugged the plastic buckets over to a relatively flat patch of ground, and collapsed.

We were both far past our limits and feeling totally unglued, which explained the anger in Pete's voice as he outlined how dire the situation was, and how much worse it was about to get.

"I don't know if you've started wrapping your head around this yet, but tomorrow morning we're gonna have to load all these supplies, re-climb those cliffs we just came down, and get right back on the Tonto."

"Are you joking?"

"No. But what's going to make it even nastier is that in addition to our supplies, we'll be hauling a huge amount of water, because according to the map, there aren't a lot of places up there where we'll be able to get back down to the river."

"Can't we just keep pulling our water out of the potholes? It smells bad and tastes like turpentine, but it's kept us alive so far."

"Kev, there aren't any more storms coming," Pete snarled, irritated at having to spell out something that I should have been able to grasp. "I don't think you fully comprehend just how harsh it's gonna be once we're back up there."

"Okay, so how much water do we need to carry?"

"It'd be suicide to leave with anything less than ten liters."

"Five each?" I mumbled, dismayed by the idea of having to stack eleven pounds of water on top of everything else we'd be carrying.

"No, dude—*ten* each."

He gave me a moment to consider that we'd be hauling more weight than either of us had ever carried before—almost sixty pounds apiece—through the hottest, driest part of the entire canyon.

"I don't think I can handle that," I confessed.

"I don't know if I can, either. But once the temps push past a hundred, those ten liters won't last us more than two or three days—which means that every time we hit a break in the cliffs, we'll have to descend a thousand feet down to the river and then climb a thousand feet back up to the Tonto with more water."

By now, the stars were smeared across the heavens in such numbers that they delineated not only the rims of the canyon, but also a looming butte on the far side of the river known as Diamond Peak, whose pyramid-shaped summit registered as a hulking silhouette in the night sky.

Pete and I both knew that Diamond marked the terminus of a dirt road that meandered down from the nearest paved highway, twenty miles to the south, via an unusually broad, gently sloping tributary. This was the only road connecting the rims of the canyon to the bottom, and it served as the takeout for most river trips, dead-ending at the edge of the Colorado less than five hundred yards away—directly opposite from the place where we were camped.*

Given what lay ahead if we kept going, was this the place, I wondered, for us to pull the plug?

Pete was wondering the same thing, but the decision would have to wait until morning. Right now, the only thing either of us could handle was to roll out our tarps and collapse on the tops of our sleeping bags—the night being far too warm to crawl into them.

I was asleep the moment I laid my head down, unaware that I had unfurled my deflated air mattress on top of an anthill.

*   *   *

The following morning, I awoke to discover that in addition to the jumping-cactus spines, my body was covered with ant bites. After

---

* Because there are only one or two rapids beyond this point as the Colorado approaches the slack water in the upper tentacles of Lake Mead, the reservoir created by Hoover Dam, most river expeditions end at the Diamond Creek Road, fifty river miles upstream from the terminus of the canyon.

shaking what appeared to be most of the colony from my sleeping bag, I went looking for Pete.

I found him perched on a rock about a hundred yards up the drainage, where he'd been sitting since 4:30 a.m. trading texts with Rich, who had confirmed that the weather was about to get a lot hotter, and that if we decided to keep pushing west, organizing an extraction would become geometrically more difficult the moment we moved beyond Diamond.

If we were thinking of quitting, this was the time to do it.

We spent the next twenty minutes wrestling with a realization that neither of us wanted to accept: that although we were absolutely desperate to be done with the canyon, the canyon didn't appear to be in any particular hurry to be done with us.

Wordlessly, Pete dug the DeLorme out of his pack, pecked out a message, and hit SEND.

Five hours later, we gathered our gear, headed to the edge of the river, and watched a blue inflatable canoe make its way across the Colorado, paddled by a friend named Scott Perry, who had driven more than 120 miles from Flagstaff to retrieve us.

After Perry ferried us to the far side, we deflated his boat and lifted it into the bed of his truck. But before climbing into the cab, Pete and I padded back down to the shore for a last glimpse of the cliffs we had descended the previous evening.

They were now framed by a sky so blue it looked like the flame on a gas stove—an image that reminded me of a passage I once read in *The Last Cheater's Waltz*, by Ellen Meloy, one of the loveliest writers of the Southwest, who was obsessed with the harshness and beauty of canyon country.

On the opening page of her book, Meloy relates a story about how she was making coffee one morning at her home in the desert when she accidentally poured a stream of scalding water on top of a Whiptail Lizard that had taken refuge for the night in the bottom of her cup. Only when the lizard's inverted body floated to the surface of the mahogany-colored water, its belly "the pale blue of heartbreak," did she realize she had boiled the poor thing alive.

Had Pete and I decided to keep moving along the tops of those cliffs, I imagined we might have been given a taste of what Meloy's lizard felt like during the final seconds of its life. As if to confirm this, Pete nudged me with his elbow and pointed wordlessly to the thermometer on his pack.

It registered 112°F, the same temperature as at Rider Canyon, far upstream, when we'd watched the mysterious lump wriggling beneath the skin of his torso, right before we'd been forced to give up for the first time.

We'd been licked not once, but twice.

PART X

Lost and Found

Silence is the tribute we pay to holiness.

—Pico Iyer

CHAPTER 37

Hard Days Ahead

The benchlands on the west side of the Shivwits Plateau encompass one of the most remarkable regions in the Lower 48. This immense section at the far western end of the canyon, an area of almost a thousand square miles, is distinctive for many reasons, including the stillness of its mornings and the luster of its grasslands, as well as the depth and drama of its night skies. But what defines the space more than anything else is its aridness.

Along an expanse of scrubland that is roughly two-thirds the size of Rhode Island, only a limited number of springs and sinkholes offer reliable sources of water. Each is tiny and most are separated from their nearest neighbors by many miles, making this one of the most perilous sections of the park to venture into on foot—a risk whose consequences were showcased several weeks after Pete and I pulled out at Diamond Creek, when three hikers who were friends of Rich's prepared to drop off the plateau's enormous promontory for what they hoped would be a rewarding adventure.

In mid-June, Floyd Roberts, a fifty-two-year-old high school teacher from Treasure Island, Florida, flew to Las Vegas to link up with his best friend and longtime hiking partner, Ned Bryant, fifty-two, a chemical engineer who was coming in from his home in Winona, Minnesota.

They were joined by Bryant's daughter, Madeleine, twenty-four, who worked as a manager at the REI store in Flagstaff.

All of them had extensive desert-hiking experience—and much like Rich, each relished challenging trips through obscure sections of the canyon. Since 1992, the men had been teaming up on ambitious back-country ventures all over the West, while Bryant and his daughter were currently about halfway through completing a full sectional traverse of the canyon. But even so, what the three of them were now proposing to do was exceptionally ambitious and dicey.

On the afternoon of the seventeenth, the temperature on the rim was 92°F, but during the next several days it was expected to rise to 110, with even higher temperatures below. Down on the Tonto, it could easily surpass 120, conditions that qualified as extreme even for June, traditionally the hottest and driest month in the canyon. Although Andrew Holycross and Chris Atwood had initially been invited to join them, both had elected to withdraw because it was just too hot. Nevertheless, Roberts and the Bryants went ahead with their plans.

*   *   *

Simply getting to the starting line took a nine-hour drive from Flagstaff. The final two hours of that journey unfolded along a deeply rutted dirt road, twenty-five miles of which were studded with volcanic boulders the size of Halloween pumpkins, a stretch that was best handled by leaving one's 4x4 behind and switching to an ATV.*

Shortly after 3:00 p.m. on June 17, the trio arrived at an old water catchment basin known as Kelly Tanks, and walked down the final six-mile section of the road toward Kelly Point, at the tip of the Shivwits, with the intention of dropping off the rim into a ravine leading to a drainage called 214-Mile Canyon. Just before reaching the edge, they

---

* Kelly Point, at the tip of the Shivwits Plateau, may well be the hardest part of the entire rim to access, a zone even more cut off than the Great Thumb Mesa. It is forty-five miles on an unmarked two-track from the far end of the Great Thumb to the nearest gas station; for Kelly Point, the closest source of fuel is more than twice that distance.

encountered a thicket of dense brush at the base of a small knoll, and the group split in two, opting to take slightly different routes. While Roberts remained in the brush and bushwhacked around the hill, the Bryants decided to go up and over. Each party assumed that they would all link up at a cairn on the opposite side of the knoll marking the start of the descent into the ravine. But when the Bryants topped the knoll and came down the far slope, Roberts was nowhere to be seen.

After an hour of waiting, the Bryants began combing the area and calling out for their missing friend until darkness descended. Perplexed and worried, they set up camp for the night next to the cairn.

In the morning, when there was still no sign of Roberts, they returned to the dirt road and searched the area until noon, when they sent a satellite text seeking advice from a veteran hiker in Phoenix named Chris Forsyth, who was also a friend of Rich's. Forsyth immediately called the park's dispatch center, triggering a search-and-rescue mission; then he and Rich began racing in their vehicles toward the South Rim, where they would later be met by a helicopter and shuttled out to the Shivwits Plateau.

Meanwhile, a ranger named Todd Seliga, who was already on patrol in the area, was given orders to rendezvous with the Bryants. After retracing Roberts's steps with the Bryants' help, Seliga dropped off the edge of the plateau to embark on an all-night solo search in a bid to find the missing hiker before it was too late.

By the morning of the nineteenth, seven Park Service ground teams with more than a dozen trackers, including Forsyth, were combing an area of roughly ten square miles around Kelly Point, while Rich was pulled onto an aerial surveillance mission, then folded into the ground search. None of them found any trace of Roberts. It was as if he had simply vanished.

Over the next several days, the teams located a single footprint that Roberts had left along the dirt road on the rim, plus several tracks on the route leading off the edge. Based on those clues and the searchers' extensive understanding of the terrain below the Shivwits, a theory emerged about what may have happened.

*   *   *

After Roberts finished contouring around to the far side of the low knoll where the Bryants had last seen him, he had apparently dropped off the rim—probably assuming that the Bryants had already begun their descent. Unfortunately, however, he wasn't descending into 214-Mile Canyon, the drainage that the group had been planning to access. Instead, thanks to a subtle and deceptive fold in the terrain, he was unknowingly plunging into the upper tentacles of 209-Mile Canyon—an entirely different tributary that, coincidentally, was the very same drainage that Pete and I had entered two months earlier on our way down to the river.

When Roberts disappeared, he was carrying a large blue backpack stuffed with nine days' worth of food and ten liters of water, which should have been enough to sustain him for several days—as long as he had the discipline, upon realizing that he had lost contact with his companions, to seek shade and refrain from exerting himself. But the footprints suggested that he may not have done either of those things.

Instead of staying put, he had apparently continued moving deeper into the canyon, then set camp and stopped for the night. By the following morning, he would have consumed at least a liter or two of his water before resuming his descent—all while failing to realize that he had no chance of linking up with the Bryants because they were still on the rim.

Even then, Roberts might have been able to survive, had he taken steps to avoid overheating and sought to minimize the water that he was losing through perspiration. But sometime on the eighteenth, he would have found it extremely difficult to adhere to that strategy when the pilot of a search-and-rescue helicopter, at the search team's request, briefly touched down near a pour-over at the edge of the Supai to inspect a sand trap, a place from where it would be impossible for a lost hiker to descend farther into the canyon without leaving tracks.

If Roberts was anywhere near that location during the few minutes the pilot spent on the ground, he quite likely tried to make a run for the chopper—a distance of at least three miles over steep terrain—and signed his own death warrant in one of two ways. If he still had his pack with him when he made that run, the exertion would have doubled or tripled his rate of perspiration while spiking his body temperature beyond the human heatstroke threshold of 105°F. But if he set his pack down to chase the helicopter, he might well have found it impossible—upon failing to draw the pilot's attention—to retrace his steps back to the pack, which was his only lifeline.

Out there on the terraces beneath the Shivwits, it can be shockingly easy to lose one's sense of direction, especially without a compass, a map, or the other tools that were probably still in the pack. Every terrain feature—boulders, bushes, low ridges—begins to look the same, and as you race off in one direction or another without finding what you're looking for, your sense of where you've been, and where you need to be, becomes increasingly scrambled.

This is only conjecture. It's entirely possible that Roberts *did* seek shade and avoided movement. But either way, one can well imagine the dismay as he waved frantically in the hopes of catching the pilot's eye, then watched the helicopter disappear over the horizon and confronted his predicament: lost, alone, enveloped in furnace-like heat, and aware—dimly or otherwise—that the time he had left was slipping away as sweat poured through the pores of his skin at a rate of more than a liter an hour in the 110-degree air.

If he managed to survive the rest of that day, he likely made it through the night, too. But sometime the following day, unable to replace the water he had already lost, he would have progressed through increasingly severe stages of dehydration and heatstroke. Even if he remained stationary, he would be dead in less than twenty-four hours.

Given that the searchers were unable to locate Roberts's body, it is impossible to know exactly what happened, other than that he disappeared. But Rich's best guess was that his final resting place was probably within a mile of the point where, less than eight weeks earlier, Pete and I had entered 209-Mile Canyon.

* * *

For the rest of that summer, as Pete and I waited for the weather to cool and steeled ourselves for the prospect of returning to the canyon, no sign of Roberts surfaced. Although Rich and a number of others kept returning to the area, no one managed to find a single piece of gear or clothing or another footprint. By the middle of October, his fate was still a mystery when Pete and I began gathering our gear in anticipation of leaving Flagstaff and making our way out to Kelly Point along the same dirt track from which Roberts had gone missing.

The fact that he was out there, somewhere, offered a stark warning of how deadly the place was—and how quickly things could go wrong, even for people who had far more experience than us. However, one unexpected twist tipped the odds in our favor, as we learned shortly before our departure, when Pete asked Rich if he could share the GPS points of several key potholes on which our survival would depend.

"Oh, don't worry too much about the waypoints to those potholes," said Rich. "I'm coming with you guys to make sure you don't lose your way—and also because there's something out there that I want you both to see."

We entered the canyon on the morning of October 23, dropping off the edge at Kelly Point, descending through the familiar upper layers of the cliffs. Then we began working our way across a broad shelf atop the Supai, suspended fourteen hundred feet beneath the North Rim and thirty-three hundred feet above the river.

By now, we were far enough west that the geology had begun to shift in some important ways. For a start, the platform we were on no longer featured endless stretches of wind-buffed slickrock, but was covered in an orange-colored soil that was sparsely studded with piñon and juniper trees interspersed with tufts of bunchgrass.

It also had a new name. Instead of the Esplanade, it was known as the Sanup, and over the next several days, we were afforded a window into its starkness and aridity as we wended into and back out of the dry washes and the parched drainages. There wasn't a single spring, and the only sources of water were tiny, shadow-draped clefts at the base of nameless cliffs.

When we arrived at those pockets, some were so thin that we lay on our stomachs, put our lips to the trembling millimeter of liquid, and slurped it directly from the rock. If anything was left after we had slaked our thirst, we pulled out our syringes and transferred the rest into our empty bottles. Those potholes were so widely scattered and so well hidden that without Rich and his detailed knowledge of the terrain, we would surely have perished like Roberts.

Mornings along those desiccated benchlands of the Sanup were flooded in sunlight and consumed by thoughts of distance and water. In the afternoons, the heat was stoked by bake-oven breezes, and the sky offered no sign of the great phalanx of rainstorms that had swept over this part of the park during the previous autumn when Rich and Chris had come through. At the end of each day, we would lay out that night's camp, carefully take stock of how much water we had left, and spend the evening gazing toward the rimlands on the far side of the abyss as twilight stole over the Sanup.

Then one night, just after dinner, Rich told us that it was time to leave the high country, at least temporarily, and move deeper into the chasm.

"We'll be heading for the river tomorrow, and it's not going to be easy," he warned. "We've got some hard days ahead of us."

*   *   *

By sunrise the next morning, we were pushing across the dawn-reddened dirt toward a tributary that would enable us to drop off the edge of the Sanup. At the head of the drainage, Rich pulled out his rope and harnesses and set up an anchor. Then we lowered ourselves into a narrow crevasse in the Redwall and entered a realm that was considerably less appealing than Olo, the slot canyon whose vibrantly tinted walls and bell-shaped chambers had left us awash in awe the previous winter.

The first part of the descent featured a series of sharp, back-to-back rappels, each of which plopped us into a pool of brown water concealing a thick layer of sticky orange sludge that reeked of rot, stagnation, and nameless putrescence. The surface of one of these pools was coated, inexplicably, with dead tarantulas. Another bore the body of a drowned chuckwalla—a large, flat-bodied lizard—floating on its back with all four legs reaching into the air, its belly distended with gas.

By late afternoon when we finally popped through the bottom of the slot at the base of the Redwall, we were slathered in mud. But instead of stopping to rest, Rich pressed us to keep moving along the floor of the drainage, which had grown wider and was now covered in gravel.

For hours, we worked our way deeper and deeper until, long after dark, we finally arrived at the mouth of the tributary, which was known as Burnt Canyon, and dropped our packs on a flat patch of ground ringed with acacia and tamarisk trees. It was almost 10:00 p.m. and impossible to see anything beyond the fifteen-foot arc of our headlamps. I was so tired I couldn't even finish a bowl of ramen noodles before nodding off to sleep. The last thing I remembered was the sound of my spoon clinking against the gravel as it slipped from my fingers.

When I opened my eyes the following morning and sat up, I could see that we were next to the Colorado. The water was thick and sluggish and an oily brown, barely inching past the banks as the current all but came to a halt upon hitting the uppermost end of Lake Mead. A layer of mist was draped above the surface of the river, and looming out of that haze I could see a wall of reddish limestone and gray sandstone rising more than three thousand feet, set back like stairsteps and extending up to the rim where the Hualapai Reservation lay.

Still a bit stunned by what it had taken to reach this spot, I glanced dully at my wristwatch. It was 7:14 a.m.

Exactly one minute later, the bottom of the canyon filled with the kind of roar that only an aircraft can make—and one minute after that, the first helicopter appeared.

*   *   *

It came from downstream, flying fast and low, no more than two hundred feet above the river, close enough that I could clearly see the pilot's headset and sunglasses through the canopy. The chopper was painted bright red with bold lines, and the words GRAND CANYON were emblazoned along its middle in white.

It seemed to be heading upstream, but right above our camp, the pilot banked into a long S-shaped turn that took him deep into the mouth of Burnt, then back out to the river and across to the far side. As he passed over our heads, the piercing whine of the engine and the whipping thud of its twin rotors registered partly on the ear, but also on the walls of the chest and the tissues of the belly. It was loud enough that we had to shout to be heard by one another.

"That's just the first," Rich yelled as the chopper hovered briefly above the terraces on the opposite side of the Colorado before touching down on top of the Tonto. "There's more on the way."

He was right. At 7:30, as if someone had flipped a switch, a second and third helicopter clattered up the canyon, swiftly followed by a dozen more. They varied in color—some were maroon, others gray, still others were white and yellow. A few of them banked and landed at various points on the Tonto along the far side of the river, but they all flew low to the ground, rarely more than three hundred feet above the surface, and together they generated a solid wave of sound.

By 8:15 a.m., when we had broken camp, shouldered our packs, and headed downstream, we had counted thirty-eight helicopters, roughly one every ninety seconds.

That was just a foretaste of what was to come.

CHAPTER 38

"The Combat Zone"

As we pressed downstream, the sky directly above the river was thronged with helicopters. They flew along both banks as well as above the main current, and in the densest parts of every sortie, as many as ten or twelve machines were visible at once, with at least one passing directly overhead every fifteen to twenty seconds. Each surge would build for several minutes, then subside into a brief lull, followed by another rush.

Just before 11:30 a.m., having counted sixty-five helicopters, we began skirting a series of landing zones along the cliffs on the far side of the river, each featuring a set of picnic tables, a short pole strung with a windsock, and a tall mast with an American flag. At the first of these, five helicopters squatted on the ground, each looking like a bright red wasp, with a sixth taking off and a seventh approaching to land. Milling around the aircraft were roughly two dozen tourists, clad in street clothing and toasting one another with champagne glasses.

During the twenty minutes it took for us to draw abreast of the landing pads and then move beyond them, we took in the scene. Upon touching down, each chopper disgorged another batch of passengers, who walked a dozen or so steps toward the edge of the cliff, where they spent a few minutes gazing down at the river or taking selfies. Then they turned and climbed back on board. Within a minute or two, the engines had spooled and the rotors were turning, and a few seconds later they were in the air, heading back to the rim, while their replacements circled to land and repeat the same cycle. Each visit seemed to last no more than ten or fifteen minutes. The rotation was smooth, well choreographed, and seemed to flow virtually without interruption—an airborne conveyor belt of tourism.

For the most part, it was impossible to hear anything, aside from the sound of the engines and rotors. But during the intervals separating the arrival of one cluster of helicopters and the departure of another, the voices of the pilots and the clients carried clearly across the bottom of the canyon.

"All right, you guys—this is what we came here for!"

"How high do you think those walls are?"

"How many bars do you have on your phone?"

"Okay, folks, let's think about heading back."

During these exchanges, even though we were moving through their field of vision, directly at eye level, no one seemed to notice us. To them, we were too small and insignificant to register. But for us, it was the opposite.

For the rest of that day, at no moment were we free from the sight of those aircraft or the roar of their engines as we struggled to make our way along a series of enormous silt banks that rose thirty or forty feet above the river—unsightly deposits left by the receding waters of Lake Mead as the reservoir continues to shrink in response to climate change. Hour after hour, we continued moving beneath the helicopters, diligently tallying their number, until, late in the afternoon when the total reached 250, we became so dispirited that we stopped keeping count. And still they kept coming.

Around 5:45 p.m., we reached the mouth of a side canyon choked with a forest of dead tamarisk trees and dropped our packs on a flat stretch of gravel. Ten minutes later, with the sun setting, the last chopper finally disappeared.

"Whenever I walk through here and hear the constant drone of aviation, it just shocks me," said Rich as we began setting up camp. "It's like a punch to the jaw."

"How come this is allowed to happen inside a national park?" asked Pete, who was incredulous at what we had witnessed.

As I would come to learn, the answer to that question was quite a story, one that went back many years—and at the center of that saga lay a series of historic injustices that had induced the last of the canyon's eleven tribes to partner with a group of air-tour companies to transform the western end of the park from a half-forgotten backwater into one of the most crowded flight corridors in the world.

As I also discovered, to understand how all of that unfolded and why, you need to know a few things about "the People of the Tall Pines."

                    *   *   *

According to modern anthropologists, the earliest ancestors of what is now the Hualapai tribe began migrating out of the Colorado River Delta near the Sea of Cortez more than a thousand years ago, and by the mid-fourteenth century were living around what is now Las Vegas. The Hualapai, however, contend they were part of this landscape ever since their emergence at an unfathomably distant point in the past from Spirit Mountain, near present-day Laughlin, Nevada.

Either way, by the time Columbus made his first voyage to the Americas, twelve different bands of the tribe were spread across some 5 million acres of plateaus and side canyons south of the Colorado River, directly adjacent to the territory of the Havasupai, with whom they shared both a common lineage and a similar language. Unlike their eastern neighbors, however, the Hualapai considered themselves not only hunters and gatherers, but warriors as well—and when whites began invading their home ranges during the early 1860s in search of silver ore and grazing lands, they fought back with ferocity and skill.

Hostilities raged unchecked until the U.S. Army, stymied at every turn, finally invited the Hualapai to a peace parley at what is now the town of Kingman, Arizona, where they tricked the men into laying down their arms. Then the soldiers rounded everyone up and herded them into a concentration camp, where they were confined until 1874, when the entire tribe was forced to march south for more than a hundred miles to a failed mining town near Yuma in a valley so sweltering that the officer in charge of the exodus called it the "Sahara of the Colorado." There they were left to "bake in the desert," suffering from sickness and malnutrition, until the following spring, when they decided they'd had enough, gathered up their belongings, and walked home, carrying their children in their arms.

They returned to discover that white settlers and ranchers had moved in and taken over much of their homeland, fencing off nearly every spring, destroying the grass by introducing herds of cattle, and decimating the wild game. To protect themselves from these interlopers, they petitioned the federal government for a reservation, a process that took another seven years. The result was far smaller than the domain they had once occupied, but nevertheless substantial: a tract of almost a million acres whose northern boundary abutted a 108-mile stretch of the Colorado River inside the Grand Canyon, which they considered the *ha 'yidada*, or "backbone of the world."

Within the boundaries of this new reservation, the Hualapai discovered that it was impossible to return to their ancestral way of life. Cut off from 80 percent of their aboriginal range and unable to survive by semi-nomadic hunting and gathering, they were consigned to what looked like permanent destitution, dependent on meager government handouts supplemented with rock-bottom wages for a limited number of menial jobs at nearby ranches and mines. They were also reviled by the white settlers, who were arriving in ever greater numbers, and whose contempt for the natives was merciless.

"The Wallapai [*sic*] Indians complain of the quality of the flour served out to them by the government, and say it is full of weevils and has an intensely bitter taste," observed an article in the *Mojave County Miner*, a paper whose views reflected the prevailing sentiment toward the tribe. "A plentiful supply of arsenic mixed with it would disguise the bitter taste. We offer this suggestion to the contractor and sincerely hope he will adopt it."

During the years that followed, each side's response to the other would prove prophetic. Undisguised malice on the part of the local whites was matched by visceral disdain among the Hualapai, plus a defiant resolve to go about their business exactly as they saw fit. In countless ways, this mutual contempt would poison relations between the two societies over the next 150 years—and during that time, the Hualapai came to absorb the same lesson that would later be taught to their closest neighbors to the east when the Havasupai convinced Congress to return 185,000 acres of their ancestral territory, only to learn that having land offered no guarantee of economic prosperity.

If the Hualapai wanted to find a way to survive and flourish, they would have to do it themselves.

*　　　*　　　*

It wouldn't be easy. For the first half of the twentieth century, more than a third of the households inside the borders of the reservation were living below the poverty line. Aside from seasonal work on local ranches and a handful of positions in tribal government, there were almost no jobs anywhere within the Hualapai homelands. To earn money, most breadwinners were forced to seek employment in Kingman or farther afield in cities such as Las Vegas or Phoenix.

By the 1970s, the tribe's leaders decided that their best hope for economic development was to leverage their proximity to the Grand Canyon and promote tourism—a strategy that suffered a serious set-back in 1984 when the completion of Interstate 40 diverted almost all highway traffic twenty-five miles south of Peach Springs, transforming the reservation's only town into a remote crossroads with a single gas station and a row of abandoned storefronts. Nevertheless, the Hualapai were resilient, resourceful, and willing to take risks. So after partially reviving the town by investing in a motel and a restaurant, they decided to place their chips on a small casino they set up in a Quonset hut near a promontory known as Eagle Point, which overlooked the canyon on the northern end of the reservation.

They called the venture Grand Canyon West, and the drive from Peach Springs took almost two hours, most of it on a gnarled dirt road. For the next several years the casino limped along—assisted by promotional schemes such as inviting the son of the legendary stunt performer Evel Knievel to jump his motorcycle across a side canyon—until an outsider finally showed up, from Shanghai of all places, with a bold new idea.

David Jin had come to the United States with dreams of starting a company that would cater to the unprecedented influx of Asian tourists who were pouring into Las Vegas in increasing numbers during the 1990s, especially from China, where booming economic wealth had begun to trickle down to ordinary citizens, many of whom were eager to travel abroad. Jin, who knew that these vacationers were also interested in seeing nearby sights, approached the Hualapai and pitched the idea of building a one-of-a-kind tourist installation on the rim of the canyon: a glass-bottomed deck, which he called a "skywalk." It would offer anyone standing on its transparent surface an unobstructed view of the four-thousand-foot drop yawning beneath their feet, making it seem as if they were walking on the air itself—or even better, Jin rhapsodized, enabling them to feel as if they were birds soaring on the updrafts.

It took several years to secure the financing and, more important, to overcome opposition from the tribe's traditionalists, who viewed the project as something of a sacrilege, as well as a risky business venture—misgivings that appeared to be vindicated when construction was finally completed and the Skywalk opened for business in the spring of 2007. Visitation was scant—a tiny fraction of that at the main entrance to Grand Canyon National Park, almost 250 miles to the east. But thanks to some dramatic developments that had already been set in motion in that very park, things were about to change.

*   *   *

For more than two decades, officials at the Grand Canyon had been fielding an increasing number of complaints concerning the commercial air-tour industry, a sector that had been enjoying rapid and largely

unchecked growth and profitability since the early 1980s, when eighteen companies were regularly offering scenic excursions by plane
or helicopter over the canyon, with an additional twenty-six outfits
providing supplemental flights. Together these carriers were averaging
123 flights a day—a number that more than doubled during the busiest months of July and August, when twenty or more flights could be
crisscrossing the chasm at once. Each year, the air-tour fleet sold tickets
to more than 350,000 customers and filled the skies over the canyon
with some 45,000 overflights, the largest number of any national park
in the country.

For such an active airspace, there was shockingly little regulation or
oversight. Tour companies were permitted to design their own safety
protocols regarding where, when, and at what heights they flew, as
well as how they communicated with other aircraft. As a result, the
airspace resembled a free-for-all, and the number of accidents began
to increase. In the mid-1980s, sixty-six air-tour passengers and per-
sonnel lost their lives in a sequence of eight different crashes, which
was followed in the summer of 1986 by a horrific midair collision
between a helicopter and a fixed-wing plane that took the lives of all
twenty-five people in both aircraft. When the first rescue party arrived
on the scene of that catastrophe, alerted by columns of smoke, the
debris as well as the bodies of most of the victims were engulfed in
forty-foot-high flames.*

All of those incidents involved helicopters or small planes, and
many of them resulted from pilot error or improper maintenance.
But in addition to the safety scandal created by the sightseeing flights,
visitors and park officials were becoming increasingly incensed by the
spread of noise pollution in a place that had once been distinguished
not only by its scenic beauty, but also by its silence.

Each day between the hours of dawn and dusk, some of the best
overlooks along the rims and several of the most popular trails were

---

* The heat of the fire was intense enough to crack rocks near the impact site and send streams
of melted aluminum trickling down the terraces.

beset by the roar of aviation. At many of these locations, a plane or helicopter flew overhead every two minutes, so that the sound of each passing aircraft overlapped with the one that followed. The din was continuous, with no moment when the canyon's tranquility was interspersed only with natural sounds such as the rush of the wind or the call of a passing raven.

In 1987, following extensive hearings, Congress passed the National Parks Overflights Act and the FAA was ordered to begin working with the park to design a set of regulations to improve air safety while reducing aircraft noise. This included forcing commercial air-tour operators to abide by no-fly zones and forbidding them from flying or landing anywhere beneath the rims. From now on, pilots would be governed by unambiguous restrictions on where they could fly, how low they could go, and how much noise they could generate.

Unfortunately, these changes fell far short of what was necessary to fully protect the soundscape. Even though aircraft were required to fly thousands of feet above the canyon and confined to well-defined corridors, visitors who found themselves beneath those flight paths still found the noise to be intolerable, a situation that persists to this day. Nevertheless, all subsequent efforts to impose additional restrictions provoked intense pushback from the air-tour industry, which forcefully— and effectively—defended its business toehold in the central part of the canyon. At the same time, these operators were aggressively seeking to expand their business even further by reaching out to the Hualapai with a bold new scheme that was about to flip the rules upside down and change the game entirely.

*   *   *

The bonanza kicked off around 1996, right when David Jin and his team were selling the tribe on his vision of providing a bird's-eye view of the canyon. The Hualapai had already begun seeking help in improving a dirt airstrip that they maintained a short distance from the rim, hoping that this might help with tourist visitation. The following year, the FAA agreed to provide $5 million for paving the runway and other upgrades.

Not long after that, the tribe's lawyers informed the FAA that the Hualapai suffered from an unemployment rate of 50 to 65 percent, and that if the tribe was forced to abide by the new safety and noise-reduction regulations that applied in the rest of Grand Canyon, the rules would damage their economic future. With the assistance of a consultant named Lamar Whitmer—the very same developer who would later arouse the fury of Renae Yellowhorse a hundred miles to the east with his proposal for a tramway to carry tourists to the bottom of the canyon—the Hualapai lobbied for a set of new flight corridors that would support their burgeoning tourism enterprise.

Eventually, the FAA not only agreed to the tribe's requests, but also consented to allow helicopters to fly as low as two hundred feet over the rim—and, astonishingly, to enter the airspace *below* the rims and skim through the river corridor inside the canyon.

With their special dispensation from the FAA, the Hualapai had finally struck gold. Not only was the tribe now sanctioned to let choppers plunge off the rim in a stomach-churning, thirty-five-hundred-foot elevator drop that seemed as exciting as any ride at Disney World, but pilots could even touch down on a series of landing pads so that their passengers could disembark, stand on the bottom of the canyon without being forced to hike a single step, and—for an additional fee—be served a glass of champagne. And thanks to a special clause in the tribe's exemption, there would be no limit to how many people could do this in any given year.

This "Hualapai exception" neatly coincided with the impending completion of the Skywalk facility. By 2007, six different helicopter air-tour companies were rushing to take advantage of the new opportunity, putting together tours catering to every taste and timetable. Over the next several years, an untapped market opened up as Las Vegas tourists were encouraged to supplement their gambling and celebrity entertainment with a sightseeing excursion to the canyon and the Skywalk, now only a thirty-minute flight or a two-and-a-half-hour ride on a luxury tour bus.

None of this was cheap. The VIP customers on the marquee tours could pay hundreds of dollars for amenities that included limo transportation to and from their hotels, motorized boat tours, and return flights timed to pop out of the canyon at sunset and fly over the Strip just as the lights of Vegas were coming on. But even the least expensive packages cost a minimum of $300 per person. Thanks to Jin, the overwhelming majority of those tourists were not from the United States, but from China—a pattern that continued even after 2012, when the Hualapai leadership wrested ownership of Grand Canyon West and the Skywalk away from the Jin family and began operating it on their own.

By 2016, the tribe and the air-tour companies had enough customers to regularly flood the bottom of the canyon with as many as four hundred helicopter flights a day from sunrise to sunset, seven days a week, in every season of the year. During the most popular times, such as Chinese New Year, the number of flights could easily push toward five hundred. Thanks to those statistics, the airstrip and the landing pads at Grand Canyon West now qualified as one of the busiest heliports in the world.

Everyone involved seemed to be profiting handsomely from the arrangement. A significant chunk of money—perhaps as much as $55 million a year—was going straight into the hands of the air-tour operators, with Papillon and Maverick, the two largest companies, taking the lion's share. Another stream of those revenues was flowing directly to the Hualapai, who were collecting royalties for use of the tribe's airspace, airport, and helipads inside the canyon while simultaneously generating income from their glass-bottomed observation deck. Altogether, the tribe was hosting 1.1 million tourists a year and enjoying annual revenues pushing toward $110 million.

It's difficult to overstate the impact of this financial infusion on the Hualapai's economic welfare. While some of the money was being handed directly to individual members, the bulk of the funds was channeled into the tribe's health, police, and EMS departments, along with a variety of important programs for the elderly. The income also paid for scholarships to help students attend college, an enormous education victory in the wake of the boarding school era. But perhaps the greatest impact of all came from the jobs that the Skywalk provided.

By this point, Grand Canyon West employed roughly a thousand people, 28 percent of whom belonged to the tribe, and was the second-largest employer in Arizona's Mohave County. With fourteen hundred enrolled members living on the reservation, the tribal government now felt it was fair to assume that anyone who wanted a job had one.

If in achieving those goals the Hualapai had employed tactics that struck critics as materialistic, it was impossible to deny that since their very first contact with settlers of European descent, the tribe had been subjected to an extended lesson in the rules of free-market economics—and that they were doing nothing more (and nothing less) than putting into practice the lessons they had been taught by their former tormentors. For many outsiders who took the trouble to acquaint themselves with the wrongs that had been visited on not just this one tribe, but all of the Native American communities with ties to the canyon, it seemed that the Hualapai had played their cards extremely well. In the eyes of some, they were beating the whites at their own game.

"We want to live in the modern age," Damon Clarke, the tribal chairman at the time, told the writer Annette McGivney of *Outside* magazine, in response to the growing concerns about both air-tour safety and industrialized tourism in the western part of the canyon. "We are developing our own means for becoming economically self-sufficient—we are finally able to make a living."

*   *   *

In the months immediately following its grand opening, the Skywalk had been viewed by many as a joke, a tourist trap unworthy of its setting. By 2016, however, no one was laughing at the Hualapai. Yet to a growing number of critics, something about Grand Canyon West didn't add up. On the one hand, the leaders were doing an impressive job promoting the tribe's welfare while securing a future in which its members could control their own destiny. But the impact of these operations on the landscape as well as the soundscape seemed glaringly at odds with claims by those very same leaders that they were carefully balancing the Hualapai's business interests with their responsibilities as stewards to protect "the land, the sky, and the tranquility"—elements that former chairman Clarke insisted were "deeply woven into our spirit, our heritage, and our culture."

That claim certainly rang hollow among many people who found themselves on the Colorado River in the far western end of the canyon. Even during my own time on the river back in the mid-2000s, the flights were so egregiously disruptive that guides were already referring to the Hualapai's air-tour zone as Helicopter Alley, and many boatmen called the section around the Skywalk "the combat zone"—partly because the unstable silt banks along both sides of the river were constantly calving off hunks of sand that would sound like gunshots as they fell into the water, but mainly because of the visual and auditory disruption of the helicopters.

In the decades since, that disruption had so intensified that among the limited number of boating expeditions that didn't opt to simply end their trip at Diamond Creek, thirty-five miles upstream, many river runners preferred to wait until after sunset and complete the final stretch of the canyon during the quiet hours, a tactic known as a night float. But if a person wanted to truly gauge the effect of those air tours on both the land and the soundscape inside this corner of the park, it was necessary to do more than slink through the Alley after dark. Instead, you had to actually *walk* through the heart of Helicopter Alley.

That's why Rich had dragged Pete and me off on such a massive detour—and why, when we finally arrived in camp that night, we found ourselves stunned by what had been done to the canyon.

CHAPTER 39

Evensong

We could have kept going, and perhaps we should have. Helicopter Alley extended for another thirteen miles down-canyon, which meant that we were only halfway through, and if the goal was to fully absorb and assess the effects of the aviation, we would need to continue for another day. But Pete and I had seen and heard enough, and the air-tour operation's impact on the bottom of the canyon was simply too depressing for us to linger. When we awoke the following morning, our only wish was to escape the noise and the chaos as fast as possible by ascending the tributary in whose mouth we had camped.

The plan was to follow the main arm of the side canyon until it slotted up, then clamber through a series of steep ascents that would eventually deliver us to the Sanup. Rich, who had used this route multiple times, knew that although the climb was challenging at points, it had no vertical pitches requiring extensive ropework.

Within half an hour, having rounded several sharp turns, we had worked our way deep enough into the drainage that the clatter of the helicopters had disappeared, replaced by the sounds to which we were accustomed: the hollow click of a falling pebble, the snicker of water droplets dribbling into a pool at the base of a spring, the warble of a Canyon Wren. After the cacophony of the previous day, these small murmurings—and the hushed intervals between them—arrived as a relief.

We spent the rest of that day squeezing through fallen boulders blocking the floor of the tributary or wriggling beneath massive chockstones wedged between the walls, moving higher and higher as each obstacle gave way to the next. When we reached the Redwall, the space between the walls tightened, and the passageway began to wind back on itself, bending and twisting like the oxbows of a creek in a marsh.

Somewhere deep inside this section, we came across the carcass of a baby Bighorn, lying on its side. The skin along its torso had been pulled back, exposing the shattered bones of its rib cage. Several feet away lay the body of a mature ram. One of its horns had been snapped off at the base, and its spine had been broken.

Whatever had unfolded here—a rockfall, an attempt to outrun a flash flood, a desperate bid to escape an ambush by a Mountain Lion—we were unable to unravel the story. But the broken bodies of these animals offered a sobering reminder that this place was neither a playground nor an amusement park.

Eventually, the climb drew us to the base of a tall cliff whose face soared more than a hundred feet above our heads. A cone of rubble provided a crude ramp for the final part of the ascent. The ramp led us up to a tiny patch of flat dirt, roughly the size of a parking space, where the face of the cliff was inscribed with a series of small petroglyphs depicting a pair of human figures, each of which seemed to be pointing down into the serpentine arms of the drainage that we had ascended. Just to the right of the panels, the trunk of a piñon tree had been positioned to serve as a crude ladder.

The bark was long gone, and the smooth trunk, as bleached as the bones of the baby Bighorn on the rocks below, appeared to be quite ancient. The tree marked the apex of an elegant prehistoric route that today is known to only a tiny number of hikers (which is why Rich asked me to refrain from revealing the name of the tributary).

We scuttled up the trunk one by one, taking care to avoid breaking off the stubs that offered placements for our hands and feet. After stepping from the top of the tree to the top of the cliff, we found ourselves standing once more on the scrub-dotted plains of the Sanup, less than eight miles west of the spot where we had followed Rich down to the river at the start of Helicopter Alley.

Even by the warped standards of the canyon, where threading between any two points invariably seems to involve five times more work than anyone would reasonably expect, this detour was in a class by itself. We had just spent three days covering twenty-four miles, descending and then reclimbing almost seven thousand vertical feet, to arrive at a spot we could have reached in less than a three hours' walk across flat ground.

"This is probably the very first time a detour of this magnitude has been incorporated into a thru-hike," said Rich. "Up to now, nobody's ever been insane enough—or, frankly, dumb enough—to try it."

"Except for us?" I asked.

"Except for us," confirmed Rich.

*   *   *

It was now about four o'clock in the afternoon, and the sharply angled autumn light had begun teasing shadows from every twig and pebble. Across the surface of the Sanup, a cool breeze was ruffling the tall grasses that grew in tufts along the low, rounded hills. Out on the edges of the plateau, a long line of rose-colored cliffs soared almost two thousand feet to the North Rim.

The open sky, the lingering light, and the rippling sea of blond grass felt expansive and exhilarating, and for several minutes we simply stood and breathed in the sheer wonder and enormity of it all—until we gradually became aware that the savanna was suffused with a familiar sound.

The helicopters were back.

Instead of filling up the sky directly overhead, they were now miles away, emerging from the depths in ones and twos and flitting purposefully over the Hualapai Reservation near the border with the park on the far side of the canyon. Despite the distance, however, they still blanketed the entire plateau with a faint metallic thrumming.

Like a cloud of mosquitoes, the droning stayed with us as we moved toward the head of yet another side canyon, where Rich guided us to a cleft in which a few quarts of rainwater or snowmelt could linger for a week or more after a storm, the only source of water within a five-mile radius. After filling our bottles, we continued pressing west for another hour until evening caught us at the crest of a low ridge that offered a sweeping view in all directions, where we set camp.

Off to the east, more than twenty miles away, we could see the hulking pediment of Kelly Point, gleaming like copper in the fading light. A bank of bruised-purple clouds had been suspended like ripe plums above the Sanup for most of that afternoon, and as we unfurled our bedrolls, the sun dipped beneath the cloud bank, sending forth a fantail of light that set off a series of flashes as sunlight reflected off the canopies and the rotors of the day's final group of helicopters, making the sunset run to Las Vegas, almost seventy-five miles to the west.

As we stared at that twinkling line, shimmering in the last of the light, Pete caught sight of something directly to the south.

"Hey, is that the airport at Grand Canyon West?" he asked.

Sure enough, it was. Perched on the rimlands along the far side of the looming chasm were a set of white metal-clad buildings, a small cylinder that looked like a storage tank, and what appeared to be a cell tower with a blinking red light. Just to the right of the largest building were the runway and the heliport, and somewhere off to the left at the edge of a massive side canyon—partially blocked from our view by a pair of juniper trees in front of us—were the horseshoe-shaped Skywalk and the block-shaped building to which it was attached.

Even at a range of seven miles, the profiles of those structures were unmistakably distinct—as if, through some strange and puzzling sleight of optics, the canyon were holding them at arm's length in a way that enabled us to see what they were with a disarming clarity and candor.

"That airport over there and the helicopters attached to it will never go away," declared Rich. "They're a permanent fixture of the landscape, and now things are so far along that I'm starting to think it's the Achilles' heel of the canyon, the thing that may eventually cause the entire park to come apart."

"What do you mean by that?" I asked.

"This used to be the wildest and quietest part of the canyon, and it should have been allowed to remain that way," replied Rich. "What's happening over there now basically negates the laws that were created to protect this place."

In the midst of this exchange, it suddenly dawned on me that Rich had dragged us off on the most convoluted detour in the history of thru-hiking because he wanted us to understand not only what the Hualapais and the air-tour industry had already done to this part of the canyon, but what stood to be lost in the future if those initiatives opened the door for developments in other parts of the park.

Thanks to the years he'd spent exploring this place prior to meeting Pete and me, Rich was keenly aware of the canyon's vulnerability—not just the fragility of every individual fiber and strand of the landscape, but how closely and inextricably each was tied to the next so that damage to any single filament tended to ripple across the entire web—and thus how easily and irrevocably it could all be lost.

For Rich, this was perhaps the paramount insight from his thru-hike. Being able to see the larger picture was critical to understanding the connections between the canyon, its ecosystem, and the development projects looming over both. Each time one of those projects succeeded, it offered a precedent and a license for other schemes. Separately, each was capable of inflicting damage on a particular portion of the canyon. Together, they had the potential to bring about a systematic unraveling of the entire fabric.

"The acceleration of this kind of activity, this wave of industrialized, high-volume tourism, has been incredible," said Rich. "Propagate forward fifteen years, is there anything left here? Have we really done what we set out to do—what Teddy Roosevelt set out to do—in letting the rest of the world come fly over Grand Canyon National Park?"

*   *   *

That was certainly one way of responding to what we were witnessing. But there were other ways of seeing it, too, and during the years to come, several members of the Hualapai tribe would help me to understand that whenever they look at the heliport and the Skywalk, they see something very different.

They see an operation that is providing an entire tribe with jobs and income on a reservation that was previously devoid of both, thereby enabling members of the community for the very first time to earn a decent living without having to move to distant cities and towns, which means that they can now stay tied to the places and the people they love most deeply. They see a visitor center at the Skywalk that includes an indoor museum that celebrates their culture by showcasing the story of their ancestors, along with an outdoor pavilion where younger members of the tribe are now able perform dances and other ceremonies that help to keep their traditions alive while simultaneously sharing those traditions with outsiders.

They also see a source of resiliency and prosperity in which the entire tribe can take immense pride, because it provides an economic foundation that simply had not been there before. And above all, perhaps, they see a means of controlling their own destiny by building a future in which neither they, nor their descendants, will ever again be torn from their land and forced by outsiders to embark on a long walk into exile and destitution.

Those perspectives, I would eventually come to conclude, are every bit as valid as Rich's perspective—although I would never find a way to fully reconcile my admiration for the Hualapai's achievements with my dismay over the manner in which the tribe's prosperity and security are now yoked to a system of air tours that inflicts such profound damage on the integrity of the canyon as a living entity. But with time, I would also come to understand that many if not all members of the tribe are aware of these contradictions as they seek to strike a balance between economic development, cultural vitality, and sound stewardship—and that this quandary is all the more daunting because it is not entirely a situation of their own making.

That evening on the Sanup with Rich and Pete, however, all these ideas still lay in the future. For the moment, staring out at the buildings arrayed along the rimlands on the far side of the canyon, I found it impossible to do anything more than simply acknowledge the obvious, which was that we and the Hualapai appeared to stand on opposite sides of a literal and figurative abyss. If there was a way to bridge that chasm, it certainly wasn't evident to me.

* * *

Looking deflated, Rich retreated to his ground tarp and sat down to organize his gear for the night. Meanwhile, as the final helicopter arrowed into the orange gap in the sky between the bottom of the clouds and the edge of the farthest horizon, the drone gradually faded away until finally, it disappeared altogether.

For a long moment amid the stillness that followed, the land seemed to inhale deeply, as if it had been holding its breath. And then, like a choir of Benedictine monks at evensong, a little band of birds concealed in the canopy of one of the junipers blocking our view of the Skywalk abruptly broke out in a flurry of chirps, warbles, and twitters. The chorus continued to build on a rising scale of volume and vehemency until, suddenly, a flock of some three dozen Piñon Jays exploded out of the brush as if shot from a cannon.

Moving as one, wingtip to wingtip, they soared a hundred feet into the sky and slid through a fluid chain of soaring arabesques and tight pirouettes, casting a blue-black silhouette against the purple clouds. And as they flew, they filled the air with a syncopated aria of birdsong.

The intensity of their performance was matched only by its transience and brevity. After less than a minute, as if in response to a signal whose frequency only they could detect, the flock completed one final, glorious turn, executed a headlong nosedive back into the juniper, and disappeared among the shadows.

For a second or two, the twigs and branches of the tree trembled with the touch of their landings and resounded with a brief coda—one last surge of twittering that subsided as the birds bedded down for the night. Then the silence and the stillness that had already begun to drape itself over the landscape just prior to their exuberant eruption tiptoed back, and twilight settled over the Sanup.

CHAPTER 40

Unfinished Business

"Rich, are you sure you're right?" I asked, my voice laced with skepticism. "Maybe this is one of those situations where there's another ridgeline on the far side, and it just keeps going?"

In the early-morning light, we were scanning a feature that had escaped our notice the previous evening. Off to the west was a line of saw-toothed escarpments whose tops were tilted together, like a set of hands emerging from the earth and folded in prayer.

"I promise you, Kev—after that line of cliffs, there's no more canyon," said Rich. "It's just the Basin-and-Range country of the Mojave, all the way to California."

"Hard to believe we made it this far," muttered Pete, who was almost as dubious as I was.

For more than a year we had spoken of the Grand Wash Cliffs in hushed tones, as if they were something storied and mythical, a destination toward which we were forever moving without ever fully embracing the possibility that we might actually reach it. But now there they were, hovering on the horizon.

Our route over the next two days would take us directly across the center of the grasslands as we skirted a series of jagged incisions marking the heads of the last of the tributary drainages, one after another, until we arrived at the westernmost of them all, which was called Pierce Canyon.

There, we would drop off the Sanup, complete one final descent to the river, extract a set of pack rafts from our remaining resupply cache, and then float through the break in the cliffs into the world beyond the canyon.

"Are you guys ready for this to be over?" Rich asked.

"I'm honestly not sure," replied Pete. "For the longest time, I thought I couldn't wait for the end, but now that we're almost there, I don't know if I'm ready to leave."

"Not much choice after we pass through those cliffs," said Rich. "Unless you guys decide you wanna just turn around and do the whole thing in reverse?"

"Let's please not do that," I huffed, hitching my pack and marching off in the direction of the Grand Wash Cliffs.

                    *   *   *

Within ten minutes, we caught the sound of aviation and watched as a cluster of tiny dots appeared above the far end of the Hualapai Reservation, and the first wave of helicopters began dipping into the canyon. But as the day drew on and our route pulled us away from the main corridor, the noise faded until, somewhere out in the middle of that immense savanna, we were able to confirm how truly Rich had spoken when he'd first told us that the outermost reaches of the Sanup were as glorious and magnificent as the slickrock plains of the Esplanade.

As we moved across that plateau of golden grass and red dirt, the rims pulled back and the sky opened up, and we were permitted to see farther than we ever had. To the north, we could make out the first line of cliffs ascending toward Zion National Park in Utah. Straight ahead, we could gaze deep into Nevada, and to the south we could glimpse Arizona's Music Mountains, whose blue lineaments loomed above the farthest edges of the Colorado Plateau, as ghostly and shimmering as the ripples of a stone dropped in a well.

Over the next few days, we saw more sky and a wider array of wild creatures than we had witnessed on all the previous sections of our journey put together. At times, it seemed as if every square foot of the Sanup were alive with animals. Muscular jackrabbits the size of terriers bounded from cover and zigzagged violently through the sagebrush. Families of bobblehead quail darted off in all directions among the underbranches of the piñon trees. There were bobcats and coyotes, Whiptail Lizards and Pocket Gophers, and Mule Deer whose racks were so enormous that we took them for elk.

It was as if we had been handed a passport to a lost corner of the West, a secret precinct whose borders were so distant that they seemed to spill off the edges of maps. From the first fissure of dawn to the last light of evening, we drank in the vision before us as greedily as if it were a pothole's final swallow of water. The shadows at play among the cactus needles. The streaming, hard-edged radiance of a sky as crisp and clear as the clap of a church bell. The unremitting openness of country whose surface was etched only by the comings and goings of the creatures that called it home. Time and again, the sight of these and many other things, the humble and the magnificent alike, brought us up short and left us spellbound, bowed before the Sanup's all-but-unbearable beauty.

Those closing days were among the most wistful and dreamlike of the entire venture, filled with impressions that would remain imprinted like stream-polished pebbles on the riverbeds of our memories. Yet what I would later recall even more vividly than the visual splendor of the canyon's final flaring was the one-act drama that opened each evening as night fell across the Sanup, when a wave of absolute silence once again washed over the land. A silence so pure and clean, flecked with starlight and chilled by currents of cold autumn air, that it seemed to form its own river, spilling down the faces of the cliffs, flooding the pockets of shallow ground, pooling and deepening until the entire plateau was bathed in a hush that seemed to charge the senses, quicken the conscience, and settle the mind all at once.

Like the land itself, we, too, found ourselves opening up and expanding as we anticipated the return of that magnificent quiescence. And as usual, it was Pete who noticed it well before I did.

Early one morning, I caught sight of him standing amid the grass and watched as he spent the next ten minutes turning in slow circles with his camera held at arm's length, training the lens first on himself, then out toward the horizon.

"What were you doing out there?" I asked when he returned.

"I'm honestly not sure."

Later that afternoon, when we arrived at a small, ordinary-looking knoll—the kind of rounded hump that was so commonplace it could be found anywhere—he spent the better part of an hour shooting the little mound from every angle one could imagine.

"Weird," I muttered. "What the hell's gotten into him?"

Up to now, Pete had primarily been drawn either to high visual drama—soaring cliffs, sweeping sunsets—or to small details, like a single ray of light riffling through the branches of a cottonwood tree. Now his focus was evidently beginning to shift, and as it realigned, a new artistic chamber appeared to open up inside him—a space in which he seemed to be grappling, for the first time, with new and confounding possibilities.

"I can't believe I'm about to say this," he confessed to me that evening as he prepared to head off to a spot where he planned to set up his tripod and get some time-lapse photos of the stars wheeling across the night sky. "But I'm starting to think that maybe the stuff that matters most out here isn't something I can even shoot."

"Why not?" I asked, expecting to hear something technical about the limitations of his camera in capturing light of a particular wavelength.

"It's got nothing to do with my equipment because it's not about optics," he said. "You can't see it—you can only hear it."

"Hear what?"

"This is the time of day when, if you really listen, you don't hear anything at all. It's the silence—that's the most important thing."

I took a moment to ponder this.

"Okay, so all this effort that you've gone to during the past year—lugging your gear, filming video, running around back and forth—it's been pointless?"

"Well, I'm still trying to figure that out," he said. "But right now, yeah, maybe."

This reminded me of the recording from *Desert Solitaire* that we'd replayed over and over during our nights out on the slickrock benches beyond Toroweap—the passage in which Edward Abbey had postulated that "when traces of blood begin to mark your trail, you'll see something, maybe."

Perhaps Pete and I weren't meant to *see* anything. Was it possible, I wondered, that what we were supposed to do was listen—and that what we were meant to hear was silence?

*   *   *

We continued edging west until at last, on a Sunday afternoon in early November, we arrived at a place where the ground fell away into the canyon's final tributary. Just before stepping over the edge, we paused to look back at the rows of terraces and cliffs behind us, each darker and more distant than the last, until they disappeared into a purple horizon tucked beneath an indigo sky. For once, we were gazing eastward on ground that we had already covered.

"Thanks for being a part of this," said Pete. "There's nobody I would have wanted to do this with more than you."

"It really hurts to admit this," I replied, "but I feel exactly the same way about you."

The drop was as rough as any of the countless descents we had already completed—and fittingly, it was one of the last of the 164 Redwall breaks that had been rediscovered by Harvey Butchart. Equally fitting: after threading through the break, an ordeal that took long enough that the evening shadows were creeping down the walls when we finally reached the floor of the drainage, we found that the ground was littered with artifacts—a roasting pit here, a pictograph there, potsherds scattered in every direction, all of it a reminder that the true discoverers of the route had occupied this and every other part of the canyon centuries before Butchart and his followers had ever set foot inside.

Darkness caught us at a bend along the drainage surrounded by steep walls on all sides, as if in the apse of a cathedral. Pieces of wood lay everywhere, strewn by flash floods, silvered with age, polished to a smooth sheen by the gravel and sand that had traveled with them. After setting camp, we huddled around our stove and prepared our final supper.

"It's kind of remarkable to see you guys here, considering the condition you were in when you first started this transect," said Rich. "Back then, I figured that your chances of making it this far were less than one percent. But, you know . . . it's really been something to watch both of you come alive inside this place."

"Rich, is everything all right?" asked Pete. "Oh my gosh, are you tearing up a bit?"

"No way," exclaimed Rich, vigorously rubbing the side of his face. "I just have some dirt caught in one of my eyelids."

"Well thank God for that," said Pete, "because if you were turning on the waterworks right now, it would be the second time that's happened—which would mean that you've sniveled twice as much as Kevin has on this trip."

"That's not true—I've actually been crying the entire time," I corrected Pete. "You guys just haven't seen it, because I've been weeping on the inside."

"Really?" said Pete. "Me too!"

*   *   *

Secretly, we both appreciated Rich's compliment, although we were also well aware of the things he wasn't saying, out of politeness and decency. None of the progress we had made over the past year—the storm-racked traverse of the Great Thumb Mesa, the weeks out on the Esplanade, the crossing of the arid terraces that had swallowed up Floyd Roberts—would have been possible without Rich's expertise and leadership.

He had provided all of those services freely and often at the expense of his own needs and goals, which prompted me to raise a question that had been nagging at me for some time:

"Tell us something, honestly. Have you ever taken anyone as clueless as Pete and me into the canyon with you for a trek like this?"

"No," he said, laughing. "Absolutely not."

"And would you ever do it again?"

He shook his head emphatically. "Unequivocally no."

"Okay, so can I ask you something?" I said. "It's a question that's been on my mind since the start of this misadventure, all the way back at Lee's Ferry."

"Sure."

"Why the hell did you help us?"

The answer, he explained, was rooted in a conversation he'd had with Chris Atwood and Dave Nally back when they had first agreed to embark on a thru-hike together, and found themselves wrestling with the question of when they should do it.

"We all agreed that it needed to happen as soon as possible," explained Rich, "because when we asked ourselves whether we'd be able to do the very same hike in ten years—in other words, if the canyon would still feel, for the most part, wild and untouched a decade into the future—we all agreed that the answer was no."

As Rich paused to collect his thoughts, I reflected on the changes that had already unfolded in Helicopter Alley during the years since I'd last worked on the river, and about the transformation that would surely overtake the Confluence if the developers who were attempting to partner with the Navajo were given a green light for their tramway project.

"That realization weighed on us pretty heavily," Rich continued, "because we understood that landscapes don't have voices, that they can't speak for themselves—and although the three of us knew an awful lot about the canyon, we also knew that none of us were storytellers."

"And the team you picked for this job, to speak on behalf of the land"—I tried to control my incredulity—"was me and McBrody here?"

"Enough with the McBro stuff, Groover Boy," snapped Pete. "It's not even funny."

"Yes it is—it's hilarious."

"No it's not—it's *stupid.*"

"What can I say?" Rich threw up his hands. "You make the best of what you've got. But I wasn't wrong about one thing."

"Which was what?" I asked.

"That you guys didn't quit," he replied after a long moment. "You two kept coming back, and you never gave up."

*　　　　*　　　　*

The next morning, we followed the drainage down through a series of long curves, descending for hours, and as we walked, the space between the walls of the tributary gradually widened, until eventually the abutments fell away altogether. Directly in front of us was a thicket of dead tamarisk trees, and in the distance we could see a set of low, sandy hills marching off to the west beneath a whitish sky.

We proceeded into the thicket, and before long the trees gave way to a muddy embankment, where we found ourselves at the edge of the river. The water was reddish brown, and the current seemed to be barely moving.

This marked the location of our final cache, three plastic buckets that had been tucked under a sandstone ledge many weeks earlier by Jean-Philippe Clark. Inside the buckets was a set of one-man inflatable pack rafts, double-bladed paddles, and life jackets. After blowing up the boats and fitting the paddles together, we slithered aboard, balancing our packs between our knees, and cast off.

Over the better part of the next hour, we spun in lazy circles as the river carried us through the Grand Wash Cliffs and escorted us out of the canyon. For part of the way, we faced downstream, staring out at the flinty folds of gravel dotted with creosote bushes and Joshua trees extending west like the rumpled folds of an unmade bed, the true beginnings of the Mojave. Then the current would gently wheel us around, and we would find ourselves gazing back into the canyon's V-shaped profile, which grew smaller with each rotation until at last the crooked sky became straight, and the cliffs were swallowed up by the clouds.

For once, there was nothing left for Pete to photograph. His camera rested by his side, and his work was complete.

Unlike Pete's journey, however, mine wasn't over just yet. There was still one last item of unfinished business for me to tie up before I could declare that I was truly done.

CHAPTER 41

Pilgrims All

O n a Thursday morning in November, ten days after passing through the Grand Wash Cliffs, I found myself once again heading back into the canyon—and for the first time, Pete wasn't with me. Instead, I was accompanied by my brother, Aaron, who had caught a flight out to Arizona from his home in Maine to keep me company as I filled in the final piece of the puzzle that Pete and I had set out to complete.

Eleven months earlier, when I had traveled back to Pennsylvania following the last of my father's chemotherapy treatments, Pete had pressed ahead on his own, pushing our line through the central part of the canyon all by himself. Now, Aaron and I would retrace that same route, starting at a point on the Navajo Nation overlooking the Confluence just a few miles from the spot where Pete and I had met with Renae Yellowhorse and learned of her battle against the tramway.

It took the rest of the day for us to descend through a break in the cliffs, scramble down to the bottom of the drainage, then wade across the waist-deep waters of the Little Colorado River to reach the start of the first segment of the Tonto Trail network. From there, a broad path pointed the way forward while eliminating any need to hop across fields of boulders or thrash through thickets of underbrush. Its appearance—a smooth brown ribbon cutting cleanly across the terrain—stood as a reminder that among the many reasons why people love trails, perhaps the most compelling is that they offer something we all long for, which is the promise to faithfully deliver us to where we need to be.

That night we camped on a sandstone terrace above the Colorado, and as we sat listening to the river and staring up at the full moon, hanging fat and heavy in the sky, a satellite text arrived from Pete, who was watching the same moon rise over the skyscrapers of Manhattan, where he was paying a visit to his goddaughter, whose fourteenth birthday he had missed back in February when we were far out on the Esplanade.

WISHING I WAS WITH YOU GUYS IN THE CANYON TONIGHT, he wrote.

WISH YOU WERE HERE TOO, I wrote back. THIS LAST SECTION WON'T BE THE SAME WITHOUT YOU.

And sure enough, it wasn't.

*   *   *

Each morning for the next week, Aaron and I awoke at first light, but made a point of lingering over coffee for an hour or two before striking camp. Then we ambled down the trail at a serene, unhurried pace, lingering for long lunches and dawdling by every spring. Toward the end of the afternoon, we stopped walking and set up camp early enough to ensure that we could spend the evening doing what we had been doing all day long—the thing that neither of us had taken the time to do properly for more than thirty years—which was to be fully in each other's presence, and to conduct an extended heart-to-heart conversation between brothers.

As the trail led us beneath a flawless autumn sky in the clear November air, we talked about our lives and our careers and our families: how they had played out, and how the results had stacked up against the hopes and dreams we'd chased as younger men. We talked about our boyhoods in Pennsylvania, and about how without ever having consciously planned things this way, each of us had fled Pittsburgh—he to a small town on the coast of Maine, and I to the deserts of the Southwest—in the hopes of finding a place where nature and the land hadn't been treated so poorly. A place where outdoor recreation involved more than shooting cans and bottles that had been dumped into a river, or schlepping through fields that doubled as junkyards and waste pits. And as we talked of all these things, we told stories about our father, who, to neither my brother's surprise nor mine, inveigled his way into every part of the conversation, even though he wasn't there.

"What's the name of this geologic layer we're on right now?" Aaron asked one afternoon at the start of an exchange that progressed, like so many others, from the specific to the paternal.

"It's called the Bright Angel Shale."

"All these tiny chips of rock, the way they form little hills and valleys—in a weird way, it looks a bit like the spilly piles inside the strip mine where Dad used to take us hiking, don't you think?"

This prompted a discussion of the wastelands that had been part of the geography of our childhood, and although neither of us said so specifically, I think we both knew that much of the damage that had been inflicted on the landscape of our birth had been unwittingly committed by men like our grandfather—men who were chasing dreams of prosperity and security not unlike the visions of the Hualapai—and that by virtue of this history, we, too, were complicit in what had been done to the land in ways that neither of us had been able to acknowledge or understand as boys.

We talked, both directly and indirectly, of what we had gained in fleeing our native ground, what we had lost by refusing to remain, and what we now knew we could never escape, no matter how far away we might wander, because all trails that appear to lead away from the place you're from will eventually circle back and drop you where you began in a manner that might, if you are attentive and very lucky, enable you to see it clearly for the first time.

"God, those spilly piles were ugly—do you remember the litter and the trash and the junked cars?" I said. "But Dad never seemed to mind, did he?"

"He didn't, which was always a mystery to me then and still is now," Aaron said. "It was almost like the ugliness didn't matter to him. Why was that?"

As I pondered those questions and talked with my brother, it began to dawn on me that the journey which had taken me from Pennsylvania to the Grand Canyon had imposed a distance and a separation from who I was and where I had come from—and that my father stood as a potent embodiment of everything I thought that I had left behind, but actually had been carrying with me the whole time, tucked inside my pack along with the rest of my gear.

"Do you think Dad feels shortchanged that I never invited him to come to the canyon when he was healthy enough to run the river or hike the trails?" I asked one afternoon.

"I'm honestly not sure," said Aaron. "But thanks to you, at least he got a chance to see it with his own eyes, before it was too late—even if he wasn't able to do what we're doing here."

Which reminded me of a story about my dad and the canyon that I hadn't fully shared with my brother, even though he'd been there to witness part of it—and which I've also left out of this account, until now.

*   *   *

Back when we'd first learned that my father's cancer had returned, and that it was terminal—which was also when Pete had first approached me with the idea of completing a transect of the canyon—Dad's doctor had a suggestion for him to consider before the first of his chemo treatments began. "If there's a trip that you want to take, an experience you want to have, a place you've always wanted to see, this is the time. Do it now—and do it with your family."

For my father, figuring out where to go didn't require a lot of deliberation. More than anything else, he wanted to see the place he'd introduced me to almost forty years earlier when he'd handed me a copy of Colin Fletcher's book—the place that I had never made the time to share with him. And so, several months before Pete and I had launched the first leg of our traverse, my family had gathered Dad up and brought him out to Arizona to see the canyon for the very first time.

I was in charge of putting the trip together, and I had planned things carefully enough that in the span of a single week, with everyone packed in two vehicles, we circled almost the entire park. We took him up to the North Rim to see the leaves of the aspens and walk among the wildflowers in the meadows of the Kaibab, and we brought him down to Lee's Ferry so he could sit at the edge of the shore and let the river run through his fingers. But for me, the most memorable spot of all, as well as the most meaningful exchange I had with him, took place at Lipan Point, a magnificent overlook on the South Rim where he got his initial glimpse of the chasm.

In addition to offering sweeping views of the river and the canyon's interior, which was the reason I'd selected it, Lipan marks the start of one of the steepest hiking routes in the park. The trail starts just a few steps from the edge of the road, where the path winds through a grove of piñons and junipers before dropping off the rim in a series of sharp switchbacks.

The pull of that trail can be powerful, and many visitors are unable to resist the urge to venture partway down, which is exactly what Aaron and his wife, Molly, did, followed closely by my two nephews—Simon, who was twelve, and Wilson, nine—along with my mom, who was seventy-two. The only exception was my dad, who took one look at the path, shook his head, and quietly sat himself down on a low stone wall.

I wasn't willing to traipse off and leave him there by himself, so I took a seat next to him, and what passed between us during the next thirty minutes was the part of this story that my brother had not yet heard.

*　　　*　　　*

As we stared into the depths, I tried to think of something to say, and perhaps the acuteness of what I imagined to be my father's predicament in that moment—a man too frail to venture more than a few yards beyond the side of the road, deprived of the chance to do anything more than passively observe the scene from above—turned my thoughts toward the proposal for the tramway on the rimlands of the Navajo Nation directly to the north, whose route, I now realized, was readily visible along the cliffs in the distance, more than a dozen miles away.

"You know, Dad, there's some talk of maybe building a cable car into the canyon not far from this spot so that people who aren't able to hike can access the inside of the canyon. If that was available right now, do you think it would be helpful? Is that something you might appreciate?"

He gave me a look of reproach. "Of course not," he said softly.

"Really?" I was mildly surprised that he was so quick to turn down a chance to move deeper into this space—to descend through the cliff bands and the terraces, to see the colors of the rock change, to discover what it would feel like to reach the bottom and gaze up at those soaring ramparts of stone. "Why not?"

"Well—because of them," he said, raising his arm.

He was pointing to the trail down which the rest of the family had disappeared.

*   *   *

"Oh, wow," said Aaron. "So he was talking about us, huh?"

"Maybe not all of you," I replied. "I think he was mostly referring to Simon and Wilson."

"How so?"

"He didn't really elaborate. But I think he felt that running a tramway down those walls would diminish the world that his grandsons will one day inherit."

Now Aaron nodded in agreement.

"And I think he understood that to mean," I continued, "that if part of protecting a national treasure like this involves banning things like cable cars and gondolas, then people like him will have to park themselves on a wall while others get to go off and explore, like you guys did."

"Do you think he was okay with that?"

"He was sitting at the edge of the grandest place on earth," I said. "I think he felt like that was more than a fair trade. It was a privilege and a gift."

"So what did you two do next?"

"Until the rest of you returned? Not much, really. We just sat there together, enjoying the view."

*   *   *

For the remainder of that week on the Tonto, it felt as if Aaron and I had the canyon to ourselves as we meandered down the trail without encountering anyone. But on the morning of our seventh day, a flurry of signals indicated that our ramble was finally drawing to a close.

First, we started seeing small groups of other hikers, almost all of whom paused to say hello and exchange a few words about the weather or the condition of the springs ahead. Then late one afternoon we reached a point where the trail met a creek lined with cottonwoods whose leaves were turning gold, and we turned to follow the creek upstream until we arrived at a campground filled with picnic tables, and a sign that read INDIAN GARDEN.

The last time I had seen this place was with Pete, on a frigid January morning in the dead of winter during our push toward the Great Thumb Mesa. At the time, it had looked completely deserted. Now people were everywhere: day hikers and runners as well as long-distance backpackers sprawled on the benches, milling along the creek, or sorting through their gear.

We set up our tent in the campground, and that night as I lay and listened to the low voices of the other campers mingling with the rushing waters of the creek and the rustling of the leaves in the trees, I found myself thinking back on the journey with Pete, especially through Helicopter Alley, and pondering how egregiously the odds seemed to be stacked against the canyon's being handed off intact to the next generation, and those to follow.

Despite all the mistakes that have been made—how much of this place has already been impaired or traded away, how swiftly the gains that were made long ago are presently in danger of being rolled back or erased, how egregiously the descendants of the land's original inhabitants have been marginalized and written out of the story—it struck me then, as it does now, that it's a miracle we have any park at all.

*   *   *

By dawn the following morning, Aaron and I were ascending the upper portion of the Bright Angel Trail, the ancient Havasupai route that now featured well-maintained drainage channels, perfectly contoured switchbacks, and rest stops equipped with benches, water spigots, shade awnings, and toilets. No other trail in the canyon caters to tourists as solicitously as the Bright Angel, and within a few minutes we spotted the day's first set of clients—a group of three women clad in pink-and-purple running suits, chatting merrily as they passed by without even noticing us. They were followed by a mother and father with two small girls, whose eyes were bright with excitement, and immediately behind them was a family of eight that included a pair of spry-looking grandparents.

An hour later, we reached a set of steep switchbacks that looked like a wilderness version of San Francisco's Lombard Street and found the trail brimming with people moving in both directions. They wore everything from cotton sweatpants and combat boots to long Amish dresses and fancy cowboy hats. There were athletes who could jog from the river to the rim without stopping, and stout middle-aged husbands and wives who couldn't move more than a few steps without pausing to lean on their walking sticks to catch their breath.

An entire class of college students was blasting music on speakers dangling from their necks, and a trio of monks clad in brown robes appeared to be observing a vow of silence—although they were quick to smile and wave. There was a group of folks clad in turquoise T-shirts indicating that they all belonged to the same church in Oklahoma City, led by a man carrying a Bible. And there was a woman in a fashionable leather jacket that would have blended well in midtown Manhattan, clutching a newspaper in one hand and a Styrofoam cup of coffee in the other.

By now it was midmorning, and more than a hundred people were moving up and down this section of the trail, and because the switch-backs were stacked tightly atop one another, we could hear all of them talking. The array of languages they spoke offered an auditory map of how far they'd traveled to see this place: Spanish and German, French and Portuguese, plus snatches of Russian and Turkish and Hindi over-lapping with fragments of Arabic and Chinese. Amid all those voices and languages, you could hear a range of other sounds, too.

A string of eight pack mules, led by a pair of wranglers clad in thick gloves and heavy leather chaps, were beating out a soft, thudding tattoo of hoofbeats, punctuated by creaking saddles and the occasional clang of a steel horseshoe striking bare stone. Directly behind the mules, a six-person trail-repair crew wearing heavy work boots was grunting beneath the weight of their picks, crowbars, and chain saws. Lancing through that symphony of sound—the polyphony of foreign words, the laughter and squeals of small children, the murmurs and groans of animal effort and human movement—came a long, piercing squeal that left us momentarily bewildered, until I realized it was the whistle of the steam engine on the tourist train, pulling into the railway station on the rim.

*   *   *

When we reached the top of the trail, the view was as stunning as ever, although the sensation of gazing into the abyss was different from that on any of my previous visits to the South Rim. After more than a year of moving through the entirety of the canyon, I could now identify every butte and mesa and pinnacle that was visible from this vantage, plus a host of others that lay far beyond the last line of cliffs and ridges to the east and west, formations whose shapes and textures I could instantly conjure in my mind.

Hundreds of features that had once seemed mysterious and foreign were now deeply familiar in a way that had never been true back in the days when I was a boatman whose grasp of the canyon had ended at the edges of the river. Thanks to where I had been and what I had seen along the way, I commanded a level of knowledge about this place that appeared, at least on the surface, to reinforce and validate the thing that Pete and I had so fervently believed when we'd started our trek:

To truly know this world, it is necessary to move through it not by plane or raft or on the back of a mule, but on foot, hauling your gear and provisions on your back while moving through the space between the river and the rims. Step by step from one hidden pocket of water to the next, day by day, until eventually the canyon is persuaded to reveal the things it keeps hidden. Only on foot, the slowest and hardest way to move, can you hope to make contact with the finest parts of this landscape.

Standing at the head of the Bright Angel with my brother, I was still convinced that this was true. But as my gaze was drawn away from the splendor in the distance and pulled toward the colorful parade of human foot traffic moving along the switchbacks directly beneath our feet, I unexpectedly found myself wondering if the exact opposite might be equally true.

Peering down at those people, I felt it safe to assume that almost none of them had experienced anything like the kind of epic Pete and I had undergone. The majority of them were evidently here for less than a day. Few were willing or able to venture much beyond the first rest stop, slightly more than a mile from the top. For a number of them, even this modest stroll probably lay at the outer edge of their comfort zone. And yet, judging by the smiles and the laughter and the giddy sense of excitement they exuded, every one of them was thrilled to be here. They were having a blast, unshakably convinced that they were in the midst of a marvelous adventure—an observation which prompted, here at the tail end of my own grand escapade, an abrupt reevaluation of what I had just done.

It dawned on me then, for the very first time, that perhaps it may not be necessary to hump a fifty-pound backpack across almost eight hundred miles of the park's most remote and inaccessible reaches to touch the magic of this place—and that although such an approach can yield some exquisitely sublime moments of wonder, it may well be possible to have a briefer but equally authentic encounter with that magic.

To take even a few steps without anything coming between you and the canyon may be all that most people who are drawn to this landscape, or any landscape, really need.

All of which brought me back to one final piece of unfinished business with my father.

*   *   *

Despite the differences in how we had chosen to lead our lives, I admired many things about my dad. But somewhere out there on the Tonto, amid the conversations with my brother, I realized that perhaps the thing I admired most was what he represented when he was at his best, which was the embodiment of gratitude.

Although my father's world was small, he regarded his home with the kind of reverence that can imbue even the humblest of places with radiance and grandeur. Which was why, in my dad's eyes, the ground on which he had most loved to hike, the waste fields and strip-mine tailings of Pennsylvania, was more than just a third-rate substitute for the magnificent wilderness areas that my brother and I would move so far from home to find. Because unlike us, he was convinced that his home, despite its many flaws, was beautiful—and unlike us, he had faith that even the parts of that world that are ugly will one day heal.

In addition to that, my dad believed that any day spent outdoors walking, even if it was on spilly piles, was a good day—and he was convinced of this because he had seen his own father, my grandfather, leave the house each morning to go into a coal mine. If you watch a man spend fifty years of his life on his knees in the darkness digging coal, my father could have told me, then you calibrate your blessings by a different set of metrics than most people. You spend less time thinking about what's been lost or taken away, and more time focusing on what's handed to you—and you treat those gifts with reverence.

Unlike my brother and me, our dad didn't need to spend a year walking through the Grand Canyon to learn these things—and he probably knew that those tourists we'd been passing on the trail didn't, either. They were pilgrims, each and every one of them, and what made them so was neither the difficulty of the path they had chosen nor the distance they intended to travel.

They were pilgrims because they had come to a holy place—a cathedral in the desert—in the hope of standing in the presence of something greater than themselves, something that would enable them to feel profoundly diminished and radically expanded in the same breath. They were pilgrims because there is something sacred in the belief that despite its ugliness and its many depravities, there are still places in our fallen and shattered world where wonder abides.

But most of all, they were pilgrims because they were seeking their benedictions on foot, the simplest and humblest means of all. Which meant that they were doing the very thing that my father had prepared my brother and me to do, each in his own way, all those years ago.

They were going for a walk in the park.

Epilogue

We come and go,

but the land is always there.

—Willa Cather

I f the journey that Pete and I completed was reckless and misguided, a vision conceived in ignorance and executed (at least in the beginning) in the worst style imaginable, it was also the purest thing either of us had ever done. An adventure like no other, in a landscape like no other, that would remain with us for the rest of our lives.

When I cast back on the days and nights that we spent wandering that wild country together, the memories of the places we moved through and the things we were permitted to see, all of it returns with a radiance whose luster never seems to dim or fade with time.

I remember how the apricot-colored cliffs reached toward the cobalt sky, how the sinking sun softened and soothed the white glare of the day, how the swallows dipped and turned amid the deepening shades of twilight, and how the starshine slid like sheets of mercury down the canyon's dark and glistening walls. I remember how the planets would wink out with the gathering of dawn, how the last of the morning shadows played among the branches of the rabbitbrush and the cholla spines, and how the hot light of noon could make the edges of the limestone twinkle like sea glass.

I remember how these and many other small things stood out against the immensity of all that stone, and the even greater immensity and depth of the time distilled within its folds. How the winds that buffeted the slickrock in the early part of evening would abate as the constellations filled the sky, rinsing the terraces in a silence so vast and brooding that it seemed to form its own ocean. I remember what it felt like to crawl to the edge of a cliff and lean on our elbows to peer down, watching the moonbeams coruscate among the ripples and eddies of the great river below—and how every now and then, if we were lucky, the canyon might call forth a choir of Bighorns bleating from the Redwall, calling out to one another against the splendor and loneliness of the night.

But among those memories, the most vivid of them all, perhaps, is a recollection from an early winter's morning far out on the Esplanade, when I arose before dawn, fired the camp stove, and carried a steaming mug of coffee out to Pete, who had been up past midnight taking time-lapse photos of the stars as they wheeled across the heavens.

*   *   *

He'd set his camera on a tripod several hundred yards from camp, and as we stood side by side, stamping our feet and waiting for the sun to rise, we gazed across an expanse of slickrock that was studded with potholes, each lidded with a thin lens of ice. More than a hundred of them were out there, glowing in the predawn shadows, each a blue eye set in the face of the sandstone.

The moment the first rays of light hit that immense patio, it set all the potholes ablaze at once, making them shimmer and dance until the entire Esplanade seemed to lift and levitate on the force field of its own beauty. Then as the crystals of ice began to evaporate, a little puff of vapor wafted into the air above the frozen surface of each pool, making it look as if the stone itself was breathing.

It occurs to me now that to be in the canyon in a moment like that was to feel as if we were balanced on a ledge just a notch or two below paradise—and to look back on such a moment is to be reminded that even in the midst of our journey, long before the end was ever in sight, Pete and I found ourselves haunted by a growing awareness that we might be moving through this landscape not only for the first time, but also the last.

The longer we spent and the farther we ventured, the more deeply we understood that in the months and years to come, it might no longer be possible to complete a walk such as this without colliding against changes so profound that the land would never again be the same, and thus that the possibility of returning would forever be closed off.

Haunted—that's how we walked. Haunted by what we saw and heard, and by the knowledge that the future that was bearing down on the canyon was, in ways both marvelous and terrible, already transforming the place.

*   *   *

In the months following the completion of our journey, Lamar Whitmer and his group of developers ramped up their campaign to secure approval for their tramway project by aggressively courting a handful of prominent Navajo politicians. Meanwhile, Renae Yellowhorse and her tiny band of volunteers continued to pour what little money they were able to raise—which paled in comparison to the $3.5 million that Whitmer's team claimed to have invested in the project—into beefing up the monthly plans on their cell phones and boosting the reach of their social media platforms, especially Facebook.

Aided by the Grand Canyon Trust in Flagstaff, they also spent heavily on gas, oil changes, and new tires as they logged thousands of miles in their dilapidated vehicles, driving the length and breadth of their vast reservation to attend fairs and community meetings. They set up booths, distributed flyers, and spent hours explaining to anyone who would listen the impact that the new resort would have on the Confluence of the Colorado and Little Colorado rivers. They also managed to enlist the support of Navajo medicine men and other traditionalists as well as that of several neighboring tribes, including the Hopi, the Zuni, and the Havasupai.

Eleven months later, all of those tribes sent representatives to the capital of the Navajo Nation in Window Rock when the legislative council convened a special session to debate the project, put it to an up-or-down referendum, and tally the votes.

The results weren't even close. Sixteen council delegates rejected the project outright, while only two voted in favor of it.

"You've gotten a taste of what we can do," Rita Bilagody, one of Yellowhorse's allies, pointedly told Whitmer that evening when she cornered him in the parking lot. "We'll do it again."

Despite her warning, however, everyone involved seems to agree that it's just a matter of time until Whitmer or someone like him decides to revive the scheme and give it another try. The money to be made on a tourist enterprise that will offer effortless access to the canyon is simply too great for profiteers to ignore—and anyone who doubts the truth of this would do well to look at what continues to unfold more than a hundred miles to the west on the Hualapai Reservation.

*   *   *

These days, air tours inside Helicopter Alley are more popular than ever, and with the exception of a lull in visits during the pandemic, the number of flights from Las Vegas to Grand Canyon West has continued to increase. The Skywalk has also grown in popularity, propelled by the Hualapai's willingness to host events such as a live-stream performance by the progressive house DJ Kaskade, who spent an evening pumping electronic dance music over the canyon while drones recorded aerial footage that was broadcast to viewers around the world, and bright pink lights played against the Supai cliffs along the rim.

Aside from a handful of long-distance hikers, self-guided boaters, and backcountry rangers who continue to be appalled by the visual and auditory impact of these operations, few outsiders seem to have taken note of what is going on. Safety within the loosely regulated airspace also remains a concern among experts—especially in light of incidents such as the one that took place not long after the tramway was defeated, when a sightseeing helicopter run by Papillon, the largest air-tour company in the canyon, spiraled out of control and crashed near the mouth of Quartermaster Canyon, the tributary that serves as the Alley's primary exit corridor—directly across from where Pete, Rich, and I witnessed the barrage of choppers on our first morning inside the "combat zone."

According to news reports, five of the passengers on the Papillon flight either perished at the crash site—several were burned alive—or died soon after in a hospital. The surviving client suffered severe burns on extensive portions of her body, while the pilot, who also survived, later had both of his legs amputated. Despite these horrors, the accident received scant attention, generated no outcry, and seems to have inspired zero public discussion about why the Hualapai and their partners are still permitted to overcrowd the airspace in the western part of the canyon.

Shortly after the accident, the tribal council released a communiqué expressing condolences to the victims and stating that blessings for those who perished had been offered near the crash site. One possible response to the announcement—cynical, perhaps, but highlighting the inappropriateness of allowing sightseeing helicopters to fly and land inside a place like the canyon—might entail pointing to the level of aircraft noise that envelops Quartermaster Canyon at almost every hour of the day, and asking how the person performing that ceremony could have offered the simplest and most universally acknowledged tribute to the dead: a moment of silence.

Another response might be to cast one's thoughts in an altogether different direction by turning away from the impulse to denounce the Hualapai, and concede that what they have done to the canyon pales in comparison to the sins committed against so many other landscapes in this country—an observation that could induce one to ask if it's really fair to condemn the Hualapai merely for having failed to do better than the rest of us.

To consider this question is to find oneself face-to-face with the possibility that the Hualapai may well have some important insights to offer about our own complicity—which, in turn, could suggest that perhaps one of our higher duties to the land (as well as to ourselves) involves making a sincere effort to talk less and listen more. Only then might it be possible to hear, among many other things, the warning that the Hualapai have been transmitting about what can happen when Native American communities are ceaselessly ignored and trivialized.

In the years to come, whatever happens in the park will be determined, in large part, by the willingness or refusal of the outside world, especially the Park Service, to regard not just the Hualapai but all who are indigenous to the canyon as neither adversaries to be defeated nor as minions who can be manipulated and instead to embrace them as partners and equals. Because in addition to having shaped the canyon's past and defined a critical part of its present, the tribes now hold the key to its future.

In the meantime, it's worth noting that a tentative vision for how a more constructive alliance might at least begin to take shape is offered by what seems to be unfolding at the park's headquarters.

*   *   *

In the autumn of the year that Pete and I were completing our hike, park administrators announced that an iconic seventy-foot-tall building on the South Rim known as the Desert View Watchtower, a monument originally designed as a visitor attraction, was being converted into an interpretive center and a heritage site to honor the indigenous people of the canyon. When it came time for the tower's rededication ceremony, which coincided with celebrating the centennial of the National Park Service, Dave Uberuaga, the superintendent at the time, stepped to the podium and issued a statement on behalf of himself and the twenty-three superintendents who preceded him in which he offered a formal apology for the pain and humiliation that had been inflicted on the canyon's tribal communities during the previous century.

"I humbly ask for your forgiveness, and your reconciliation," he said.

It was the first time in the one-hundred-year history of the Park Service that anyone in a position of authority at the Grand Canyon had ever uttered words like that. And since then, it has become clear that Uberuaga's gesture of contrition and atonement was not only sincere, but is part of a larger effort to reframe the relationship between the park and the tribes.

In the summer of 2023, Joe Biden traveled to northern Arizona to sign a presidential proclamation incorporating almost 1 million acres of public lands on both the north and south sides of the canyon into the country's newest national monument. Baaj Nwaavjo I'tah Kukveni, which translates as "Ancestral Footprints of the Grand Canyon," may be difficult for many non-indigenous people to pronounce; but the name, a linguistic composite of both Havasupai and Hopi, symbolizes an effort to address a number of injustices connected with the forcible removal of Native Americans from land that later became part of the park.

The monument, which now protects thousands of cultural and religious sites as well as a host of plants, animals, and springs that lie just beyond the formal borders of the park, stands as a victory for all of the tribes—although the ceremony itself held special significance for those who continue to call themselves "the guardians of the Grand Canyon."

Moments before the president signed the proclamation into law, he was introduced by a high school student named Maya Tilousi-Lyttle, the great-great-great-great-granddaughter of Billy Burro, the last Havasupai resident of Indian Garden, who, ninety-five years earlier, had been forcibly evicted by park rangers from the idyllic creekside oasis beneath the South Rim, and told that his people could never return.

*   *   *

Also in 2023, the Park Service announced that it had begun to identify a number of significant landmarks in the canyon whose names needed to be amended. In the first of these changes, Grand Canyon's superintendent Ed Keable, one of Uberuaga's successors, announced that after extensive consultation with the People of the Blue-Green Water, Indian Garden would henceforth be known as Havasupai Gardens.

In addition to making the necessary modifications to all signposts and official maps, Keable's staff and the tribe would explore how to co-manage the site in a range of innovative ways that might include encouraging the Havasupai to begin replanting the area with traditional crops such as corn, squash, and sunflowers. There was also discussion of inviting tribal members to explain to visitors how their ancestors had created the route they called *Gthaty He'e*, the Coyote's Tail Trail, before they were banished from the park and their path was renamed the Bright Angel Trail.

Oddly enough, these ideas arose from Keable's willingness to do exactly what Dianna Uqualla had urged Pete and me to do when she spoke to us at this very same trailhead: to slow down, to pay attention, and to attend to the stories that the animals and the land—and the people who are most deeply connected to both—are trying to share.

She offered this advice because she grasped something important that I did not fully understand at the time, which is that although this park, like all our nation's parks, may initially look and feel like a place where the cares and the complexities of the larger world are held at bay, it is very much the opposite. She was suggesting, I think, that the true purpose of places such as this is to lay the groundwork for—and at times demand—a heightened confrontation that is more challenging, more unsettling, and infinitely more rewarding than a simple vacation.

*   *   *

One person who continues to seek challenges and rewards in this landscape is Rich Rudow, whose passion for the world beneath the rims burns as fiercely as ever, although it has morphed in ways that neither he nor those who know him best could have anticipated. On the one hand, he continues to probe the chasm's deepest and most inaccessible niches by methodically working his way through an ever-diminishing roster of unexplored slot canyons. However, he now devotes the lion's share of his time to volunteer work with backcountry rangers, especially those whose jobs involve patrolling the remotest reaches of the canyon.

During these ventures, Rich keeps faith with the people he has lost. Whenever he's able, he visits the spot in Owl Eyes Bay where Ioana Hociota, the wife of his good friend Andrew Holycross, slipped and fell to her death in the winter of 2012, to pay his respects before the cairn that was erected in her memory.

In the midst of all those activities, Rich has never given up searching for Floyd Roberts, who vanished amid the 120-degree heat wave that descended on the western part of the canyon in the summer of 2016. To this day, Roberts's body has yet to be found—a testament to the fearsome austerity of the Sanup Plateau.

* * *

In a very different way from Roberts, the Sanup also took hold of me and refused to let go—because it was out there, amid the distant horizons and the endlessly streaming light, that I first began to understand that there was something about my journey that I found troubling. Which brings me to one last detail that I've neglected to mention until now.

By the time we had floated down the river through the Grand Wash Cliffs, I had come to realize that the canyon is far too complex, too mysterious, too *grand*, for it to ever be known in full. And in light of that fact, it seemed to me that declaring my odyssey complete and having my name added to the official list of thru-hikers, along with that of Kenton Grua and those who followed him, might perhaps amount to a kind of delusion. An expression of hubris commensurate with the arrogance that Pete and I had displayed by imagining that we could launch our traverse off the couch, without any preparation or training.

For better or worse, it seemed important for me to find a small but sincere way of affirming what I had come to learn about the land—a gesture of respect akin to the ritual of thanks that tribal people perform by scattering a pinch of tobacco or corn pollen next to a spring. After giving the matter some thought, the idea that finally came to me—perhaps fittingly—was inspired by the first of the tribes that we had met, during our encounter with Renae Yellowhorse, overlooking the place where the waters from two different rivers meet and merge to become one.

Among the eleven tribes of the canyon, none surpasses the Navajo in the art of weaving textiles, especially rugs, which are created by the women of the community and considered to be works of art. The layouts of those rugs, by tradition, are conceived by the weaver, carried in her memory, and passed down from mother to daughter. The designs are renowned not only for their beauty and symmetry, but also for a curious hallmark that involves a break in the pattern at the border, which, when viewed from a distance, can easily be mistaken for a loose thread, even though it has been incorporated directly into the fabric.

This minor but deliberate flaw is known as a *ch'ihónít'i*, or "spirit line," and its purpose has been interpreted in a variety of ways, one of which suggests that it is an expression of restraint. By ensuring that the rug will always remain incomplete—and therefore imperfect—the break stands as an acknowledgment of the need to remain humble, a renunciation of vanity that helps the weaver to maintain a proper sense of balance in the world.

Not all rugs have a spirit line, and in those that do, they can sometimes be hard to discern. But if you look carefully, you will see the defect in the line along the edge, a reminder—for those who choose to see it in this manner—that humility, like all desert flowers, needs a bit of watering from time to time.

The more I thought about this, the more convinced I became that, like a Navajo rug, the layout of my own journey could benefit from having a loose thread. And so, somewhere along the final stretch of my hike, I orchestrated a breach in my line through the canyon.

The gap that I left wasn't large, no more than a few hundred yards or so, and it was essentially symbolic. But it is more than enough to disqualify me from being credited with having completed a transect of the canyon, and thereby ensures that my name can never be added to the list of thru-hikers.

It's possible, of course, that this amounts to its own form of vanity, an affectation that might well strike others as silly or sanctimonious. Nevertheless, I'm glad I did it, because in addition to the fact that it helps keep me grounded, the gap reaffirms my belief that there can be coherence and even beauty in stories, like this one, whose endings fail to tie off perfectly.

Which brings me to the two people who started this whole thing.

                    *   *   *

When my journey finally came to an end, my hope was to finish this book as quickly as possible and place it in my father's hands, thereby completing the circle that we had begun drawing together, without either of us really knowing it, back when he'd first given me a copy of Colin Fletcher's work more than forty years earlier. Despite my best efforts, however, I fell short of that goal because I couldn't write faster than my dad's death.

Four years after we brought him west to see the canyon, a month before he would have celebrated his eightieth birthday, he passed away at home in Pennsylvania without being given a chance to read this story. As it turned out, however, he was able to experience our trek in a different way—and for that, I owe a debt of gratitude to the finest friend I've ever known.

Upon returning to the mountains of Colorado, Pete sat down at his desk and got to work on a coffee-table book showcasing the finest of all the photographs he'd taken between Lee's Ferry and the Grand Wash Cliffs. It offered a visual chronicle of our entire hike, and he mailed me a copy just in time for what would be my father's last Christmas.

As Dad opened the book and held it in his lap while sitting in front of the fireplace, I snapped a picture of him with my cell phone. From the photo, it's clear that he was studying it intently, paging through the images and drinking everything in. But in that moment, I think he was doing something else, too.

He was counting his blessings as he prepared to head off on the grandest walk of all.

Robert M. Fedarko

August 16, 1939–July 14, 2019

BENEDICTO

May your trails be crooked, winding, lonesome, dangerous, leading to the most amazing view. May your mountains rise into and above the clouds. May your rivers flow without end, meandering through pastoral valleys tinkling with bells, past temples and castles and poets' towers into a dark primeval forest where tigers belch and monkeys howl, through miasmal and mysterious swamps and down into a desert of red rock, blue mesas, domes and pinnacles and grottos of endless stone, and down again into a deep vast ancient unknown chasm where bars of sunlight blaze on profiled cliffs, where deer walk across the white sand beaches, where storms come and go as lightning clangs upon the high crags, where something strange and more beautiful and more full of wonder than your deepest dreams waits for you—beyond that next turning of the canyon walls.

—Edward Abbey, *Desert Solitaire*

Author's Note

P art of the power wielded by places of great natural beauty resides in their capacity to evoke profoundly irrational responses from people who love them deeply. In my case, this involves an impulse to celebrate and share the beauty of the Grand Canyon with others in the hope that some of those people might one day rise to its defense, twinned with a fervent wish for the landscape itself to remain untrammeled, because visitors in larger numbers inevitably wind up destroying the very qualities that evoke reverence and awe in the first place.

While conceding the contradiction inherent in those longings, I'd like to offer some respectful admonitions, beginning with the fact that this book is in no way intended to serve as an invitation for readers to rush out into the canyon's backcountry, nor is it meant to offer a guide for navigating the terrain between Lee's Ferry and the Grand Wash Cliffs on foot. Indeed, it is emphatically the opposite.

Although this is a work of nonfiction, the descriptions of several key sites have been deliberately modified to disguise their precise locations, while in other instances the details regarding routes have been omitted or masked. These informational gaps represent an imperfect effort on my part to protect especially sensitive areas inside the world between the rims, and to avoid contributing to the deluge of information that is already overwhelming many of these places with levels of visitation that they simply cannot handle.

I realize that despite this warning, some readers may nevertheless feel inspired to repeat what Pete and I did. If you happen to number yourself among this group, please consider taking a better approach than the one that we adopted—first and most important by devoting a substantial amount of your time and energy to research, preparation, and homework.

A good place to begin that effort is by reaching out to the generous and openhearted community of desert hikers, backpackers, and canyoneers who not only understand how to move through this harsh and exquisitely delicate landscape, but also how to protect it. You will find that these experts are often quite happy to share their hard-won knowledge with newcomers who are looking not to exploit the canyon for their own ends, but to learn from it and grow.

If you do venture into this park, regardless of whether your itinerary takes you down the most heavily trafficked trails or draws you deep into the most remote reaches of the outback, you are obliged to familiarize yourself with and faithfully follow the rules. Although Pete and I committed many, many mistakes, we were rigorous about obtaining the necessary permits from the National Park Service and adhering to the guidelines of "leave no trace" camping. You should do the same. (For more information, go to Grand Canyon National Park's backcountry web page at https://www.nps.gov/grca/planyourvisit/back country-permit.htm.)

These regulations may sometimes seem annoying, but they form a key part of the Park Service's effort to uphold its core mission. That mission, it's important to emphasize, does *not* entail providing unfettered access to every location inside the park for all people at any time. Instead, it hinges on balancing the myriad and often competing demands of recreationists with the overarching and far more vital mandate to preserve the country's most precious natural spaces so that these treasures can be handed off, intact, to future generations of

Americans. This amounts to a kind a covenant whose purpose is to nurture and sustain the hope that, despite the imperfections and flaws of this park and many others, something wondrous will be passed on to our descendants.

It's one of the best things about this country, and it's something worth celebrating.

Also, when you enter this space, please consider going with your family and taking your kids—especially if they're young. You will find that your appreciation of the canyon's wonders will be expanded, quite radically, by the wonder in your children's eyes. Their response will leave you not only invigorated and made whole, but touched by a rare kind of fulfillment: the realization that you are instilling memories and values that, with a bit of luck, will help to anchor and inspire your offspring for the remainder of their lives.

Finally, I'd like to express one additional request—an entreaty with which some readers will surely disagree, but one that I hope others will consider.

Please do not lobby the Park Service or your congressional representatives to build a trail running the length of the Grand Canyon. There is neither a historic nor a topographic precedent for such a path, and creating one would only serve to erode and annul the wildness that still abides there.

In other words, it would be a violation of the very thing that makes the canyon holy.

Acknowledgments

When I completed the final leg of our hike, I had little idea that an even longer journey was about to begin. A decade later, a pile of debts has accumulated, all arising from the simple truth that this book, like the walk itself, represents the work of an entire community. In the course of completing both projects, the obligations I have incurred to a host of people—as well as the river of gratitude flowing from me to each and every one of them—run as deep as the canyon itself.

Pete and I would never have made it more than a few hundred yards beyond Lee's Ferry without the unstinting support and selfless participation of a group of long-distance hikers who knew the terrain and its secrets far better than we could ever hope to, and who embraced our goals in a manner that humbles us to this day. They adopted our journey as their own, I think, because they believed—rightly or otherwise—that coming to the aid of a pair of hapless storytellers might somehow support a larger effort to venerate and protect the world beneath the rims.

The first person on the list of people to thank is Rich Rudow, who was directly tied to every aspect of the planning and execution of our transect. Without him, we would have been truly lost. We are also indebted to Chris Atwood, Dave Nally, and Mike St. Pierre for the kindness they displayed during the first and cruelest phase of the journey; and we are deeply grateful to Mathieu Brown, Justin Clifton, Aaron Divine, Amy Martin, Blake McCord, Kelly McGrath, Harlan Taney, Marieke Taney, Anne Mariah Tapp, and the heroic John-Philippe Clark, each of whom played a critical role in getting us through the rest of the hike. A special note of thanks is reserved for Tom Myers, who, like the terrain he cherishes, stands in a class all by himself. And I need to tip my hat to Matt Mallgrave and John Seybold for helping see us through, too.

I want to thank three other members of the canyon's backpacking society—Ned Bryant, Matthias Kawski, and Andrew Holycross—for their willingness to entrust me with the stories of people they loved whose lives were tragically lost inside the chasm, and whose spirits remain there to this day.

When it comes to matters of the spirit, no group is more tightly wedded to this landscape than the canyon's eleven Native American tribes. I am indebted to a number of individuals for helping me to develop a rudimentary understanding of the profound role that indigenous people play in the chasm's past, present, and future.

Among the Navajo, I would like to extend my deepest thanks to Renae Yellowhorse, Dolores Wilson-Aguirre, Rita Bilagody, Larry Foster, Frank and Frances Martin, Jason Nez, the Reid family (Earlene, Betty, and William), Sarana Riggs, the late Wilson O. Wilson, and the rest of the Save the Confluence team. I am profoundly grateful to Coleen Kaska, Carletta Tilousi, Dianna Sue White Dove Uqualla, and other members of the Havasupai tribe whom we met. Among the Hopi, I would like to express my thanks to Lyle Balenquah, Ed Kabotie, Merv Yoyetewa, and members of the Hopi Cultural Preservation Office. I am indebted to Octavius Seowtewa from the Zuni nation, and Richard Graymountain Jr. of the San Juan Southern Paiute tribe. And I would like to express my thanks to Damon Clarke of the Hualapai tribe, who I have not had the privilege of meeting but whose views I appreciate and value—a sentiment that I wish to extend to the rest of the Hualapai tribal council, along with the hope that I may one day be able to speak with them directly.

*   *   *

In addition to the tribes themselves, I have also benefited immensely from contact with non-tribal experts, many of whom have devoted a significant portion of their lives and careers to working respectfully with tribal people and have developed lasting connections rooted in respect and affection, even when both parties are not able to see eye-to-eye. Among this group, I want to acknowledge and express my gratitude to Robert Breunig, the former executive director of the Museum of Northern Arizona; Helen Fairley of the U.S. Geological Survey; Kelley Hays-Gilpin at Northern Arizona University and the Museum of Northern Arizona; Dennis Gilpin at the Museum of Northern Arizona; and Peter Pilles with the U.S. Forest Service.

I also want to express my profound thanks to an extraordinary group of people who have dedicated a significant portion of their lives and careers to living, teaching, and working among the tribal communities of the canyon, including Stephen Hirst (author of *I Am the Grand Canyon*) and his wife, Lois, former Peace Corps volunteers who spent sixteen years teaching among the Havasupai at the Supai Village school, and have since worked tirelessly on behalf of the tribe; Tom and Cynthia Nicas, who devoted almost two decades to teaching school and providing health-care services among the Hualapai at Peach Springs; and Denny Preisser, a fellow Pennsylvanian, who spent twenty years working as a teacher and librarian among the Navajo at Kayenta before shifting to Seligman, where students from the Hualapai tribe now benefit from his skills and kindness. I am also grateful to John Tvetan, Pearish Smith, and Elena Kirschner, health-care professionals whose insights from years spent among the Hopi and Navajo have been deeply appreciated.

In addition to the people mentioned above, my education in tribal matters was also facilitated by the staff, board members, and affiliates of the Grand Canyon Trust, an organization whose influence on me was initially shaped by the writing of the late Charles Wilkinson, one of the Trust's original founders, whose works are essential texts for anyone seeking to understand the industrial development of the Southwest, especially on the Colorado Plateau, and the impact these events have had on Native American communities. I am indebted to the following current or former staff members at the Trust—Darcy Allen, Ethan Aumack, Deon Ben, Mike Chizhov, Roger Clark, Ashley Davidson, Libby Ellis, Natasha Hale, Bill Hedden, Ellen Heyn, Amanda Podmore, Mike Popejoy, Amber Reimondo, Tony Skrelunas—and to the following current or former board members: Ethel Branch, Pam Eaton, John Echohawk, Jim Enote, Holly Holtz, Sarah Krakoff, Steve Martin, and Rebecca Tsosie. I am grateful to the Trust for its support of the nine-city speaking tour that Pete and I embarked on in 2017 and 2018; for enabling me to participate in tours of the Navajo, Hopi, and Paiute lands in 2017; and for generously permitting me to work at the Kane Ranch, where significant portions of this book were written. Finally, I want to thank Stephanie Smith, the Trust's marvelously talented GIS director and cartographer, who is responsible for the maps in this book.

To the extent that I can claim to have a rudimentary understanding of the Colorado River, it is thanks to the generosity and kindness of members of the Grand Canyon River community who have already been mentioned in the acknowledgments of *The Emerald Mile*. In an echo of those thanks, I would like to again express my gratitude to John Blaustein, Regan Dale, the late Rudi Petschek, and Monte Tillinghast, all of whom supported me in important ways during the years of my apprenticeship on the river; to the many guides who helped me during the summers in which I rowed the *Jackass*; to the late Martin Litton, who served as both an inspiration and a conservation lodestar; and to Michelle Grua, who has faithfully kept the flame of her late husband's memory burning, and whose generosity in sharing his journals is deeply appreciated.

*   *   *

The canyon is enriched by many layers of scholarship and writing, and during the past twenty years, I have benefited enormously from the marvelous work done by a host of experts whose insights and understanding so decisively surpass whatever knowledge I've managed to cobble together. I have highlighted the books and articles on which I drew in the Readers' Guide and the Bibliography, but I would like to spotlight a number of these professionals who not only have been exceptionally helpful to me over the years, but are, in many cases, also my neighbors and friends in Flagstaff. Among these, I want like to thank George Bain, Daiva Chesonis, Craig Childs, Michael Collier, John Dillon, Margie Earhart, Dane Gruver, Tom Gushue, Dan Hall, Lynn Hamilton, Rose Houk, Matt Kaplinski, Annette McGivney, John Napier, John O'Brien, Ken Phillips, Richard Quartaroli, Wayne Ranney, Glenn Rink, Scott Thybony, Gwendolyn Waring, Larry Stevens, and Emma Wharton.

I am awed and inspired by the dedication, skill, and passion of the staff at Grand Canyon National Park, people whose patience and decency too often go unrecognized, and whose commitment to the landscape is surpassed only by the beauty and majesty of the park itself. In addition to former superintendents Dave Uberuaga, whose support was absolutely critical to the success of our hike, and Christine Lehnertz, I want to thank Betsy Aurnou, Joëlle Baird, Jan Balsom, Kim Besom, Matt Jenkins, Todd Seliga, and Elyssa Shalla. I would also like to extend a special note of appreciation to Ed Keable, one of the finest superintendents in the hundred-year history of the park, for his immense contributions to improving the park's relationship with the tribes of the canyon. And I want to express my gratitude to the staff at the park's partner, the Grand Canyon Conservancy, whose mission is to serve as the park's advocate and voice, including Theresa McMullen and Christy Spivey, as well as Betsy Sylvester, whose geological illustration greatly enhanced this book.

Any mistakes found in these pages are entirely my own fault, and I welcome hearing from readers who wish to draw my attention to errors so that I can correct them in future editions of the book. But whatever I managed to get right was thanks to the expertise and generosity of the people mentioned above, as well as a number of organizations that have provided assistance, expertise, and inspiration over the years. Among these, I am deeply grateful to American Rivers, whose commitment to the health and preservation of the country's rivers has no equal, especially Sinjin Eberle in Durango and Matt Rice in Denver, who are also cherished friends.

I would like to thank everyone affiliated with the Museum of Northern Arizona in Flagstaff, especially Mary Kershaw—every facet of this wonderful institution, from its exhibits and lectures to its docent-training program, played a vital role in the research for this book. I'm also extremely grateful to the Honors College at Northern Arizona University, where I was privileged to teach with Bruce Aiken, Shonto Begay, Kevin Gustafson, and Dawn Kish as part of the Canyon Country Aesthetics Seminar, funded by the late Richard and Alice Snell. And I'd like to express my deep appreciation to the staff—especially Peter Gwynne and Sadie Quarrier—at *National Geographic*, which funded our entire expedition.

In the early stages of writing this book, I was fortunate to be offered a writer's residency at the Aspen Institute's Aspen Words program. The month I spent in Colorado was made possible by the generosity and kindness of Isa Catto and Daniel Shaw, together with the fabulous support provided by Marie Chan, Jamie Kravitz, Elizabeth Nix, and Caroline Tory. Their passion for books and for supporting writers is matched only by the people who work at the Bright Side Bookshop in Flagstaff, each and every one of whom deserve my thanks—especially the store's co-owner, Lisa Lamberson, as well as Sarah Badger and Cori Cusker, both of whom read and provided valuable feedback on this book.

It has been my immense (and undeserved) good fortune to be surrounded by the extraordinary members of the editorial staff at Scribner, where I am indebted to Nan Graham, Susan Moldow, Brian Belfiglio, Annie Craig, Mark Galarrita, Kyle Kabel, Jaya Miceli, Sydney Newman, Abigail Novak, Ashley Gilliam Rose, Stu Smith, Rafael Taveras, and Brianna Yamashita. In addition to these good people, I want to make special mention of my editor, the magnificent Colin Harrison, a force of nature whose support of this book as well as *The Emerald Mile* extended far beyond what any writer could ever hope for; to the wonderful Emily Polson, without whom this book would never have made it to press and whose talents as a emerging editor are nothing short of dazzling; and to the remarkable Katie Rizzo.

Aside from Colin Harrison, there has been only one other person who has been with me from the very beginning of my obsession with the Grand Canyon—someone whose passion and dedication have sustained me through some extremely challenging times. Perhaps the finest thing I can say about Jennifer Joel is that when writers imagine landing the agent of their dreams, she is the embodiment of what they're hoping to find. My gratitude also extends to her enormously talented colleagues at CAA: Sloan Harris, Sindhu Vegesena, Will Watkins, and Jake Smith-Bosanquet.

*   *   *

Many years ago when Pete McBride first proposed that he and I collaborate on a series of magazine assignments that would take us around the world and eventually bring us back to our beloved home ground in the Southwest, I'm not sure that he chose well in picking me. But I have no hesitation in declaring that it was my immense good fortune to have been selected by him. Together we have seen some marvelous places and met some remarkable people, but the finest part of it all has been being able to call him a friend, and to know his parents, Pabo and Moutie, as well as the rest of his family in the mountains of Colorado.

My most heartfelt thanks are reserved for my family, which now has grown to the point where it extends from one end of the country to the other. I want to recognize my brother, Aaron, who completed the final section of my traverse with me and who remains the finest brother anyone could ever wish for; his wife, Molly, and my marvelous nephews, Simon and Wilson; my mother, Rita, who keeps my father's memory alive in Pittsburgh while serving as an inspiration to all of us through her optimism, resiliency, and shining spirit; and our extended family in Pittsburgh and throughout western Pennsylvania, as well as Rochester, New York. I would also like to extend a special thanks to my cousin Brian Charlton, whose passion for history has achieved something special at the Donora Smog Museum. Pap would have been thrilled and proud by what you've achieved.

As for the Avery-Wildes family, when I was first swept into this magnificent and boisterous clan, I had no idea that I was being admitted into a society whose members are less concerned with the number of books one has written than with the far more important questions of whether you made the right-hand cut on your last run through Bedrock Rapid, or kept up on the family's annual rim-to-rim canyon hike. All I can say is that it has been a joyous ride, and I'm so very lucky to be a part of it all.

Although I once thought that it was the canyon that stole my heart, I now know that's not really true, because the keepers of everything that matters most to me are Cora, Thad, and Maddox.

Finally, and speaking of matters of the heart, there is my wife, Annette, the foundation of our world. Like the Vishnu Schist and its bright seams of Zoroaster Granite, nothing runs deeper, stands stronger, or is more beautiful.

She's bedrock.

Readers' Guide
and Chapter Notes

For a comprehensive bibliography that includes a list of all of the books, articles, and other sources cited in the pages that follow, please go to the author's website, KevinFedarko.com.

Prologue

The Edward Abbey quote is from *The Journey Home: Some Words in Defense of the American West*.

For books that have been exceptionally helpful to me in understanding and appreciating the canyon's richness and complexity, see Wallace Stegner, *Beyond the Hundredth Meridian: John Wesley Powell and the Second Opening of the West*; Stephen Pyne, *How the Canyon Became Grand*; Donald J. Hughes, *In the House of Stone and Light: A Human History of the Grand Canyon*; and Ann Zwinger's *Downcanyon: A Naturalist Explores the Colorado River through the Grand Canyon*.

Edward Abbey's short essay "In the Canyon" in *Down the River* is a treasure, as is Donald Worster's landmark article "Environmental History: The View at the Grand Canyon," available on the National Park Service's website. *The Hidden West: Journeys in the American Outback*, by Rob Schultheis, is one of the finest portraits ever written of the landscape of the canyon country of the American Southwest.

Andrew Holycross, who knows a thing or two about mammals as well as snakes, has objected to my reference to a Bushy-Tailed Wood Rat because this creature is not commonly found inside the canyon—and thus it would have been more accurate to invoke its cousin, the Desert Wood Rat, as metaphor to describe Pete McBride's hyponatremia-induced muscle cramps. Holycross is 100 percent correct. Complaints from wildlife enthusiasts and rodent devotees should be addressed to me, not him.

PART I   Wild Country

John Wesley Powell's quote is from the report on his expeditions to the canyon that he submitted to Congress in 1875.

CHAPTER 1   Into the Abyss

The natural history of the canyon has been given ample treatment in a variety of sources, all of which have been used in this chapter.

For geology, the finest general-interest work is Wayne Ranney's *Carving Grand Canyon: Evidence, Theories, and Mystery*, followed closely by J. P. Graham's *Grand Canyon National Park: Geologic Resources Inventory Report* and Ivo Lucchitta's *Hiking Arizona's Geology*. Another excellent resource is *Grand Canyon Geology: Two Billion Years of Earth's History*, by Michael Timmons and Karl Karlstrom, a professor in the Department of Earth and Planetary Sciences at the University of New Mexico who has contributed more to the understanding of the geology of the canyon than almost anyone else. The magnificent Trail of Time exhibit on the South Rim was created by Karlstrom together with his wife, Laura Crossey, a professor in the same department at UNM whose research focuses on the geochemistry and geomicrobiology of springs and travertines, with the assistance of Ryan Crow at the U.S. Geological Survey, who studies the neotectonic evolution of the Grand Canyon.

If you're lucky enough to walk the Trail of Time exhibit—which should be a required feature of every visit to the canyon—be sure to obtain a copy of Karlstrom and Crossey's *Grand Canyon Trail of Time Companion Book* before you set out.

To learn about the fascinating origin of the canyon's many layers of rock, see *Ancient Landscapes of the Colorado Plateau*, by Ron Blakey and Wayne Ranney, in which the evolution of the region's landscape history comes to life on the page through a colorful suite of paleogeographic maps. For a deeper and more technical perspective on the rock layers of the canyon, see *The Colorado Plateau: A Geological History*, by Donald Baars, and *Grand Canyon Geology*, by Stanley Beus and Michael Morales.

For the layperson who is interested in developing an understanding of both geology and deep time, there is no finer place to start than John McPhee's monumental trilogy, *Annals of the Former World*, which places great demands on the reader, but offers commensurate rewards. In addition to McPhee's writings, I've also found the following works to be exceptionally helpful: *How the Mountains Grew: A New Geological History*, by John Dvorak; *A Brief History of the Earth: Four Billion Years in Eight Chapters*, by Andrew H. Knoll; and two books by Marcia Bjornerud, *Reading the Rocks: The Autobiography of the Earth* and *Timefulness: How Thinking Like a Geologist Can Help Save the World*.

The total area of Grand Canyon National Park is 1,904 square miles in planview, 23 percent larger than Rhode Island. However, adding the cliff faces increases the canyon's surface area by slightly more than 32 percent to 2,517 square miles, about the planview area of Delaware. The volume of the Grand Canyon is almost exactly a thousand cubic miles, 15 percent less than the volume of Lake Michigan. For more information, see "Physiographic Rim of the Grand Canyon, Arizona: A Digital Database," by George Billingsley and Haydee Hampton.

For references to paleontology, see V. Santucci and J. Tweet's "Grand Canyon National Park: Centennial Paleontological Resource Inventory," Christa Saddler's *Life in Stone: Fossils of the Colorado Plateau*, and David Thayer's *An Introduction to Grand Canyon Fossils*. Regardless of which set of books you might select, I strongly recommend pairing each of those texts with Brian Gootee's superb *Geologic Timeline of the Grand Canyon*. (For further details, please turn to Maps and Tables at the end of this readers' guide.) Regarding relative ages, the oldest known rock in the canyon, the Elves Chasm Gneiss, is 1.84 billion years old. The earth is estimated to be 4.5 billion years old, and the age of the universe is currently dated at 13.77 billion years.

For information on birds, see *Grand Canyon Birds: Historical Notes, Natural History, and Ecology*, by Bryan Brown, Steven Carothers, and R. Roy Johnson. For details on snakes' and scorpions' heat-tolerance thresholds, see Jeremy Schmidt's *Grand Canyon National Park: A Natural History Guide* (which is also packed with a wealth of other details).

Information on the discovery of a cave cricket, bark louse, and two eyeless albino millipedes in a cave along the North Rim can be found in Mark Harvey and J. Judson Wynne's "Troglomorphic Pseudoscorpions (*Arachnida: Pseudoscorpiones*) of Northern Arizona, with the Description of Two New Short-Range Endemic Species." Sightings of the Sooty Grasshopper Mouse along the South Rim of the canyon and the southeastern corner of the national park were noted by Vernon Bailey in 1935 in "Mammals of the Grand Canyon Region." Laurence Stevens offers a superb and fascinating treatment of the relationship between geography and biology within the Grand Canyon in "The Biogeographic Significance of a Large, Deep Canyon: Grand Canyon of the Colorado River, Southwestern USA."

For a window into natural history during the years following the creation of Grand Canyon National Park in 1919, see *The Best of Grand Canyon Nature Notes: 1926–1935*, edited by Susan Lamb. For a splendid work of fiction whose characters were inspired by the community of scientists and natural historians along the South Rim, see Margaret Erhart's novel *The Butterflies of Grand Canyon*, which has received far less attention than it deserves.

References to the canyon's layered ecology can be found in Rose Houk's *An Introduction to Grand Canyon Ecology*, and deeper context for a historical understanding of the relationship between altitude and ecology receives excellent treatment in Andrea Wolf's *The Invention of Nature: Alexander Humboldt's New World*. Humboldt's thinking offered a foundation for C. Hart Merriam's studies of the canyon, which receive special attention in Gwendolyn Waring's marvelous work *The Natural History of the San Francisco Peaks: A Sky Island of the American Southwest*, which serves as an excellent companion to her equally thorough *A Natural History of the Intermountain West: Its Ecological and Evolutionary Story*, as well as the Arizona-Sonora Desert Museum's *A Natural History of the Sonoran Desert*, edited by Steven Phillips, Patricia Wentworth Comus, and Mark Dimmitt.

The quotation from Theodore Roosevelt comes from *A Compilation of the Messages and Speeches of Theodore Roosevelt, 1901–1905*, edited by Alfred Henry Lewis. The account of Vladimir Nabokov's discovery and naming of a new butterfly can be found in "An Absence of Wood Nymphs: Vladimir Nabokov, Famed Author of *Lolita*, and a Renowned Lepidopterist, Seeks His Favorite Butterfly in Arizona," by Robert Boyle in *Sports Illustrated*. More information about the Schmidt pain scale rating of the sting of a Tarantula Wasp can be found on Joseph Jameson-Gould's wildly entertaining blog, *Real Monstrosities: A Journey amongst the Weird, the Wonderful and the Downright Ugly of the Natural World*, at http://www.realmonstrosities.com/.

CHAPTER 2 The Man Who Walked Through Time

Colin Fletcher's life has now received comprehensive treatment in a thorough and meticulous biography by Robert Wehrman, *Walking Man: The Secret Life of Colin Fletcher*. For details on Fletcher's canyon hike, personality, and other aspects of his life, see Fletcher's *The Man Who Walked Through Time*, Wehrman's biography, as well as two other articles by him: "Colin Fletcher, the Father of Modern Backpacking" in *Adventure Journal* and "Fumbling toward Fulfillment: The Metamorphosis of Colin Fletcher" in *Adventures Northwest Magazine*; plus the obituary for Fletcher that Dennis Hevesi wrote, "Colin Fletcher, 85, a Trailblazer of Modern Backpacking, Dies," for the *New York Times*.

Details on the number of tributaries within the canyon come from two studies. A 1995 paper authored by Theodore Melis, Robert H. Webb, Peter G. Griffiths, and T. J. Wise ("Magnitude and Frequency Data for Historic Debris Flows in Grand Canyon National Park and Vicinity, Arizona") references a total of 530 offshoots of the main canyon; but this study was restricted to the stretch of river from Lee's Ferry to Diamond Creek. A later paper, published in 2004 by Griffiths, Webb, and Melis ("Frequency and Initiation of Debris Flows in Grand Canyon, Arizona") cites 740 tributaries that are known or thought to transport sediment via runoff between Lee's Ferry and the Grand Wash Cliffs.

Additional information on the legend of Tiyo, the Hopi boy who floated through the canyon in a hollow log, can be found in Maren Hopkins's master's thesis, "A Storied Land: Tiyo and the Epic Journey down the Colorado River"; and aside from Fletcher's account of his walk, the only other book about the canyon to which I was exposed as a boy was Marguerite Henry's *Brighty of the Grand Canyon*.

CHAPTER 3 Hell with the Lid Off

Anyone who is interested in learning more about the history of pollution in Pittsburgh should consult the work of Joel Tarr, especially *Devastation and Renewal: An Environmental History of Pittsburgh and Its Region* and "The Changing Faces of Pittsburgh: A Historical Perspective." Two other excellent works on the city's industrial saga are John Hoerr's *And the Wolf Finally Came: The Decline and Fall of the American Steel Industry* and Cliff Davidson's "Air Pollution in Pittsburgh: A Historical Perspective" in the *Journal of the Air Pollution Control Association*.

For details on the Donora smog disaster, the most comprehensive work is Andy McPhee's *The Donora Death Fog: Clean Air and the Tragedy of a Pennsylvania Mill Town*. Also see Edwin Kiester's article "A Darkness in Donora," in *Smithsonian Magazine*; Alexis Madrigal's "Aghast over Beijing's Air Pollution? This Was Pittsburgh Not That Long Ago," in the *Atlantic*, and Liam Baranauskas's superb treatment, "The Historically Hazy Story of Donora's Deadly Smog," in *Atlas Obscura*. Additional information can be sought by contacting the Donora Historical Society and Smog Museum (for contact information, see Other Resources at the end of the readers' guide).

PART II The Witchery of Whitewater

The Kenneth Grahame quote is from *The Wind in the Willows*.

CHAPTER 4 The *Jackass* Chronicles

The finest book on the history of Grand Canyon river running, David Lavender's *River Runners of the Grand Canyon*, is amplified and enlivened by a quartet of marvelous river books: *The Hidden Canyon: A River Journey*, by John Blaustein (which has the added benefit of text written by Edward Abbey and an introduction from Martin Litton); François Leydet's classic *Time and the River Flowing: Grand Canyon*, which was commissioned and published by the legendary conservationist David Brower; the highly entertaining *We Swam the Grand Canyon: The True Story of a Cheap Vacation That Got a Little Out of Hand*, by Bill Beer; and Christa Saddler's marvelous anthology, *There's This River . . . Grand Canyon Boatman Stories*, a copy of which rides in the ammo box of every river guide on the Colorado.

The author and boatman Brad Dimock, who knows more about the design, construction, and history of wooden boats than anyone else in the canyon, has written a trio of nonfiction books that deserve a place on any river lover's shelf: *Sunk without a Sound: The Tragic Colorado River Honeymoon of Glen and Bessie Hyde*; *The Very Hard Way: Bert Loper and the Colorado River*; and *The Doing of the Thing: The Brief and Brilliant Whitewater Career of Buzz Holmstrom* (cowritten with Vince Welch and Cort Conley).

I would be remiss in failing to highlight Louise Teal's *Breaking into the Current: Boatwomen of the Grand Canyon*, a well-deserved tribute to the women who work in the canyon as river guides. Equally important are a trio of guidebooks that serve as vital additions to a river trip, each of which specializes in a different aspect of the canyon (which is why it's important to purchase all three). For natural history, Larry Stevens's *Colorado River in Grand Canyon: A River Runner's Map and Guide to Its Natural and Human History* (2013 edition); for human history, *Belknap's Waterproof Grand Canyon River Guide* (2022 edition), by Buzz Belknap and Loie Belknap Evans; and for geology and geomorphology, *Grand Canyon Geologic River Guide*, by Ryan Crow et al.

Finally—and with some hesitation, if only because it probably contains more details than most people care to know—I suggest that readers who are interested in learning more about the toilet system on commercially guided river expeditions in the canyon have a look at "They Call Me Groover Boy: My Life at the Helm of a Colorado River Latrine Raft," which I wrote for *Outside* magazine.

CHAPTER 5 The Emerald Cannonball

The standard history on dories is John Gardner's classic *The Dory Book*, which, much like the boats he extols, is a thing of beauty—although it is gracefully complemented by Roger Fletcher's tribute, *Drift Boats & River Dories: Their History, Design, Construction, and Use*. For additional details, see Dan Alsup's *Driftboats: A Complete Guide*.

For a comprehensive history on the design and construction of the Glen Canyon Dam, see Russell Martin's excellent *A Story That Stands like a Dam: Glen Canyon and the Struggle for the Soul of the American West*. For readers who are interested in learning more about the speed run, perhaps the best place to start is with Lew Steiger's story "Speed," the first story ever written on the speed run, which is included in Christa Saddler's *There's This River . . .*, cited above.

It is also worth noting that the runoff inside the canyon in the spring and early summer of 1983, which peaked at ninety-three thousand cubic feet per second, was neither unusual nor unprecedented, and that several other runoffs in the previous few decades, especially in the summer of 1957, exceeded its crest by almost 35 percent—facts that have led a handful of nitpickers to argue that Kenton Grua's speed run is overrated.

I disagree with those critics for two reasons: first, because the deadliest and most challenging feature on the river in the spring of 1983, Crystal Rapid, wasn't much more than a riffle until it was transformed by a massive debris flow in the winter of 1966 (which meant that it barely even registered for the handful of boaters who experienced the high-water surge of 1957); and second, because none of the previous big runoffs in the twentieth century had menaced the Glen Canyon Dam. The dam didn't even begin impounding water until early 1963, and Glen's parapet wasn't topped out until the autumn of that year.

In short, the speed run of 1983 coincided with, and collided against, two dramatic challenges—a series of wrecks at Crystal Rapid and a crisis at the Glen Canyon Dam—which simply didn't exist in the summer of 1957. Nothing like the runoff of 1983, or the speed run that was powered by it, has ever been seen in the Grand Canyon.

CHAPTER 6 "Kind of a Crazy Idea"

For additional details on the claims made on the front and back covers of Fletcher's books, see *Grand Obsession: Harvey Butchart and the Exploration of the Grand Canyon*, by Elias Butler and Tom Myers. This valuable work also contains an in-depth analysis on exactly how much ground Fletcher covered during his hike, and how much additional distance he would have needed to cover to traverse the entire canyon.

For more information on the Grand Canyon Enlargement Act, which expanded the size of the park in 1975, see chapter 30, "In Sinyella's Shadow." Also see Jeff Ingram's exhaustively detailed and highly informed political history of the canyon, *Celebrating the Grand Canyon*, at https://gcfutures.blogspot.com/, which reflects more than half a century of direct involvement with the politics of wilderness conservation, as well as a deep commitment to preserving the canyon for future generations.

For a thorough analysis of the history of Grand Canyon thru-hiking as well as fascinating key details on Grua's transect, see Tom Myers's excellent article "Down the Gorge with Uncle George: Hiking the Length of Grand Canyon." And for a comprehensive chronological list compiled by the Grand Canyon Hikers & Backpackers Association that includes all the hikers who have completed either continuous or sectional traverses of the canyon during the modern era, please go to https://gchba.org/through-hike-list/.

A number of details regarding Grua and his thru-hikes can be found in *The Emerald Mile: The Epic Story of the Fastest Ride in History through the Heart of the Grand Canyon*, especially in chapter 10, "The Factor." One piece of information that was not included in the book, however, is that Grua succumbed to an aortic dissection while riding his mountain bike on the Schultz Creek Trail, at the edge of Flagstaff, in August 2002. He was found lying on the ground next to his bike, just beyond a parking lot, by a passerby. He was still breathing and had a heartbeat when the ambulance arrived, and was transported to Flagstaff Medical Center, where resuscitation efforts ultimately failed. He was fifty-two years old.

Although Grua was unique, the canyon is a magnet for eccentric characters whose passion for the landscape is matched only by their desire to protect it. For a riveting portrait of the wildland firefighting crews on the North Rim more than thirty years ago, see *Fire on the Rim: A Firefighter's Season at the Grand Canyon*, by Stephen Pyne; for a marvelous glimpse into what life is like on a trail crew, see Nathaniel Farrell Brodie's *Steel on Stone: Living and Working in the Grand Canyon*; for the story of a man whose fixation on moving through the canyon on foot probably matches or exceeds that of Grua, see *Running Wild: Through the Grand Canyon on the Ancient Path*, by John Annerino; and for a series of arresting portraits of a variety of people who work in or around the park, see *Grand Canyon Stories: Then & Now*, by Leo Banks and Craig Childs.

One additional note for bird-watchers: there is a single record of a Harlequin Duck in the canyon, an individual that remained in the eastern part of the river corridor for nearly a year back in the early 1990s.

CHAPTER 7   The Real Deal

None of my comments on the limited nature of the hikes that are offered to commercial river passengers when I worked on the river are meant to diminish how marvelous those excursions are, but simply to place them in the context of the longer and generally more rigorous endeavors undertaken by long-distance backpackers. Even the shortest of those river hikes—such as the walks up to the granaries at Nankoweap, the pools at North Canyon, or the stair-step cascades at Elves Chasm—are pure magic for everyone. Some river concessionaires offer specialized river trips for exceptionally fit clients that feature adventurous day hikes, some of which can be quite lengthy and formidable.

Readers who are interested in learning more about the system of dams that shackles the Colorado, making it possible for cities such as Phoenix and Tucson to thrive and expand, should consult a number of excellent books. The place to start is with Marc Reisner's monumental *Cadillac Desert: The American West and Its Disappearing Water*, which is every bit as trenchant, provocative, and relevant today as it was when it was first published in 1986. For additional material and a deeper understanding of key themes in Reisner's work, see Michael Hilzik's *Colossus: Hoover Dam and the Making of the American Century*; Donald Worster's *Rivers of Empire: Water, Aridity, and the Growth of the American West*; and Philip Fradkin's *A River No More: The Colorado River and the West*.

For an alternative viewpoint on how the dams inside the Grand Canyon were blocked, see Byron Pearson's *Still the Wild River Runs: Congress, the Sierra Club, and the Fight to Save Grand Canyon* and *Saving Grand Canyon: Dams, Deals, and a Noble Myth*, also by Pearson. For a contemporary overview on what has been done to the Colorado, see David Owen's *Where the Water Goes: Life and Death along the Colorado River*, and for a magnificent profile of two men who shaped the river's destiny during the twentieth century, go to the chapter on David Brower and Floyd Dominy in John McPhee's literary gem *Encounters with the Archdruid*.

CHAPTER 8 Fricking *Grand*

Readers should be aware that although the canyon's backcountry has almost no amenities, the most heavily trafficked pathways within the canyon's central corridor—the Bright Angel, the South Kaibab, and the North Kaibab trails—offer extensive support services, including water spigots or rain barrels, shade structures, and emergency telephones, plus two ranger stations. Phantom Ranch, where all three trails converge at the bottom of the canyon, boasts an additional ranger station as well as cabins, hot showers, a dining hall, an outdoor lecture venue, a gift shop, and an outstanding lemonade machine.

Although there is still no guidebook to thru-hiking the entire canyon, a number of books offer valuable information on the challenge of moving through this landscape on foot. The most comprehensive guide to hiking a variety of trails and routes, with valuable information on physical conditioning, trip reservations, permit applications, and weather conditions is *Hiking the Grand Canyon: A Detailed Guide to More than 100 Trails*, by John Annerino, reissued in 2017 in a "Commemorative Hiker's Edition," which includes a pullout map. Readers who are interested in keeping to the trails can consult Ron Adkinson's *Hiking Grand Canyon National Park*, and *A Naturalist's Guide to Hiking the Grand Canyon* by Stewart Aitchison. For river-runner hikes that can be conducted from the edge of the Colorado, see *Grand Canyon River Hikes*, by Tyler Williams, and for a guidebook that combines trail information with background on the canyon's rock layers, see *Hiking the Grand Canyon's Geology*, by Lon Abbott and Terri Cook. For general information on hiking, see two excellent websites that are packed with hiking information, Bob Ribokas's "Grand Canyon Explorer" and Doug Nering's "Grand Canyon Off the Trail: An Explorer's Catalog of the Grand Canyon of the Colorado."

Hikers who are keen to explore the canyon's backcountry should be warned that although the following books are all considered classics, they are intended only for experts and are not suitable for beginners. *Grand Canyon Treks*, *Treks II*, and *Treks III*, by Harvey Butchart, which are now individually out of print but have been combined into a single edition by Spotted Dog Press, contain valuable secrets, especially on breaks in the Redwall Limestone, but the writing is, to put it mildly, highly condensed and cryptic. Ditto for *Hiking in the Grand Canyon Backcountry*, by J. D. Green and Jim Ohlman.

As for *Hiking Grand Canyon Loops: Adventures in the Backcountry (Hikes I and II)*, by George Steck, perhaps the most important thing to note is that in addition to the fact that the first fifty pages include one of the finest introductions that has ever been written to hiking in the canyon, one of the book's sections begins with a useful cautionary warning from Long John Silver, which all prospective canyon hikers should bear in mind: "Them that die'll be the lucky ones."

In general, although all of the above works are deeply inspiring and studded with a wealth of hard-won information, each offers a blueprint that will enable novices to get themselves into a great deal of trouble from the get-go. Prudent readers who prefer to experience hiking vicariously may wish to turn instead to the anthology *On Foot: Grand Canyon Backpacking Stories*, edited by Rick Kempa, or—even better—seek out perhaps the finest story ever to chronicle a full Grand Canyon thru-hike, "Amongst the Canyon Walls: Traversing the Length of Grand Canyon by Foot," which was written by Elyssa Shalla and photographed by Matt Jenkins, her husband, both of whom work as rangers at the Grand Canyon. This magnificent article, which includes Shalla's blunt warning "It is not possible to hike the length of the canyon off the couch," can be accessed online at https://express.adobe.com/page/OYN4y/.

The definitive source on just how perilous the canyon can be is *Over the Edge: Death in Grand Canyon*, by Michael Ghiglieri and Tom Myers, which totals almost six hundred pages, weighs nearly two pounds, and includes details and analysis on every fatality in the last 150 years. For a more specific treatment that addresses why Grand Canyon probably qualifies as the most dangerous national park in the United States (it had the highest number of search-and-rescue callouts, 828, of any national park in the country in the three-year period between 2018 and 2020, with seventy-seven deaths from drownings, heatstroke, or cardiac arrest during hikes, plus twenty-eight fatalities of visitors who fell), see "The Risk of Death in the National Parks: Beware of the Facts," by Brad Bennett and Tom Myers, in *Wilderness Medical Society Magazine*.

For detailed information on how many people hike the backcountry, see the Park Service's web page on general statistics at https://www.nps.gov/grca/learn/management/statistics.htm, then consult "2022 Backcountry and River Use Statistics," by Steve Sullivan, at the Grand Canyon Backcountry Information Center.

CHAPTER 9 A Shortcut

For a brief profile of Rich Rudow, published in *Outside* when he received the magazine's Adventurer of the Year Award, see "2012 *Outside* Adventurers of the Year," by Tim Neville.

Much of Rich's research on hiking the canyon's backcountry and putting together his own thru-hike took place at Grand Canyon National Park's Research Library on the South Rim, where he accessed the journals of Robert Benson and Harvey Butchart. In addition to the journals Rich consulted, he also pored over a variety of maps, each of which enabled him to tease forth different aspects of the terrain. The most inspiring (and fascinating) of these cartographic resources include the U.S. Geological Survey's excellent sectional geographic maps of the canyon.

Although the "high route" that Rich designed was unique and unprecedented, prior to his successful completion of it in the autumn of 2015, a version of that route had already been done. Late in 2011, Rich learned that Andrew Holycross and Ioana Hociota were hoping to launch a thru-hike along the north side of the canyon that would enable them to move along a variety of ledge systems high above the river, and were interested in seeing Robert Benson's notes, which Rich had copies of. The three of them met for the first time over coffee and immediately decided that they would all tackle the hike together, with Rich doing the lion's share of the work in designing the route—a plan that fell apart early the following year, when Hociota tragically fell to her death in Owl Eyes Bay. Months later, Holycross decided to complete Rich's high-line in memory of his wife, which he did in the autumn of 2012.

For a detailed account of mapmaking in the canyon, see "Mapping the Heart of the Grand Canyon: Behind the Herculean Effort to Create a Scientifically Accurate Cartographic Masterpiece," an excerpt in *Outside* magazine of Greg Miller's fabulous book *All Over the Map: A Cartographic Odyssey*, which chronicles what it took for Bradford Washburn to put together the *National Geographic* map of the canyon's central corridor in 1978. For an equally fascinating glimpse into what it took to produce the map that preceded Washburn's, see an article by François Matthes and Richard Evans, "Map of Grand Canyon National Park," published in the *Military Engineer* in 1926.

CHAPTER 10 Who *Are* These Clowns?

Additional details on Brady's Pincushion Cactus (*Pediocactus bradyi*), which has been listed as a critically endangered species since October 1979, can be found at the National Park Service website (https://www.nps.gov/articles/bradys-pincushion -cactus.htm).

There are a number of excellent reference books on Grand Canyon botany, starting with the definitive *River and Desert Plants of the Grand Canyon*, by Kristin Huisinga, Lori Makarick, and Kate Watters. Also see Anne Epple's *A Field Guide to the Plants of Arizona*; Arthur Phillips's *Grand Canyon Wildflowers*; Donald Peattie's *A Natural History of Western Trees*; and Francis Elmore's *Shrubs and Trees of the Southwest Uplands.*

Finally, anyone interested in the botanical history of the canyon needs to obtain a copy of *Brave the Wild River: The Untold Story of Two Women Who Mapped the Botany of the Grand Canyon*, Melissa Sevigny's eloquent and long-overdue tribute to the canyon's botanical trailblazers, Elzada Clover and Lois Jotter.

CHAPTER 11 Happy Trails

In addition to the previously cited *A Story That Stands Like a Dam*, excellent treatments of the lost world of Glen Canyon, now submerged beneath the waters of Lake Powell, can be found in Eleanor Inskip's *The Colorado River through Glen Canyon before Lake Powell: Historic Photo Journal, 1872 to 1964*; Jared Farmer's *Glen Canyon Dammed: Inventing Lake Powell and the Canyon Country*; and Gregory Crampton's *Ghosts of Glen Canyon: History beneath Lake Powell*. But perhaps my favorite work on Glen is Wallace Stegner's essay "Glen Canyon Submersus," which can be found in *The Sound of Mountain Water.*

The standard history of Lee's Ferry is P. T. Reilly's monumental *Lee's Ferry: From Mormon Crossing to National Park*, edited by Robert H. Webb. It is admirably supplemented by W. L. Rusho's *Lee's Ferry: Desert River Crossing.*

All readers who are fascinated by snakes (as well as those who couldn't care less about them) should purchase a copy of Andrew Holycross and Joseph Mitchell's magnificent *Snakes of Arizona*, an 860-page doorstop that celebrates the taxonomy, distribution, habitat, diet, predators, parasites, and reproductive habits of every species of snake found in Arizona. The book retails for sixty dollars but is also available in a special edition that includes a leatherbound slipcase for $249.95.

PART IV The Shakedown

The Bill Bryson quote is from *A Walk in the Woods: Rediscovering America on the Appalachian Trail*.

CHAPTER 12 Dirty Business

Several excellent books shed light on various aspects of the human history along the rim country in the area surrounding Lee's Ferry. For Mormon history, see *Mormon Country*, by Wallace Stegner; *A Frontier Life: Jacob Hamblin—Explorer and Indian Missionary*, by Todd Compton; and *Mormon Enigma: Emma Hale Smith—Prophet's Wife, "Elect Lady," Polygamy's Foe*, by Valeen Avery and Linda King Newell. For a marvelous glimpse of what the Navajo and Hopi cultures were like during the 1930s, when both reservations were far more remote and inaccessible than they are today, see Edward Hall's *West of the Thirties: Discoveries among the Navajo and Hopi*. For information on the epic exploratory journey undertaken by a pair of Spanish friars who were attempting to find a route from Santa Fe to California, see *The Dominguez-Escalante Journal: Their Expedition through Colorado, Utah, Arizona, and New Mexico in 1776*, edited by Ted Warner.

Readers who are interested in the uniquely colorful terrain that lies east of the canyon should see *The Painted Desert: Land of Wind and Stone*, by David Edwards and Scott Thybony. The history of the two bridges that span the Colorado River just downstream from Lee's Ferry is covered in Jerry Cannon's *The Navajo Bridge: Challenging Nature's Barriers to Transportation*. For a delightful book of poems and photographs that evoke the landscape along the western end of the Navajo Reservation, including Tuba City and the Painted Desert, search out a copy of *Secrets from the Center of the World*, by the U.S. Poet Laureate Joy Harjo and the photographer Stephen Strom.

The uplift history of the Colorado Plateau and the incision rates of the Colorado River have long been a subject of contentious debate, and many sources can be found, but there are no treatments of this complicated topic for general-interest readers, only scholarly articles. For a summary and overview, see "Rise of the Colorado Plateau: A Synthesis of Paleoelevation Constraints from the Region and a Path Forward Using Temperature-Based Elevation Proxies," by Emma Heitmann et al.

The rate at which the Colorado River cuts down into Grand Canyon's bedrock is complicated and variable across the length of the canyon. In the eastern canyon, incision rates are estimated at about 500 feet per million years. Incision rates west of the Toroweap Fault, however, are calculated to be only about 250 to 330 feet per million years. For more information, see "Using Fill Terraces to Understand Incision Rates and Evolution of the Colorado River in Eastern Grand Canyon," by Joel Pederson et al., and "Steady Incision of Grand Canyon at the Million Year Timeframe: A Case for Mantle-Driven Differential Uplift," by Ryan Crow et al. To understand where various layers of rock initially emerge from beneath the river along the first twenty-five miles of its passage through the canyon, see *Grand Canyon Geologic River Guide*, from the U.S. Geological Survey by Crow et al.

CHAPTER 13 The Godfather of Grand Canyon Hiking

Details on the Hermit Shale can be found in Ranney's *Carving Grand Canyon*, and in McPhee's *Annals of the Former World*. For more information on the canyon's thirteen geomorphic reaches, see Stevens's previously cited article "The Biogeographic Significance of a Large, Deep Canyon."

Grand Obsession by Butler and Myers, is the definitive biography of the godfather of Grand Canyon hiking. Beautifully written and exhaustively researched, the book not only lays out every aspect of Butchart's story but also offers a rich and highly informed portrait of the canyon's backcountry, as well as the history of its trails and routes. For anyone interested in hiking the canyon, the book is as indispensable as a map and a compass.

Additional information on Butchart and the history of thru-hiking can be found in Myers's previously cited "Down the Gorge with Uncle George," and also in the introduction to Butchart's *Grand Canyon Treks*, written by Wynne Benti. Butchart's "still unknown territory" quote comes from his unpublished essay "The Canyon Nobody Knows," cited in Butler and Myers's *Grand Obsession*, which is also the source for the "made of piano wire" remark quoted by Rich Rudow, which is credited to Bob Packard.

Although Butchart is credited with first ascents on 28 of the 138 prominent peaks inside of the canyon, some or all of these summits may have been climbed by prehistoric tribal people who inhabited this landscape long before the arrival of white Europeans. The most valuable of the documents Butchart created were not his guidebooks, but his logbooks, which total more than a thousand pages. The donation of those materials to the public record and their transfer to electronic files was spearheaded by two of Butchart's friends, William Mooz and Wayne Tomasi.

CHAPTER 14 Rock Bottom

Pete's condition may have been exacerbated by his having driven down from Colorado the night before we drove out to our first campsite, without giving his body a chance to acclimatize to the heat. Most people adapt to excessive heat by reducing electrolytes lost through perspiration; after about a week, the body withdraws many of its salts from sweat, which no longer stains clothing or tastes salty.

The source for this and many other details of dehydration, heatstroke, and hyponatremia can be found in Kenneth Kamler's well-written and informative *Surviving the Extremes: What Happens to the Body and Mind at the Limits of Human Endurance*, and Frances Ashcroft's equally informative *Life at the Extremes: The Science of Survival*.

For additional information on heat-related conditions and their effect on the human body, see *Waterlogged: The Serious Problem of Overhydration in Endurance Sports*, by Timothy Noakes, and "Water Requirements and Soldier Hydration," part of the U.S. Army's Borden Institute Monograph Series, by Scott Montain and Matthew Ely.

Readers who are interested in the history of how we came to understand the impact that heat can have on human performance should turn to *Physiology of Man in the Desert*, by Edward Adolph, who conducted a series of experiments in the desert outside Yuma, Arizona, during the Second World War that provide a baseline for much of what we know today.

CHAPTER 15 Snakebit

The break in the Redwall Limestone at South Canyon that Pete and I used to exit the canyon also served as an escape route 126 years earlier for several members of a legendary trip that ran into even more trouble than we did. The expedition, whose purpose was to conduct the preliminary survey for a railroad along the bottom of the canyon that would enable coal to be transported from Colorado to the coast of California, was named after Robert Brewster Stanton, who completed its mission after three members—including its leader—drowned within the first twenty-five river miles downstream of Lee's Ferry.

For a lively account of that ill-starred journey, start with Lavender's highly entertaining (and previously cited) *River Runners of the Grand Canyon*. Readers who are interested in learning more about Robert Stanton's critique of John Wesley Powell should go to Stanton's own account, *Down the Colorado*, and also consult *The Colorado River Survey: Robert B. Stanton and the Denver, Colorado Canyon and Pacific Railroad*, edited by Dwight Smith and Gregory Crampton.

Finally, for a fascinating account of an effort to match the extensive series of 445 photos that Stanton took during his expedition and compare them with a series of modern replicas taken at the same locations—thus offering a unique demonstration of the human impact on the canyon over a century—see Robert Webb's *Grand Canyon, a Century of Change: Rephotography of the 1889–1890 Stanton Expedition*.

PART V Rebooting

The "Walk on!" quote is attributed to the Buddha by Bruce Chatwin in *The Songlines*. Although Chatwin's writing is superb, his grasp of hard facts was, at times, rather slippery. I've been unable to confirm this remark through other sources, so it may be apocryphal.

CHAPTER 16 Acts of Contrition

The basic principles of ultralight backpacking were laid down and formally codified, for the most part, by a former aerospace engineer from Colorado named Ray Jardine, who developed a set of ideas and techniques while hiking the Pacific Crest Trail back in the late 1980s with his wife, Jenny, that would turn the world of long-distance backpacking on its head. For information on Jardine and his philosophy—which essentially boils down to the adage that the less you carry, the farther and faster you're able to travel—see "Ray Jardine and the Revolution of Lightweight Wilderness Travel," by Pete Gauvin in *Adventure Sports Journal*; "Ultralight: The Ray Jardine Way," by Peter Potterfield in *Backpacker* magazine; as well as two of Jardine's own books: *Beyond Backpacking: Ray Jardine's Guide to Lightweight Hiking* and *The PCT Hiker's Handbook: Innovative Techniques and Trail Tested Instruction for the Long Distance Hiker.*

In many ways, the concepts at the heart of what is now called the Ray Way were anticipated and put into practice long before Jardine arrived on the scene. In 1955, inspired by a discarded copy of *National Geographic*, a sixty-seven-year-old grandmother from Mercerville, Ohio, hiked the entire length of the Appalachian Trail in canvas tennis shoes carrying a handmade drawstring laundry sack in which she hauled her umbrella, army blanket, and a plastic shower curtain for a tent. For more information on this remarkable woman and her subsequent career as a long-distance hiker, see *Grandma Gatewood's Walk: The Inspiring*

Story of the Woman Who Saved the Appalachian Trail, by Ben Montgomery, and Katharine Seelye's "Overlooked No More: Emma Gatewood, First Woman to Conquer the Appalachian Trail Alone," in the *New York Times*.

For additional details on ultralight gear in the Grand Canyon, see "Ultralight Winter Backpacking through Canyon Country," by Matt Jenkins. For information on food and nutrition for extended hikes in the canyon, see Mike St. Pierre's "Prepping for a Grand Canyon Thru-Hike: A Guide to Multi-sport Expedition Planning" and "Ultralight Backpacking Food Prep for Extreme Thru-Hikes," also by St. Pierre, at the Hyperlite Mountain Gear website. As a starting place for analyzing nutritional requirements and calculating the caloric equivalent by weight of one's food, see "What to Eat When Hiking? 4 Rules for Backpacking Food," by Lara Sein.

CHAPTER 17 Back Again, Wiser?

The possibility that Point Hansbrough may qualify as the most deeply incised large river meander on earth comes from an interview with Larry Stevens, director of the Springs Stewardship Institute in Flagstaff. Details about the riparian ecosystem along the bottom of the canyon on the stretch between Fence Fault and the Little Colorado come from *The Colorado River through Grand Canyon: Natural History and Human Change*, by Steven Carothers and Bryan Brown, and "Colorado River Riparian Ecosystem Rehabilitation in Glen and Grand Canyons, Arizona," by Lawrence Stevens et al.

Details on mesquite trees come from *Mesquite: An Arboreal Love Affair*, by Gary Paul Nabhan. For information on a Bighorn Sheep's ability to conserve water (and many other fascinating details), see *The Desert Bighorn: Its Life History, Ecology, and Management* by Gale Monson and Lowell Sumner, and *The Wilderness of the Southwest: Charles Sheldon's Quest for Desert Bighorn Sheep and Adventures with the Havasupai and Seri Indians*, by Neil Carmony and David Brown. For additional facts about Bighorns as well as information on White-Winged Doves, see Ann Zwinger's article "White-Winged Doves and Desert Bighorns," in *Counting Sheep: 20 Ways of Seeing Desert Bighorn*, edited by Gary Paul Nabhan.

Information about the remains of prehistoric animals and other artifacts in the Redwall Limestone caves around Point Hansbrough can be found in "Grand Canyon National Park," edited by Santucci and Tweet. Also see the articles "An Inventory of Paleontological Resources Associated with Caves in Grand Canyon National Park," by Jason P. Kenworthy, Vincent L. Santucci, and Kenneth L. Cole; and "Extinction of Harrington's Mountain Goat," by J. I. Mead et al.

Additional context and information on prehistoric mammals in the canyon can be found in *Twilight of the Mammoths: Ice Age Extinctions and the Rewilding of America*, by Paul S. Martin, and "Shasta Ground Sloth Food Habits, Rampart Cave, Arizona," by R. M. Hansen.

Finally, I should note that in some sections of the canyon, a set of previously unclassified dolomites sits directly atop the Muav Limestone. This rock unit, which is Cambrian in age, has recently been given a name, the Frenchman Mountain Dolostone. Just downstream from Malgosa Canyon, where we first encountered the Muav, we also saw this formation.

CHAPTER 18   The Greater Unknown

Prior to John Wesley Powell's first river expedition down the Colorado River in the summer of 1869, people speculated that the Grand Canyon's interior might be too harsh and inaccessible to accommodate human settlement (see Stegner's *Beyond the Hundredth Meridian*). But a number of land expeditions had already made contact with a variety of tribes along the edges of the canyon, including ones led by Lieutenant Joseph Ives (who interacted with members of the Mojave, Hualapai, and Havasupai tribes in late winter and early spring of 1858 after leaving a steamboat and venturing onto the Coconino Plateau), and Jacob Hamblin, who interacted with members of the Paiute, Hopi, Havasupai, and Navajo tribes in a series of trips conducted between 1858 and 1863.

Details of the Powell expeditions are from his *Report of J. W. Powell: Exploration of the Colorado River of the West and Its Tributaries*. The first and one of the finest books on Powell remains *Beyond the Hundredth Meridian*; a valuable companion piece is Donald Worster's *A River Running West: The Life of John Wesley Powell*. For an inspiring and well-written account of Powell's first expedition, see *Down the Great Unknown: John Wesley Powell's 1869 Journey of Discovery and Tragedy through the Grand Canyon*, by Edward Dolnick; and for a sampler of Powell's work, see *Seeing Things Whole: The Essential John Wesley Powell*, edited by William deBuys.

Additional information on the archaeological sites that Powell encountered can be found in a series of exceptionally helpful books and articles that include *Anthropology of the Numa: John Wesley Powell's Manuscripts on the Numic Peoples of Western North America, 1868–1880*, edited by Don and Catherine Fowler; and "John Wesley Powell and the Anthropology of Canyon Country: A Description of John Wesley Powell's Anthropological Fieldwork, the Archaeology of the Canyon Country, and Extracts from Powell's Notes on the Origins, Customs, Practices, and Beliefs of the Indians of That Area," written by both Fowlers, together with Robert Euler.

For information on the fragments of Folsom and Clovis projectile points found in the canyon, see "The Ancient Ones: Ten Thousand Years of Hunting and Gathering at Grand Canyon," by Francis E. Smiley, and "Prehistoric Peoples of the River Corridor," by Jan Balsom, Ellen Brennan, Jennifer Dierker, and Ian Hough. Both papers can be found in *The Archaeology of Grand Canyon: Ancient Peoples, Ancient Places*, edited by Francis E. Smiley, Christian E. Downum, and Susan G. Smiley. Balsom and her cowriters prominently cite the work of Ashley Bailey, whose unpublished master's thesis at Northern Arizona University is entitled "Lithics from the Edge: Flaked Stone Assemblages from Grand Canyon National Park."

One of the finest presentations of the eleven Native American tribes whose ancestral lands either abut or lie inside the Grand Canyon is Sarah Krakoff's exceptionally well-researched article for the *University of Colorado Law Review*, "Not Yet America's Best Idea: Law, Inequality, and Grand Canyon National Park." Krakoff's work is admirably supplemented by *We Call the Canyon Home: American Indians of the Grand Canyon Region*, published by the Grand Canyon Conservancy, which includes direct input from each of the tribes, under the editorship of Stephen Hirst.

Also see "Who Owns the Grand Canyon?," by Michael Anderson and Paul Hirt; two fine introductory works by Christopher Coder: *An Archaeological Perspective of Human History at Grand Canyon* and *An Introduction to Grand Canyon Prehistory*; Janet Balsom's article "A Little Knowledge Goes a Long Way: A History of Archaeological Research at the Grand Canyon"; and "Below the Rim: Humans Have Roamed the Grand Canyon for More Than 8,000 Years. But the Chasm Is Only Slowly Yielding Clues to the Ancient Peoples Who Lived Below the Rim," by David Roberts, in *Smithsonian Magazine*.

A work that stands in a class all by itself is Helen Fairley's monumental review of the archaeology, anthropology, and cultural traditions of the canyon's tribes, *Changing River: Time, Culture, and the Transformation of Landscape in the Grand Canyon—A Regional Research Design for the Study of Cultural Resources along the Colorado River in Lower Glen Canyon and Grand Canyon National Park, Arizona*. For additional information on the history of archaeology in the canyon, see *On the Edge of Splendor: Exploring Grand Canyon's Human Past*, by Douglas Schwartz; and for a similar treatment on the history of archaeology in both Glen Canyon and across the entire Southwest, respectively, see two classics by Don Fowler: *The Glen Canyon Country: A Personal Memoir*, and *A Laboratory for Anthropology: Science and Romanticism in the American Southwest, 1864–1930*.

Historical texts specific to the Navajo, Havasupai, and Hualapai tribes are cited in entries for chapters that follow, but for additional information on the Hopi tribe, see "Öngtupqa niqw Pisisvayu (Salt Canyon and the Colorado River): The Hopi People and the Grand Canyon," by T. J. Ferguson et al. For a study of the Ghost Dance traditions, see *The Ghost Dance of 1889: Among the Pai Indians of Northwestern Arizona*, by Henry Dobyns and Robert Euler. The quote from the U.S. Army general who called the Yavapai "wild animals" comes from David Holthouse, "Revenge of the Verdes," in the *Phoenix New Times*, and the quote from the army officer who called La Paz, where the Hualapai tribe was exiled, the "Sahara of the Colorado" is from *We Are an Indian Nation: A History of the Hualapai People*, by Jeffrey Shepherd.

Finally, for an exceptionally cogent articulation of the ties that bind the native peoples of the Southwest to a particular landscape, see the "Proclamation" that was issued for Bears Ears National Monument upon its establishment by the Obama administration in December 2016, prior to its shameful evisceration by the Trump administration, and its subsequent restoration by the Biden administration.

CHAPTER 19 Where Water Comes Together

Details on Navajo history are gleaned from a variety of sources, including *Diné: A History of the Navajos*, by Peter Iverson; *The Navajo Treaty of 1868: Treaty between the United States of America and the Navajo Tribe of Indians*, by Berhard Michaelis; and *Dreaming of Sheep in Navajo Country*, by Marsha Weisiger. Also see *Navajo Place Names: An Observer's Guide*, by Alan Wilson and Gene Dennison, and *Navajo Sacred Places* by Klara Bonsack Kelley and Harris Francis.

For valuable background on the origins of the Bennett Freeze and the Navajo-Hopi land dispute, events that lie beyond the scope of this book but nevertheless played an important role in the Escalade tramway project, see Krakoff's previously cited "Not Yet America's Best Idea" article, as well as *Bitter Water: Diné Oral Histories of the Navajo-Hopi Land Dispute*, which was edited and translated by Malcolm Benally.

For additional background on the politics of the Escalade tramway, see "Who Can Save the Grand Canyon? A Holy War Is Being Fought over a Proposal to Build a $500 Million Commercial Development, on the Rim of America's Natural Treasure," written by David Roberts for *Smithsonian Magazine*. For historical background on a previous attempt to construct a tramway in the canyon, see "The 1919 Transcanyon Aerial Tramway Survey," by Jim Ohlman. And for an excellent overview and analysis of a variety of development threats, including the Escalade tramway project, that loom over Grand Canyon National Park, see *Grand Canyon for Sale: Public Lands versus Private Interests in the Era of Climate Change*, by Stephen Nash.

The quote from Lamar Whitmer about how the tramway would employ "an awful lot of people in an impoverished area and help them save their culture" comes from an interview Pete McBride conducted with Whitmer, which was recorded on film.

The stanza from the Raymond Carver poem comes from *Where Water Comes Together with Other Water: Poems.*

PART VI The Sudden Poetry of Springs

The Terry Tempest Williams quote is from her magnificent book *Refuge: An Unnatural History of Family and Place.*

CHAPTER 20 The Return of the Hiking King

Information on distances for various segments on the Tonto Trail can be gleaned from an extremely helpful pdf on the Grand Canyon National Park website, which can be accessed by going to the "Backcountry Trail Distances" page and clicking on the link for the Tonto Trail (see https://www.nps.gov/grca/planyour visit/upload/tonto_distances.pdf).

For a comprehensive account of Rich Rudow's thru-hike that offers details about the challenges he faced together with Dave Nally and Chris Atwood, as well as a series of photographs chronicling their route, see the article Rudow wrote, entitled "The Grandest Walk: A 700-Mile Thru-Hike below the Rims," which can be accessed at the Hyperlite Mountain Gear website.

For a suite of exceptional photographs of the traverse that Pete McBride and I completed, accompanied by text that Pete wrote, see *The Grand Canyon: Between River and Rim.* Five other photo treatments of the canyon that I find wonderful are *Grand Canyon: Views beyond the Beauty,* by Gary Ladd; *Grand Canyon: Time below the Rim,* also photographed by Gary Ladd, with text by Craig Childs; *Grand Canyon National Park: 100 Views,* with text by Scott Thybony; *Grand Canyon: Little Things in a Big Place,* with photographs by Michael Collier and text by Ann Zwinger; and Blaustein's previously cited work, *The Hidden Canyon.* For an exceptional photographic treatment of the landscape of the entire Colorado River system, obtain a copy of Michael Collier's *Water, Earth, and Sky: The Colorado River Basin.*

The history of photography in the canyon has been afforded an excellent treatment by Stephen Trimble in *Lasting Light: 125 Years of Grand Canyon Photography.* For a valuable look at two of the earliest (and certainly the most famous) of the canyon's photographers, see *The Kolb Brothers of Grand Canyon,* by William Suran.

On the related subject of painting the canyon, a number of wonderful books merit attention, including *Bruce Aiken's Grand Canyon: An Intimate Affair,* by

Susan McGarry Hallsten and Bruce Aiken; *Gunnar Widforss: Painter of the Grand Canyon*, by Bill and Frances Belknap; and *Grand Canyon Calling: An Artist's Relationship with the Grand Canyon*, by Serena Supplee.

Information on the flash flood that John McCue survived in Phantom Creek on September 11, 1997, which took the lives of Patty and John Moran, McCue's sister and brother-in-law, can be found in Ghiglieri and Myers's *Over the Edge: Death in Grand Canyon*.

CHAPTER 21 Gems

In 1979, when Grand Canyon National Park commissioned its initial inventory of perennial waters native to the canyon, investigators reported a total of fifty-seven sources, including twenty-one spring-driven streams and thirty-six seeps. Since that first study, an extensive effort to document additional water features in and around the canyon—work that has been coordinated by the National Park Service and the Springs Stewardship Institute in Flagstaff—has resulted in another 616 sites being added to the map, although Larry Stevens, the institute's director, believes that when the survey is finally complete the number will easily exceed a thousand.

For a scholarly analysis of various aspects of desert seeps and springs, see *Aridland Springs in North America: Ecology and Conservation*, edited by Lawrence Stevens and Vicky Meretsky; "Declines in an Aridland River's Base Flow due to Increasing Air Temperature: Implications for Springs Ecosystems," by Edward Schenk, Jeff Jenness, and Lawrence Stevens; and "Springs Ecosystem Distribution and Density for Improving Stewardship," by Katie Junghans, Abraham Springer, Lawrence Stevens, and Jeri Ledbetter.

The statement that the collective acreage of seeps and springs amounts to less than 0.01 percent of the canyon's total surface area, but supports a species concentration that is at least one hundred times greater than that of the surrounding desert, comes from "A Study of Seeps and Springs" on the Grand Canyon National Park website (see https://www.nps.gov/grca/learn/nature/seepspringstudy.htm).

Information about the pair of springs below the South Rim that are home to a unique cluster of redbud trees whose blossoms are white rather than purple, and the statement about seeps in other parts of the canyon supporting one-of-a-kind specimens of stone flies, damselflies, beetles, and butterflies, come from an interview with Larry Stevens. Details about the plants at Indian Garden (now known as Havasupai Gardens) come from *Indian Garden Cultural Landscape Report, Grand Canyon National Park*, by John Miller Associates.

CHAPTER 22 The Woman in the White Deerskin Dress

Any consideration of Havasupai history begins with *I Am the Grand Canyon: The Story of the Havasupai People*, by Stephen Hirst. Details about the tribe's nuanced and comprehensive grasp of desert botany comes, in part, from *Havasupai Habitat: A. F. Whiting's Ethnography of a Traditional Indian Culture*, edited by Steven Weber and David Seaman.

For details about goods that were traded and exchanged at Havasupai harvest festivals, see "Natural Disasters within Transitional Societies: The Havasupai Indians at Supai, Arizona," by Michael Anderson. Context on white cattlemen who began swarming the Havasupai's winter rangelands on the Coconino Plateau can be found in *Polishing the Jewel*, Michael Anderson's superb administrative history of Grand Canyon National Park. Background on President Benjamin Harrison's efforts to protect the Grand Canyon can be found in "The Decades-Long Political Fight to Save the Grand Canyon," by Francine Eunuma, in *Smithsonian Magazine*. The quote from Polly Mead Patraw comes from "Polly and Preston Patraw Oral History," Grand Canyon Museum Collections.

Perhaps the most illuminating study of the history of interpretation of Grand Canyon National Park for visitors is Sarah Gerke's 2010 Arizona State University PhD dissertation, "A History of Park Service Interpretation at Grand Canyon National Park." For additional information on the Hopi and Navajo artisans at Hopi House, see "Hopi House," also by Gerke. For a deeply informed study of the history of contentious land-use issues in and around the Grand Canyon, see *A Place Called Grand Canyon: Contested Geographies*, by Barbara Morehouse.

Anyone interested in learning about the beauty of Havasupai basketmaking should obtain of copy of *Havasupai Baskets and Their Makers: 1930–1940*, written by Barbara and Edwin McKee with Joyce Herold. For details on birds that move up and down the canyon walls seasonally—which include Townsend's solitaires and Clark's nutcrackers—turn to Houk's *An Introduction to Grand Canyon Ecology*.

PART VII In the House of Tumbled Stones

The Craig Childs quote is from *Virga & Bone: Essays from Dry Places*.

CHAPTER 23 The Great Thumb

The Great Thumb Mesa was named by Frank Bond, who viewed the mesa from the air prior to submitting his nomination to the U.S. Board on Geographic Names in 1932. For details, see *Grand Canyon Place Names*, by Gregory McNamee.

Four separate routes lead off the Great Thumb from the Esplanade to the river: the Enfilade, Fossil Bay, Matkatamiba, and Havasu Canyon. As for the Thumb's dimensions, it is only about fourteen miles long if one is measuring from the head of Forester Canyon (four miles shorter than the isthmus of the Shivwits Plateau concluding at Kelly Point on the north side of the canyon); but if one is measuring from the head of Royal Arch Creek (a starting point with which the Havasupai Tribe would surely concur), the Thumb extends for a full twenty miles. The narrowest point of the Thumb is just over half a mile wide, while the narrowest part of Kelly Point is a full mile.

The history of Grand Canyon National Park has been thoroughly chronicled by a number of historians, beginning with Anderson's previously cited *Polishing the Jewel* and an excellent companion volume by the same author, *Living at the Edge: Explorers, Exploiters and Settlers of the Grand Canyon Region.* For an informative glimpse into some of the characters who enlivened the community at the canyon's South Rim at the end of the mining era and the start of the tourist industry, see *John Hance: The Life, Lies, and Legend of Grand Canyon's Greatest Storyteller,* by Shane Murphy; "The Man Who Tried to Claim the Grand Canyon," by Adam Sowards; and Debra Sutphen's "'Too Hard a Nut to Crack': Peter D. Berry and the Battle for Free Enterprise at the Grand Canyon, 1890–1914."

Readers interested in exploring the story of the National Park Service should consider a range of sources, beginning with John Ise's standard history, *Our National Parks Policy—a Critical History.* One of the most provocative and informed examinations of how the parks were brought forth is Alfred Runte's *National Parks: The American Experience.* Also see *An American Idea: The Making of the National Parks,* by Kim Heacox; as well as Robert Keiter's deeply informed *To Conserve Unimpaired: The Evolution of the National Park Idea,* and "The American Invention of National Parks," by Roderick Nash.

Regarding the little warbling bat that flitted above our camp on the Great Thumb, several species of bats do actually sing—although the sounds they make are normally too faint to be detected and often require amplification with a direction microphone to be heard. That we heard the song of this bat offers testament to the silence and the stillness that one can encounter in remote sections of the canyon, such as the Thumb.

To learn more about this phenomenon and to hear a recording of several bat songs, check out "Is That a Lark I Hear?" by the NPR journalist Robert Krulwich.

CHAPTER 24 The Storm

Although the primary focus of this chapter is our navigation through the snow-storm that overtook us on the Great Thumb Mesa, this part of the book offers an opportunity to provide citations for a number of valuable works on the vital and overlooked subject of the fraught relationship between Native Americans and national parks.

Some of the most important and provocative texts include *Dispossessing the Wilderness: Indian Removal and the Making of the National Parks*, by Mark David Spense; *Indian Country, God's Country: Native Americans and the National Parks*, by Philip Burnham; and *American Indians & National Parks*, by Robert Keller and Michael Turek. For additional treatments, also see "Ethnic Cleansing and America's Creation of National Parks," by Isaac Kantor, and "The Tribes vs. Donald Trump," by Abe Streep.

Two of the finest books ever written about Native Americans in the Southwest and their fight to protect their lands from development and exploitation are *Fire on the Plateau: Conflict and Endurance in the American Southwest* and *The Eagle Bird: Mapping a New West*, both written by Charles Wilkinson.

CHAPTER 25 Beneath the Eyes of the Owl

Like its predecessor, this chapter—which is focused primarily on the challenges of moving through Owl Eyes Bay, just beyond the outermost extremity of the Great Thumb Mesa—provides a chance to highlight several important ancillary works, in this case on the subject of wilderness preservation. The place to begin is with Roderick Nash's classic and still timely *Wilderness and the American Mind*—although fans of Aldo Leopold would probably argue, with some justification, that the "first book" on the ethics of land preservation is *A Sand County Almanac: With Essays on Conservation from Round River*.

Regardless of where you start, it's important to follow up these texts with two vital treatments: Edward O. Wilson's *Half-Earth: Our Planet's Fight for Life* and William Cronon's controversial, challenging, and important essay "The Trouble with Wilderness; or, Getting Back to the Wrong Nature." And please be sure to take a look at the beautiful and elegant speech given by former executive director of the Grand Canyon Trust Bill Hedden, the transcript of which has been published under the title "In Praise of a Wild West: A 21st-Century Vision for Western Public Lands," in *High Country News*. It is well worth reading.

CHAPTER 26 *Casa de Piatra*

Owl Eyes Bay looms large in the minds and folklore of the canyon's backcountry hiking community. In 1963, just before the start of Colin Fletcher's famous hike, the bay remained the only section that Harvey Butchart had not yet hiked—primarily because at the time it was unclear to Butchart whether it would be possible to complete a traverse of the bay's upper slopes, which were steep enough to serve as a barrier to the eastward dispersal of the horses and elk that occasionally dwell on the Esplanade directly to the west. So shortly before Fletcher was scheduled to pass through Owl Eyes, Butchart drove out to the Great Thumb Mesa, dropped onto the Esplanade, and completed the passage—partly to make sure it was safe, but also because he was concerned that the intrepid Welsh hiker might beat him to the punch.

During the half century since Butchart and Fletcher first made it through, the bay has seen very little foot traffic, and by the time our party arrived in the winter of 2016, fewer than a dozen people during the modern era may have passed beneath the ominous blank stare of those hollow eyes. Under the conditions in which we found ourselves, Owl Eyes surpassed its reputation as an exceptionally dangerous place to travel. However, context is everything whenever one is assessing danger, and this truth bears some elaboration in connection with the events that had befallen Ioana Hociota four years earlier.

On the day that Hociota and Matthias Kawski entered Owl Eyes in late February of 2012, patches of snow dotted only the shadiest parts of the slopes, and the afternoon temperature was in the high sixties. Under these relatively dry conditions, the two hikers mostly traveled high on the slopes, where a fall would quickly be arrested by dense bushes and well-seated boulders, and the risk of plunging over the edge was low. Upon reaching the midpoint of the bay around noon, they were so completely within their comfort zone and so far ahead of schedule that they took time for a leisurely lunch, during which Hociota lounged barefoot to air out her feet, and beamed for commemorative photos.

After leaving their lunch spot, Hociota and Kawski took slightly different routes. Hociota's was fifty feet away from the cliff edge and protected by bushes and boulders, but it took her above a narrow, steep chute that was obscured by a massive boulder roughly the size of a tractor trailer. A loose rock or a misstep above that hidden chute—perhaps the only place on her route where catastrophe was even possible—is what took her life.

Like much of the remote backcountry in the canyon, Owl Eyes is relatively safe for expert hikers under ideal conditions, but can quickly become a dangerous place under other circumstances. The tragedy that unfolded illustrates how even highly accomplished hikers with deep experience and excellent judgment, walking with caution under the best of circumstances, can pay the ultimate consequences from unseen hazards. In the canyon, irreducible risk is omnipresent.

Details of Hociota's life and her fall, as well as an elaboration of the points made here, have been provided by Andrew Holycross. Her story has also been chronicled in two other places: "A True Story about Three People, Passion, a Place—and Triumphing over Tragedy," by Scott Seckel, and "Grand Canyon Hiker Dies Close to Her Goal," KNAU Radio.

Following his wife's death, Holycross created and endowed the Ioana Elise Hociota!!! Memorial Mathematics Scholarship at Arizona State University. (The triple exclamation points reflect Hociota's fierce drive and her irrepressible joie de vivre.) The scholarship is intended to promote opportunity and diversity in mathematics while honoring Hociota's background as well as her intellectual interests. Any immigrant or international student with an interest in pure mathematics may apply for the scholarship. For more information, see "Other Resources" at the end of the readers' guide.

PART VIII Beneath the Ramparts of Time

The "wildness" quote is from *The Abstract Wild*, by Jack Turner.

CHAPTER 27 The Godscape

One of the most fascinating books ever written about the vast sandstone benches west of the Grand Scenic Divide is also perhaps the most vivid and expressive text in the history of American geology.

When Clarence Dutton, a protégé of John Wesley Powell, produced *Tertiary History of the Grand Cañon District* for the fledgling U.S. Geological Survey in 1882, it not only showcased Dutton's unique ability to write about the geography of the canyon with evocative literary flair, but also highlighted the work of three great visual artists, each of whom offered a different lens through which to appreciate and interpret the landscape.

Dutton's book was illustrated with drawings and paintings by Thomas Moran, an artist of the Hudson River School whose paintings—in particular his massive canvas entitled *Grand Canyon of the Yellowstone*—were instrumental in securing support for the bill that set aside Yellowstone as the world's first national park. Moran's images in *Tertiary History* were accompanied by the topographical drawings of William Henry Holmes, whose three-part *Panorama from Point Sublime* stands as what Wallace Stegner once called "the most magnificent picture of the Grand Canyon ever drawn, painted, or photographed."

In 2001, Dutton's magnum opus was republished by the University of Arizona Press in a volume that includes an introduction by Wallace Stegner and a foreword by Stephen Pyne, both of which are essential texts on the canyon. But the heart of the book is Dutton's prose—language as complex, convoluted, and pure as the canyon itself, especially his portrait of the Supai terraces that dominate the canyon's interior reaches west of the Great Thumb Mesa, for which he coined the name by which we know them today: the Esplanade.

CHAPTER 28 Drenched in Wonder

Todd Martin's *Grand Canyoneering: Exploring the Rugged Gorges and Secret Slots of the Grand Canyon* is the most authoritative and comprehensive guide to the slots of the Grand Canyon. The book documents 105 canyoneering routes within the park boundaries, 68 of which require rappelling, 63 of which necessitate swimming or wading, and 78 of which usually take more than one day to complete. Many of these routes also require the use of pack rafts to facilitate a return to one of the canyon rims.

Martin has intentionally omitted a number of the most delicate, beautiful, and challenging slots in the hopes that they will remain protected—the need for which is covered admirably by Matt Jenkins in "Canyoneering at Grand Canyon National Park: Monitoring Pockets of Wilderness in the Canyon Corridor."

For additional information on navigating through technical slot canyons in Arizona and southern Utah, see *Canyoneering Arizona*, by Tyler Williams, and *Technical Slot Canyon Guide to the Colorado Plateau*, by Michael Kelsey. A book that beautifully evokes the wonder of a landscape riddled with slot canyons is Ann Zwinger's celebration of the southeastern Utah Canyonlands, *Wind in the Rock*.

CHAPTER 29 Olo

Although Olo Canyon may well have already been explored by entering its mouth at the edge of the Colorado, its first recorded ascent took place in April of 1983, when Robert Benson climbed through its interior all the way from the river to the base of a hundred-foot rappel that separated him from the top of the Redwall. Olo's first recorded descent was made by Rich Rudow, Todd Martin, and Brian Alleyn in October of 2008.

A number of scholarly articles offer insight into the forces that carve and shape slots such as Olo, including "Episodic Incision of the Colorado River in Glen Canyon, Utah," by Christopher D. Garvin et al., in *Earth Surface Processes and Landforms*; "New Insights into the Mechanics of Fluvial Bedrock Erosion through Flume Experiments and Theory," by Michael Lamb et al., in *Geomorphology*; and "Inner Gorge–Slot Canyon System Produced by Repeated Stream Incision (Eastern Alps): Significance for Development of Bedrock Canyons," by Diethard Sanders et al., in *Geomorphology*.

For a marvelous film that chronicles Rich Rudow, Todd Martin, Dave Nally, and a number of other canyoneers as they descend a slot much like Olo, see *Last of the Great Unknown: The Story of Grand Canyon's Hidden Slot Canyons, the Canyoneers Who Systematically Explored Their Drainages, and the Secrets Hidden Deep within Their Walls*, directed by Dan Ransom.

CHAPTER 30 In Sinyella's Shadow

This chapter draws extensively from a variety of sources, many of which have already been cited, including *I Am the Grand Canyon*, by Hirst; "Not Yet America's Best Idea," by Krakoff; *A Place Called Grand Canyon*, by Morehouse; "A History of Park Service Interpretation at Grand Canyon," by Gerke; *Living at the Edge, Polishing the Jewel*, "Who Owns the Grand Canyon?" and "Natural Disasters within Transitional Societies," by Anderson; and the *Celebrating the Grand Canyon* blog, by Ingram, who was directly involved in the campaign for the 1975 Grand Canyon National Park Enlargement Act as a representative of the Sierra Club.

The quote about the Havasupai calling themselves "the forgotten tribe" comes from an author interview with Carletta Tilousi. For Havasupai views on uranium mining, see "Why Do We Need to Mine Uranium in the Grand Canyon?" by Carletta Tilousi, in *Newsweek*.

CHAPTER 31 The People of the Blue-Green Water

In *Pure Land: A True Story of Three Lives, Three Cultures, and the Search for Heaven on Earth*, Annette McGivney chronicles the tragic stories of Tomomi Hanamure, a Japanese woman who was murdered in the spring of 2006 as she hiked to Havasu Falls, and Randy Redtail Wescogame, the eighteen-year-old Havasupai youth who killed her. Combining journalism with memoir, McGivney offers readers a glimpse into the hardships and challenges that the Havasupai have been forced to confront during the late twentieth and early twenty-first centuries as they continue to grapple with—and move beyond—the injustices that have been committed against them.

PART IX Boneland and Bedrock

Annie Dillard's quote is from *The Abundance: Narrative Essays Old and New*.

CHAPTER 32 All In

For details about the settlement of the Arizona Strip by the descendants of white Europeans, as well as a profile of the community that took root along this remote stretch of the West, see *Far from Cactus Flat: The 20th Century Story of a Harsh Land, a Proud Family, and a Lost Son*, by Lyman Hafen. Also see *John H. Riffey: The Last Old-Time Ranger* and *The Last Homesteader on the Arizona Strip*, by Jean Luttrell. For a modern-day portrait of this same subculture, see *The Last Cowboys: A Pioneer Family in the New West*, by John Branch.

Details on the archaeological and anthropological history of the Shivwits Plateau as well as sections of the Esplanade to the east and west of Toroweap can be found in a number of sources already cited, including "Not Yet America's Best Idea," by Krakoff; *An Archaeological Perspective of Human History at Grand Canyon* and *An Introduction to Grand Canyon Prehistory*, by Coder; and Fairley's *Changing River: Time, Culture, and the Transformation of Landscape in the Grand Canyon*. Also see sources on Paiute history cited in the notes for chapter 33.

For information on the microecology of desert potholes, see "These Tiny Desert-Dwelling Crustaceans Are Incredibly Patient: Tadpole Shrimp Hunker Down, Waiting for Water Conditions to Be Just Right," by Jessica Hester, in *Atlas Obscura*; and "Creature Feature: A Fairy of a Different Sort," by Hadley Kunz, in *National Parks Traveler*. For a more scholarly treatment of this subject, see "Desert Potholes: Ephemeral Aquatic Microsystems," by Marjorie Chan et al., in *Aquatic Geochemistry*. Also see "Inside Canyonlands: Potholes," a short video recorded by Karen Henker on the Canyonlands National Park website.

CHAPTER 33 Ghosts of a Former World

In addition to previously cited sources on the history and culture of the Southern Paiute, further information can be found in *From the Sands to the Mountain: Change and Persistence in a Southern Paiute Community*, by Pamela Bunte and Robert Franklin. For a poignant and inspiring look at contemporary Paiute people, accompanied by some very fine photo portraits, see *Southern Paiute: A Portrait*, by Logan Hebner. For information on the Ghost Dance traditions in the western part of the Grand Canyon rim country, see "The Mormons and the Ghost Dance of 1890," by Gregory Smoak; and "Ghost Dancing the Grand Canyon: Southern Paiute Rock Art, Ceremony, and Cultural Landscapes," by Richard Stoffle et al., in *Current Anthropology*.

The history of rock art in the Southwest has been covered in a number of illuminating books, including *Rock Art of the Grand Canyon Region*, by Don Christensen, Jerry Dickey, and Steven Freers; *Indian Rock Art of the Southwest*, by Polly Schaafsma; and *Rock Art of the American Southwest*, by Scott Thybony. Also see two articles by Polly Schaafsma: "Shaman's Gallery: A Grand Canyon Rock Art Site," in *Kiva*, and her 1988 report for Grand Canyon National Park, "Shaman's Gallery: A Grand Canyon Rock Art Site."

For a provocative article on the possible connection between polychrome pictographs and shamanistic trances, see "Trance and Transformation in the Canyons: Shamanism and Rock Art on the Colorado Plateau," in *The Archaeology of Horseshoe Canyon*, by Polly Schaafsma; and for a short profile of Schaafsma herself, see "Polly Schaafsma: Imagery and Anthropology," by Gwinn Vivian, in *New Mexico Historical Review*.

For the finest work I've ever read on the magnificence of darkness—a book that simultaneously stands as a hymn to the glory of the night sky, a scientific treatise on the concept of "celestial vaulting," a plea for the preservation of darkness by reducing light pollution, and a gorgeous piece of nature writing—see *The End of Night: Searching for Natural Darkness in an Age of Artificial Light*, by Paul Bogard.

CHAPTER 35 Badlands

The most comprehensive history of mining in the canyon is *Quest for the Pillar of Gold: The Mines and Miners of the Grand Canyon*, by George Billingsley, Earle Spamer, and Dove Menkes. It is ably supplemented by Michael Anderson's article "Mining," at the Nature, Culture, and History at the Grand Canyon website.

The information on the Copper Mountain Mine in the vicinity of Parashant Canyon comes from the Arizona Department of Mines and Mineral Resources Mining Collection at the Arizona Geological Survey, and from "Radioactive Occurrences and Uranium Production in Arizona," by R. B. Scarborough. A reconnaissance field and laboratory study of radionuclide activity levels at a portion of the Copper Mine site was completed by Ray Kenny for the National Park Service. He published his results, "Management Report: Assessment of Radionuclides in Breccia Pipe Mine Spoils, Grand Canyon National Park, AZ: Phase III: Copper Mountain Mine," in 2002.

Uranium is known to have been produced at a dozen mines—Orphan, Ridenour, Hack 1, Hack 2, Hack 3, Arizona 1, Pigeon, Kanab North, Pinenut, Hermit, Chapel, and Pinyon Plain (formerly known as Canyon).

For a devastating exposé on the effects of uranium mining on the Navajo Nation, which helps to explain the deep distrust of the uranium-mining industry among the tribes of the canyon, see *Yellow Dirt: An American Story of a Poisoned Land and a People Betrayed*, by Judy Pasternak. For a glimpse of more recent developments in the uranium industry, see "Uranium Miners Pushed Hard for a Comeback. They Got Their Wish," by Hiroko Tabuchi, in the *New York Times*; and "Will Trump Dump on Grand Canyon? Experts Say Risk of Mining Not Worth Reward," by Miriam Wasser, in the *Phoenix New Times*.

A broader context for understanding the impact of private industry on public lands and fragile desert ecosystems across the intermountain West, including ranching, is provided by Christopher Ketcham's *This Land: How Cowboys, Capitalism, and Corruption Are Ruining the American West*. For details on the damage that cattle can inflict on arid-land springs—and how swiftly the land can recover when cattle are removed—see "Collaborative Rehabilitation of Pakoon Springs in Grand Canyon–Parashant National Monument, Arizona," by Kelly Burke et al., in *The Colorado Plateau VI: Science and Management at the Landscape Scale*, edited by Laura Huenneke, Charles van Riper III, and Kelley Hays-Gilpin.

Information on the lava dams that repeatedly blocked the Colorado River— including an evocative description of the massive outburst floods that were created when those dams eventually failed, draining their reservoirs in a matter of hours or days while depositing boulders up to one hundred feet in diameter along the walls of the canyon—can be found in *Tuweep Geology Bulletin* on the Grand Canyon National Park's website.

Details on how the blossoming cycle of Ocotillo has evolved to coincide with the migration of hummingbirds can be found in "Pollinator Availability as a Determinant of Flowering Time in Ocotillo (*Fouquieria splendens*)," by Nickolas Waser, in *Oecologia*.

CHAPTER 36 Rock Bottom, Again

Ellen Meloy's tale about accidentally boiling the lizard that had spent the night at the bottom of her coffee cup can be found on the opening pages of *The Last Cheater's Waltz: Beauty and Violence in the Desert Southwest*. Readers who are intrigued by this story and want to explore more of Meloy's writing should seek out a copy of *Raven's Exile: A Season on the Green River*, which many fans (including me) regard as her finest work.

Something about the Green River seems to inspire fabulous writing, because this is also the setting for one of Ann Zwinger's loveliest books, *Run, River, Run: A Naturalist's Journey Down One of the Great Rivers of the American West*, which is well worth reading. And no desert lover's library can be considered complete if it lacks a copy of Craig Childs's classic *The Secret Knowledge of Water: Discovering the Essence of the American Desert*.

PART X Lost and Found

Pico Iyer's quote is from his essay "The Eloquent Sounds of Silence," published in *Time* magazine. It was cited on the opening page of the Department of the Interior's 1995 report on the effects of aircraft overflights on the National Park system.

CHAPTER 37 Hard Days Ahead

The account of the events leading to the disappearance of Floyd Roberts derives partly from news reports and the Grand Canyon National Park's case incident report, but is based primarily on an author interview with Ned Bryant, as well as subsequent interviews with Rich Rudow. For additional information, see "Search On for Missing Florida Hiker in Grand Canyon," by Alexis Egeland, in the *Arizona Republic*; "Update: Hiker Remains Missing in Western Grand Canyon," Grand Canyon National Park website; and "Cold Cases," Investigative Services, U.S. National Park Service.

An alternative theory about Roberts's disappearance is that he may actually have set his pack down in the dense juniper thickets atop Kelly Point shortly after having lost contact with the Bryants, and been unable to locate it again. If true, this would explain his failure to deploy items from his pack such as clothing or toilet paper that might have alerted searchers to his location.

According to this theory, after spending the night without food or water, Roberts moved down the steep terrain leading off Kelly Point in an unsuccessful effort to make contact with a search-and-rescue helicopter that landed briefly on a Supai pour-over just above 209-Mile Canyon. By this point, he would have been without water for more than twenty-four hours in extreme heat, and probably expired somewhere inside the 209-Mile basin.

Rich and other searchers believe this hypothesis fits the scant evidence that has come to light so far.

CHAPTER 38 "The Combat Zone"

The most comprehensive general history of the Hualapai tribe is Shepherd's *We Are an Indian Nation*. Valuable material can also be found in a number of previously cited works, including Krakoff's "Not Yet America's Best Idea." Also see "Hualapai Reservation," by Sarah Gerke, on the Nature, Culture, and History at the Grand Canyon website.

A critically important and absolutely fascinating chapter of Hualapai history—the tribe's court battle against the Santa Fe Pacific Railroad and the Hualapai's landmark victory at the U.S. Supreme Court—has been given a superb treatment by Christian McMillen in *Making Indian Law: The Hualapai Land Case and the Birth of Ethnohistory*. Although the details of this case lie far beyond the scope of this book, McMillen's work is an essential text for anyone who is interested in the history of the tribe.

The quote suggesting that arsenic be added to the flour supplied to the Hualapai following their return from La Paz is from an editorial in the *Mojave County Miner* on October 8, 1887, cited by Hirst in *I Am the Grand Canyon* and in "About the Hualapai Nation," on the Hualapai Department of Cultural Resources website.

Following our hike, Pete and I made two separate trips to Grand Canyon West, once from Flagstaff and a second time from Las Vegas, to get a firsthand look at the helicopter air tours, the motorized-boat tours on the Colorado, and the Skywalk, as well as various other attractions such as the restaurant and the Wild West show that the tribe runs on the rim of the canyon. We would have liked to have met, spoken to, and perhaps even walked with the Hualapai on their own land, but this proved impossible. The tribe does not issue hiking permits, with or without a guide, and multiple requests for an interview with the tribal leadership were denied.

Although this was disappointing, we understand the tribe's reluctance to speak with journalists, given that their operation has often been written about in a manner that fails to offer an even-handed view of how challenging it is for the tribe to balance the desire to practice good stewardship with the imperative to promote economic prosperity.

Details about Robbie Knievel jumping a side canyon in the spring of 1999 come from "Robbie Knievel Jumps Motorcycle 223 Feet across Grand Canyon," *Los Angeles Times*.

For details on the story of David Jin and the development of the Skywalk, see "Tribe Brings on the Tourists: Hualapai Nation Plans Ambitious Development at Grand Canyon," by Emma Brown, in *High Country News*; "Hey, Sin City, Top This: Grand Canyon West's Skywalk," by Christopher Reynolds, in the *Los Angeles Times*; "Sovereignty and the Skywalk," by Emily Guerin, in *High Country News*; and "Grand Canyon Skywalk Developer David Jin Dies in L.A.," by Ken Ritter and Felicia Fonseca, in *Las Vegas Review Journal*.

For background and details on the 1986 collision over the canyon, see "Aircraft Accident Report: Grand Canyon Airlines, Inc., and Helitech, Inc., Midair Collision over Grand Canyon National Park, June 18, 1986," issued by the National Transportation Safety Board; "June 18, 1986: Grand Canyon Airlines, Inc. / Helitech Inc: Accident Synopsis and Historical Summary," by Michael McComb, at the impressively researched Grand Canyon Aviation Archaeology website, Lostflights.com; and "Air Crash Kills 25 at Grand Canyon," by Judith Cummings, in the *New York Times*.

Two key reports, both of which are accessible online, offer important information on the state of the Grand Canyon air-tour industry following the 1986 collision, the frequency and intensity of aircraft overflights above the canyon, and the impact of aviation noise on this as well as other national parks. See "Report to Congress: Report on Effects of Aircraft Overflights on the National Park System—Full Report," issued by the National Park Service; and "Special Flight Rules Area in the Vicinity of Grand Canyon National Park: Actions to Substantially Restore Natural Quiet—Final Environmental Impact Statement FES 12-21," issued by the Grand Canyon National Park.

For readers interested in the impact of aviation on the canyon, the reports mentioned above are certainly worth reading, but for a sense of the outrage that aviation noise can provoke among visitors, also see "The Sound and the Fury," by T. R. Reid, published by the *Washington Post*—an article that feels as timely and relevant today as it must have when it was originally published on March 23, 1986. For context and details on Grand Canyon National Park having more sightseeing overflights than any other park in the country, see "Buzzing the National Parks," by Jim Robbins, in the *New York Times*.

Anyone who thinks that the problems created by aviation noise in the 1980s and 1990s are now a thing of the past may wish to access the following investigative articles: "Grand Canyon Air Tours: Conservationists Hear Noisy Flights, Tribe Sees Economic Returns," by Ron Dungan, in the *Arizona Republic*; and "Is Grand Canyon West Turning into 'Las Vegas East' and Ruining the Park's Wilderness? Or Is It Saving a Native American Tribe?," by Annette McGivney, in *Outside* magazine. Also see "Critics: Grand Canyon Flight Regulation Will Increase Noise," by Bill Theobald, in the *Arizona Republic*.

For details on the amenities and the expense of VIP air tours over the Grand Canyon, see "Helicopter Sightseeing at the Grand Canyon," by Dan Sweet, in *Rotor Magazine*.

Quotes from Hualapai tribal chairman Damon Clarke come from an opinion piece written by Clarke and his fellow councilmember Candida Hunter, "Hualapai Tribe: Don't Tell Us How to Respect the Grand Canyon," for the *Azcentral* website.

CHAPTER 39 Evensong

The blending of three of North America's four deserts in western Grand Canyon—Mojave, Great Basin, and Sonoran—is beautifully evoked by Ann Zwinger in *The Mysterious Lands: A Naturalist Explores the Four Great Deserts of the Southwest*, a book that was written about a different part of the Southwest, but nevertheless conveys the austerity, aridity, and aesthetic richness of the most remote reaches of the canyon. Readers who are interested in learning more about this remarkable (and overlooked) ecosystem should also turn to *A Natural History of the Mojave Desert*, by Lawrence Walker and Frederick Landau.

For a brief essay that will enhance one's appreciation of the connection between the Colorado Plateau's biology and its human ecology, see Steven Trimble's foreword to Tony Joe et al.'s *Safeguarding the Uniqueness of the Colorado Plateau: An Ecoregional Assessment of Biocultural Diversity*, a book which also includes an array of valuable writing by Tony Joe, Luisa Maffi, Gary Paul Nabhan, and almost half a dozen other writers.

Although this may sound a bit odd, assistance in opening the doorway to an appreciation for a place as harsh as western Grand Canyon is offered by a pair of writers who have devoted their thoughts, energy, and considerable talents—as well as their preference for moving on foot—to parts of the world that seem to have little in common with the canyon. See *Arctic Dreams: Imagination and Desire in a Northern Landscape*, by Barry Lopez, one of the finest books ever written on nature, land, and human culture, and Robert Macfarlane's marvelous *Landscape Trilogy: Mountains of the Mind, The Wild Places*, and *The Old Ways: A Journey on Foot*.

CHAPTER 40 Unfinished Business

A number of works explore, celebrate, and help to expand one's appreciation for the power and importance of silence. Begin with an essay that has already been cited—Pico Iyer's incomparable and humbling "The Eloquent Sounds of Silence"—and from there, attend to the messages in the following books: *Silence in the Age of Noise*, by Erling Kagge; *A Book of Silence*, by Sara Maitland; *In Pursuit of Silence: Listening for Meaning in a World of Noise*, by George Prochnik; and finally, *The Power of Silence: Against the Dictatorship of Noise*, by Robert Cardinal Sarah.

CHAPTER 41 Pilgrims All

The three most popular and heavily trafficked trails in the canyon's central corridor—the Bright Angel, the South Kaibab, and the North Kaibab—attract more than eighty thousand permitted overnight backpackers each year, as well as numerous day hikers and mule riders. The history of these routes is chronicled in a wonderful book by Seth Muller, *Canyon Crossing: Experiencing Grand Canyon from Rim to Rim*.

After my brother, Aaron, and I set up our tent in the backpackers' campground at Havasupai Gardens, we walked over to the ranger station, a wooden building with a wide front porch, where we were greeted by the two rangers on duty, Betsy Aurnou and Elyssa Shalla. Both were friends of Tom Myers, and having heard that we would be passing through, they had invited us to come by for dinner.

Inside, the kitchen table was loaded with roasted eggplant and acorn squash, burritos stuffed with cheese and rice, a tray of tiny chocolate cupcakes, plus a box of red wine. It was by far the best meal of the entire hike, and for the next three hours, as the moonlight spilled across the porch and the stars winked through the branches of the cottonwoods outside, we talked of their work in the park, and their feelings about the canyon.

READERS' GUIDE AND CHAPTER NOTES

As Shalla was sharing a few details about how she and her husband, Matt Jenkins—the park's North Rim manager, who had been hoping to join us for dinner before he was called to the North Rim for a search-and-rescue mission—had completed a continuous thru-hike of the canyon in January of 2016, it dawned on me that it was she who had written the article I'd read warning that it is not possible to hike the length of the park without adequate preparation.

Although Shalla was far too discreet to mention anything, she was well aware of how much trouble Pete and I had gotten ourselves into, and that we were (and remain to this day) poster boys for how *not* to hike the canyon.

Epilogue

The Willa Cather quote is from the final chapter of her novel O *Pioneers!*

For details of the helicopter crash in Quartermaster Canyon on the Hualapai Reservation, see "Screams Echoed throughout the Canyon," by Amie Gordon, in the *Daily Mail*. Also see "Grand Canyon Helicopter Crash: Experts Say Crowded Airspace Is 'a Recipe for Disaster,'" by Alden Woods, in the *Arizona Republic*, which is also the source for the quote from Gary Robb, a Kansas City attorney who specializes in helicopter-crash litigation.

For information on Kaskade's live-stream concert at the Skywalk, see "How Kaskade Became the First DJ to Perform on the Grand Canyon West's Skywalk," by Sarah Pittman, in *Pollstar*.

For a series of articles that chronicle the Navajo fight against the Escalade tramway project and the victory achieved by Renae Yellowhorse and the other members of Save the Confluence, see the "Stopping Grand Canyon Escalade" page at the Grand Canyon Trust website.

Details regarding the changes that have unfolded at the Desert View Watchtower are laid out in "A New View: Has the Long-Troubled Relationship between Grand Canyon National Park and Local Indigenous People Entered a More Harmonious Era?," by Laura Allen, in *National Parks* magazine.

For background and context on the establishment of Baaj Nwaavjo I'tah Kukveni National Monument, see "Fact Sheet: President Biden Designates Baaj Nwaavjo I'tah Kukveni—Ancestral Footprints of the Grand Canyon National Monument," Briefing Room: Statements and Releases, the White House, August 8, 2023, and "Biden Designates Baaj Nwaavjo I'tah Kukveni—Ancestral Footprints of the Grand Canyon National Monument," by Amber Reimondo, at the Grand Canyon Trust website. (Among other protections, the designation permanently prohibits staking any new uranium mines within the monument's boundaries and will permit only two of nearly six hundred preexisting claims to continue moving forward—one of which is the Pinyon Plain Mine.)

For additional information on the subject of Navajo rugs, see *Weaving a World: Textiles and the Navajo Way of Seeing*, by Roseann Sandoval Willink and Paul Zolbrod; *Navajo Rugs: The Essential Guide*, by Don Dedera; *Unbroken Web: The Art of Ellen & Lucy Begay—a Collector's Perspective*, by Gary Beaudoin; "Navajo Rugs," by Hattie Clark, in the *Christian Science Monitor*; and "Elle Meets the President: Weaving Navajo Culture and Commerce in the Southwestern Tourist Industry," by Laura Jane Moore, in *Frontiers: A Journal of Women Studies*.

The "Benedictio" quote from Edward Abbey is from the preface (dated June 1987) of the University of Arizona Press 1988 hardcover reprint of *Desert Solitaire*.

Last but not least, my mother asked me to include a few additional details about my father that she feels need to be mentioned.

He was a devoted reader who cultivated a love of books for his entire life—a passion that he never lost, even during his final weeks when his eyesight failed him. And his jovial manner of speaking, which was one of his trademarks, was an expression of his kindness and decency—aspects of his character that he retained, with great courage and determination, right up to the very end.

Maps and Tables

BACKCOUNTRY TRAIL DISTANCES
Grand Canyon National Park. https://www.nps.gov/grca/planyourvisit/trail-distances.htm.

GEOLOGICAL MAP OF THE GRAND CANYON
Generated by George Billingsley and others at the U.S. Geological Survey. https://rclark.github.io/grand-canyon-geology/#11/36.1495/-111.9874.

GEOLOGICAL TIMELINE OF THE GRAND CANYON
Brian F. Gootee. Arizona Geological Survey Open-File Report OFR-19-02, with supplemental resource document for Geological Timeline of the Grand Canyon. 2019. https://repository.arizona.edu/handle/10150/631779.

HISTORIC GRAND CANYON MAPS
The 1893 Grand Canyon Forest Reserve, the 1906 Grand Canyon Game Preserve, the 1908 Grand Canyon National Monument, the 1919 Grand Canyon National Park, and the present-day boundaries of the park following the 1975 Grand Canyon Enlargement Act. "Historic Boundaries Map." Grand Canyon Trust. https://www.grandcanyontrust.org/grand-canyon-historic-boundaries-map. All

of these maps, together with an eclectic and valuable mix of other cartographic representations, can be found at Jeff Ingram's web page, *Celebrating the Grand Canyon.* https://gcfutures.blogspot.com/p/some-maps.html.

TONTO TRAIL DISTANCES TABLE, EAST AND WEST
Grand Canyon National Park. https://www.nps.gov/grca/planyourvisit/upload/Tonto_Distances.pdf.

Other Resources

AMERICAN CANYONEERING ASSOCIATION
(435) 826-4714
http://www.canyoneering.net

CLINE LIBRARY SPECIAL COLLECTIONS AND ARCHIVES
AT NORTHERN ARIZONA UNIVERSITY
1001 Knoles Drive
Flagstaff, AZ 86011
(928) 523-2173
https://nau.edu/special-collections/

COALITION OF AMERICAN CANYONEERS
https://www.americancanyoneers.org

CROW CANYON ARCHAEOLOGICAL CENTER
23390 Road K
Cortez, CO 81321
(800) 422-8975
https://crowcanyon.org/

DONORA HISTORICAL SOCIETY AND SMOG MUSEUM
595 McKean Avenue
Donora, PA 15033
https://sites.google.com/site/donorahistoricalsociety/home

GRAND CANYON CONSERVANCY
P.O. Box 399
Grand Canyon, AZ 86023
(800) 858-2808
https://www.grandcanyon.org

GRAND CANYON HIKERS AND BACKPACKERS ASSOCIATION
P.O. Box 30233
Flagstaff, AZ 86003
https://gchba.org/

GRAND CANYON NATIONAL PARK MUSEUM COLLECTION
2 Albright Avenue
Grand Canyon Village
Grand Canyon National Park, AZ 86023
(928) 638-7769
https://www.nps.gov/grca/learn/historyculture/muscol.htm

GRAND CANYON NATIONAL PARK RESEARCH LIBRARY
20 South Entrance Road
Grand Canyon Village
Grand Canyon National Park, AZ 86023
(928) 638-7768
https://www.nps.gov/grca/learn/historyculture/reslib.htm

THE GRAND CANYON TRUST
2601 North Fort Valley Road
Flagstaff, AZ 86001
(928) 774-7488
https://www.grandcanyontrust.org/

IOANA ELISE HOCIOTA!!! MEMORIAL MATHEMATICS SCHOLARSHIP
Arizona State University
For donations or application, see https://www.asufoundation.org/colleges
-and-programs/schools-and-colleges/the-college-of-liberal-arts-and-sciences/ioana
-elise-hociota-memorial-mathematics-scholarship-CA101332.html.

MAP AND GEOSPATIAL HUB, ARIZONA STATE UNIVERSITY
300 East Orange Mall
Tempe, AZ 85287
(480) 727-2565
Room 334, Hayden Library
https://lib.asu.edu/geo

MUSEUM OF NORTHERN ARIZONA
3101 North Valley Road
Flagstaff, AZ 86001
(928) 774-5213
http://musnaz.org

RAVEN'S PERCH MEDIA
Bibliographical and Historical Resources in the Grand Canyon and Lower
Colorado River Regions of the United States and Mexico
Contact: earlespamer@gmail.com
https://ravensperch.org/

SPRINGS STEWARDSHIP INSTITUTE
414 North Humphreys Street
Flagstaff, AZ 86001
(928) 440-3191
https://springstewardshipinstitute.org/

Photograph, Illustration, and Map Credits

Insert 1

1–2, 4–6, 13–21: Photographs by Pete McBride
3: Illustration by Betsy Sylvester
7: Doris A. and Lawrence H. Budner Theodore Roosevelt Collection, DeGolyer Library, Southern Methodist University
8: NAU.PH.568.8131. Kolb, Emery. Special Collections and Archives, Cline Library, Northern Arizona University
9: NAU.PH.568.5615. Kolb, Emery. Special Collections and Archives, Cline Library, Northern Arizona University
10: Bettmann via Getty Images
11–12: Courtesy of the author

Insert 2

1–16, 19–24: Photographs by Pete McBride
17–18: Stephanie Smith, Grand Canyon Trust

Interior

Pp. iv, 1, 69, 111, 155, 190, 193, 205, 214, 243, 281, 323, 371: Photographs by Pete McBride
Pp. xiv–xv, 112, 206–7, 324–25: Stephanie Smith
Pp. 29, 66: Photographs by John Blaustein
P. 48: Rudi Petschek
Pp. 56–57: Stephanie Smith, Grand Canyon Trust
P. 434: Courtesy of the author

About the Author

Kevin Fedarko has spent the past twenty years writing about conservation, exploration, and the Grand Canyon. He has been a staff writer at *Time* magazine, where he worked primarily on the foreign affairs desk, and a senior editor at *Outside*, where he covered outdoor adventure. His writing has appeared in *National Geographic*, the *New York Times*, and *Esquire*, among other publications. His first book, *The Emerald Mile: The Epic Story of the Fastest Ride in History Through the Heart of the Grand Canyon*, which won a National Outdoor Book Award and the Reading the West Book Award, was a *New York Times* bestseller. He lives in Flagstaff, Arizona.